AF361420

Patterns of Political Leadership
Egypt, Israel, Lebanon

By R. Hrair Dekmejian
State University of New York at Binghamton

State University of New York Press
Albany, New York, 1975

For Babu John of Gamiss
and his descendants—
Anoush, Gregory, Armen, Haig

Published with assistance from
the University Awards Committee
of State University of New York

Published by State University of New York Press
99 Washington Avenue, Albany, New York 12210
© 1975 State University of New York
All rights reserved
Printed in the United States of America

Library of Congress Cataloging in Publication Data

Dekmejian, R   Hrair, 1933–
   Patterns of political leadership: Egypt, Israel,
Lebanon.

   Bibliography: p.
   Includes index.
   1. Elite (Social sciences)—Egypt.   2. Elite (Social
sciences)—Israel.   3. Elite (Social sciences)—
Lebanon.   I. Title.
JQ1758.A91D44   301.44′92′0956   74-20940
ISBN 0-87395-291-X
ISBN 0-87395-292-8 microfiche

Contents

Tables

Figures

Preface

It is ironic that the present study of three Middle Eastern elites was begun in the wake of one war and completed in the aftermath of another. The October 1973 War, even more than that of June 1967, underlined the stubborn persistence of the Arab-Israeli conflict and the central role played by political leaders throughout its tragic evolution.

It is not, however, this writer's intention to add one more opus to the burgeoning literature on the Arab-Israeli dilemma. The central concern here is leaders and the process of leadership in three Middle Eastern countries which happen to be deeply involved in the protracted conflict between the Arabs and Israelis. This conflictual milieu has provided the major logic behind my choice of the countries in this study—Israel and Egypt being the main antagonists and Lebanon constituting a more "neutral" basis of comparison. My second reason was the considerable contrast that exists among the three political systems and their respective elites. Finally, the present comparative study of Middle Eastern leaders constitutes a natural extension of my earlier work on the Egyptian leadership.

The most important disclaimer that I wish to make is that the three elite studies are not intended to be exhaustive, much less definitive. The constraints of time and treasure worked to limit the study primarily to ministerial elites. Even so, the collection and analysis of data on approximately 400 leaders, no less than the intellectual inspiration to begin, required the help of numerous colleagues and students, whom I herewith gratefully acknowledge.

A special debt of gratitude is due to my former professors at Columbia University who stimulated my interest in the study of political leadership, particularly Dankwart Rustow, Richard Neustadt, J. C. Hurewitz, and Charles Issawi. I owe even more to colleagues at the State University of New York at Binghamton—Professors Eduard Ziegenhagen, Khalil Semaan, Harold Nieburg, Morris Budin, Louis Gawthrop, Robert Jordan, Don Peretz, Becky Grajower, Walter Filley, Safia Mohsen, and James Caldwell—for their suggestions and patience in answering my frequent requests for advice. With respect to three other colleagues—Professors Malcolm Kerr of the University of California, Los Angeles, Arthur Goldberg of the University of Rochester, and A. Haluk Ulman of Ankara University—my gratitude transcends the present volume. The contribution of my colleague Paul Smith was unique in the context of an earlier collaborative effort on elites from which parts of the present study developed. A greater debt is due Professor Arthur K. Smith, Jr., Chairman of the Department of Political Science at the State University of New York at Binghamton for his unstinting intellectual and moral support. My colleagues, Professors Michael Brecher, McGill University; Amos Perlmutter, American University; and Emmanuel Guttman, Hebrew University, were generous with their time and valuable comments. A number of close friends of Middle Eastern origin provided much information and insights particularly Drs. Taysir Nashif, Henri Janian, Garabed Fattal, Ohannes Bezazian, Muntasir Labban, Ara Misakyan, and Oshagan Minassian. I am also deeply indebted to Muhammad Husami, Hikmat Fayiz, Nubar Najarian, Zahi Khuri, Tahsin Bashir, and Sana Hasan who helped with the Lebanese and Egyptian data, not to mention Mr. Jalal Zuwiyya, Middle East bibliographer at the State University of New York at Binghamton, who helped generously.

The assistance of the University Awards Committee of The Research Foundation of State University of New York is deeply appreciated, as are the modest contributions from the Center for Comparative Political Research at the State University of New York at Binghamton. Particular thanks are also due to Professors I. William Zartman and Marvin Zonis, and Mr. Rowland Mitchell for organizing the American Council of Learned Societies–Social Science Research Council Workshop on Elites in February 1972 which provided an intellectually memorable occasion for this author.

A word must be said about the role of students in the completion of this study. A large number of undergraduate and graduate students contributed either as researchers, typists, translators, or critics in my courses on political leadership, comparative politics, and Middle Eastern politics. In this connection, I should like to mention Michael Schreiber, Raymond Kortbawi, Janice Murphy, Walid Kaddoura, Aram Nigogosian, Virginia Rober, Nazih Halabi, Mark Haven, and Bana Barazi. Also special thanks to Mark Silverman, the designer of this book, and Margaret Mirabelli for her editorial work on a most complex manuscript. I remain deeply grateful to Norman Mangouni, Director of the State University of New York Press whose expert and patient guidance went beyond the call of duty. Few authors are lucky enough to find the kind of encouragement and assistance which Norman provided me so frequently. Finally, I owe an inestimable debt to my assistants Clement Koutsoukis and Margaret J. Wyszomirski for their help. Clement's methodological assistance was most useful. As for Margaret, words cannot describe her immense contributions to this volume, both in intellectual and practical realms.

Aside from one's colleagues and students, one's family suffers the most from the intrusion of yet another publication into their lives. It is my hope that if and when my children read this modest contribution they will be able to judge whether the book was worth all the effort.

Richard Hrair Dekmejian

Binghamton, January 1975

"Power is the Great Aphrodisiac."
—Henry Kissinger, 1971

1

The Comparative Study of Political Elites

This study was undertaken in the belief that in a world of continuous conflict and crisis, there exist few subjects more worthy of systematic scrutiny than the phenomenon of leadership. In view of the destinal impact that national-level leaders often have, it is surprising that intellectually sound studies of elites are not more abundant. Indeed, leaders are often the most talked about and least known component of a polity. Although highly visible by virtue of their leadership positions, their backgrounds, behavior, and attitudes are often shrouded in secrecy—a possible reason why many scholars prefer to study parties, pressure groups, or the mass base rather than elites.

Nevertheless, negligence of the study of political leadership might well be to our peril. One need only consider the ramifications of the irresponsible exercise of executive power particularly in the Vietnamese conflict and in the Watergate affair. It is significant that American political science has traditionally been more concerned with Congress, political parties, voting behavior, interest groups, and the Supreme Court, than with the presidency and the executive branch. With few exceptions, little social background analysis has been done of the White House staff, much less the cabinet itself.[1] It is interesting to note that the recent spurt of psychological and psychohistorical analyses of presidents (e.g., Barber, Mazlish, Wills) only came after the manifestation of unrestrained presidential power at home and abroad.

Still fewer are genuinely comparative, empirical studies of leaders—either as individuals or in groups. By far the best known cross-national analyses of elite groups are the two by Lasswell and his associates.[2] Another collective effort under Edinger focuses on elites in selected industrialized polities.[3] A more recent study, edited by R. Barry Farrell,[4] is devoted to the comparative analysis of communist elites. Equally noteworthy are Quandt's methodological, empirical monograph [5] and studies of Marvick,[6] Wilkinson,[7] Lipset and Solari,[8] and Huntington and Brzezinski.[9] In the area of comparative elite attitudes, there are the works of Moskos and Bell,[10] not to mention the major collective undertakings of Lerner and Gorden,[11] and Karl Deutsch and his colleagues,[12] which focus on West European leaders. Comparative single-leader studies are even fewer; these include Wolfenstein's study of Lenin, Trotsky, and Gandhi,[13] Barber's study of US presidents,[14] and the distinguished effort under Dankwart Rustow's editorship.[15]

Macroequivalence: Universality of the Leadership Function

Students of comparative social inquiry have used a variety of units of analysis ranging from decision-making to political socialization, from political parties and legislatures to elites. However, there are distinct advantages to the use of political elites as an unit of comparative analysis.

The most overwhelming consideration is the universality of leaders and the leadership phenomenon. While each societal unit has its own particular authority structure, leaders and leadership have constituted an inescapable part of human social existence at all levels of society; indeed, "in any organization of any size, leadership becomes necessary to its success and survival." [16] A closely related consideration is the relative ease with which one may identify a national-level political leadership group, although the boundary problem remains, i.e., at what point does one draw the line between the top leadership and the next level.[17]

One can only wonder what comparative analysis would be like had it proceeded from Eastern to Western cultures rather than vice versa. It is quite possible that neither parties, nor pressure groups, nor, say, interest aggregation would occupy the center stage of comparative inquiry. Indeed, the bane of American social science has been a pervasive ideological compulsion to view the world through our own *Weltanschauung*, which results in the choice of analytical categories that proceed from our own American-Western political experience. How else can one explain our often abortive quest for political parties and legislatures in places where these do not really exist. Even if it is granted that the interest articulation and aggregation functions of western parties are universal, clearly they are not a central function in most traditional autocracies or modern dictatorships. In contrast, the leadership function is not only universal but is a central facet of virtually all political systems both at the national and subnational levels.

Among the other characteristics which contribute to the attractiveness of leadership as a unit of analysis are its precision and elegance, particularly in quantitative research. Finally, if politics is defined in terms of power, nothing can be more central to it than the study of those who hold power—the political elite.[18] This is particularly true of the new states where the frequent absence of institutionalized power not only makes leadership decisive, it makes effective leadership imperative to systemic survival.[19]

The present study deals with cabinet elites of three countries primarily in terms of social background characteristics, recruitment, and circulation, and only secondarily with their attitudes and behavior. This is mainly due to the easy availability of recruitment data, in contrast to difficulties in obtaining reliable information on elite attitudes and behavior. Whenever possible the interaction of background characteristics and performance is analyzed in some detail, mostly through longitudinal analysis. The three countries are Lebanon (1943–1973), Israel (1948–1973), and Egypt (1952–1973).

The identification of cross-nationally comparable leadership groups constitutes a most basic methodological problem.[20] Actually two related tasks need to be performed: first, one must identify the group in each polity which possesses the critical mass of political power; second, one must consider the comparability of these politically powerful groups. At the most general level it is possible to enumerate at least five characteristics which may be useful in identifying a national-level political elite group. These are

1. The possession of a disproportionate amount of political power relative to all other groups and individuals in society.
2. The sharing of a private political culture, distinct from the mass

culture, in which the leaders have more in common with each other than with their constituents.
3. The possession of significant mutual ties—economic, political, matrimonial, familial, socializational—all of which bring together the elite in a network of interrelations uncharacteristic of most members of society.
4. The possession of a self-view which emphasizes the uniqueness, exclusiveness, and political centrality of the group, i.e., the self-view of the group that it *is* an elite.
5. The existence of a widespread popular view that the group *is* an elite.

These characteristics have been utilized in various degrees throughout this study. The last two have been considered only indirectly to the extent that the data permits. Clearly, the first characteristic is the most important identifying feature of an elite. If power is considered a concomitant of political leadership, then the problem is to find the locus of power and to identify the individuals who exercise it. For each of the three countries under study, the cabinet constitutes the most important institutional power collectivity. While the validity of this judgment will gradually appear in subsequent chapters, the initial choice of the cabinet as the focus was based on direct observation as well as on expert opinions found in studies of the three polities.[21] This should not be taken to mean that the acquisition of any cabinet office automatically endows one with power, although this occurs frequently. Yet it seems that politically powerful people somehow end up in the cabinet in the three polities in question. One can venture to hypothesize that the quest for cabinet office by those possessing power is attributable to the natural desire of leaders to gain visibility and prestige. Perhaps more important, by entering the cabinet, the powerful legitimize their power.

Of course the three cabinets cannot be considered equally powerful or important. Indeed, there is some variation between them. As presidential-type systems, Egypt and Lebanon possess weaker cabinets than Israel, which has a cabinet-type government. Thus, in terms of relative systemic power, Israel's cabinet should be ranked first, followed by those of Lebanon and finally Egypt. These variations, however, are not significant enough to make a qualitative difference, thus while the three cabinets are not equal, they are comparable.

In establishing the general conditions of equivalency, additional components of the political system need to be considered. The three elite groups function within the context of substantially different party systems. Israel's multiparty system stands in sharp contrast to Egypt's single party, the Arab Socialist Union (ASU). And both are a far cry from Lebanon's small and confessionally based political parties and groups. Indeed, in Lebanon the country's sects and ethnic groups are more politically significant than are the parties, since elections to the chamber take place from lists based on confessional quotas in each electoral district. Israel's list-type electoral system is equally important to its political process and contrasts with Egypt's relatively constricting one-party framework for elections to the National Assembly and the ASU.

Despite these differences, ministers serving within the cabinet framework occupy the highest posts in each country's political structure and therefore conditions of structural as well as nominal equivalence exist. To the extent that cabinet members function as the responsible heads of various ministries, there is substantial equivalence among the three elites. In cases where ministers also act as party leaders, the area of functional equivalence becomes restricted. This is because Lebanese and Egyptian ministers do not function as party leaders to the extent that Israeli ministers are accustomed to doing.

It should also be noted that the three elite groups function within distinct political cultures. On the one hand, there is the free-wheeling, thoroughly capitalistic, heterogeneous, and pluralistic culture of Lebanon, which stands in stark contrast to the more disciplined and centralized societies of Egypt and Israel. The latter two cultures remain substantially ideological, while the Lebanese tends to manifest a more materialistic *Weltanschauung* that suggests an "end of ideology" milieu. Other factors in the individual political milieux include dissimilar imperial experiences, differing popular expectations and demands upon each leadership group, as well as variations in national wealth, size of country, and population. Finally, all three countries can be classified as new nations in different phases of development. These are some of the main factors that determine the broad context in which the three leadership groups operate, and as such they receive due consideration in the subsequent cross-national analysis.

This study sets out to accomplish two specific aims. It attempts to present in-depth studies of the cabinet leadership groups of Lebanon, Israel, and Egypt. A composite profile of each group is systematically presented in separate chapters providing a wealth of hard data for the area specialist. It then strives in the concluding chapter to utilize this data to test a number of hypotheses cross-nationally. Throughout, social background data is analyzed aggregately and longitudinally.

An eclectic methodology is employed combining historical analysis with empirical and quantitative approaches [22] to achieve a high degree of analytical depth. The historical method permits consideration of elite socialization over time, as well as the analysis of background material on the three political systems. On the other hand, the empirical-quantitative method assures precision and certainty, and as such is more suitable in inductive analysis that aims to arrive at more general hypotheses, principles, or theories.[23] Because of its rich detail, the generation and scrutiny of aggregate-type data tends to reduce journalistic impressionism in political analysis and contributes to overall accuracy.

Despite an inductive-empirical approach, several basic theoretical assumptions are necessary to provide a starting point. Most students of leadership assume that the elite is a reflection of society.[24] This is a valid assumption, given a sufficient time lag for adjustments to take place as changes in social forces change elite composition and/or vice versa. Implied is a close relationship between elite recruitment and social and political change, or as Seligman states, recruitment patterns both reflect and affect society.[25] Thus, recruitment is both a dependent and an independent variable. As a dependent variable, recruitment patterns will reflect a society's political culture, structures, and values; as an independent variable recruitment patterns manifest the pathways to power and status, and thus influence stability.[26] Closely related are the key concepts of elite legitimation and representativeness. In contrast to traditional societies, most contemporary polities regard elite representativeness as a major determinant of elite legitimacy, the other factor being elite performance, both actual and symbolic. Therefore, representativeness and effective performance vary directly with elite legitimacy, which is treated as a dependent variable.[27] However, this study makes no attempt to explore systematically the influence of social background variables on elite attitudes and behavior—a topic of lively controversy in political research.[28] Rather, an attempt will be made to show the coincidence of several social background variables with certain broad elite behavior patterns.

Microequivalence

Based on these theoretical assumptions, the framework is designed to generate and analyze social background data under basic categories common to the three elite groups and environments. Here inquiry should focus on microequivalence, i.e., comparison of specific elite attributes in differing political cultures. Although the use of a common framework cross-nationally will sharpen comparability, it also can mute or deemphasize unique characteristics. Therefore, care must be taken to use the framework flexibly, even modify it, to bring out the peculiar in each case study.

However, in considering microlevel attributes of leaders in each polity, the problem of equivalence once again emerges since variables such as age and education may have different meanings in each political culture, or their meanings may have changed over time. Thus, in establishing microequivalence one has to account for the peculiar influences of each milieu upon these variables. For instance, it is not enough to know that elite X is older than elite Y, but one must ascertain the meaning of these findings in each culture. What might be considered ''old'' in one polity may be regarded as ''young'' in another. Nevertheless, the use of a single methodological framework can contribute to the integration of comparative studies and thus avoid the problem of many edited anthologies on elites, where disparate chapters by several authors employ diverse theories and methods. Clearly, in such cases integration is sacrificed and so is comparative analysis.

Fundamentally we seek to answer several basic questions: where do cabinet leaders come from in each of the three political systems; what leadership techniques do they use; how much cooperation and conflict is there among them; and what happens to them after they leave their leadership positions. In short, inquiry will center on the sources, recruitment patterns, cohesion, strategies, tenure, and disposition of Lebanese, Israeli and Egyptian leaders— factors which determine what has been called since Pareto, the ''circulation of elites.'' The following specific categories of variables were used to classify detailed biographical data on each minister.

A. Age: (1) at first political office; (2) at first cabinet office; and (3) at leaving cabinet office.
B. Occupation: (1) positions held before first political office; (2) before first cabinet office; and (3) after leaving cabinet office.
C. Education: (1) level of achievement; (2) area(s) of specialization; and (3) name of educational institution(s).
D. Family identification and class by birth and by marriage.
E. Religion.
F. Geographical affiliation.
G. Political career: (1) first office held and tenure; (2) sequence of offices including tenure in each, from first to last office in government.
H. Political identification with (1) party; (2) group; (3) class; (4) ideology.

The foregoing approach enables one to acquire two types of research dividends. It accords the scholar an in-depth understanding of the ruling elements in each country and it renders possible the identification of certain differences and similarities between the three elite groups. This, in turn, can provide clues to explain more basic questions about contrasting political cultures, rates and levels of modernization, direction of social change, and the likelihood of stability or instability. Another promising aspect of this approach is its ability to shed much needed light on the protracted conflict between Israel and its Arab neighbors, of which Egypt is the most important. In view of the leading roles that elites have played on both sides of the conflict, a comparative study should illuminate some of the basic reasons behind the disparity of Israeli and Arab power. Different leadership styles, recruitment patterns, and educational backgrounds are likely to emerge, not to mention significant contrasts in the respective elite cultures. Ultimately, it should be possible to test various hypotheses by relating rate of circulation, elite disposition, and political risk to systemic stability. Finally, in the context of the Arab-Israeli confrontation, the study will focus on two central questions of elite effectiveness: [29] how successfully did the three systems recruit and prepare future leaders for their leadership roles and to what extent did the prevailing elite selection system in each country contribute to social integration by allocating roles in ways satisfactory to citizens, groups, and society as a whole.

A major source of distortion in the aggregate method is the implicit assumption that leaders are equally powerful, i.e., since each is counted once without weighing, a prime minister can be equated with an inconsequential minister of posts or sports. In order to compensate for this distortion, an attempt is made to identify the more powerful ministers. Moreover, both presidents and prime ministers are studied separately as two elite groups distinct from the cabinets.

The foregoing variables can also reveal the attributes of each elite collectivity and the political system itself. Age is an indicator of political generations; it can serve as the demarcation between elite generations, each of which may also be distinguished by unique experiences, including the collective socialization of a great event which members of one generation may have either witnessed or participated in. Age can also measure elite homogeneity as well as demarcate generational gaps between the rulers and the ruled. Education and occupation are primarily determinants of socialization that help shape the elites' *Weltanschauung* and, to an extent, behavior. Moreover they are also related to the class origins and class aspirations (social mobility) of elites and provide important clues about the predominant values, priorities, and structure of a society. In the determination of the elite-mass gap, education and occupation are fundamental, as they are in the analysis of elite homogeneity. Place of birth and family background reveal something about elite origins, class background, and/or various types of group identification, as do ethnic and religious affiliation, both of which also influence attitudes. Finally, all the variables in combination provide the entire progression from birth to elitehood—the so-called *cursus honorum,* or the pathways to power.

Sources of Data

The accumulation of detailed, reliable, biographical information on a large number of political leaders is a laborious task that demands an inordinate amount of time, patience, and financial resource. The problem is especially acute in many non-Western states, where biographical directories and related data on elites do not abound and available information is often replete with errors. The quest for data therefore, must be pursued through other means, notably the press, both domestic and Western, and must often go back several decades. Because the various sources frequently diverge, it is necessary to collate information on each minister from multiple sources in order to achieve a high degree of reliability and completeness. The author gathered supplementary material through native contacts in the course of a research visit to the Middle East. As a final step, six knowledgeable individuals from the Middle East and the United States were used as judges (two for each country) to provide a general check on the data and to advise in instances of grossly conflicing data. In this fashion, it was possible, with few exceptions, to collect information on about 400 ministers, which was then utilized to construct a composite picture of the three elite groups.

2

Political Elites in a Sectarian Democracy: Lebanon

In many ways Lebanon has one of the world's most unique political systems. The Land of the Cedars is the Middle East's oldest democracy as well as a haven for capitalist enterprise. Its Phoenician commercial heritage, no less than the growth of Middle East oil production, has made Lebanon a major commercial center both regionally and internationally. Lebanon's unique features include one of the world's smallest armies, not to mention a most heterogeneous popular base consisting of many religious sects and ethnic groups.

The fact that Lebanon's confessional, capitalist democracy functions at all is a wonder. Yet, except in a few instances, the political system has continued to exhibit signs of dynamism despite the unsettling effect of the Arab-Israeli conflict. In this context, Lebanon's heterogeneous political leadership has played a critical role as the subsequent data analysis will show.[1]

Our consideration of the Lebanese elite is limited to the cabinet and the presidency. Although these constitute the most important sectors of the total political elite, a number of politically important individuals can be located in the bureaucratic, military, legislative, and economic spheres of Lebanese society. However, many of these individuals have served in the cabinet at some time in their careers and as such have been included in our sample.

Za'imism and Dynasticism

It is difficult to formulate an operational definition of the type of Lebanese leadership associated with za'imism. Despite Hottinger's [2] laudable attempt to advance such a definition, differing views of the zu'ama' (pl.) persist in the literature.[3] Nor is the Lebanese perception a clear guide to their identity. What everyone agrees upon is that the zu'ama' constitute a category of Lebanese leaders who are central to the political process.

One obstacle to viable classification is the great dissimilarity among the zu'ama'. Some have a rural base while others are urban dwellers. Not only do they come from seven diverse religious backgrounds, but they also differ widely in age, ideology, social background, motivation, wealth, leadership style, and extent of power. Therefore, at a given moment, one can find different zu'ama' possessing varying amounts of power, which are subject to variation especially after elections and cabinet changes. Nevertheless, there do exist a number of common features among the zu'ama' which may serve as a basis for classification.

There appear to be at least four main traits in the Lebanese perception by which the populace intuitively identifies a za'im:

1) The possession of political power centered in one geographical area of Lebanon.
2) The possession of personal wealth or access (through family or other ties) to economic power.
3) The possession of social prestige by virtue of family name or reputation.
4) The ability to attract a client group and promote its interests through the use of his own influence.

Despite expectations of their gradual demise, the zu'ama' have continued to maintain and even expand their power in the political system, especially since the end of General Shihab's presidential term of office (1964). Indeed, in the closely fought presidential contest of 1970, the zu'ama' exercised a decisive influence over the outcome—the election of President Sulayman Franjiyyah, himself a za'im. The failure of Lebanese political parties to expand and develop national constituencies also gave the zu'ama' a new lease on life. As the 1972 elections demonstrated, even the Kata'ib (Phalange) Party of Shaykh Pierre Jumayyil acts less as a party and more as an ideologically oriented client group. The perceptions and expectations of Phalangists regarding the shaykh seem little different from those of a client group vis-à-vis its za'im.[4]

Clearly no inquiry into the nature of the Lebanese elite could be complete without an examination of the zu'ama', since this group constitutes a primary recruitment base for the elite. Not only are the zu'ama' well represented in the Chamber, but the more powerful of them find their way into the cabinet and other important governmental posts. Yet little can be gained from a narrow focus on the zu'ama' alone. The Lebanese political elite includes leaders who can not be classified as zu'ama', as well as others who may be in the process of developing the attributes of za'imship. It would be more profitable, therefore, to consider the zu'ama' within the larger context of the power elite, which would include the rest of the political elite (cabinet, chamber, bureaucracy), the economic elite, and the social elite. Such an approach might elucidate the historical role of the zu'ama' as well as the inter-elite relationships within and outside the extended family structure of the zu'ama'. In the end the Lebanese extended family (*a'ilah*) may prove to be of greater utility in understanding the political process and the leaders' role in it than the concept of za'im.

The Great Families

The formative period [5] of modern Lebanon's power elite goes back to the half-century before the Battle of Ayn Dara in 1711. Indeed, it was after the fall of the Ma'anid Amir Fakhr al-Din II (c. 1633) and the defeat of Yemenite Druzes led by the Alam al-Dins that the Shihab family's rule became predominant. The Shihabs ranked first among the great feudal families of the Mountain, followed by the Abi al-Lama' and the Arslans, all of whom were give the princely title of *amir*. Next in line came the families with the rank of *shaykh,* including the Druze Junblats and Talhuqs and the Maronite Khazins. Almost equally important were the Shi'ite Himadih shaykhs, not to mention the Khuri and Karam shaykhs, both of whom were Maronite.

These nine families did not constitute the totality of Lebanon's early elite. There were others—Dahdah, Imad, Abu-Nakad, Abd al-Malik, Dandash, Azar, and Dahir—to mention the most important. Yet few of the latter survived politically the turbulent years of Lebanese history; that is, survived long enough for one of its sons to reach cabinet office in independent Lebanon. In contrast, the first nine families displayed strong dynastic continuity and, along with a newly emergent elite, became the founders of modern Lebanon.

Not all of the nine families have been equally powerful; nor have they always succeeded in holding political power. Yet despite temporary lapses, the families returned to claim a share of political influence, although this amount has varied over the years. Overall, the foremost clans in terms of power have been the Shihabs, the Khuris, the Junblats, and the Arslans.

The process of elite formation in contemporary Lebanon has been most powerfully affected by the clan system. The early years of the present century witnessed the emergence of a second and larger category of leaders who could not boast of belonging to the major clans. Nonetheless the social-economic credentials of this new group were sound from the Lebanese perspective. This new elite came from families of local notables—large landowners, rich urban merchants, and bankers—who acquired political power either during the last days of Ottoman rule or under the French mandate. Like their more famous predecessors, the new zu'ama' tended to operate through the clan system, and with the passage of time they have also tended to manifest dynastic continuity.

The following families can be considered among the second elite group: [6]

Abdallah	Cham'un	Karami	Sharaf al-Din
Abi Shahlah	Da'uq	Khalil	Skaff
Abu Haydar	Fadl	Lahhud	Sulh
Abu Jawdih	Far'awn	Majdalani	Taqi al-Din
Abu Khatir	Franjiyyah	Ma'luf	Taqla
Aql	Ghusn	Mu'awwad	Trad
As'ad	Haydar	Murr	Twayni
Baydun	Hilu	Naqqash	Usayran
Bayhum	Hrawi	Nahhas	Zayn
Bulus	Husayni	Rizq	
Bustani	Iddih	Salam	
Butrus	Jumayyil	Sarraf	

Nationalism and Elite Formation

The advent of nationalism in Lebanon, first among the Christians and then among the Muslims, did not have the same unifying effect that it has had in other countries. The confessional divisions in the Lebanese body politic prevented the emergence of a unified nationalism at the outset. With the coming of the Young Turks and their pan-Turanist policy of Turkification, the Christian and Muslim segments of the population began to converge in their increasingly anti-Turkish attitudes—a process which led to involvement in clandestine activities within secret nationalist societies. The Turks responded by massive repression and the hanging of nationalist leaders during 1915 and 1916.

Despite confessional differences, the anti-Turkish activities of the nationalist elite, no less than their joint suffering and martyrdom, created among them a sense of spiritual unity and consciousness. Since many leading families were deeply involved in nationalist activities, some of their members were either hanged or imprisoned by Jemal Pasha, the Young Turk commander of the Syrian Front. Significantly, those who were executed revealed little about their colleagues or the nationalist societies to which they belonged.[7]

A large portion of the leaders who were hanged, exiled, or imprisoned came from well-known families. Some of those who lost their lives were succeeded by brothers, sons, or cousins, many of whom are still politically active. Of those who were imprisoned or who escaped, some survived to take leading roles under the mandate and after independence. For example, ten of the hanged belonged to eight prominent Lebanese families which subsequently contributed at least one minister each. The victims of Jemal Pasha's retribution included Sa'id Aql, Mukhtar Bayhum, Abd al-Karim al-Khalil, Salih Haydar, Amir Arif Shihab, Shaykhs Philippe and Farid al-Khazin, Sayf al-Din al-Khatib, and the Mahmasani brothers.[8]

The annals of the struggle against the Turks reveal a host of other well-known family names, whose members were involved in some capacity in the nationalist movement. These families included the Arslan, Sulh, Da'uq, Haydar, Husayni, Iddih, Jumayyil, and Salam.[9] It was no mere coincidence that these same families who fought for the nationalist cause later became the major recruitment source for a large portion of Lebanon's ministerial elite. Each of the families mentioned contributed at least one minister to the cabinet between 1943 and 1973. This is testimony to the political endurance of the large Lebanese clans; it also underlines the important role that the anti-Turkish struggle played in elite socialization. Thus, despite the fractionalized milieu of Lebanon's formative years, common involvement in the nationalist effort provided the elite with a degree of cohesion and viability essential for her survival.

However, one should not exaggerate the impact of the events of 1915 and 1916 on the emerging Syrian-Lebanese elite, since elite cohesion was weakened when the French strove to separate Lebanon from Syria under their mandate system. Also, among the leaders who were hanged, the Christians were in the minority, perhaps reflecting their apprehensions about fighting for an Arab state with a Muslim majority. On balance, therefore, the hangings and persecutions seem to have contributed to the molding of an elite by increasing its prestige among the public and by reinforcing the elite's image of itself as an elite group capable of future rulership (see figure 7).

The Feudal Landowners

Perhaps the most outstanding characteristic of the Lebanese elite is that a significant number of its members are large landowners. Indeed, a clear relationship existed between large landownership and the acquisition of political power in Lebanon even in pre-Ottoman times. It is often difficult to determine which came first, land or power; suffice it to say that the two variables were mutually reinforcing and usually resulted in extending a clan's influence. Additionally, as landowners, the rural elite possessed effective control over specific, often semi-autonomous, geographic regions of the country, including the inhabitants, who provided both labor and soldiers—i.e., a base from which family members could launch their political careers.

With the emergence of the commercial-financial metropolis of Beirut, the value of the feudal lands in the mountains declined, especially in the postwar period. Many rural proprietors began selling portions of their holdings and pursuing professional or commercial interests in the modern sectors of the economy. Nevertheless, land remains an important ingredient of political power. An examination of the family backgrounds of ministers yields a highly significant finding: approximately three-fourths of 159 ministers had ties to the land either through their clan or by direct personal ownership. Of these, 11 ministers could be classified as landowners who considered themselves as nothing but "proprietaire terrain"—indeed, save their involvement in politics, they had no other occupation but landowning. Other ministers owned various amounts of land but chose to delegate responsibility for running these estates to relatives or appointed representatives. In certain cases while the minister himself did not own large tracts, other members of his clan did; that is, he came from a landed family.

The greatest of the landed clans number about 19 not including such presently diffuse families as the Khuris and the Shihabs. Table 1 indicates the distribution of these landowners in terms of their specific geographic and religious affiliation. Confessionally,

TABLE 1. *Lebanon: Great Landowning Families* [10]

REGION	FAMILY	SECT	N OF MINISTERS
	Franjiyyah	Maronite	2
	Karami	Sunni	2
North Lebanon	Mu'awwad	Maronite	1
	Karam	Maronite	1
	Ghusn	Orthodox	2
	Abbud	Sunni	1
	As'ad	Shi'ite	2
	Khalil	Shi'ite	1
South Lebanon	Salam	Sunni	1
	Sulh	Sunni	3
	Zayn	Shi'ite	2
	Usayran	Shi'ite	1
	Arslan	Druze	1
Mount Lebanon	Junblat	Druze	2
	Abi al-Lama'	Maronite	1
	Khazin	Maronite	1
	Haydar	Shi'ite	1
Biqa'	Skaff	Catholic	2
	Himadih	Shi'ite	1

Shi'ites claim 6 landowners, with 5 for the Maronites, 4 for Sunnis, 2 for Druzes, and 1 each for the Catholics and the Orthodox. The geographical location of the clans' estates have always been politically significant, since they have often determined the character of interclan politics in each locality, e.g., Franjiyyah and Mu'awwad vs. Karam and Dwayhi in Zgharta; Khalil and Usayran vs. As'ad and Zayn in the south. One should hasten to add that land was not always the determining factor; often it was the pursuit of power in the context of parliamentary elections, presidential balloting, or candidacy to the speakership of the Chamber that caused interclan conflict.

As the table shows, the Sulhs have given three ministers, two of whom have been prime minister and the Franjiyyahs contributed two, one of whom is now president of the Republic. In addition, two Karamis, father and son, were both prime ministers. And there were two ministers from each of these clans: Ghusn, Zayn, Skaff, Junblat, and As'ad. The As'ads, both father and son, served as speaker of the Chamber for many years.

With six clans, the Shi'ites lead the other sects in big landlords. However, taken proportionately the Shi'ite landowners possess greater weight than might be suggested numerically, since they represent a sect smaller than the Maronites, with five landowning families. Therefore the Shi'ite leadership both in the cabinet and Parliament is far more feudally oriented than is the leadership of the other sectarian groups.

Inter-elite Ties: Marriage

The practice of establishing and/or reinforcing inter-clan ties through marriage has had a long tradition in Lebanese political history. The great shaykhly families of Lebanon have often used marriage as an instrument to strengthen their positions of power. Among the factors that entered marriage calculations were the clan's respective power position, rank, wealth, and social prestige. In the past the Shihab and the Abi al-Lama' families frequently intermarried; as Lebanon's two foremost clans of amirs, such intermarriage was considered mutually advantageous. The same could be observed about the main Druze families, whose frequent inter-marriages were based primarily on family status.[11]

An examination of modern Lebanon's clan structure brings to light a number of politically significant inter-elite ties through marriage. Interestingly, some of the historic marriage patterns (i.e., Shihab—Abi al-Lama') are still observable today.

The data presented in figures 1, 2, 3, 4, indicate certain of the more important marriage ties between ministerial families. Each figure represents a different cluster of marriage ties which run substantially, but not exclusively, along confessional lines. The figure 1 cluster is virtually all composed of Christian families, the sole exception being the Twayni-Himadih marriage—an Orthodox Christian to Druze tie being a relatively rare occurrence. The predominant sect in figures 1 and 2 is Maronite, with important Catholic and Orthodox connections. Perhaps the single most significant tie, which writers on Lebanese politics unfailingly mention, is the

Figure 1   *Family Networks: Marriage*

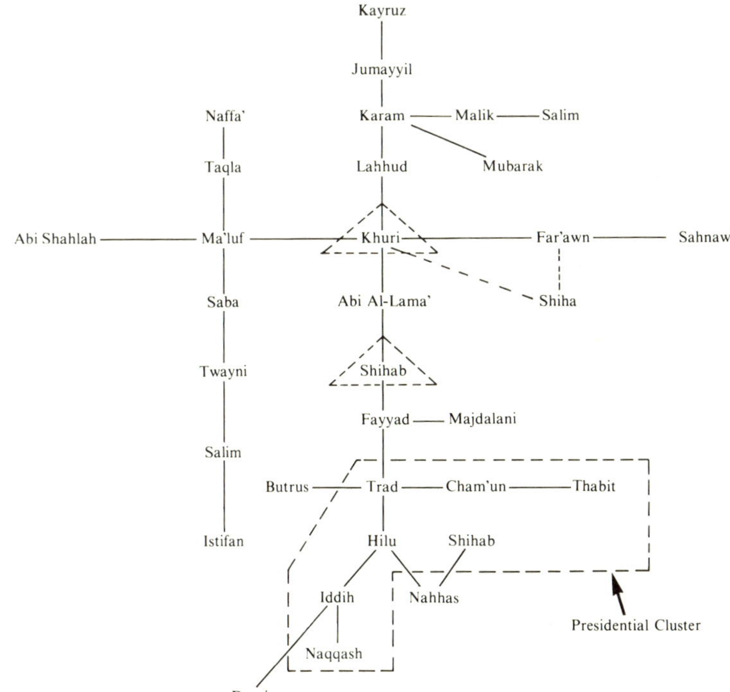

Figure 2 *Family Networks: Marriage*

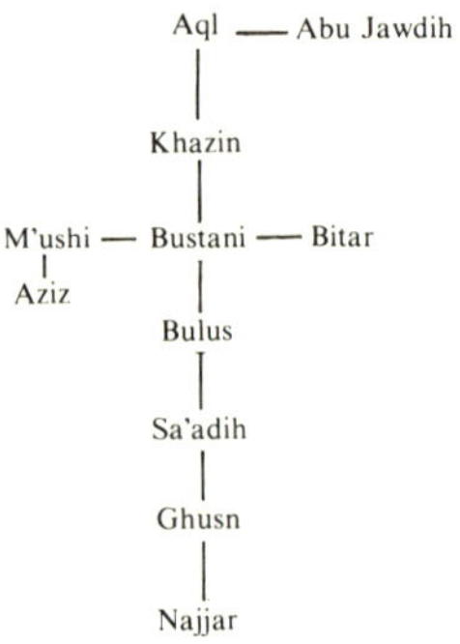

Figure 3

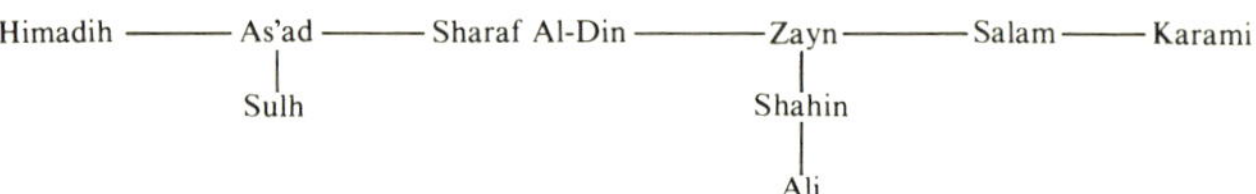

Figure 4

Khuri-Far'awn-Shiha connection which joins two Catholic bankers with the Maronite Khuri clan. The Catholic big-business Sahnawi family is also tied into this cluster. The role of the Shiha-Far'awn combination in helping Bishara Khuri's presidential aspirations against ex-President Emile Iddih is well known. Equally renowned is their peace-making role in the 1958 crisis when they joined with General Shihab, Raymond Iddih, and Charles Hilu to form the "Third Force." [12] It is significant that of the foregoing individuals only Shiha stayed away from cabinet office. He preferred to remain behind the scenes to play the roles of kingmaker, honest broker, advisor, and national reconciler, depending on Lebanon's needs. In the lower part of figure 1 one can note a "presidential" cluster, consisting of the families from which Lebanese presidents have come: Naqqash, Iddih, Hilu, Trad, Cham'un, Thabit, with ties to the Shihabs once removed. Also one can identify certain key families with a large number of marriage ties (e.g., the Orthodox Trads and the Catholic Ma'lufs), who serve as linkages between the more important clans.

Figures 3 and 4 present chains of powerful Shi'ite feudal clans with some Sunni marriage ties. Figure 3 shows the connections among the major Shi'ite landowning families of Himadih (Hirmil-Biqa') and the As'ads, the Zayns, the Sharaf al-Dins, and the Shahins (South Lebanon). Additional marriage ties link Shi'ite landowning families to the large Sunni landowning clans of the South—the As'ads to the Sulhs and the Zayns to the Salams. In turn, the Sunni Alis of North Lebanon are linked to the Shi'ite Shahins of South Lebanon. Figure 4 presents yet another Shi'ite marriage "confederation," which brings together the other major South Lebanese landowning clans of Arab (Tyr), Khalil (Tyr), and Usayran (Zahrani) with the Biqa' clan of Haydar (Ba'albak). Significantly the two foregoing Shi'ite alignments have been rivals in Lebanese politics, especially during the 1958 crisis, when the figure 4 clans were pro-Cham'un and the figure 3 clans anti-Cham'un. Other politically important marital liaisons include: Ma'luf to Taqla, Khuri, Saba, and Abi Shahlah; and Abdallah to Bayhum. Regionally significant ties exist between Safi al-Din and Bazzi (Shi'ite, South Lebanon); Yafi and Salha (Sunni, Beirut); Arslan and Junblat (Druze, Mount Lebanon); Skaff and Abu Khatir (Catholic, Zahli); Hibri and Mahmasani (Sunni, Beirut).

Ties with nonpolitical or nonministerial clans also can be significant for the launching and perpetuation of ministerial careers. This is especially true of ties to socially and/or financially prominent families such as the Sursuq, Huwayyik, Shiha, Isa al-Khuri, Hubaysh, and Mukarzil. Finally a great deal of inbreeding takes place within the large clans themselves. Marriages between two members of a clan (both having the same last name) are frequently consummated, since custom does not prohibit unions between even close cousins. More than thirty ministerial families displayed some inbreeding.

This analysis does not suggest that politics is the main intention behind inter-clan matrimony; indeed, money, prestige, and love may singly or in combination result in inter-elite ties. All that is suggested here is that this type of inter-elite tie exists and that the elite frequently uses marriage to perpetuate itself. Furthermore sub-elite groups use marriage to achieve social and political mobility. While the elite has a strong sense of exclusiveness and the desire to marry into a "good" family, it is not a closed elite, especially to those with money. In the final analysis, the persistence and proliferation of inter-clan matrimonial ties constitutes another indication of a power elite in Lebanon.

Linkages: Politics and Economics

One need not possess the economic determinism of a Marxist to hypothesize about the powerful influence that the economic sphere exercises over Lebanese politics. Because of Lebanon's location and laissez-faire milieu, the interaction between the economic and political spheres has been unusually close. Without belaboring any deterministic arguments, one might inquire into the location, scope, and intensity of the economic-political interaction—an inquiry that once again brings into focus the political and economic components of the elite.

Our findings, based on background analysis, indicate that the political elite, especially at the ministerial level, provides a primary link between the economic and political spheres of Lebanese life. These linkages can take three forms. A minister can provide a linkage by virtue of his membership in both the political and economic elite. The political family also provides a link between the political and economic spheres; this occurs when a close relative of a minister (brother, cousin, or spouse) belongs to the economic elite. While this family-type connection may be less close (and therefore politically less productive) than when the minister himself provides the linkage, its significance is by no means negligible. Finally, the political and economic spheres can be linked through inter-elite alliances between individuals or families. These alliances are often reinforced by marriage ties, joint business ventures, and political coalitions, or any combination thereof. For example, a politician might pursue a ministerial career with the financial help of a rich industrialist friend, or vice versa.

Overlapping Elites

Observations gleaned from the data suggest not only a mere convergence at the elite level of Lebanon's political and economic spheres, but an uncommon degree of overlapping between the economic and political elite. And considering the primacy of free-enterprise economics in the country, the political elite might be viewed as an extension of the economic elite.

To begin with, about 31 of Lebanon's 159 ministers belong to the banker-industrialist-businessman category. By any measure these 31 ministers come from the very top of Lebanon's economic structure (see table 2). These men own and/or administer many of the country's main enterprises, including tourism, finance, industry, airlines, mass media, commerce, and construction. While all 31 are considered economically prominent, about one-half are generally regarded as being among the country's topmost entrepreneurs: Najib Alam al-Din, Ali Arab, Emile Bustani, Najib Abu Haydar, Ahmad Da'uq, Michel Iddih, Pierre Iddih, Henry Far'awn, Georges Karam, Michel Khuri, Yusif Salim, Najib Salha, Basil Trad, Jean Skaff, and of course, Antoine Sahnawi. In virtually all these cases, political power (cabinet office) came after the acquisition of economic power and apparently because of it although there have been instances where the sequence has been reversed.

TABLE 2. *Lebanon: The Economic Elite*

Najib Abu Haydar	Husayn Mansur
Najib Alam al-Din	Musa Mubarak
Ali Arab	Gabriel Murr
Nasib Barbir	Fuad Najjar
Emile Bustani	Georges Naqqash
Ahmad Da'uq	Antoine Sahnawi
Michel Dumit	Sa'ib Salam
Henry Far'awn	Yusif Salim
Boulos Fayyad	Nicolas Salim
Pierre Hilu	Najib Salha
Michel Iddih	Jean Skaff
Pierre Iddih	Basil Trad
Georges Karam	Farid Trad
Michel Khuri	Gibran Twayni
Nassim Majdalani	Husayn Uwayni
Nasri Ma'luf	

To be sure the economic elite component within the ministerial elite would be still larger, if two hidden factors were considered. Actually the total number of ministers engaged in substantial business activity would exceed the 31 men already identified if less rigorous criteria for economic elitehood were employed. Moreover, the landowners should be considered in the determination of the economic elite within the ministerial elite. As indicated in table 1, about 19 ministers came from large landowning backgrounds. With one exception (Skaff), the 19 landowning ministers did not coincide with the 31 business-category ministers. Thus, a valid estimate of the presence of the country's economic elite in the cabinet would include the 19 big landowners as well as the 31 big businessmen for a total of 50 ministers or about 30 percent of the total political elite.

Beyond the substantial linkage provided by the foregoing ministers, the political and economic spheres also interact within the larger context of the extended family system. The large clans themselves serve as links in cases where political and economic elites come from the same clan. Indeed, it is quite common for individual members of a family to specialize in different endeavors; while one brother or cousin may decide in favor of a full-time politician's career, another member may further the clan's business interests. This division of labor is especially common in the close-knit medium-size families which are not excessively diffuse; nor is it unusual for two or more members of a family to compete as candidates for parliament or the cabinet. In some instances the various political aspirants of a family agree to take turns at acquiring political office. Therefore any family which has both economic and political elites within its fold can fulfill the link function. There were over 75 such families, many of whom not only possessed economic and political branches, but professional and artistic ones as well.

The occupational backgrounds of ministerial family members reveal substantial diversification. On the basis of data obtained on ministerial families since the mandate, it is possible to construct a generalized model or tree diagram showing the possible areas of occupational involvement. In the case of tightly knit families, occupational diversity may be synonymous with family control over the various areas of national endeavor. The generalized model of figure 5 illustrates the typical pursuits of an extended family whose members have achieved distinction in different fields. To be sure, some families tend to be more active politically, while others concentrate on economic activities. The Franjiyyahs have been more involved on the political side than the economic. The same may be said about the Zayns. Other ministerial families which have been more political than economic include the Cham'uns, the Lahhuds, and the Naqqashes. In contrast, the Sahnawis must be considered primarily an economic family, a member of which served as minister for brief periods. Other ministerial families with greater economic than political involvement include the Da'uqs, the Ma'lufs, the Abu Jawdihs, and the Alam al-Dins. Finally, certain of the large clans are equally involved in both the economic and the political spheres, not to mention the cultural and professional aspects of life. These usually large families are involved comprehensively in most of the occupational fronts identified in figure 5. No less than 19 ministerial families may be identified as fitting most of the branches of figure 5 in varying degrees. In terms of comprehensiveness, the larger families clearly had the advantage. The Shihabs and the Khuris, both very large clans, each had a membership sufficient to cover all branches in figure 5, some by more than one family member. Next on the ladder of occupational diversity came the Khazin, Skaff, Aql, Trad, Iddih, Jumayyil, Far'awn, Bustani, Baydun, Bayhum, Abi al-Lama', and Taqla, to mention only the largest families.

The larger families were also well represented in the professions, particularly in law, journalism, and medicine. Journalism was especially important since it provided the political families with access to the media and thus to the wider public. In addition, certain of the great families had achieved cultural prestige by producing some of Lebanon's greatest writers, poets, musicians, and artists. Ministerial families of cultural distinction include Abi al-Lama' (musician), Abi Shahlah (poet), Ammun (painter), Aql (writer, poet, and musician), Bayhum (writer), Himadih (poet), Khuri (poet), Trad (poet), Hilu (musician), Murr (poet), Mubarak (poet), Naffa' (poet), Taqi al-Din (musician), and Uwayni (writer).

While accelerated modernization and size contribute to the weakening of family bonds, primordial habits do not die easily. To counteract centrifugal trends, some families have formed formal or informal associations which bring members of the clan together periodically for consultation, mutual aid, and planning. The well-known Shihab Family Association exemplifies one such organization.

Figure 5 *Generalized Model of Familial Occupational Diversity*

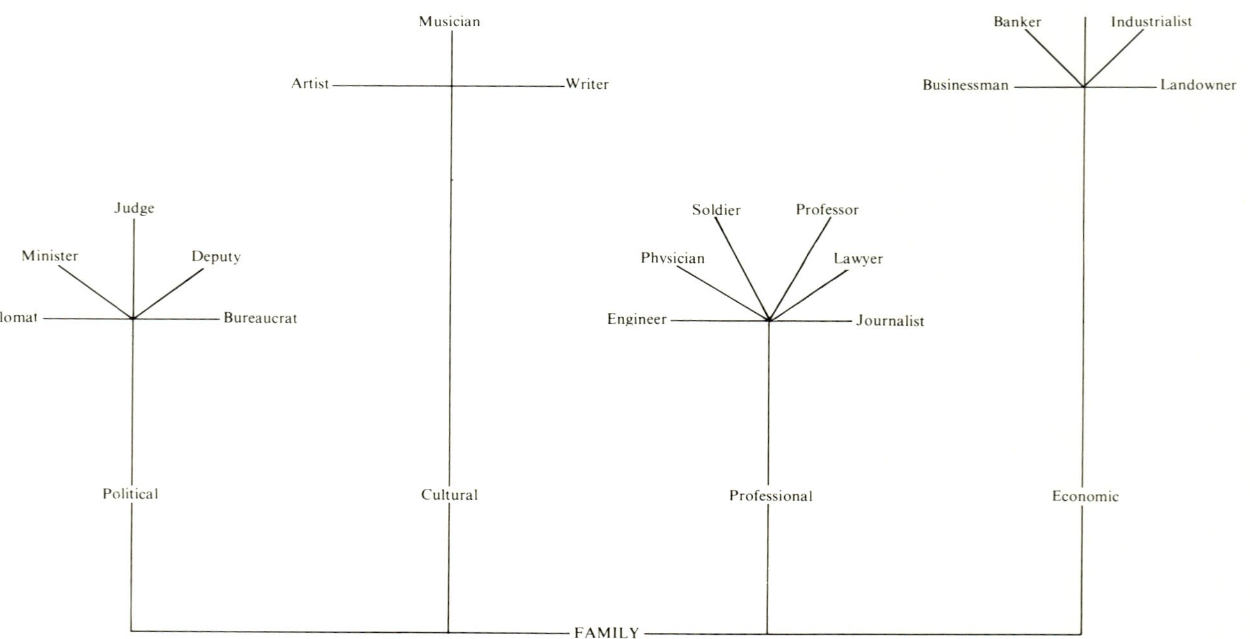

Inter-elite Ties: Business

Marriage and politics are not the only connections among the families of the ministerial elite. Important economic ties exist especially in the areas of finance, commerce, and industry. These ties occur by virtue of joint ownership and/or management of various enterprises. Some of the more significant connections appear on figure 6, which shows the interrelations between a number of major companies and economically prominent ministerial families. In tracing the relevant economic ties one can focus on a particular family such as the renowned Sahnawis. This family has interests in eleven of the enterprises listed in figure 6 and through these maintains direct ties with a total of 15 other families. Alternatively, one can focus on a company to determine inter-family ties. As shown in figure 6, the SODAFI enterprise brings together the Far'awn, Iddih, Hilu, Dumit, and Taqla families. But the chain of ties does not end there, because the Iddih interests in the Beirut-Riyad Bank connect them with the Mansurs and the Khalils; there are also Iddih ties through MEBRCO with Sahnawi and Taqla for a second time. If various connections of the Taqla and the Far'awn were projected, it would substantially enlarge the net of inter-elite economic ties.

Figure 6 illustrates the centrality of the Sahnawis within the Lebanese economic elite. No less than 15 direct business ties link the Sahnawis with other ministerial families. However, this figure does not represent the entirety of Sahnawi economic connections. Other economically important ministerial families include Iddih, Khuri, Salha, Baydun, Far'awn, Taqla, Da'uq, and Khazin.

This analysis should not suggest that the foregoing families constitute the entire Lebanese economic elite although they are a prominent part of it. There exist other economically prominent families who have failed or who lack the disposition to pursue political office at the highest level of the power structure. Examples of economic elite families who have not achieved political prominence, include the Araman, Arida, Asayli, Shammas, Daw, Dabban, Fattal, Frayha, Ja'ja', Jid'awn, Jallad, Haji-thomas, Jabbur, Jabr, Kittanih, Matar, Nammur, Nasif, Nihmi, Sa'ad, Sabir, Sahb, Sawaya, Shubayr, Sadnawi, Sursuq, Thabit, Tannus, Trabulsi, Yazbik, Yusif, and Zaydan. While these families have not

Figure 6 *Family Networks: By Business*

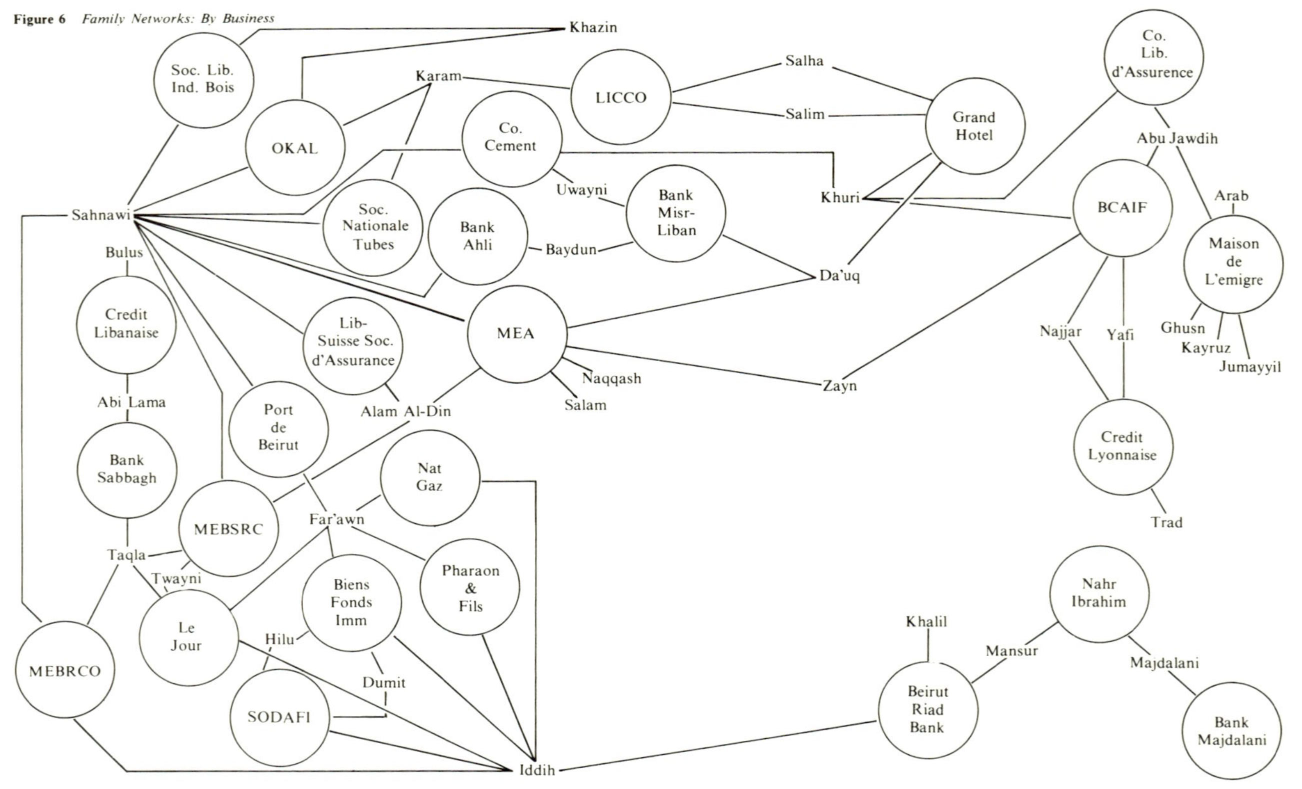

28

achieved cabinet office yet, the convertibility of economic power into political power in Lebanon makes it very likely that some will gain entrance into the Chamber and eventually the cabinet.

The Lebanese Presidency

Scholars and observers agree that the Lebanese presidency is the most important source of power in the political system. Since the promulgation of the constitution under the French mandate in 1926, a total of eleven individuals have been president. Five have taken office after the granting of independence in September of 1943. In view of their centrality to the Lebanese political process, the eleven presidents constitute a primary elite group.

Despite his importance in Lebanese politics, the president cannot rule alone. In a strictly balanced pluralistic democracy such as Lebanon, the president needs to retain the confidence of the main religious sects, the various landed and urban zu'ama', and the major economic interest groups, in order to rule effectively. In other words presidential performance should be such that at the very least it does not threaten the basic interests or rights of the main communities, groups, and leaders of the country.

Therefore, the president's first priority will be the maintenance of the status quo in the confessional distribution of power within all government bodies, especially the cabinet. But beyond the confessional balance there is the highly complicated problem of putting together in the cabinet a viable governing coalition. While ideally this coalition should include most of the main zu'ama' and leaders of the principal interest groups, in practice, only a few Lebanese cabinets have been so comprehensively representative. To begin with, the president may decide on a small, tightly knit cabinet rather than a large unwieldy one. In a small cabinet the seats will be carefully assigned to the president's allies, who are often major denominational leaders who banded together in Parliament to elect the president. Lesser allies or neutral zu'ama' will be excluded unless the president should enlarge the cabinet substantially. Since there are often too many elites and interests to satisfy at the cabinet level, these will form the opposition. Often vis-à-vis certain powerful zu'ama', presidential authority is limited. For example, it has been impossible to bring together ex-President Cham'un and Minister Kamal Junblat, who have been major antagonists since the 1958 crisis. Also Ministers Majid Arslan and Kamal Junblat have shown similar reluctance to serve together.

Collectively, the eleven presidents project a highly varied profile in background characteristics (see table 3). The predominance of lawyers among the cabinet-level elite also holds for the presidents. No less than seven presidents had been lawyers; of these Charles Dabbas and Charles Hilu were also journalists, Alfred Naqqash a judge and Petro Trad a banker. One president, Fu'ad Shihab, came from a military background, while Ayyub Thabit was a physician. Geographically, six were Beirutis, four came from Mount Lebanon, and one from North Lebanon.

In terms of education, nine presidents attained Bachelor or higher degrees. At least three had been educated in France and the rest in Lebanon—at St. Joseph University. More significant was their confessional affiliation—not everyone was a Maronite. Two—Dabbas and Trad—came from the Greek Orthodox community, while Thabit identified himself as a Protestant, although his antecedents had been Maronites. It is noteworthy, however, that all five presidents of independent Lebanon have been Maronites, in keeping with the precedent established by the National Pact.

TABLE 3. *Lebanon: Presidents*

PRESIDENT	TENURE	SECT	OCCUPATION
Charles Dabbas	May 1926–January 1934	Orthodox	Lawyer
Habib Pasha al-Sa'ad	January 1934–January 1936	Maronite	Landowner
Emil Iddih	January 1936–April 1941	Maronite	Lawyer
Alfred Naqqash	April 1941–May 1943	Maronite	Lawyer
Ayyub Thabit	May 1943–July 1943	Protestant/ Maronite	Physician
Petro Trad	July 1943–September 1943	Orthodox	Lawyer
Bishara al-Khuri	September 1943–September 1952	Maronite	Lawyer
Camille Cham'un	September 1952–September 1958	Maronite	Lawyer
Fu'ad Shihab	September 1958–September 1964	Maronite	Soldier
Charles Hilu	September 1964–September 1970	Maronite	Lawyer
Sulayman Franjiyyah	September 1970–	Maronite	Landowner

The Prime Ministers

After the presidency the prime ministry is Lebanon's most powerful and prestigious office. Since traditionally the president appoints a Sunni Muslim as prime minister, the office derives special importance vis-à-vis Lebanon's Islamic half—as the presidency has to its Christian half. Moreover, as a Sunni leader, the prime minister speaks for the second largest sectarian group in Lebanon, the largest being the Maronites.

The prime minister usually serves for a short period of time, always at the pleasure of the president. Thus, constitutionally, the prime minister is not the president's equal, since he lacks an independent source of power. Under a strong-willed president, the prime minister often accepts presidential dictates concerning cabinet appointments. Yet despite the great institutional and constitutional weaknesses of his office, the prime minister may return to office repeatedly, while the president has to leave office after six years. Thus presidents have come and gone, but prime ministers have repeatedly returned to office.

As shown in table 4, there were a total of twelve prime ministers since independence (September 1943). Collectively they present an even profile in many respects. All were Sunnis, except General Fu'ad Shihab, a Maronite who acted both as head of state and as prime minister during the twelve-day emergency period created by President Khuri's resignation from office. At all other times the tradition of appointing a Sunni prime minister has been maintained. In terms of frequency of holding the premiership, Rashid Karami and Abdallah Yafi lead the group with eight cabinets apiece. Sami Sulh is next with seven cabinets, while his cousin Riyad Sulh and Sa'ib Salam led six cabinets each. Husayn Uwayni headed four cabinets and the remaining six prime ministers—Nazim Akkari, Ahmad Da'uq, Abd al-Hamid Karami, Sa'adi Munla, Fu'ad Shihab, and Khalid Shihab—headed one cabinet each. Between them the two Sulh cousins headed thirteen of the forty-five cabinets or nearly one-third of the total. The longest continuous cabinet (twenty-eight months from October 1961 to February 1964) was headed by Rashid Karami—a length rare in Lebanese politics. Rashid Karami is also the youngest of Lebanon's prime ministers, having first taken office (May 1955) at thirty-four; he was followed by Sa'ib Salam, who was forty-seven when he headed his first cabinet (July 1952). The two oldest prime ministers have been Khalid Shihab (60) and Ahmad Da'uq (67).

At least three different types of prime ministers can be discerned depending on the needs of the political environment. First, one can

TABLE 4. *Lebanon: Prime Ministers (September 1943–May 1972)*

PRIME MINISTER	Beginning of term	Frequency in office	Sect	Geographic Base	Deputy/ Nondeputy	Age	Educational Level	Occupation
Akkari, Nazim	9/9/52	1	Sunni	Tripoli	ND	50	AA	Bureaucrat
Da'uq, Ahmad	5/60	1	Sunni	Beirut	ND	67	BA	Engineer
Karami, Abd al-Hamid	1/45	1	Sunni	Tripoli	D	50	BA	Cleric
Karami, Rashid	7/55,7/58,10/58 10/61,7/65,12/66, 1/69,11/69	8	Sunni	Tripoli	D	34	BA/ License	Lawyer
Munla, Sa'adi	5/46	1	Sunni	Tripoli	D	—	BA/ License	Lawyer
Salam, Sa'ib	14/9/52, 4/53,8/60,5/61, 10/70,5/72	6	Sunni	Beirut	D	47	BA+	Businessman/ Landowner
Shihab, Fu'ad	18/9/52	1	Maronite	Mount Lebanon	ND	49	BA+	Soldier
Shihab, Khalid	7/52	1	Sunni	South Lebanon	ND	60	AA	Landowner
Sulh, Riyad	7/43,6/44,12/46 4/47,6/48,10/49	6	Sunni	South Lebanon	D	49	—	Lawyer
Sulh, Sami	8/45,2/52,9/54, 7/55,11/56,8/57,3/58	7	Sunni	Beirut	D	55	—	Lawyer
Uwayni, Husayn	3/51,2/64,9/64 11/64	4	Sunni	Beirut	ND	51	AA	Businessman
Yafi, Abdallah	4/51,8/53,3/54, 3/56,6/56,4/66, 2/68,10/68	8	Sunni	Beirut	D	50	Ph D	Lawyer

identify the full-time politicians, who as deputies and Sunni zu'ama' are in the thick of everyday political battles; they include Salam, Yafi, Munla, the two Sulhs, and the two Karamis. The second category consists of senior statesmen, who as neutrals are entrusted with caretaker, nonparliamentary cabinets to conduct elections; the main examples are Da'uq and Uwayni. Third are those called upon by the president to serve as prime minister in times of crisis and rapid change. These crisis premiers have included Nazim Akkari, Fu'ad Shihab, and Khalid Shihab—all nonparliamentary types at least partially isolated from political pressures. While much of the decision-making usually falls upon the political types, the two other kinds of prime minister have contributed greatly to Lebanon's stability.

In terms of regional identification, the prime ministers have come mainly from the two large cities, a fact reflecting the presence of heavy Sunni concentrations in Beirut and Tripoli. The two Karamis, Munla, and Akkari came from Tripoli, while Da'uq, Salam, Sami Sulh, Uwayni, and Yafi were Beirutis. Both Riyad Sulh (Saida) and Khalid Shihab (Hasbaya) were from South Lebanon, and Fu'ad Shihab, the only Christian, was born in Mount Lebanon. In fact the Sulhs moved from Saida to Beirut in their quest for national office,[13] not only to be close to the center of power but because of the capital's large Sunni population. The Sulh's presence in Beirut added two more aspirants to the premiership, thus maximizing competition and factionalism within the Sunni community, which already possessed more than its share of zu'ama'. The same is less true of Tripoli, for the Karamis have thus far been able to overcome internal challenges to their leadership with continuous success. The main competition for the premiership is customarily set between Karami of Tripoli and whoever happens to be the strongest Sunni za'im in Beirut. After the passing of Sami Sulh and Uwayni, Yafi and Salam became the two contenders for the premiership. Yafi was prime minister until January 1969, followed by Karami. With Sulayman Franjiyyah's election as president, Salam became prime minister both of the October 1970 and May 1972 cabinets. But Salam is approaching seventy and one can reasonably expect new leaders to emerge from the Beirut Sunnis as aspirants to the premiership.[14]

In terms of social background, all twelve premiers came from well-known families, some more prominent than others. The Karamis, the Sulhs, the Shihabs, and the Salams have come from landowning families. Sa'ib Salam also had business interests, as did Ahmad Da'uq and Husayn Uwayni. Akkari and Munla are somewhat less prominent. As to disposition, Akkari became secretary-general to the cabinet; Munla, Yafi, and Khalid Shihab have retired. Riyad Sulh was assassinated (1951) and Sami Sulh, Uwayni, the older Karami, Da'uq, and General Fu'ad Shihab have passed away.

The premiers' educational level and specialization varied greatly as table 4 indicates. The best educated was Yafi, with a doctorate in law from the Sorbonne. Sa'ib Salam and Fu'ad Shihab come next, both having gone beyond the BA level. Six others—Da'uq, the Sulhs, the Karamis, and Munla—have done BA-License level work. The remaining three—Uwayni, Akkari, and Khalid Shihab—placed below the BA level and constitute 25 percent of the group. Thus the prime ministers have generally been less educated than either the presidents or the ministerial elite as a whole.

As might be anticipated, law was the major field of specialization—five of the twelve were lawyers. Fu'ad Shihab had specialized in military science, and Salam in economics. Abd al-Hamid Karami was the lone mufti in the group and Da'uq was the sole engineer. Khalid Shihab, Uwayni, and Akkari did not posses college-level academic specializations.

The President and Changing Elite Coalitions

If the presidency is the center of gravity in the Lebanese political system, the zu'ama' in their sectarian settings represent disparate centers of power without whose cooperation the country could become ungovernable. Therefore, the study of the dynamics of Lebanese politics should center on the interaction of presidential power and the ever-shifting balance of elite coalitions and cleavages. What follows is a chronological analysis of political dynamics with an attempt to identify relationships between social background characteristics and elite behavior.

Charles Dabbas, the first president, was chosen by the French, the Senate, and the Chamber in 1926. His election was the result of his pro-French orientation no less than the necessity to find a compromise candidate. As a Greek Orthodox, Dabbas was more acceptable to the Sunnis, Shi'ites, Druzes and the other minorities than a Maronite candidate. Even the Maronites welcomed Dabbas's election because of his reputation as a devoted Lebanese nationalist.[15] Significantly, his two-term presidency was a success. Despite French tutelage and the interconfessional struggle, Dabbas established an important precedent—that of an effective presidency—by his own exemplary performance. Once such an auspicious precedent had been set, one could expect the presidency's legitimacy to carry through into later periods.

Because Dabbas was a Greek Orthodox, he appointed Maronites as premier; these included August Adib Pasha, Habib Pasha al-Sa'ad, Emile Iddih, and Bishara Khuri. Of this group al-Sa'ad succeeded Dabbas as president and was in turn succeeded by Iddih, a well-known Lebanese nationalist lawyer of pro-French orientation. It was during Dabbas's presidency that the first pair of rival coalitions emerged among the elite. These coalitions, led respectively by Emile Iddih and Bishara Khuri, preoccupied Lebanese politics well into the fifties. Iddih enjoyed French support as well as backing from the French-language newspaper *L'Orient,* published by George Naqqash and Gabriel Khabbaz. Khuri's partisans included the Catholic banking families of Shiha and Far'awn. Indeed, Michel Shiha's sister was Khuri's wife and his paper *Le Jour* became Khuri's main journalistic proponent.

Despite Khuri's greater political abilities, it was Iddih who won the first round by being elected president (1936) by a majority of one vote. The conflict continued, however, as Khuri demanded from France full restoration of the constitution which had been suspended in 1932. As the head of the Constitutionalist Bloc in Parliament, Khuri put forth a program of pro-Arabism, national unity, and independence which Lebanon's Muslims could support. Meanwhile pro-Syrian agitation had reached a climax during 1936, when the Muslims were joined by Antun Sa'adih's Syrian National Party in advocating Lebanese unity with Syria. The French responded by concluding a treaty with the Iddih regime that provided sectarian representation in government within a framework of independence after three years. Despite Muslim popular opposition, the Muslim deputies joined the Christians in approving the treaty since they began to perceive a vested interest in Lebanon's future. On 4 January 1937 President Iddih asked the Sunni deputy Khayr al-Din al-Ahdab to assume the premiership. Al-Ahdab set a precedent, for the premiership was successively occupied by Sunnis— Khalid Shihab and Abdallah al-Yafi—until September 1939, when the French again suspended the constitution as the war broke in Europe. Iddih's presidential powers were curtailed, although he was permitted to continue in office by appointment. However, the cabinet was dismissed, and Abdallah Bayhum was asked to act as secretary of state, as he had done in 1934. By mid-1940 France had collapsed and the Vichy French took control of Lebanon. These developments, coupled with food riots in April 1941, brought President Iddih's resignation. General Dentz, the Vichy high commissioner, appointed Alfred Naqqash (Maronite) president with Ahmad Da'uq (Sunni) as undersecretary. When the Free French under General Georges Catroux took over Syria-Lebanon with British help, they proclaimed the independence of these countries; Naqqash was reappointed as president and Da'uq became premier, to be followed by the Sunni Sami al-Sulh.

Soon, the emerging Lebanese confessional system became entangled with the Iddih-Khuri rivalry and the growing Anglo-French tension in the Middle East. The Khuri faction (Constitutionalists) joined with Muslim and Arab nationalist elements in supporting Britain, while ex-President Iddih's National Bloc and the Christian element generally backed the French. Iddih's policy was to secure an independence tempered by connections to France, which would secure Lebanon against neighboring Arab states. In contrast, Khuri had been trying to reach an understanding with the Sunni Muslim Sulh family based on complete Lebanese independence within the framework of close ties to the Arab sphere. Thus, the broad outlines of the National Pact emerged, starting in 1942 amid British demands that the Gaullist General Catroux restore the constitution and permit new elections. In March 1943, Catroux, President Naqqash, and Premier Sami al-Sulh resigned their positions and the French appointed Ayyub Thabit as president and premier to oversee the forthcoming elections. As a Christian and as a pro-Iddih politician, Thabit was strongly disposed against the Muslims. His attempt to assign the Christians ten more Chamber seats than the

Muslims brought widespread protests that resulted in Thabit's replacement (July 1943) by the Greek Orthodox banker-lawyer, Petro Trad. The principle they agreed upon was to maintain a six-to-five ratio in favor of the Christians, making the size of the Lebanese Chamber a multiple of eleven. President Trad proceeded to hold the elections for the Chamber which were won by Khuri's Constitutionalists. On 21 September 1943 the Chamber elected Khuri as president. The Sunni leader Riyad al-Sulh was asked by the new president to form a confessionally based cabinet that would include Lebanon's six major denominations. The cabinet of six that took over on 25 September 1943 included the leading personalities of Khuri's coalition, some of whom would continue in elite roles well into the seventies. Aside from Riyad al-Sulh (Sunni), the cabinet consisted of Habib Abi Shahlah (Orthodox), Majid Arslan (Druze), Camille Cham'un (Maronite), Adil Usayran (Shi'ite), and Salim Taqla (Catholic).

The legitimacy which this elite derived from electoral victory was soon augmented. When the French proved reluctant to end mandatory rule, the Khuri government pushed through the Chamber (November 1943) several constitutional amendments relating to Lebanon's sovereignty. The French response was to imprison President Khuri, Prime Minister Sulh, and Ministers Cham'un, Taqla, and Usayran; Arslan and Abi Shahlah fled to the Mountain and set up a temporary government. Meanwhile the French had suspended the constitution, dissolved the Chamber, and reappointed Iddih as president.

These developments produced an unprecedented unity among the Lebanese, including such opponents as the Kata'ib and the Najjadah, and demonstrations rocked the country. On 22 November President Khuri and his ministers were released from prison in a triumphant atmosphere. The mandate was gradually terminated as France withdrew from Syria and Lebanon under British pressure.

As table 5 indicates, Khuri appointed a total of nine different prime ministers for the fifteen cabinets of his nine-year presidency (1943–1952). Riyad al-Sulh headed six, an indication of his key role as co-author of the National Pact and co-leader, with Khuri, of the anti-Iddih coalition. Despite his heavy dependence on Riyad al-Sulh, President Khuri also brought other Sunni leaders to the

TABLE 5. *Lebanon: Prime Ministers by Presidencies*

Khuri, Bishara	Riyad al-Sulh
	Abd al-Hamid Karami
	Sa'adi Munla
	Husayn Uwayni
	Abdallah al-Yafi
	Sami al-Sulh
	Nazim Akkari
	Sa'ib Salam
	Fu'ad Shihab
Cham'un, Camille	Khalid Shihab
	Sa'ib Salam
	Abdallah al-Yafi
	Sami al-Sulh
	Rashid Karami
Shihab, Fu'ad	Rashid Karami
	Ahmad Da'uq
	Sa'ib Salam
	Husayn Uwayni
Hilu, Charles	Husayn Uwayni
	Rashid Karami
	Abdallah al-Yafi
Franjiyyah, Sulayman	Sa'ib Salam

premiership, for he hoped through cooptation, to satisfy the Sunni partners of his coalition and thereby minimize defections. These prime ministers included Abd al-Hamid Karami and Sa'adi Munla from Tripoli and Abdallah al-Yafi, Husayn al-Uwayni, and Sami al-Sulh from Beirut. In his last month in office Khuri tried to head off a governmental crisis by bringing three others to the premiership—Nazim Akkari, Sa'ib Salam, and Fu'ad Shihab. Similarly, cabinet posts were rotated among the other main zu'ama' of the Khuri coalition to maintain near-optimum satisfaction for the sects, subgroups, and interests involved. At the outset, Khuri's Druze allies included most major Druze leaders, notably Arslan, Junblat, and Jamil Talhuq.[16] Among the Greek Orthodox, there were Habib Abi Shahlah, Nicolas Ghusn, Gabriel al-Murr, Gibran Nahhas, and Philippe Bulus. The Sunnis included Sulayman Ali and Muhammad Abbud. Of the Shi'ites, the Khuri regime had coopted the powerful landowners Sabri Himadih, Ahmad al-As'ad, Adil Usayran, and others.[17]

Rounding out what Michael Hudson aptly calls Khuri's "grand

coalition'' [18] were the powerful Catholic bankers and some Maronites. While Khuri's alliance with the Beirut Catholics was reinforced by marriage ties (see figure 1) as well as political and financial interests,[19] it was more difficult to hold the Maronite elite coalition [20] together, since the powerful among the Maronite ministerial group regarded themselves as potential candidates for the presidency; these included Camille Cham'un, Hamid Franjiyyah, Emile Lahhud, and Charles Hilu.

An examination of successive cabinet lists [21] reveals the patterns of factional change and elite turnover and simultaneously provides insight into presidential strategy. Thus, the first two cabinets were headed by Riyad al-Sulh and included one representative from each of the six major denominations. But the third cabinet (January 1945) represented a substantial change in elites and coalitions as Riyad al-Sulh was replaced by Abd al-Hamid Karami. The stand-off between the Riyad al-Sulh and Karami factions brought forth the neutralist Sami al-Sulh as prime minister, under whom the cabinet was increased from six to eight. By assigning one additional cabinet post to the Maronites and one to the Sunnis, it was possible for President Khuri to accommodate an additional za'im from each of these sects.[22] While both geographically and politically the Sami al-Sulh cabinet was well balanced, its chance of survival was not great in view of the on-going confrontation between the proponents of Riyad al-Sulh and those of Abd al-Hamid Karami.

The contending factions within the Khuri coalition in 1946 included:

Constitutional Bloc and Allies	*Independent Bloc and Allies*
Riyad al-Sulh (Sunni)	Abd al-Hamid Karami (Sunni)
Yusif Salim (Catholic)	Henri Far'awn (Catholic)
Philippe Taqla (Catholic)	Alfred Naqqash (Maronite)
Wadi' Na'im (Maronite)	Kamal Junblat (Druze)
Majid Arslan (Druze)	Sa'ib Salam (Sunni)
Habib Abi Shahlah (Orthodox)	Sa'adi Munla (Sunni)
Hamid Franjiyyah (Maronite)	Abdallah al-Yafi (Sunni)
Kazim al-Khalil (Shi'ite)	Ahmad al-As'ad (Shi'ite)
Adil Usayran (Shi'ite)	Jamil Talhuq (Druze)
	Gabriel al-Murr (Orthodox)
	Sabri Himadih (Shi'ite)

While each faction hid behind a veneer of opposing policies, their primary interest was to acquire and hold power, and power in the Lebanese political culture is perceived not merely in terms of deputyship, but of ministerial position. The strongest Sunni leader, Riyad al-Sulh, desired to replace his neutralist cousin Sami al-Sulh as prime minister, a post also coveted by Sunnis of the Independent Bloc—Karami, Yafi, Munla, and Salam. Similarly, there was a struggle between Arslan and Talhuq for the Druze seat, the latter being supported by Junblat. As for the Shi'ites, two southern landlords, Khalil and Usayran, opposed Ahmad al-As'ad, another big landowner from the South. The same factionalism applied to the Catholics and Maronites.

Caught between the factions, President Khuri asked Sa'adi al-Munla of Tripoli to head an eight-man cabinet in May 1946.[23] By presidential design the cabinet had few major political personalities. Being a weak cabinet, it was difficult for Prime Minister Munla to last more than six months. In December 1946 Riyad al-Sulh returned once again to head four successive cabinets until February 1951—a longer period of continuous tenure than any other prime minister in Lebanese history.

In terms of recruitment, these four cabinets recreated the old Khuri coalition—at least a part of it. The December 1946 cabinet included Far'awn and Yafi, both anti-Riyad al-Sulh members of the Independent Bloc, as well as Sabri Himadih. Gabriel Murr became a permanent fixture in the Orthodox position for the next five years. The old Constitutionalist Bloc was represented by Arslan, also a permanent appointee to the Druze seat. A second Druze seat was created for Junblat who went back into the opposition during 1947 and thus began his career as Lebanon's foremost maverick politician. Khuri's emerging rival, Cham'un, joined the December 1946 and April 1947 cabinets, as did Elias Khuri, both Maronites. Throughout these cabinets, some seats were rotated among competing zu'ama' to minimize defections. The only major figure who remained outside the fold was Abd al-Hamid Karami and, of course, Iddih's National Bloc—Khuri's old enemies. Yet despite such virtuosity in coalition politics, Khuri's hold progressively weakened for a variety of reasons. While Riyad al-Sulh's five-year premiership provided much needed continuity, it also drove into opposition the other three Sunnite candidates for the premiership—Sami al-Sulh, Sa'ib Salam, and Abdallah Yafi.[24]

Equally significant was Cham'un's defection. As an aspirant to the presidency, Cham'un could not tolerate another presidential term for Khuri, who had induced the Chamber to extend his term of office; hence Cham'un opted out of Riyad al-Sulh's last two cabinets and was replaced by his rival—Hamid Franjiyyah.

Other causes of Khuri's decline included growing corruption, the Arab defeat in Palestine, the Syrian National Party (PPS) uprising in 1949 and the execution of its leader, Antun Sa'adih by the Khuri-Sulh regime. These, coupled with Riyad al-Sulh's departure from the government in February 1951 and subsequent assassination, and the reduction of electoral strength in the 1951 elections, manifested the weakening of the regime. The two post-election cabinets under Yafi (April 1951) and Sami al-Sulh (February 1952) proved unable to maintain stability despite the large-scale cooptation that increased cabinet size to ten.[25] The challenge came from the so-called Socialist Alliance which was composed of Junblat's Socialist Progressive Party, ex-President Iddih's National Bloc led by his son Philippe, the Kata'ib, the Najjadah, the Syrian National Party, and Cham'un himself. During the first two weeks of September 1952, the Sami al-Sulh cabinet fell and was succeeded by a three-man crisis cabinet under Nazim Akkari. Five days later (14 September 1952) a second three-man cabinet was formed by Sa'ib Salam, which lasted four days. Amidst increasing strikes and turmoil and lacking army support, Khuri left the presidency, after appointing General Fu'ad Shihab premier on 18 September 1952. Shihab's three-man cabinet was instructed to keep the peace, preside over the election of a new president, and carry out the transfer of power. Five days later (23 September 1952) Camille Cham'un was elected president of Lebanon.

Coalition Patterns of the Cham'un Period (1952–1958)

In terms of reputation and personality no politician in Lebanon could equal Camille Cham'un. Despite his association with the British, he had accrued considerable popularity by opposing Ottoman Turkish rule and later by defending the Arab cause at the UN. These attributes, coupled with Cham'un's attractive personality, keen intelligence, and well-known courage, augured an auspicious beginning. Soon, however, the new president became enmeshed in the great power game in the Middle East amidst growing Arab nationalist sentiment inspired by Nasir of Egypt. From the outset, Cham'un encountered trouble from allies and opponents alike. Kamal Junblat insisted on serious leftist reform—nationalization of industry, land redistribution, social security—in addition to dominance in the cabinet. Moreover, Cham'un could not find a prime minister acceptable to all factions. He finally recruited Amir Khalid Shihab, a member of the Sunni branch of the Shihab clan from South Lebanon, who had been active as a Constitutionalist during mandatory rule. At the head of a four-man nonparliamentary cabinet,[26] Shihab acquired from parliament bold, new powers to reform the bureaucracy, the judiciary, and the press. Since these reforms cut into the interests of many leaders, Khalid Shihab's government fell in April of 1953, amid increasing opposition from a Chamber still dominated by the politicians of the Khuri period. Indeed, as a nonpolitical cabinet the Shihab government aroused hostility in the Chamber. While its composition gave the cabinet an aura of impartiality, as nondeputies the ministers lacked the legitimacy that elections bestow. Thus, Cham'un turned to Sa'ib Salam, a deputy, to form a mixed cabinet where deputies would outnumber nondeputies by five to three; its primary function would be to conduct the parliamentary elections. Despite its caretaker status, the Sa'ib Salam cabinet (30 April 1953) consisted of Cham'un's allies, including Pierre Iddih of the National Bloc, whose father had been ex-President Khuri's opponent. Most of the ministers were new recruits and as such represented Cham'un's emerging policy of undermining zu'ama' power, especially in rural areas. This policy was also incorporated in the new electoral law for the 1953 elections.[27]

The first post-election cabinet reflected the president's reaction to the electoral results. Under Yafi's premiership Cham'un brought in the newly elected Iddih, leader of the anti-Khuri National Bloc, along with Gabriel Murr, who had been pro-National Bloc. Significantly, Bashir al-A'war was made Druze minister instead of Junblat, who soon turned against Cham'un, his former ally. The Shi'ite cabinet member was Kazim al-Khalil, a foe of both the As'ads and the Himadihs. Former President Alfred Naqqash came in as an independent, as did Nicolas Salim; also Rashid Karami was coopted, reflecting the need to include a major Sunni personality from the North. In the next cabinet, also headed by Yafi (March 1954), the Druze post was assigned to ex-Constitutionalist (pro-Khuri) Majid Arslan—a new Cham'un ally and opponent of Junblat. However, both Yafi cabinets lacked strength since they were not recruited from a broadly based coalition of zu'ama'. Indeed, many of the latter had been alienated by Cham'un's electoral policies. In September 1954, the president made his second attempt at governmental reform under a new, stronger cabinet headed by Sami al-Sulh.[28] It had a larger membership and a stronger coalition of elites relative to the previous Yafi cabinets. This was the first of five successive ten-man cabinets under Cham'un's presidency where the Maronites and the Sunnis together controlled 60 percent of the portfolios. The choice of Sami al-Sulh was expected to add strength to the government; since his cousin's assassination, he had emerged as the strongest Sunni leader, certainly stronger than Yafi. Significantly Sulh's entrance into the Cham'un coalition in September 1954 marked the start of a close, four-year relationship between this prime minister and the president. Sami al-Sulh returned to head five cabinets and remained allied to the president throughout the '58 crisis until the end of Cham'un's term of office.

The new cabinet did not succeed in implementing the reforms because of vehement protest from opposition politicians, including Yafi, Pierre and Raymond Iddih of the National Bloc, and Hamid Franjiyyah. In July 1955 a reshuffled cabinet was placed under Sulh's premiership;[29] it was no coincidence that the new government included two of the very foes of the proposed reforms: Hamid Franjiyyah and Pierre Iddih. Franjiyyah's role as foreign minister was considered especially important, since he was pro-Cairo. As the inter-Arab cold war began to intensify, Franjiyyah and Iddih quit the cabinet (7 September 1955), precipitating a change of government two weeks later. The next cabinet was entrusted to another Sunni za'im, Rashid Karami. By this choice Cham'un accomplished the dual purpose of giving the young Tripoli leader his first chance to become premier as well as neutralizing pan-Arabist criticism directed at his emerging pro-Western stance. Indeed, by April 1955 Cham'un had already manifested interest in the Baghdad Pact and although Lebanon in March 1956 declined to join the pact, there was a general feeling that Cham'un was supporting the Hashemites of Iraq and Jordan against the emerging Arab nationalist leader, Abd al-Nasir. Despite his pro-Arabist record as a diplomat at the United Nations, Cham'un, who had been close to the British, was now seen as supporting the two major clients of Britain in the Middle East.

While the Karami cabinet included mostly new pro-Cham'un politicians,[30] it was full of contradictions in policies and personalities. Karami and Cham'un were not compatible, nor did they agree on foreign policy. As a result in March 1956 Yafi was returned to the premiership. While Yafi was considered slightly less pro-Cairo than Karami, Cham'un in a clever move, reinforced the Arabist contingent by appointing ex-Prime Minister Sa'ib Salam as minister of state.[31] Within three months, however, Yafi had to reshuffle his cabinet, which subsequently had to deal with the disruptions arising from the Suez War of October 1956.

The first major test for Cham'un and the Yafi cabinet came with Nasir's nationalization of the Suez Canal Company (July 1956). Cham'un quickly supported the nationalization but without great enthusiasm. When Israel attacked Egypt, the Lebanese president reportedly advocated severing relations with Britain and France and invited the Arabs to a conference in Beirut. At the conference the president joined the Arab states in condemning the aggression, but refused to sever relations with Britain and France. He later claimed that a severance of diplomatic ties would make it impossible to act as mediator to effect Anglo-French withdrawal from Egyptian territory.[32] At that point Yafi and Salam asked Cham'un to withdraw Lebanon's ambassadors from Paris and London. The president refused, citing to his ministers a verbal message from Nasir asking him to act as mediator.[33] Nevertheless, Yafi and Salam resigned from the cabinet, to be replaced by Sami al-Sulh, who lacked a strong Arabist orientation.

There seems to be a direct relationship between the incidence of crisis and the increase of nondeputies in Lebanese cabinets. As indicated in table 6, starting with the September 1954 cabinet, growing numbers of nonparliamentarians were in evidence as they were during the crisis year of 1952. In the Sulh cabinet of November 1956, only two of the six ministers (Arslan and Sulh) were deputies—since this was an emergency cabinet to deal with the aftermath of the Suez War of 1956.

TABLE 6. *Lebanon: Deputy and Nondeputy in Each Cabinet*

CABINET	DEPUTY	NONDEPUTY
September 1943	6	—
July 1944	6	—
January 1945	5	1
August 1945	8	—
May 1946	8	—
December 1946	8	1
April 1947	7	1
July 1948	8	—
October 1949	10	1
February 1951	—	3
April 1951	9	2
February 1952	10	—
9 September 1952	—	3
14 September 1952	1	2
18 September 1952	—	3
30 September 1952	—	4
April 1953	5	3
August 1953	8	—
March 1954	8	—
September 1954	9	2
July 1955	9	1
September 1955	8	2
March 1956	6	4
June 1956	7	3
November 1956	2	5
August 1957	8	—
March 1958	14	—
September 1958	3	5
October 1958	5	5
May 1960	1	7
August 1960	17	1
May 1961	7	1
October 1961	14	1
February 1964	—	11
September 1964	—	10
November 1964	12	2
July 1965	1	12
April 1966	8	2
December 1966	1	9
February 1968	7	5
October 1968	3	1
January 1969	15	1
November 1969	16	—
October 1970	1	16
May 1972	18	—

General Shihab became minister of defense to symbolize the army's support of the regime. The remaining ministers were not deputies but recent pro-Cham'un recruits.[34] But on 1 March 1957 amid domestic and inter-Arab polarization, General Shihab left the cabinet [35] just as the government was getting ready to accept the Eisenhower Doctrine. After a brief debate in the Chamber, the government asked for a vote of confidence. As opposition deputies walked out in protest, the Chamber voted thirty to one in support of Premier Sulh.

Another major problem facing the government was legislation concerning the size of parliament. While the regime favored a small Chamber of forty-four deputies, the opposition favored increasing the membership to eighty-eight; they finally decided on a sixty-six member Chamber. Meanwhile, seven opposition deputies had resigned (5 April 1957), protesting the Eisenhower Doctrine, as the pro-Cham'un deputies proceeded to redraw the country's constituencies to favor the president's allies. Soon the dissidents organized themselves into the "National Front," which gave the president a memorandum requesting a neutral caretaker cabinet, a Chamber of eighty-eight deputies, abolition of the state of emergency, institution of self-contained constituencies, and abstention from concluding foreign agreements until after the elections.[36] Furthermore, the National Front demanded adherence to the National Pact of 1943 and the principle of inter-Arab neutrality. While the opposition received much of its support from the Sunnis, many Shi'ites and Christians also took part in the growing antigovernment coalition. The main opposition leaders were Maronite Hamid Franjiyyah, Sunnis Sa'ib Salam, Abdallah al-Yafi, and Rashid Karami, Catholic Philippe Taqla, and Shi'ites Ahmad al-As'ad and Sabri Himadih. As the electoral battle was joined the two sides accused each other with a bitterness unprecedented in Lebanese elections. Former Foreign Minister Henri Far'awn's belated attempt to neutralize the existing polarization proved unsuccessful.[37]

The election constituted a defeat for Cham'un's enemies. Some of Lebanon's most important leaders were thrown out of office, which in turn threw the political system into disequilibrium. In Beirut, both Yafi and Salam were defeated by Prime Minister Sami al-Sulh's list. While Ahmad al-As'ad lost to the pro-Cham'un ex-

Minister Kazim al-Khalil, his son Kamil won. Even more significant, Kamal Junblat lost to a list headed by the progovernment Catholic Na'im Mughabghab because of gerrymandering. Nevertheless the regime's sweep was not strong enough to unseat Karami, Franjiyyah, Mu'awwad, Himadih, or Taqla.

As anticipated, it was Cham'un's closest ally Sami al-Sulh who once again formed a new cabinet (August 1957) consisting of pro-Cham'un politicians.[38] In the newly elected Chamber the pro-Cham'un majority elected Adil Usayran as speaker over the anti-Cham'un Himadih. In fact, because of presidential interference, neither Himadih nor his father-in-law, Ahmad al-As'ad had been successful in obtaining the speakership since 1953.[39] What especially disturbed the opposition was the fear that the president would use his majority faction in the Chamber to amend the constitution to allow him a second term. Some suspected that Cham'un would use the Eisenhower Doctrine to sustain himself in power indefinitely. Many recalled Cham'un's opposition to President Khuri's successful attempt to succeed himself, and who could forget Cham'un's role in causing Khuri's resignation in 1952? A second Cham'un term antagonized Hamid Franjiyyah, Pierre Jumayyil, and Raymond Iddih, since it would be tantamount to blocking their quest for the presidency.

As Lebanon was plagued by turmoil in late 1957, the Chamber continued its acrimonious debate; its traditional role of conflict resolution could not be fulfilled under circumstances of growing ideological polarization. In February 1958 inter-elite and interdenominational ties were further strained by the sudden establishment of the UAR. Amid demonstrations and disorders the president decreed the formation of a new cabinet, again under Sulh, one of his few remaining Sunni allies.

Consisting of an unprecedented fourteen ministers,[40] the cabinet of 14 March 1958 was designed to enlarge the pro-Cham'un coalition by coopting as many leaders as possible. This action was expected to increase the president's power to deal with internal and external challenges. Cabinet membership also had been chosen in a manner that would give the president a Chamber majority if he decided to succeed himself. Most important among the newcomers, however, were the well-known critics of the government, Pierre Iddih and Joseph Shadir. Iddih's inclusion meant a play for the old anti-Khuri faction of ex-President Iddih, Pierre's deceased father. Joseph Shadir not only assured the cooperation of Jumayyil's Kata'ib Party, but the loyalty of the Armenian community, since he was the first Armenian to become a minister.

A number of events precipitated the government's fall. Three Muslim ministers resigned, upsetting the confessional ratio and thereby weakening the government. On 8 May, Nasib al-Matni, an anti-Cham'un journalist, was assassinated. Two days later armed insurrection began in Beirut and Tripoli and spread to other parts of Lebanon. The enemies of the regime had combined into the United National Opposition Front, which called for the president's resignation. By the spring of 1958 two large coalitions stood face to face, vying for power. A third, smaller coalition, "the Third Force," emerged in the role of mediator. Tables 7, 8, and 9 present lists of the three groups with their geographical and religious identifications.

In addition to the anti-Cham'un zu'ama' who held ministerial rank, support for the insurgents (table 7) came from the Druze tribal chieftain Shibli al-Aryan, the Sunni deputy Ma'ruf Sa'ad, the Najjadah leader Adnan al-Hakim, as well as the Ba'ath, the Communists, and the Armenian Hunchaks and Ramgavars.

TABLE 7. *Lebanon: Antigovernment Coalition*

PLACE	NAME	SECT
	Sa'ib Salam	Sunni
	Abdallah al-Yafi	Sunni
Beirut	Husayn al-Uwayni	Sunni
	Nasim Majdalani	Orthodox
	Abdallah Mashnuq	Sunni
	Hamid Franjiyyah	Maronite
North Lebanon	Rashid Karami	Sunni
	Rene Mu'awwad	Maronite
	Ahmad al-As'ad	Shi'ite
South Lebanon	Ali Bazzi	Shi'ite
	Kamil al-As'ad	Shi'ite
	Kamal Junblat	Druze
Mount Lebanon	Fuad Ammun	Maronite
	Taqi al-Din al-Sulh	Sunni
Biqa'	Salim Haydar	Shi'ite
	Philippe Taqla	Catholic
	Sabri Himadih	Shi'ite

The pro-Cham'un coalition (table 8) consisted of most of the leaders from the August 1957 and March 1958 cabinets. Other ministers associated with the Cham'unites included Na'im Mughabghab and Majid Arslan. The most important political groups which joined in the fighting on Cham'un's side were Pierre Jumayyil's Kata'ib, the Syrian National Party, and the anti-Communist Armenian Revolutionary Federation (Dashnak).

TABLE 8. *Lebanon: Progovernment Coalition*

PLACE	NAME	SECT
	Sami Sulh	Sunni
	Khalil Hibri	Sunni
Beirut	Pierre Jumayyil	Maronite
	Joseph Shadir	Armenian Catholic
North Lebanon	Charles Malik	Orthodox
	Camille Cham'un	Maronite
Mount Lebanon	Na'im Mughabghab	Catholic
	Majid Arslan	Druze
Biqa'	Joseph Skaff	Catholic

The Third Force

No study of Lebanon's leadership would be complete without an account of the Third Force, which attempted to mediate between the two warring sides in the 1958 crisis. The group of leaders that became identified as the Third Force coalesced after the 1957 parliamentary elections in which many anti-Cham'un leaders were defeated. Foreseeing the possibility of intercommunal strife, the Third Force attempted to prevent it. Indeed, its members had both individual and collective reasons for creating a group independent of the two warring factions. In general the motivating factors were probably a mix of individual self-interest and the desire to preserve the Lebanese ship of state. Collectively, the Third Force had every reason to want a pacified Lebanon in the shortest possible time. Over half the leaders listed in table 9 represented Lebanon's banking and business interests, the very areas of life which had suffered from the war and had so much to gain from peace. Lebanese business needed peace, and within Lebanon's economic and psycholog-

TABLE 9. *Lebanon: The Third Force*

NAME	SECT
Yusif Salim	Catholic
Henri Far'awn	Catholic
Georges Naqqash	Maronite
Charles Hilu	Maronite
Joseph Hitti	Maronite
Raymond Iddih	Maronite
Najib Salha	Sunni
Bahij Taqi al-Din	Druze
Ghassan Twayni	Orthodox
Gabriel Murr	Orthodox
Paul M'ushi	Maronite
Bishara Khuri	Maronite
Fu'ad Shihab	Maronite

ical milieu, business has always been considered more important than anything else except confessionalism. Ex-Foreign Minister Henri Far'awn, the leader of the Third Force, was considered Lebanon's foremost banker. Along with his friend and partner, Michel Shiha, Far'awn had once helped Bishara Khuri win the presidency. Closely allied to these Catholic bankers of Beirut was Charles Hilu himself an ex-minister and an aspirant to the presidency. Reinforcing the bankers were two big businessmen, Joseph Salim and Najib Salha. Nor did most of the other Third Force leaders—Naqqash, Iddih, Twayni, Murr—lack business connections and an upper-class economic position—both inducements to conclude interfaith peace.

Politically the Third Force elite consisted of either Cham'un's personal rivals or former members of his coalition. Far'awn's early support of Bishara Khuri's bid for the presidency had not especially endeared him to the Cham'unites. Another Third Force member, Charles Hilu, had served briefly as minister under Cham'un, yet had once been a Far'awn ally and after the mid-fifties had rivaled Cham'un as a presidential aspirant. Once a frequent cabinet appointee, Gabriel al-Murr had been sidetracked in Cham'un's last three years. Yusif Salim, a Far'awn business ally, saw in Cham'un a threat to his business prospects; [41] also he had been a part of the Khuri-Sulh coalition in and out of the cabinet in 1945. Another pro-Khuri exminister was Bahij Taqi al-Din, who never got near the cabinet under Cham'un. As Maronites, Joseph

Hitti and Alfred Naqqash were considered potential rivals for the presidency. Ghassan Twayni, a neutral newspaperman, found his path to the cabinet blocked. Finally, there was Raymond Iddih of the National Bloc, who considered himself a candidate to succeed Cham'un to the presidency, the same office that his father, Emile Iddih, had held during the mandate years.

It follows that when the Third Force came out against extending Cham'un's presidency, it was advocating a policy dictated not only by national interest but also by the self-interest of most of its members. The main exception was Far'awn, who opposed constitutional change for fear that it could destroy Lebanese democracy. He had opposed President Khuri's drive for a second term, he could do no less with President Cham'un. Whatever the members' motives, the Third Force was the most vocal and effective group to play a mediatory role. It was highly representative denominationally. Given its broad distribution and the high prestige of its members, the Third Force was uniquely suited to reduce tensions and work toward peace. Yet even this high-powered group could not achieve peace without the support of four other behind-the-scenes actors—the anti-Cham'un Maronite patriarch, Monsignor M'ushi, ex-President Khuri, General Shihab, and the Americans—an impressive coalition of forces by any measure.

Events moved in rapid succession after mid-1958, pushing Lebanon toward chaos. Shocked by the July 14th Revolution in Iraq and in response to President Cham'un's appeal, President Eisenhower dispatched the US Marines to Lebanon (15 July). Soon the UN mediating effort was partly assumed by the Americans, who began to cooperate with the Third Force. These efforts led to the election of General Shihab as president (July 1958) and the acceptance by both sides that there had been "no victor and no vanquished" in the conflict. The presidential election induced a changing of the guard which brought both new and old personalities together in new coalitions that could bridge the cleavages brought about by the fighting. In retrospect perhaps the greatest utility of Lebanon's cabinet system has been its use as an instrument of reconciliation; this was never more true than after the civil war.

The Shihab Cabinets (1958–1964)

General Shihab had been summoned to power for the second
time in six years; but unlike his brief stay in 1952, now he was
coming as the elected head of state. His troubles began when the
predominantly Maronite Kata'ib Party declared a strike in the
name of Christian interests after one of its journalists was ab-
ducted. More significantly, the Kata'ib wanted guarantees of Lebanese independence and a share of power in the new government,
which it considered unrepresentative of the nation and at variance
with the ''no victor, no vanquished'' formula.

The cabinet which the Kata'ib opposed was headed by Rashid
Karami, leader of Cham'un's opposition in Tripoli. The remaining
ministers [42] were neutrals including Charles Hilu, a Third Force
leader. The sole exception was Philippe Taqla, who had been one
of the leaders of the resistance against Cham'un. In its totality the
first cabinet under President Shihab was not well suited for reconciliation, since it was ''tilted'' toward such main Cham'un opponents as Karami and Taqla. More important, the cabinet included
not one member of Cham'un's constituency, not even the Kata'ib.
This situation moved the Kata'ib to trigger a protracted boycott
that led to disturbances. Finally on 15 October 1958 the president
formed a new cabinet of four ministers—two Maronites and two
Sunnis. It was given substantial emergency powers and once again
placed under Prime Minister Karami, a Sunni. The second Sunni
was Husayn al-Uwayni, also an insurgent. On the Maronite side
were two perpetual rivals, Raymond Iddih of the National Bloc
and Pierre Jumayyil of the Kata'ib. The new cabinet represented
the Sunni concentrations in Tripoli and Beirut as well as the Third
Force, to which Raymond Iddih belonged. Jumayyil was the only
outright pro-Cham'unite in the cabinet.

Backed by a strong soldier-president, the emergency cabinet
won a vote of confidence on 17 October. Karami hailed his cabinet
as one of national salvation and reiterated its commitment to the
National Pact of 1943. In the end, the new cabinet came to represent a reestablishment of balance between various interests.
Equally significant was the reconciliation among the elite as reflected by their willingness to serve together in the cabinet. Of

course the most effective instrument of this reconciliation was the induction into the cabinet of pro-Cham'un politicians. The process of reconciliation through cabinet recruitment continues in Lebanese politics today. The sole major politician who was not returned to cabinet office since the 1958 civil turmoil has been ex-Premier Sami al-Sulh. As the principal pro-Cham'un Sunni leader during the civil war, he was never forgiven by his enemies.[43]

The original cabinet of four survived until October 1959, when Raymond Iddih resigned because of disagreements with his fellow Maronite, Jumayyil. Next came an expansion of the government to satisfy a larger number of interests.[44] In general the expanded cabinet consisted of moderates, half of whom were nondeputies. Once again it was tilted in favor of the insurgents. In other words, the lineup showed three main insurgent leaders (Karami, Uwayni, Taqla) and two allies (Bazzi and Najjar) versus Jumayyil and his two allies, Butrus and Zuwayn.

During 1959 life returned substantially to normal. In order to accommodate more interests and personalities a new electoral law was passed increasing the number of deputies from sixty-six to ninety-nine. This brought a new openness to the political system and contributed greatly to reconciliation and general normalization of political life. The new electoral law was to be implemented by an extraparliamentary cabinet of eight ministers under the venerable Ahmad Da'uq. The new ministers were regarded as neutrals, the sole exception being Philippe Taqla.[45] The election went peacefully and was one of the fairest in Lebanon's history. Pro-Shihab candidates won overwhelmingly because of the president's prestige and the support of those constituencies which had backed the 1958 insurrection. While Cham'un [46] and Raymond Iddih did win their seats, most of their supporters lost in the pro-Shihab tide of victory. The fact that Cham'un could win testified to the possibility of achieving reconciliation in the system.

Most of the major leaders involved in the 1958 crisis became deputies and ministers: Sa'ib Salam, Nasim Majdalani, Kamal Junblat, Ahmad al-As'ad, Rashid Karami, Sulayman Franjiyyah (for his ill brother), Rene Mu'awwad, and Sabri Himadah. For these men the insurrection had paid off—after exclusion from office by Cham'un now they were back in power. Only Yafi was not elected, and as a result Salam remained the only major Sunnite candidate for the premiership except Rashid Karami. On 1 August 1960 Salam formed what was Lebanon's largest cabinet to date. It contained eighteen ministers, representing most of the political parties, groups, and zu'ama'—virtually a miniature of the ninety-nine member Chamber. Because of its unprecedented size the cabinet could provide niches for a greater number of politicians than ever before. Even though still tilted in favor of the insurrectionists—Salam, Franjiyyah, Taqla, Majdalani, Junblat, and Mashnuq—it also included exloyalists such as Arslan, the two Jumayyils, and Skaff. For the first time the Armenian Orthodox community was represented at the cabinet level by deputy Khatchig Babikian, who belonged to the pro-Cham'un Dashnak Party. The remaining ministers were neutrals. While its broad representativeness contributed to national reconciliation, it complicated the formulation of unified cabinet policy resulting in periods of cabinet inaction. Thereafter President Shihab sometimes bypassed formal channels by operating through his personal "kitchen cabinet" which consisted of military and civilian aids.[47]

The cabinet resigned after several strikes were capped by Syrian National Party (PPS)-Kata'ib clashes in the Biqa' in May 1961. Prime Minister Salam formed a second cabinet on 20 May 1961 composed of only eight ministers, seven of whom came from his previous cabinet. The strongest members of the cabinet had been retained.[48] Despite the consolidation, however, the cabinet did not last for long. In October 1961 bombings and internal disorders increased anti-Salam sentiment in the Chamber, especially among those members of Salam's first cabinet who were left out of his second. There had also been the maverick maneuverings of Junblat in defiance of Sa'ib Salam, who seemed to have lost President Shihab's confidence. As a result a new cabinet came into power on 31 October 1961 under Salam's rival Rashid Karami. Composed of fourteen ministers, the Karami cabinet was broadly based both confessionally and factionally. This factor coupled with presidential backing made it possible for the cabinet to endure until February 1964, when it resigned for the forthcoming elections. With a tenure of twenty-seven months this cabinet has the distinction of longevity among all previous governments. The cabinet's endurance as well as Karami's third return to the premiership under Shihab were clear indications of the compatible partnership between president and premier reminiscent of the Khuri-R. Sulh and Cham'un-S. Sulh combinations.

The new cabinet coalition included two antagonistic Druzes, Junblat and Arslan; two rival Shi'ite factions, represented by Kamal al-As'ad and Ali Bazzi; and the Maronites were Rene Mu'awwad (Franjiyyah Bloc), Jumayyil (Kata'ib), and Hunayn (National Bloc). The rest were pro-Karami or neutral ministers.[49] The strength of the government was repeatedly tested, beginning with the abortive PPS coup d'etat (January 1962), clashes on the Syrian border, and student strikes. Yet because of presidential support and its makeup, the cabinet survived all these crises, any one of which would have probably brought down past cabinets.

On 20 February 1964 a caretaker cabinet of ten took over under the Beirut Sunni leader, Husayn al-Uwayni, to oversee the elections. In Uwayni's selection one could discern another nod toward the Cairo Arab leadership; like Karami, Salam, and Yafi, Uwayni had been a Sunni anti-Cham'un leader in 1958, as were the Christians Fu'ad Ammun and Philippe Taqla.[50] From the Third Force there were Charles Hilu and Georges Naqqash—two middle-of-the-road journalists. The remaining ministers were neutrals,[51] in keeping with the tradition of a nonpartisan electoral cabinet.

The 1964 elections were not conducted as fairly as those of 1960, since there were charges of army pressure in favor of a Chamber which could reelect General Shihab for a second term.[52] After initial indecision, however, President Shihab decided against another presidential term.

The Hilu Cabinets (1964–1970)

Significantly, the person who won the presidency belonged to neither of the warring sides in 1958. Charles Hilu, like his military predecessor, had stayed out of partisan quarrels and therefore lacked major political enemies. As a lawyer, journalist, ambassador, and cabinet minister, Hilu knew Lebanese politics, but was not a center of controversy. Indeed he had served in parliament for only one term. His major distinction was his leadership (along with Henri Far'awn) of the Third Force. Hilu had personal and business ties to the Catholic bankers Far'awn and Shiha, the latter having been Hilu's employer in journalism. Also Hilu had marriage ties with other presidential families including the Trads, the Iddihs, the Cham'uns, the Thabits, the Shihabs, and the Naqqashes (see figure 1). Yet despite such centrality within the Lebanese political and economic elite, President Hilu lacked the depth of support that his predecessor possessed. At least Shihab could count on the army's organizational support and on the legitimacy he had gained during and after the 1958 conflict. By contrast, Hilu was a politician, who became a compromise candidate for the presidency. He therefore had to move cautiously, to govern without alienating the increments of political support he might need to be an effective president. Hence he reappointed Husayn al-Uwayni (24 September 1964) along with most of his previous nonpartisan cabinet. Despite receiving a vote of confidence, the new cabinet was doomed to failure because it had no deputies in it. Then Uwayni formed his third cabinet (19 November 1964) consisting of fourteen members, twelve of whom were deputies. This was an unusually affluent cabinet composed of men (Salha, Sahnawi, Arab, and Majdalani) who had financial or business interconnections before entering the cabinet. Politically, the cabinet brought together a broad coalition of elements loyal to the Cham'un and Karami factions; also included was a Constitutionalist, a Progressive Socialist, and a Phalangist (Kata'ib).[53]

The government's greatest challenge came during June 1965 with the exposure of a new PPS coup plot. On 20 July the Uwayni cabinet fell; five days later Rashid Karami formed a new cabinet of ten. With the single exception of Premier Karami, the cabinet was extraparliamentary so that it could implement long expected reforms such as purging the bureaucracy and the police and suppressing the Ba'ath Party. The cabinet's make-up was determined by the president's desire to accord it prestige and an aura of legitimacy and fairness; hence the appointment of personalities of repute such as Najib Alam al-Din, Georges Hakim, Wajdi Mallat, Georges Naqqash, and Emile Tyyan.[54] By late March 1966, the president was under increasing pressure to stop reform and to institute a parliamentary government. It was significant that Hilu followed the tradition set by his predecessors Shihab and Cham'un of instituting a reform program at the start of the presidential term; President Franjiyyah followed suit in 1970.

A new cabinet of ten ministers came into being on 10 April 1966, under Abdallah al-Yafi. This was Dr. Yafi's sixth cabinet since Lebanon's independence. Aside from Yafi and Taqla, all the remaining ministers were deputies and they represented most of the interest groups in the Chamber; the cabinet was labeled "a government of national union." [55]

Crisis after crisis eroded the effectiveness of the Yafi cabinet. In September there was a workers' strike, but far more serious were the communal clashes in Zgharta which required army intervention. On 15 October the Intra-Bank crashed and a month later the mayor of Ba'albak was shot because of a clan feud; also there was an unsatisfactory vote of confidence. On 2 December Dr. Yafi resigned and once again Karami returned at the head of a ten-man coalition cabinet drawn from his own Democratic Parliamentary Front, Junblat's Progressive Socialist Party, the Armenian deputies group, plus the old Shihabites. However, the coalition was not strong enough and Karami had to form a cabinet of independents (7 December 1966), consisting of prominent citizens.[56] The substantial social and economic prestige and great technical competence of this cabinet were resources much in demand during the hard days of mid-1967.

Tripartite opposition to Karami materialized in early April 1967, when ex-President Cham'un, Raymond Iddih, and Pierre Jumayyil joined in criticizing the prime minister for pro-UAR leanings. With the advent of the Six-Day War, the government found itself in an untenable position regarding the disposition of its small army against Israel. With the support of Cham'un, Jumayyil, and Iddih, General Bustani successfully resisted Karami's pressures to involve the army in war. In August these leaders formed an alliance of their respective parties to contest the March 1968 elections. On 5 February 1968 the Karami government resigned in favor of a ten-member caretaker cabinet under Yafi to supervise the parliamentary elections. However, all the ministers were deputies except the noted banker Henri Far'awn and Yafi himself. In contrast to most earlier election cabinets, Yafi's was not nonpartisan. Indeed some of the ministers who were seeking office were presiding upon their own electoral contest. Seven of them were reelected,[57] thus making it possible for the cabinet to continue with minor changes.[58] In the election the Tripartite Alliance of Cham'un, Jumayyil, and Iddih increased its strength to twenty-nine seats while Karami's Democratic Parliamentary Front dropped to twenty-five seats. In early May Kamal al-As'ad became speaker of the Chamber of Deputies defeating Sabri Himadih, who had Prime Minister Yafi's support. In June general instability caused by the threat of war, guerrilla activity, and the concomitant economic decline prompted another cabinet reshuffle. The attempted assassination of ex-President Cham'un exacerbated the situation and rekindled the old Junblat-Cham'un polemic. Amid increasing instability the government resigned 9 October; but President Hilu asked Dr. Yafi to form another cabinet which because it lacked a consensus resigned almost immediately. Attempting to end the eight-day impasse, President Hilu submitted his own resignation (20 October) but withdrew it when Yafi finally succeeded in forming a government that included two Sunnis and two Maronites—Yafi, Uwayni, Jumayyil, and Iddih. At the same time Himadih defeated his brother-in-law Kamal al-As'ad in the contest for the speakership.

Yafi's cabinet would have probably lasted, had it not been for the continuing instability caused by the warfare between the Israelis and the Palestinian guerrillas. After the shock produced by the Israeli commando raid on Beirut International Airport (29 December 1968), it was a foregone conclusion that a new cabinet would emerge to deal with the task of national defense. On 15 January 1969 Karami returned to head an unusually large cabinet designed to unite the people of Lebanon at a time of external and internal danger. The sixteen-man cabinet included Iddih and Jumayyil but their partner in the Tripartite Alliance, ex-President Cham'un, was not included.

Despite winning a vote of confidence in the Chamber, Karami's cabinet underwent a major reshuffle (23 January 1969) necessitated by the resignations of Jumayyil, Iddih, Ma'luf, and Mansur—and four new ministers were brought in.[59] At least six groups were represented in the cabinet; the Center Bloc, the Franjiyyah, the Junblat, and the Arslan factions, the Hay'at al-Wataniya Party and Karami's faction; there were also two independents, a Constitutionalist, and a Dashnak.[60]

In the wake of shooting between the army and the Palestinians (April 1969) Karami presented his resignation to the president but agreed to stay on until the formation of a new cabinet. From mid-May on, Karami tried in vain to form a viable cabinet, for both the Tripartite Alliance and Junblat manifested increasing intransigence. While the Tripartite Alliance advocated ending of guerrilla activity, Junblat supported commando actions against Israel. Meanwhile, President Hilu declared (31 May) his solidarity with the Arab cause in Palestine but opposed commando bases in Lebanon.

Toward the end of October clashes between Palestinian commandoes and the Lebanese Army so intensified that Karami resigned (21 October). On 2 November an agreement was concluded through Nasir's mediation limiting the scope of commando activity. Karami returned as head of another government (25 November 1969), which represented most shades of Lebanese opinion. With the exception of Iddih's National Bloc, Karami's parliamentary cabinet was all-encompassing, even including Cham'un's National Liberals together with Junblat, the two Jumayyils, the Center Bloc, the Nahjists, Arslan's Druze faction, and the Dashnaks.[61]

Caught between their Israeli enemies and the Palestinian commandoes, the Lebanese elite found itself in a state of virtual impotence as the Cairo Agreement was repeatedly violated both by the guerrillas and the Lebanese Army. On 17 March 1970 fourteen persons died in clashes between Kata'ib members and the commandoes. The thirty-two-hour Israeli raid on 12 May increased inter-elite conflict at a time when President Hilu's hold on the country was weakening since his term of office was ending. Also contributing to inter-elite conflict was the country's increasing preoccupation with the forthcoming presidential elections. Karami's Democratic Parliamentary Front and the Nahjists met on 4 May to nominate ex-President Fu'ad Shihab as presidential candidate. A month later, the Tripartite Alliance leaders Cham'un and Iddih met to nominate their colleague Jumayyil to the presidency. By late July it was not clear whether Shihab would agree to return as president. As a result, several candidates were put forth: Jamil Lahhud, Sulayman Franjiyyah, Habib Kayruz, Raymond Iddih, Camille Cham'un, and Pierre Iddih.

As election day approached there was no sign of a caretaker

cabinet to preside over the contest. By early August Cham'un and Iddih were also seeking the presidency. Meanwhile, Junblat announced his support for General Jamil Lahhud, and Najjadah leader Adnan al-Hakim proposed himself as a candidate in an attempt to challenge the Maronites' exclusive right to the presidency. Finally, there were two compromise candidates, Minister of Economy, Sulayman Franjiyyah and Governor of the Central Bank, Elias Sarkis. Eventually, the seventeen-member Center Bloc of Sa'ib Salam and Kamal al-As'ad nominated Franjiyyah. Next, ex-President Cham'un, an opponent of Salam, As'ad, and Franjiyyah during the 1958 conflict, gave his support to Franjiyyah by withdrawing himself from the race; Raymond Iddih followed suit. On the same day the forty-member Nahjist group (pro-Shihab) met and nominated Sarkis as their candidate. On the third ballot Franjiyyah defeated Sarkis by one vote when Junblat and Jumayyil switched their support to him; but Speaker Sabri Himadih declared that Franjiyyah's fifty votes fell short of a two-third majority. Pandemonium broke out in the Chamber and both Junblat and Karami reportedly urged the speaker to declare Franjiyyah the winner before serious trouble began in the streets. Finally, Himadih relented. A quest for the presidency begun by Hamid Franjiyyah was now realized by his younger brother, Sulayman, who had stepped into Hamid's shoes as za'im in 1960 when the latter suffered a stroke.

Franjiyyah's Presidency: A New Coalition

In many ways the Franjiyyah election was a turning point in Lebanese politics. The election at once reflected the shifting of elite coalitions and the emergence of new ones; it also meant that the crisis of 1958 had finally been committed to history. Perhaps the most dramatic move in the whole affair was the support Cham'un gave to Franjiyyah, who with his brother Hamid had led the insurrectionists in North Lebanon. Even before the 1958 fighting Hamid had been Cham'un's rival for the presidency. Indeed, in voting for Franjiyyah, Cham'un had aligned his group with most of his enemies of yesteryear including Sa'ib Salam, Kamal al-As'ad, and Kamal Junblat. The rationale of this grand coalition was the need to stop Shihab's return or the emergence of a pro-Shihab candidate supported by Karami and the Nahjists. To that end Cham'un and Jumayyil, who had been anti-Shihab, and Iddih, Salam, Junblat, and As'ad who had supported Shihab, had banded together behind Franjiyyah.

Prime Minister Karami resigned on 3 October and two days later President Franjiyyah paid his largest political debt by asking Sa'ib Salam to form a new cabinet drawn from outside the Chamber. The twelve-man government (13 October 1970) was composed of young technocrats and businessmen, most of whom were relatively unknown. Without counting Salam, the average age of the ministers was thirty-nine. The best known was Ghassan Twayni, the editor-publisher of *Al-Nahar* and a Harvard graduate. The remaining ministers included four professors, one lawyer, three engineers, one doctor, and one economist. The purpose of this nonpolitical cabinet, according to Salam, was "to carry out a revolution from the top." Despite grumbling in parliament, the new government received an overwhelming vote of confidence. Meanwhile Kamil al-As'ad, an early Franjiyyah supporter, was elected as speaker. Thus, the three top positions in the state were controlled by three members of the Center Bloc—Franjiyyah, Salam, and As'ad.

The cabinet's major problem centered on the continuing war between the Israelis and the Palestinian guerrillas, not to mention growing lawlessness and economic problems. During March 1972 it became clear that the Franjiyyah-Salam administration had no intention of creating a caretaker cabinet to supervise the forthcoming parliamentary elections. Instead, Prime Minister Salam asserted his intention to maintain a "strict neutrality."

The elections were held, and with few exceptions all the major zu'ama' won: Arslan, Iddih, Salam, As'ad, Skaff, and Jumayyil. Junblat allied himself with his rival Arslan and carried with him five others to victory, while his old opponent, Cham'un, won only one seat besides his own. On 25 May President Franjiyyah called on Sa'ib Salam to form a new cabinet drawn from the Chamber. Thus, the Center Bloc again kept control of the three highest government posts: the presidency, the premiership, and the speakership.

The new eighteen-man cabinet included many of the old

zu'ama', six of whom were over sixty years of age. Only four ministers were carried over from the last cabinet. Also in the new government were two old Constitutionalists—the perennial Majid Arslan, who had been in twenty governments since 1943, and Sabri Himadih, who was brought into the cabinet since As'ad had replaced him as speaker. Other groups in the new cabinet coalition were Iddih's National Bloc (Mukhaybar and Hunayn) and Cham'un's National Liberals (Khalil and A'war). The return of Khalil and A'war to the cabinet after an absence of about fourteen years indicated the culmination of the reconciliation between the old Cham'unites and their enemies.[62] Finally, after initial reluctance, the Kata'ib and the Armenian Dashnak parties joined the government. Thus, Salam's coalition included a wide spectrum of interests and leaders within a large cabinet where all but one were deputies. Hence the cabinet's success in getting a strong vote of confidence (77 to 15) from the Chamber. Through his choices Franjiyyah had rewarded almost all of the leaders who had supported his presidential bid: Salam, As'ad, Cham'un, Iddih, Jumayyil, Himadih, Arslan, and the Armenians. Pro-Karami and pro-Shihab (Najhist) leaders were left out. Junblat's last minute support of Franjiyyah was not rewarded. During the rest of 1972 and early 1973 the cabinet's make-up did not change radically.[63] Despite the Crontale Missile controversy, worker-student strikes, Israeli attacks, and Lebanese-Palestinian clashes, Sa'ib Salam gave no indication of resigning. As a founding member of the pro-Franjiyyah Center Bloc coalition, the prime minister continued in power with presidential approval and support. It was not until April 1973 that Salam resigned as a result of fighting between the Lebanese army and the Palestinian guerrillas. The term of his successor, deputy Amin Hafiz of Tripoli, was shortlived because of the protracted army-guerrilla fighting.

Elite Profiles

Tenure: Cabinets and Ministers

The foregoing analysis of elite coalitions illustrates that Lebanese cabinets have a high turnover rate; no less than 159 individuals served in 45 cabinets which have come to power in the nearly thirty years from 1943 to 1972. The average tenure of these cabinets was approximately 7.5 months. The cabinet of longest duration, headed by the veteran Sunni politician Rashid Karami (October 1961), lasted 2½ years. Not counting certain abortive cabinets which lasted only a day, the shortest cabinet in Lebanese history was that of 14 September 1952, organized during the national emergency which culminated in the forced resignation of President Bishara Khuri; it lasted exactly 4 days.

The frequency of cabinet changes is attributable to intermittent crises, parliamentary and presidential elections, cabinet dissension, and the will of a president, who may force cabinet changes to increase elite circulation and thereby satisfy as many major leaders, factions, and/or sects as desirable.

Examined confessionally, tenure was longest for the Druze ministers and shortest for Maronite ministers, with the other sects somewhere in between (see table 10). The long tenure of the Druzes is largely attributable to Arslan's phenomenal longevity; he has been in 22 cabinets for a total of 16 years. Another perennial Druze minister has been Kamal Junblat with service in 6 cabinets for a total of over 5 years. Between them, these two ministers account for over half the Druze tenure and thus reflect the traditional strength of Druze tribal zu'ama' and the concomitantly low level of intra-elite competitiveness. In contrast, the short Maronite ministerial tenure indicates the relative weakness of the Maronite zu'ama' and the resulting milieu of heightened competitiveness.

Age

Based on a total of 142 ministers for whom definite ages were indicated, the average age of Lebanese politicians at first cabinet office was 47 years—not too old even though one-half of Lebanon's population is below 20 years of age.[64] Considerably higher was their average age at leaving cabinet office—53 years old. The Shi'ite ministers, at an average age of 40 years, entered the cabinet earlier than the ministers from the other minorities (see table 11). The highest average ages were those of the Sunni and Maronite ministers which exceeded 49 years. Just below them were the Catholics with an average age of 48 years, followed by

TABLE 10. *Lebanon: Confessional Representation over Time*

SECT

CABINETS		Maronite		Sunni		Shi'ite		Orthodox		Catholic		Druze		Armenian Orthodox and Catholic		Size
		N	%	N	%	N	%	N	%	N	%	N	%	N	%	
25 September	1943	1	16.7	1	16.7	1	16.7	1	16.7	1	16.7	1	16.7	—	—	6
3 July	1944	1	16.7	1	16.7	1	16.7	1	16.7	1	16.7	1	16.7	—	—	6
9 January	1945	1	16.7	1	16.7	1	16.7	1	16.7	1	16.7	1	16.7	—	—	6
22 August	1945	2	25	2	25	1	12.5	1	12.5	1	12.5	1	12.5	—	—	8
22 May	1946	2	25	2	25	1	12.5	1	12.5	1	12.5	1	12.5	—	—	8
14 December	1946	2	22.2	2	22.2	1	11.1	1	11.1	1	11.1	2	22.2	—	—	9 *
7 April	1947	2	25	2	25	1	12.5	1	12.5	1	12.5	1	12.5	—	—	8
26 July	1948	2	25	2	25	1	12.5	1	12.5	1	12.5	1	12.5	—	—	8
1 October	1949	3	30	2	20	1	10	1	10	1	10	2	20	—	—	10 *
14 February	1951	1	33	1	33	—	—	1	33	—	—	—	—	—	—	3
7 April	1951	3	30	2	20	2	20	1	10	1	10	1	10	—	—	10
11 February	1952	3	30	2	20	2	20	1	10	1	10	1	10	—	—	10
9 September	1952	1	33	1	33	—	—	1	33	—	—	—	—	—	—	3
14 September	1952	1	33	1	33	—	—	1	33	—	—	—	—	—	—	3
18 September	1952	1	33	1	33	—	—	1	33	—	—	—	—	—	—	3
30 September	1952	1	25	1	25	1	25	1	25	—	—	—	—	—	—	4
30 April	1953	2	25	2	25	1	12.5	1	12.5	1	12.5	1	12.5	—	—	8
16 August	1953	2	25	2	25	1	12.5	1	12.5	1	12.5	1	12.5	—	—	8
1 March	1954	2	25	2	25	1	12.5	1	12.5	1	12.5	1	12.5	—	—	8
16 September	1954	3	30	3	30	1	10	1	10	1	10	1	10	—	—	10
9 July	1955	3	30	3	30	1	10	1	10	1	10	1	10	—	—	10
19 September	1955	3	30	3	30	1	10	1	10	1	10	1	10	—	—	10

Date	Year															
19 March	1956	3	30	3	30	1	10	1	10	1	10	1	10	—	—	10
8 June	1956	3	30	3	30	1	10	1	10	1	10	1	10	—	—	10
18 November	1956	1	16.7	1	16.7	1	16.7	1	16.7	1	16.7	1	16.7	—	—	6
18 August	1957	2	25	2	25	1	12.5	1	12.5	1	12.5	1	12.5	—	—	8
14 March	1958	3	21.4	3	21.4	2	14.3	2	14.3	1	7.1	2	14.3	1	7.1	14
24 September	1958	2	25	2	25	1	12.5	1	12.5	1	12.5	1	12.5	—	—	8
14 October	1958	2	25	2	25	1	12.5	1	12.5	1	12.5	1	12.5	—	—	8
14 May	1960	2	25	2	25	1	12.5	1	12.5	1	12.5	1	12.5	—	—	8
1 August	1960	4	22.2	4	22.2	3	16.7	2	11.1	2	11.1	2	11.1	1	5.5	18
20 May	1961	2	25	2	25	1	12.5	1	12.5	1	12.5	1	12.5	—	—	8
31 October	1961	3	21.4	3	21.4	2	14.3	2	14.3	2	14.3	2	14.3	—	—	14
20 February	1964	3	30	3	30	1	10	1	10	1	10	1	10	—	—	10
25 September	1964	3	30	3	30	1	10	1	10	1	10	1	10	—	—	10
19 November	1964	3	21.4	3	21.4	2	14.3	2	14.3	2	14.3	2	14.3	—	—	14
25 July	1965	3	25	3	25	2	16.6	1	8.3	2	16.6	1	8.3	—	—	12
10 April	1966	3	30	3	30	1	10	1	10	1	10	1	10	—	—	10
6 December	1966	3	30	3	30	1	10	1	10	1	10	1	10	—	—	10
8 February	1968	3	30	3	30	1	10	1	10	1	10	1	10	—	—	10
20 October	1968	2	50	2	50	—	—	—	—	—	—	—	—	—	—	4
16 January	1969	3	18.8	3	18.8	3	18.8	2	12.5	2	12.5	2	12.5	1	6.3	16
26 November	1969	3	18.8	3	18.8	3	18.8	2	12.5	2	12.5	2	12.5	1	6.3	16
13 October	1970	3	25	3	25	3	16.7	2	16.7	1	8.3	1	8.3	—	—	12
27 May	1972	4	22.2	4	22.2	3	16.6	2	11.1	2	11.1	2	11.1	1	5.5	18

* These two cabinets may be considered exceptions because of irregularities in their confessional balance.

the Orthodox and the Druzes at 46 and 44 years respectively. The relative youth of the Shi'ites may be attributed to the tendency to enter politics without spending time in college. This hypothesis is based on the findings in tables 19 and 20, which indicate a relatively low level of education for Shi'ite leaders.

TABLE 11. *Lebanon: Average Age at First Cabinet Office—Aggregate Count*

SECT	AVERAGE AGE
Sunni	49.3
Maronite	49.2
Shi'ite	40.0
Orthodox	46.6
Catholic	48.0
Druze	44.8

Overall the average age of the cabinet elite does not show major fluctuations throughout Lebanon's thirty years of constitutional government. The first cabinet after independence (September 1943) was composed of relatively young politicians, with an average age of 41; the average of the second cabinet (July 1944) stood even lower at about 37—the country's youngest. However, there have frequently been older cabinets as indicated in table 12, including many with an average age over 50. In the October 1968 cabinet, the average age was over 63, making it Lebanon's oldest cabinet.

Table 12 also reveals that caretaker and emergency cabinets (i.e., February 1951; 9, 14 and 18 September 1952; May 1960; February 1964; October 1968) have substantially higher average ages than the cabinets preceding or succeeding them. This is because caretaker (election) and emergency cabinets include older, well-known politicians and/or widely respected senior statesmen, expressly brought in to stress systemic legitimacy, respectability, and impartiality. Implicit are the traditional Middle Eastern notions of showing respect for old age and deference to the wisdom of elders.

Overall, the ministers' average age level did increase somewhat; that is, the cabinets of the sixties were generally older than those of the fifties. This was mostly due to the fact that certain key members of the elite have grown old in office. Most notable among these is Amir Majid Arslan, who entered independent Lebanon's very first cabinet at 38 and served repeatedly, the last being in May 1972, at the age of 67. Other near-permanent fixtures have included Sa'ib Salam, Abdallah al-Yafi, Kamal Junblat, Sabri Himadih, Husayn al-Uwayni, Philippe Taqla, Gabriel Murr, Georges Hakim, Rashid Karami, Joseph Skaff, Sami al-Sulh, and Pierre Jumayyil. These ministers, along with others who served frequently, have contributed to the aging of the cabinets especially during the sixties.

Despite the generally upward trend in age, there was a reversal beginning with the two 1969 cabinets and continuing in the first cabinet of the Franjiyyah-Salam administration (October 1970). Chiefly through the appointment of ten new and young extra-parliamentary ministers, the October 1970 cabinet registered a low of 42 years—an average cabinet age only slightly above that of the September 1943 cabinet. Although the May 1972 cabinet registered an age upswing, there is no reason to suppose that average cabinet age will continue to increase indefinitely; rather it can be expected to level off near the present figure (47) as the veterans die or retire.

Education by Cabinet

Judging from the composite index of educational level in table 12, the elite's average educational level fluctuated substantially, especially in the early years of independence. Overall, however, educational level increased from an index of 1.8 for the September 1943 cabinet to an all-time high of 3.0 for the October 1970 cabinet. This increase took place in two successive stages, as table 12 reflects. Until the 14 September 1952 cabinet, indices below 2.0 predominated, indicating the large number of ministers with only BA and lower degrees. Since 1952 the educational-level index (with one exception) has consistently registered above 2.0, mostly due to the rise in doctorates. Each of the 13 cabinets since 1961 has had a number of doctorate holders, in contrast to many previous cabinets, 13 of which had not included even one PhD or MD.

TABLE 12. *Lebanon: Age and Educational Level*

CABINET		AVERAGE AGE	No College N	%	AA N	%	BA/BS/License N	%	MA/MS/Certificate N	%	Doctorate N	%	Educational Level Index *	Total Membership **
September	1943	41	—	—	1	16.7	5	83.3	—	—	—	—	1.8	6
July	1944	37.5	—	—	2	33.3	4	66.7	—	—	—	—	1.7	6
January	1945	53	3	50	—	—	2	33.3	—	—	1	16.7	2	6
August	1945	48.4	1	12.5	—	—	6	75	—	—	1	12.5	2	8
May	1946	46	—	—	1	12.5	7	87.5	—	—	—	—	1.9	8
December	1946	45.5	1	11.1	1	11.1	4	44.4	1	11.1	2	22.2	2.2	9
April	1947	46	1	12.5	1	12.5	6	75	—	—	—	—	1.9	8
July	1948	47.5	1	12.5	2	25	4	50	—	—	1	12.5	1.8	8
October	1949	48	3	27.3	2	18.2	4	36.4	—	—	2	18.2	2	11
February	1951	50.5	—	—	2	66.7	1	33.3	—	—	—	—	1.3	3
April	1951	45	1	9.1	1	9.1	8	72.7	—	—	1	9.1	2.1	11
February	1952	44.5	2	20	2	20	6	60	—	—	—	—	1.6	10
9 September	1952	51	—	—	1	33.3	2	66.7	—	—	—	—	1.7	3
14 September	1952	50	—	—	—	—	3	100	—	—	—	—	2	3
18 September	1952	50	—	—	1	33.3	1	33.3	1	33.3	—	—	2	3
30 September	1952	48	—	—	1	25	1	25	1	25	1	25	2.5	4
April	1953	47	—	—	2	25	4	50	2	25	—	—	2	8
August	1953	49	—	—	—	—	7	87.5	—	—	1	12.5	2.3	8
March	1954	52	—	—	1	12.5	6	75	—	—	1	12.5	2.1	8
September	1954	51	—	—	2	18.2	8	72.7	—	—	1	9.1	2	11
July	1955	49	—	—	2	20	6	60	1	10	1	10	2.1	10
September	1955	45	1	10	1	10	6	60	1	10	1	10	2.2	10
March	1956	46.5	—	—	1	10	3	30	4	40	2	20	2.7	10
June	1956	47.5	—	—	1	10	5	50	2	20	2	20	2.5	10
November	1956	51.5	—	—	1	14.3	3	42.9	1	14.3	2	28.6	2.6	7

Month	Year	%											Index	**
August	1957	51	—	—	1	12.5	5	62.5	1	12.5	1	12.5	2.3	8
March	1958	50.5	—	—	4	28.6	7	49.9	1	7.1	2	14.2	2.1	14
September	1958	48.3	—	—	—	—	7	87.5	—	—	1	12.5	2.3	8
October	1958	47.5	1	11.1	1	11.1	6	66.6	1	11.1	—	—	1.8	9
May	1960	56.5	1	12.5	1	12.5	5	62.5	1	12.5	—	—	2	8
August	1960	46.2	2	11.1	2	11.1	5	27.8	5	27.8	4	22.2	2.5	14
May	1961	52.4	—	—	1	12.5	3	37.5	4	50	—	—	2.4	8
October	1961	45.9	1	6.6	1	6.6	9	59.9	2	13.2	2	13.2	2.4	15
February	1964	58.0	1	9.1	2	18.2	4	36.4	1	9.1	3	27.3	2.5	11
September	1964	59.8	1	10	3	30	1	10	1	10	3	30	2.6	10
November	1964	51.5	2	14.2	2	14.2	6	42.7	1	7.1	3	21.4	2.2	14
July	1965	50.5	—	—	—	—	7	53.9	2	15.4	4	30.8	2.8	13
April	1966	53.9	—	—	1	10	4	40	3	30	2	20	2.2	10
December	1966	52.4	—	—	—	—	6	60	3	30	1	10	2.5	10
February	1968	56.2	—	—	2	16.7	8	66.7	—	—	2	16.7	2.2	12
October	1968	63.3	—	—	1	25	1	25	1	25	1	25	2.5	4
January	1969	51.5	—	—	1	6.3	13	81.3	1	6.3	1	6.3	2.1	16
November	1969	54.8	—	—	2	12.5	9	56.3	3	18.7	2	12.5	2.3	16
October	1970	42.2	—	—	—	—	7	41.1	3	17.6	7	41.1	3	17
May	1972	47.1	3	16.7	2	11.1	8	44.4	2	11.1	3	16.7	2.1	18

* Index is calculated by assigning a point system to each degree level. Thus, No degrees = 0; AA/Baccalaureate = 1; BA/BS/License = 2; MA/MS/Diploma/Certificate = 3; and Doctorate = 4. Therefore, Index = total of degree points/denominational total of mins. at all levels.

** Total membership is all of the ministers who have served in each cabinet at any time during its tenure.

Despite the overall increase, the average educational level of cabinet elites continues to vary. There was a sharp drop of the index from 3.0 for the October 1970 cabinet to 2.1 for the May 1972 cabinet, because nonpolitical, highly trained technician-ministers were replaced by a group of older parliamentary politicians, 5 of whom had less than BA level education (see table 12).

The absence of dramatic trends in educational level is matched by the lack of clear-cut patterns in educational specialization. Despite the sharp fluctuations, lawyers represent the largest category in every cabinet, ranging from 88 percent to 20 percent. However, there is no clear trend in the fluctuating presence of lawyers in each cabinet, nor are there any causal relationships between these changes and other societal factors. All that can be discerned (table 13) is a drop in the number of lawyers in most of the extraparliamentary and/or caretaker cabinets, particularly those of February 1951, September 1952, May 1960, February 1964, and September 1964. A similar drop occurred in the technicians' cabinet of October 1970, where less than 30 percent were lawyers. Clearly, the large presence of lawyers has persisted since the early years of the republic; given Lebanon's legalistic political culture, it is reasonable to assume that the lawyers' share of ministerial posts will remain substantial in the future.

In a number of other specializations one can discern new trends. Beginning in 1953 engineering occurs with great frequency and in larger percentages. After 1953, only 7 out of 21 cabinets lacked engineers, indicating a growing systemic concern with small-scale industrialization and related aspects of development. Since the mid-fifties, similar increases are discernible in social studies and medicine. Also beginning in 1953 the proportion of ministers with no specializations (primarily those with a baccalaureate or less and frequently landowners) decreased, rarely rising above 20 percent of any given cabinet. Before 1953 the percentage was generally above 20 percent and even rose to 67 percent in February of 1951.[65] Thus, while lawyer-generalists still predominate, recent cabinets have included specialist ministers from a broader educational spectrum than in earlier years.

Education: Place of Study

Few countries are as well endowed with educational institutions as Lebanon: four universities and over twenty-five colleges, lycees, and institutes. This represents a very high university/ population ratio even when compared with some Western countries. However, it should be noted that this highly developed system serves not only Lebanon but virtually all the countries of the Arab East.

Of the four universities only the Lebanese University is home-grown (1953). The others have various degrees of foreign sponsorship, affiliation, and support. Of these, the oldest is the American University of Beirut, which was founded in 1868 by American missionaries as the Syrian Protestant College. A French Jesuit institution, Université de St. Joseph, was founded in 1875. The Arab University of Beirut, founded in 1960, is under Egyptian sponsorship and administration. Many of Lebanon's colleges and lycees were also foreign-established.

Notwithstanding the existence of the American University of Beirut, the Lebanese have patterned their educational system after the French. Given the French imperial presence and Lebanese receptiveness to France's *mission civilisatrice,* the result could be nothing less than a French-type school system. Out of thirty lycees and colleges, twenty have French affiliations; of these, over three-fourths have strong Roman Catholic ties and members of various religious orders often are involved in administration and teaching.

Education and Elite Socialization

The data shows that a large portion of Lebanon's leadership is the product of these lycees and colleges, and therefore these institutions can be regarded as having had a significant role in the socialization of the Lebanese elite. The two colleges which have graduated the largest number of future ministers are the college of the University of St. Joseph and the College St. Joseph of Ayntoura, Lebanon's oldest institution of higher learning, founded in 1734 by Jesuits and reopened by the Lazarist Fathers in 1834.[66] These two institutions have educated approximately 20 percent of

TABLE 13. *Lebanon: Educational Specialization by Cabinet*

CABINET		Law N	Law %	Social Science N	Social Science %	Religion N	Religion %	Medicine N	Medicine %	Engineering N	Engineering %	Military N	Military %	Humanities N	Humanities %	No Specialty N	No Specialty %	Unknown N	Unknown %	TOTAL
September	1943	4	67	1	17	—	—	—	—	—	—	—	—	—	—	1	17	—	—	6
July	1944	4	67	—	—	—	—	—	—	—	—	—	—	—	—	2	33	—	—	6
January	1945	2	33	—	—	1	17	1	17	—	—	—	—	—	—	1	17	1	17	6
August	1945	5	63	—	—	—	—	1	13	1	13	—	—	—	—	1	13	—	—	8
May	1946	6	75	1	13	—	—	—	—	—	—	—	—	—	—	1	13	—	—	8
December	1946	6	67	—	—	—	—	1	11	—	—	—	—	—	—	2	22	—	—	9
April	1947	5	63	—	—	—	—	—	—	—	—	1	13	—	—	2	25	—	—	8
July	1948	4	50	—	—	—	—	1	13	—	—	—	—	—	—	3	38	—	—	8
October	1949	3	36	—	—	—	—	2	18	—	—	—	—	—	—	3	27	2	18	11
February	1951	1	33	—	—	—	—	—	—	—	—	—	—	—	—	2	67	—	—	3
April	1951	9	82	—	—	—	—	—	—	—	—	—	—	—	—	2	18	—	—	11
February	1952	5	50	—	—	—	—	—	—	1	10	—	—	—	—	3	30	1	10	10
9 September	1952	2	67	—	—	—	—	—	—	1	10	—	—	—	—	1	33	—	—	3
14 September	1952	2	67	1	33	—	—	—	—	—	—	—	—	—	—	—	—	—	—	3
18 September	1952	1	33	—	—	—	—	—	—	—	—	1	33	—	—	1	33	—	—	3
30 September	1952	3	75	—	—	—	—	—	—	—	—	—	—	—	—	1	25	—	—	4
April	1953	4	50	1	13	—	—	—	—	—	—	—	—	—	—	2	25	1	13	8
August	1953	7	88	—	—	—	—	—	—	1	13	—	—	—	—	—	—	—	—	8
March	1954	6	75	—	—	—	—	—	—	1	13	—	—	—	—	1	13	—	—	8
September	1954	8	73	—	—	—	—	—	—	1	9	—	—	—	—	2	18	—	—	11
July	1955	7	70	—	—	—	—	—	—	1	10	—	—	—	—	2	20	—	—	10
September	1955	5	50	1	10	—	—	1	10	1	10	—	—	—	—	1	10	1	10	10
March	1956	4	40	2	20	—	—	1	10	2	20	—	—	—	—	1	10	—	—	10
June	1956	5	50	2	20	—	—	1	10	1	10	—	—	—	—	1	10	—	—	10
November	1956	4	57	—	—	—	—	—	—	—	—	1	14	1	14	1	14	—	—	7
August	1957	4	50	1	13	—	—	—	—	1	13	—	—	1	13	1	13	—	—	8

March	1958	6	43	1	7	—	—	1	7	1	7	—	—	1	7	4	29	—	—	14
September	1958	5	63	1	13	—	—	—	—	2	25	—	—	—	—	—	—	—	—	8
October	1958	4	44	—	—	—	—	1	11	1	11	—	—	—	—	2	22	—	—	9
May	1960	2	25	—	—	—	—	—	—	4	50	—	—	—	—	1	13	1	13	8
August	1960	8	45	4	22	—	—	2	11	—	—	—	—	—	—	3	17	1	6	18
May	1961	4	50	2	25	—	—	1	13	—	—	—	—	—	—	1	13	—	—	8
October	1961	10	67	2	13	—	—	1	7	—	—	—	—	—	—	2	13	—	—	15
February	1964	3	27	—	—	—	—	2	18	3	27	—	—	—	—	2	18	1	10	11
September	1964	2	20	—	—	—	—	2	20	3	30	—	—	—	—	2	20	1	10	10
November	1964	5	36	2	14	—	—	2	14	1	7	—	—	—	—	3	21	1	7	14
July	1965	6	46	2	15	—	—	2	15	3	23	—	—	—	—	—	—	—	—	13
April	1966	7	70	—	—	—	—	1	10	—	—	1	10	—	—	1	10	—	—	10
December	1966	7	70	1	10	—	—	1	10	1	10	—	—	—	—	—	—	—	—	10
February	1968	8	67	—	—	—	—	—	—	2	17	—	—	—	—	2	17	—	—	12
October	1968	2	50	—	—	—	—	1	25	—	—	—	—	—	—	1	25	—	—	4
January	1969	11	69	2	13	—	—	—	—	2	13	—	—	—	—	1	6	—	—	16
November	1969	11	69	2	13	—	—	1	6	—	—	—	—	—	—	2	13	—	—	16
October	1970	5	29	4	24	—	—	3	18	5 *	29	—	—	—	—	—	—	—	—	17
May	1972	8	44	2	11	—	—	2	11	1	6	—	—	—	—	4	22	1	6	18

* One of these was a physicist.

the elite. The rest attended the various Colleges des Freres, the Patriarchal College, College de la Sagesse, the Marist College, Girard Institute, and several lesser known institutions. Also, a small percentage of the elite, usually from Sunni backgrounds, went to the Maqasid College, an Islamic institution.

The extent to which Lebanese leaders have been exposed to the French-type educational process becomes clear when one considers that a total of 91 ministers out of 159 (57.2 percent) were partly or fully educated at a French and/or French-influenced Lebanese school. In contrast, only 31 out of 159 (19.5 percent) ministers were partly or fully educated in American or U.S. sponsored institutions, in or out of Lebanon. The empirical evidence obviously suggests that the role and influence of American education and educational institutions in Lebanon has been overstated.

St. Joseph vs. American University of Beirut

Those familiar with Lebanon's student scene invariably will remember the endless debates about the advantages and disadvantages of going to St. Joseph or the American University of Beirut. Although founded seven years after the AUB, St. Joseph University has educated a far greater percentage of future ministers than its American counterpart. Undoubtedly, France's imperial position and cultural influence in Lebanon accounts for St. Joseph's greater role in educating the elite. Nevertheless, the disparity between the two institutions is glaring: 49 out of 138 leaders for whom there is educational data, or 35.5 percent, received degrees from St. Joseph University; only 20, or 14.5 percent, hold AUB degrees. The St. Joseph figure may be even higher, since there are 21 ministers with various degrees, particularly in law, but without definite school identification. In all likelihood most of these *Licenses* were taken at St. Joseph. On the other hand, AUB's impact has been much greater outside Lebanon, particularly in the other countries of the Mashriq. Lebanon's two other institutions of higher learning—Beirut Arab University and the Lebanese University—are too new to have had a large impact on the country's public life (see table 14).

St. Joseph's unique place in Lebanon's educational system and

TABLE 14. *Lebanon: Educational Institution and Country—Number of Degrees*

FRANCE		BRITAIN		UNITED STATES		GERMANY		EGYPT		TURKEY		SYRIA		LEBANON		SWIT-ZERLAND	
36		**8**		**12**		**2**		**3**		**3**		**3**		**70**		**1**	
Grenoble Tech	2	Exeter	1	Columbia	2	Freiburg	1	Cairo Univ.	2	Genl. Staff College	1	Ecole Militaire de Damas	1	Amer. Univ. of Beirut	20	Univ. of Lausanne	1
Aix la Chapélle	2	Univ. of London	4	Harvard	2	Koch Institute	1	American Univ. of Cairo	1	Imperial Law Univ.	2	Damascus Univ.	2	Univ. de St. Joseph	49		
Ecole Nationale du Pont et Chausée	1	Oxford	1	Johns Hopkins	1									Beirut Arab Univ.	1		
Ecole Superieure d'état Major	1	St. Olafs	1	MIT	2												
Ecole Superieure de Guerre	1	Staff College	1	Oklahoma State	1												
Ecole Engineurs de Paris	1			Syracuse	2												
Ecole Nationale des Ingeneurs (Lille)	1			Univ. of S. Calif.	1												
Univ. of Lyon	5			Yale	1												
Cochin Hospital	1																
Univ. of Montpellier	3																
Ecole de l'Infantrie St. Mainmarte	1																
Sorbonne	15																
Pasteur Institute	1																
Ecole Polytechnique	1																

its great influence can not be satisfactorily explained without reference to the key role played by its renowned Faculté Francaise de Droit, founded in 1913. Unlike St. Joseph's equally well-known Faculté de Médecine, its law school has no counterpart at the AUB. Anyone desiring to study law in Lebanon had to go to St. Joseph; at least 40 ministers held *Licenses* in Law from this Jesuit institution.

In quantitative terms, Lebanon's universities awarded 70 degrees, in contrast to 68 given by foreign universities (see table 15). As one would expect, France claimed the largest portion of foreign degrees granted: 36 degrees, or 26 percent of the total. This was over one-half of all foreign degrees granted. The most popular French institution was the Sorbonne, which awarded a total of 15 degrees. The fact that France led in the granting of foreign degrees again points to its early primacy in Lebanese cultural life (see table 14).

American institutions trailed the French; of 12 degrees, 5 were given by Ivy League universities. British universities claimed 8, and Egypt and Turkey gave 3 diplomas each. Germany gave 2 and Switzerland one. In general, Lebanese students went to foreign countries for specialized, advanced training in engineering, military science, law, medicine, and economics.

Cosmopolitanism versus Localism

The aggregate analysis of elite educational background enables one to develop indices of cosmopolitanism versus localism. One possible approach is to calculate the total number of degrees (BA and above) awarded to the elite by Lebanese institutions and the total number of degrees given by foreign colleges and universities. As table 15 indicates, out of 138 degrees, 70 were Lebanese and 68 were foreign. Here the assumption is that foreign degrees denote foreign exposure and presumably a cosmopolitan *Weltanschauung*.

TABLE 15. *Lebanon: Aggregate Distribution of Degrees*

LEBANESE DEGREES	FOREIGN DEGREES	TOTAL N OF DEGREES (BA AND ABOVE)
70	68	138

Another approach would be to find the number of ministers who were products of Lebanese universities, of foreign universities, or of a combination of the two. This distribution is presented in table 16 where out of 106 ministers on whom data on places of education was available, 34 (32.1 percent) had a purely foreign university education, in contrast to 51 (47.2 percent) who had a purely Lebanese education. The remaining 21 (19.8 percent) had a mixed Lebanese-foreign education. By adding the "mixed" and the "foreign" categories it was discovered that 55 ministers had some foreign educational exposure, in contrast to 51 who were educationally home-grown.

TABLE 16. *Lebanon: Educational Exposure*

FOREIGN	MIXED	LEBANON
34	21	51

Educational Level

As table 17 shows, 15 (or 9.4 percent) of the 159 ministers either lacked a baccalaureate degree or failed to make public their level of education. Most of these ministers were traditional zu'ama', elder statesmen, often from rural areas, who had been active during the formative years of the republic. Another group of 15 ministers also belonging to the elder-statesman category had completed the baccalaureate or its equivalent. A much larger group of 86 ministers held Bachelor degrees or *Licenses*. This constituted the largest group of degree holders, accounting for 53.5 percent of

TABLE 17. *Lebanon: Levels of Education—Aggregate Count*

LEVEL	N	%
AA/Baccalaureate	15	9.4
BA/BS/License	85	53.5
MA/MS/Diploma/Certificate	17	10.7
Doctorate	27	17.0
No Information/No Degree	15	9.4
Total	159	

the total elite. The large size of this contingent is primarily attributable to the inclusion of the Licensates. It will be noted subsequently that Licensates in law exist in profusion.

As one goes up the educational ladder there is a sharp drop— only 17 ministers (10.7 percent) hold the Master's degree or its equivalent. A larger number (27 or 17 percent) reached the doctorate level (Ph.D./MD).

Educational Specialization: Aggregate Count

In considering the Lebanese elite's fields of study (Bachelors and above), one is immediately struck by the great number who

TABLE 18. *Lebanon: Educational Specialization—Aggregate Count*

GENERAL CATEGORY	SPECIALIZATION	N	%
Law 75 47.2%	Law	68	42.8
	Law and Economy	5	3.5
	Law and Humanities	1	0.6
	Law and Political Science and Criminology	1	0.6
Engineering 22 13.8%	Engineering	14	8.8
	Engineering and Math	1	0.6
	Engineering and Commerce	1	0.6
	Engineering and Social Studies	1	0.6
	Agronomy	5	3.1
Medicine 12 7.6%	Medicine	10	6.3
	Medicine and Literature	1	0.6
	Medicine and Physics and Math	1	0.6
Miscellaneous 20 12.4%	Political Science	5	3.1
	Political Science and Economy	2	1.3
	Economics	4	2.5
	Military Science	3	1.9
	History	1	0.6
	Pedagogy	1	0.6
	Philosophy and Math and Physics	1	0.6
	Physics	1	0.6
	Pharmacology	1	0.6
	Religion	1	0.6
No Education/ No Specialization 30 18.9%			

specialized in law. Indeed, a legal education, usually completed at St. Joseph University, is a hallmark of the Lebanese political elite. As shown in table 18, no less than 75 ministers, or 47 percent, were lawyers. If one discounts the 30 who did not reach the Bachelor's level, the lawyer component will equal about 58 percent of the remaining ministerial elite.

The second largest specialization category was engineering, with 22 ministers or 13.8 percent of the total elite. A subcategory of some importance—agronomy—is represented by 5 ministers, which points to Lebanese interest in agriculture, especially the growing of fruits for export. The total engineering contingent would probably be larger if Lebanon possessed the raw materials and aspiration for large-scale industrialization.

The third largest category of specialized study was medicine. Since the field is traditionally respected in the Middle East, the physician is accorded an inordinate amount of prestige in society. There were 12 physicians, which constituted 7.6 percent of the elite.

The social sciences were comparatively underrepresented. There were 5 political scientists, 4 economists, and one who combined those two disciplines. In a country that thrives on finance and commerce one would have expected a larger contingent of economists at the ministerial level. The next category was the military, constituting 1.9 percent of the elite; it included generals Lahhud, Nawfal, and Shihab—the last being a former president of the Republic. The remaining fields—religion, history, philosophy, physics, pedagogy, and pharmacology—claimed one each. Shaykh Pierre Jumayyil, leader of the Kata'ib, was the sole pharmacist.

Education and Confessionalism

Tables 19 and 20 illustrate the different levels of education among the ministers belonging to the various confessional groups of Lebanon. For example, Sunnis possessed the highest number of doctorates (9) and the Maronites had the most Bachelors and Licensates (33). In order to facilitate the cross-confessional comparison of overall educational levels, it is necessary to develop a composite index. This is done in table 20, which converts the data in

TABLE 19. *Educational Level versus Confessional Affiliation—Aggregate Count*

EDUCATIONAL LEVEL	Sunni N	%	Shi'ite N	%	Maronite N	%	Orthodox N	%	Catholic N	%	Druze N	%	Armenian * N	%
No Education/ No Information	3	9.7	5	20.3	4	7.7	2	9.5	0	0	1	8.3	0	—
AA/Baccalaureate	6	19.4	2	8.3	3	5.8	2	9.5	1	5.8	1	8.3	0	—
BA/BS/License	8	29.0	13	54.2	33	63.5	9	42.9	16	94.1	5	41.7	1	—
Certificate/ MA/MS/Diploma	5	16.1	0	0	7	13.5	2	9.5	0	0	2	16.7	1	—
Doctorate	9	25.8	4	12.5	5	9.6	6	28.6	0	0	3	25.0	0	—

* Since there are only two individuals in this category percentages would be meaningless.

TABLE 20. *Lebanon: Overall Educational Level Index * by Sect*

	MARONITE	SUNNI	SHI'ITE	ORTHODOX	CATHOLIC	DRUZE
Educational Index	2.1	2.4	1.8	2.4	1.9	2.4

* On calculation of educational index see note on table 12.

table 19 into indices of overall educational level. Table 20 indicates that the Orthodox, Sunni, and Druze ministers enjoyed the highest overall levels of education, while the Shi'ite ministerial group scored the lowest. One might venture the hypothesis that the more traditional and rural-based a group—e.g., the Shi'ites—the less their propensity for higher education. A further hypothesis might attempt to correlate the Shi'ites' traditionalism, rural location, and relatively low educational level with their comparatively low level of representation in the cabinet (see table 21).

A correlation of specialization within confessional affiliation reveals few surprises. Overall, law was the most popular field of study, with the Maronites and the Catholics leading the rest; over 59 percent of the Catholics and 60 percent of the Maronites had specialized in law. In contrast only 34 percent of both the Sunnis and Shi'ites studied law while the Orthodox scored 43 percent and the Druze 25 percent. The relatively high Maronite and Catholic percentages in law are probably due to their easier access to St. Joseph University.[67]

Representation and Confessionalism

Given the confessional nature of the Lebanese political system, the subject of representation assumes overwhelming importance. In no other country is the question of sectarian balance as crucial as in Lebanon.

The original formula for the country's denominational representation was promulgated in Articles 24 and 95 of the 1926 Constitution. This was reiterated in the National Pact of 1943, an unwritten part of the Lebanese constitution, which provided for parliamentary inclusion of diverse minorities with representation based on the principle of parity and the sharing of power at the top between Maronites and Sunnis. Since 1943 the number of deputies in the Chamber has always been a multiple of 11; the ratio of Christians to Muslims being six to five. Thus the parliamentary representation of each denomination was proportional to its size: Maronite 30 percent, Sunni 20 percent, Shi'ite 19 percent, Orthodox 11 percent, Catholic 6 percent, Druze 6 percent, Armenian Orthodox 4 percent, Armenian Catholic 1 percent, Protestant 1 percent, and others 1 percent. One would expect that the cabinet would reflect the parliamentary representation of each denomination.

With the passage of time the cabinet in general has become more representative. As shown in table 10 originally the six major sects were equally represented; this has evolved into a more proportional representation of these six with the addition of a seventh—the Armenians. More specifically, the early ten-member cabinet pattern comes closest to approximating the minorities' percentages in parliament (not including the Armenians) i.e., Maronites 30 percent, Sunnis 20 percent, Shi'ites 19 percent, Orthodox 11 percent, Catholics 6 percent, Druzes 6 percent. All cabinets except the early ten-man and sixteen-man ones overrepresent the Sunnis, while all cabinets except the early ten-man and three-man ones underrepresent the Maronites. The Shi'ites also are generally underrepresented in comparison to their parliamentary proportion. With only a few exceptions a fifty-fifty Christian-Muslim cabinet balance is maintained in contrast to the six-to-five parliamentary ratio.

Another method of determining the cabinet's denominational proportions is to compare parliamentary representation with the aggregate cabinet representation of each group. Two convenient methods to calculate the total cabinet "presence" of each denomination are shown in table 21. The first method consists of calculating the total number of months spent in cabinet by all the ministers of each denomination. The second method of measuring relative denominational cabinet presence is to compute the total number of ministerial positions held by each religious group and measure this against the overall total of 159 ministers.

A comparative analysis of each denomination's parliamentary representation with their cabinet presence reveals certain interesting insights into Lebanese politics. As shown in table 21, Sunnis, Catholics, Orthodox, and Druzes have a substantially higher cabinet presence than warranted by their parliamentary representation. The Sunnis' cabinet presence is 3 percent in excess of their parliamentary representation; the Orthodox are over 1 percent higher. As to the Catholics and Druzes, their respective cabinet presences are about twice their parliamentary representation.

A diametrically opposed effect can be observed when one analyzes the representational distribution of Maronites, Shi'ites, and Armenians (see table 21). It is immediately apparent that relative to their parliamentary shares, all three minorities were accorded lower aggregate representation in the cabinet, both in total period of ministerial service and in the number of ministerial positions oc-

TABLE 21. *Lebanon: Confessional Representation—Cabinet and Parliament*

PARLIAMENTARY REPRESENTATION		SECT	CABINET REPRESENTATION *		CABINET POSTS	
N	%		N	%	N	%
30	30.3	Maronite	886	25.9	105	25.5
20	20.2	Sunni	806	23.7	102	24.7
19	19.2	Shi'ite	480	14.1	55	13.3
11	11.1	Orthodox	421	12.3	52	12.6
6	6.1	Catholic	376	11.0	46	11.1
6	6.1	Druze	408	11.9	48	11.6
4	4.0	Armenian Orthodox	32	0.9	4	.96
1	1.0	Armenian Catholic	7	0.2	1	.2
1	1.0	Protestant	—	—	—	—
1	1.0	Minorities	—	—	—	—

* Cabinet Representation is determined by total number of months each denomination has spent in cabinet office.

cupied. In terms of length of cabinet service and number of ministerial posts, the Maronites' 30.3 percent parliamentary representation drops to under 26 percent in the cabinet, the Shi'ites' 19.2 percent parliamentary share drops to 14.1 percent in the cabinet, and the Armenians' (Orthodox and Catholic) who had 5.0 percent in Chamber representation, were given just over 1 percent of the cabinet seats.

While it is difficult to explain these disparities,[68] some partial explanations are possible. The 5 percent lower Maronite presence in the cabinet is counterbalanced by their permanent retention of the presidency, which is the most powerful position in the country's political structure. The Sunni cabinet presence of approximately 24 percent, an increase from their 20.2 percent in the Chamber, is attributable to their permanent hold on the premiership. While the presidency is not calculated as part of Maronite cabinet representation, the premiership is made an integral share of the Sunnite cabinet allotment. Despite this fact, the Maronite-Sunni cabinet shares are almost equal, as indicated in table 21, with the Maronites holding a thin edge of about 2 percent in time served and about 1 percent in number of positions held.

The 19.2 percent Chamber representation of the Shi'ites is reduced by over 5 percentage points within the cabinet—more than any other group. While the Shi'ites have almost as large a deputy bloc as the Sunnis, their cabinet share is about 10 percent less. The only compensating factor is that the Shi'ites retain the speakership of the Chamber, which is not a cabinet post and therefore not calculated as part of the cabinet percentages. Thus, unlike the premiership (Sunni), the speakership of the Chamber (Shi'ite), the presidency of the Republic (Maronite), and the vice presidency of the Chamber (Orthodox) do not enter in cabinet representation levels. Although both the Maronites and the Shi'ites have a 5 percent negative variation between their Chamber and cabinet representation, it becomes clear that proportionally speaking the Shi'ites' reduction in cabinet presence was larger than the Maronites', who had a high (30.3 percent) Chamber allocation initially.

The other real losers in cabinet representation are the Armenians—the smallest and newest of Lebanon's principal minorities. The total Armenian (Orthodox and Catholic) share of Chamber seats is about 5 percent; this is one deputy less than the

Druze or the Catholics. Yet each of the latter groups claims over 11 percent of the cabinet positions, while the Armenians are granted just over 1 percent. Any explanation of this disparity is bound to reflect poorly on Lebanese democracy. One plausible explanation is that as latecomers—most came after the 1915 massacres in Turkey—the Armenians have not as yet been sufficiently integrated into Lebanese society to be granted their due share of cabinet portfolios.

Representation: Christian versus Muslim

Having explored the representational structure of Lebanon's major denominations, it is now possible to calculate the aggregate Muslim-Christian distribution—a basic and peculiar feature of the political system. The data in table 22 presents the Muslim-Christian line-up in parliament as well as in the cabinet (computed both in terms of total positions and of tenure). In the Chamber, the balance favors the Christian side by about 10 percentage points, or a six-to-five ratio. This difference narrows in the cabinet. As indicated in table 22, cabinet presence measured both in total number of positions and in aggregate tenure of Muslim versus Christian ministers is 49.6 percent to 50.4 percent respectively. Although these figures favor the Christians slightly, they also indicate a more realistically balanced situation than that existing in the Chamber, particularly in view of probable demographic changes.

TABLE 22. *Lebanon: Christian versus Muslim Representation*

| | PARLIAMENTARY REPRESENTATION | | CABINET REPRESENTATION | | CABINET REPRESENTATION | |
RELIGION	*Number of Seats*		*Tenure in Months*		*Number of Positions*	
	N	%	N	%	N	%
Christian	54	55.5	1722	50.4	208	50.4
Muslim	45	45.5	1694	49.6	205	49.6

Regional Affiliation

Two types of regional identification have been considered in analyzing the background characteristics of these 159 cabinet members: birthplace and governmental service in a particular locality. Table 23 presents a breakdown by districts and provinces of the birthplaces of the 144 ministers who served since independence (1943). For the remaining 15 ministers, mostly now deceased, data on places of birth were not available.

More than half of the total number of ministers were born in the provinces of Mount Lebanon and Beirut, which contributed 41 and 39 individuals respectively. Next was South Lebanon with 23 ministers, followed closely by North Lebanon with 22. Only 11 ministers (6.9 percent) were born in the Biqa' province. Finally, 8 were

TABLE 23. *Lebanon: Geographical Identification— Place of Birth*

PROVINCE	REGION	N	%
	Akkar	4	2.5
North	Batrun	2	1.3
Lebanon	Bsharri	2	1.3
22	Kurah	5	3.1
13.8%	Tripoli	6	3.8
	Zgharta	3	1.9
	Alay	5	3.1
Mount	Ba'abdah	11	6.9
Lebanon	Jbayl	1	0.6
41	Kisrwan	6	3.8
24.3%	Matn	10	6.3
	Shuf	8	5.0
Beirut 39 24.5%			
	Marji'yun	4	2.5
South	Jazzin	1	0.6
Lebanon	Nabatiyah	6	3.8
23	Tyre	8	5.0
14.5%	Saida	3	1.9
	Zahrani	1	0.6
Biqa'	Ba'albak-Hirmil	3	1.9
11	Biqa'-West	2	1.3
6.9%	Zahli	6	3.8
	Cyprus	1	0.6
Foreign	Egypt	5	3.1
8	Palestine	1	0.6
5.0%	Syria	1	0.6
Unknown		15	9.4

foreign-born: Egypt (5), Cyprus (1), Syria (1), and Palestine (1). Most of these were born to Lebanese parents.

As indicated in table 23, 39 ministers were born in Beirut proper, which is considered a province administratively. The district of Ba'abdah in the province of Mount Lebanon contributed 11 officials to the cabinet—the highest of any district. Second place went to Matn with 10, including Pierre Jumayyil and the two Murrs. Not far behind was Shuf, where 8 ministers were born, including Kamal Junblat, Najib Alam al-Din, Fuad Ammun, Camille Cham'un, and Sa'id Himadih, some of whom also represented the district. The South Lebanon district of Tyre (Sur) also claimed 8 future ministers, including such notable figures as Kazim al-Khalil, the Salims, and Muhammad Safi al-Din. The districts of Tripoli (North Lebanon), Kisrwan (Mount Lebanon) and Zahli and Nabatiyah (South Lebanon) claimed 6 ministers each. The remaining birthplaces were distributed unevenly among the other districts with the exception of Bint Jbayl—the only electoral district which was not the birthplace of a minister.[69]

Table 24 presents the regional affiliation of ministers by governmental service, as a result of deputyship, governorship, judgeship, or similar position in a particular area of the country. Of the 138 ministers on whom such data is available, 49 (30.8 percent) served in Mount Lebanon, 36 (22.6 percent) in Beirut, 22 (13.8 percent) in South Lebanon, 21 (13.2 percent) in North Lebanon and 10 (6.3 percent) in the Biqa'. If tables 23 and 24 are taken as indicators of the elite's regional representativeness, then one must conclude that Mount Lebanon and Beirut have been very strongly represented in Lebanese cabinets. The question remains as to whether these two areas have been overrepresented in proportion to their population; however, due to the unreliability of population statistics, this is not a feasible approach.[70]

Perhaps a sounder approach to the issue of representation is to compare the percentages of seats apportioned among the five provinces with the percentages of ministers born in each province and percentages of ministers who served as deputies from each province. As reflected in table 25, North Lebanon, with 20 percent of parliamentary seats, was the birthplace of only 15 percent of the ministers; moreover, only 16 percent of the ministers have been deputies from North Lebanon. Thus, North Lebanon has had a low

TABLE 24. *Geographical Identification—Government Position*

PROVINCE	REGION	N	%
North	Akkar	4	2.5
Lebanon	Batrun	3	1.9
21	Bsharri	1	0.6
13.2%	Kurah	4	2.5
	Tripoli	5	3.1
	Zgharta	3	1.9
	North Lebanon (General)	1	0.6
	Alay	4	2.5
Mount	Ba'abdah	9	5.7
Lebanon	Jbayl	1	0.6
49	Kisrwan	7	4.4
30.8%	Matn	13	8.2
	Mount Lebanon (General)	6	3.8
	Shuf	9	5.7
Beirut		36	22.6
	Marji'yun	4	2.5
	Jazzin	2	1.3
South	Nabatiyah	4	2.5
Lebanon	Tyre	4	2.5
22	Saida	—	—
13.8%	Zahrani	2	1.3
	Bint Jbayl	3	1.9
	South Lebanon (General)	3	1.9
	Ba'albak-Hirmil	4	2.5
Biqa'	Biqa'-West	—	—
10	Zahli	5	3.1
6.3%	Biqa' (General)	1	0.6
Unknown or None		21	13.2

TABLE 25. *Lebanon: Regional Representativeness—Parliamentary and Ministerial*

PROVINCE	% PARLIAMENTARY REPRESENTATION	% OF MINISTERS BORN IN PROVINCE	% OF MINISTER-DEPUTIES FROM REGION
North Lebanon	20	15	16
Mount Lebanon	30	28	29
Beirut	16	27	26
South Lebanon	18	16	22
Biqa'	15	7.5	8
Foreign-born		5.5	

aggregate ministerial presence or representation relative to its parliamentary contingent. This phenomenon is especially pronounced in Biqa' where the province's ministerial presence was merely half of its percentage share of Chamber seats. A slight loss is observable in the case of Mount Lebanon. Although South Lebanon registered a percentage loss of ministers born within its boundaries, it gained perceptibly in the percentage of ministers representing the area as deputies. The sole region which consistently gained was Beirut; holding only 16 percent of parliamentary seats, Beirut was the birth place of 27 percent of the ministers and was represented by 26 percent. It follows that Beirut is markedly overrepresented at the cabinet level and that North Lebanon and Biqa' are notably underrepresented.

Political Opportunity: The Main Determinants

A number of variables control the political opportunity of individuals who seek admission to the cabinet. In Lebanon—a pluralistic society par excellence—the determinants of political opportunity or eligibility include frequency of cabinet changes, cabinet size, denominational and geographic balance, interest-group influence, education, social and economic background, political affiliation, and personal loyalty.

The Lebanese cabinet changes at highly irregular intervals; cabinets have been known to last from several days to two and one-half years. Cabinet changes or reshuffles are caused by significant external and internal developments, ranging from elections to crises threatening the security and integrity of Lebanon itself. The frequency of cabinet turnover since independence has been quite high, with forty-five cabinets during a period of approximately 29 years or one cabinet every 7.6 months. While the high rate of turnover has in one sense signified instability, it has also promoted stability by promoting elite circulation, both horizontally and vertically. In this way the cabinet has acted as a key mechanism of conflict resolution in the political system.

Another factor that influences political opportunity is cabinet size. Lebanese cabinets have fluctuated between three and eighteen members; while most cabinets average ten members, in recent years their size has tended to be larger, reflecting an official attempt to widen the cabinet's representational base. It follows that cabinet size, combined with frequency of cabinet turnover, produces substantial opportunities for elite recruitment and circulation. Cabinet size and frequency of cabinet change have been partially responsible for the relatively large number of individuals—159—who have served in the Lebanese cabinet.

Political Opportunity and Competitiveness

Lebanon's unique confessional system constitutes another determinant of political opportunity. Since virtually all the aspirant elite pass through the recruitment processes of their respective communities, their opportunities to reach positions of leadership in their own denominations are dependent on intra-community competition. Only rarely are the main sectarian groups of Lebanon internally united. Various degrees of competition exist in each community between rival leaders, as table 26 indicates. For each

TABLE 26. *Lebanon: Confessional Competitiveness*

SECT	NUMBER OF MINISTERS	NUMBER OF CABINET POSITIONS
Maronite	52	105
Sunni	31	102
Shi'ite	24	55
Orthodox	21	52
Catholic	17	46
Druze	12	48
Armenian Orthodox	1	4
Armenian Catholic	1	1

denomination the table provides the total number of ministers and the total number of cabinet offices occupied since 1943. By comparing the two sets of figures it is possible to calculate a competition ratio:

$$\frac{\text{Number of ministers from each sect}}{\text{Number of Cabinet posts allocated to each sect}}$$

Thus, 52 ministers filled 105 Maronite positions; hence, the proportion of ministers to seats was approximately 1 to 2. In contrast only 31 ministers filled the 102 Sunni seats for a minister-seat ratio of 1 to 3. A comparison of the Sunni and Maronite ratios reflects the rapid turnover of Maronites, which is at least partly due to a high degree of intra-Maronite competitiveness.

Except for the Druze, all the remaining sects show greater internal competitiveness than the Sunni, though they do not reach the Maronite level. The Druze, with a ratio of 1 to 4 are the least competitive. The low number (12) of Druze cabinet leaders has partly been due to the tenacity of two major zu'ama' (Arslan and Junblat) who have occupied cabinet seats repeatedly, thereby reducing competition.

Similar conclusions about competitiveness within the communities may be gleaned from table 27. In calculating the average tenure in months for all the ministers of each denomination, one finds the highest level of competition among the Maronite elite, whose average tenure in cabinet was a mere 17 months. The Sunnis averaged 26 months, but again the Druzes manifested the least competitiveness: their average cabinet tenure was 34 months, exactly twice the Maronite average.

TABLE 27. *Lebanon: Average Tenure By Sect*

SECT	NUMBER OF MINISTERS	TENURE IN MONTHS	AVERAGE TENURE IN MONTHS
Maronite	52	886	17
Sunni	31	806	26
Shi'ite	24	480	20
Druze	12	408	34
Orthodox	21	421	20.1
Catholic	17	376	22.1
Armenian Orthodox	1	32	—
Armenian Catholic	1	7	—

The relative positions of the remaining denominations are the same as those in table 26 and therefore require no elaboration. What might prove revealing, however, is the obvious disparity between the Christian and Muslim ministers as calculated in table 28.

TABLE 28. *Lebanon: Competitiveness—Christian versus Muslim*

RELIGION	N OF CABINET POSTS	N OF MINISTERS
Christian	208	92
Muslim	205	67
Total	413	159

While 92 Christian ministers occupied 208 Christian cabinet seats, only 67 Muslims occupied 205 seats, indicating a much shorter tenure for the Christian ministers. Clearly this means greater competition among the Christian elite and more political opportunity for Christian aspirants. The opposite is true of the Muslim community—they display lower competitiveness, hence lower political opportunity.

Political Opportunity and the Parliament

The role of Lebanon's parliament as a primary gateway to the cabinet will be analyzed subsequently. The present discussion will consider parliament as a forum of competition for cabinet jobs. Of the 317 deputies who served in parliament between 1943 and 1972, 119 or 37.5 percent have become ministers. As shown in table 29, the structure of political opportunity from parliament to the cabinet varies in different regions of the country.[71] Table 29 presents the total number of deputies from each province who have served since 1943 as well as the number of those who have gone on to the cabinet. By comparing these findings it is possible to determine the relative opportunities for cabinet aspirants in each province.

TABLE 29. *Lebanon: Regional Competitiveness*

PROVINCE	TOTAL N OF DEPUTIES SINCE 1943	N OF MINISTERS	PERCENTAGE
North Lebanon	63	17	27
Mount Lebanon	98	37	38
Beirut	51	28	55
South Lebanon	61	24	39
Biqa'	44	13	30

It is obvious that deputies from Beirut had a much greater chance of becoming ministers than those from any other region. While 55 percent of Beirut deputies became ministers, only 27 percent of the North Lebanon deputies went on to enter the cabinet. Mount Lebanon was by far the most competitive province, with a total of 98 deputies since 1943.

Additional factors that affect political opportunity include family background, party identification, political reliability, wealth, and, of course, confessional affiliation. These variables are examined under subsequent headings.

Political Opportunity and the Family

A major determinant of political opportunity is one's family background including family name, prestige, and ties. While other facets of familial influence in Lebanese economic and political life have been explored earlier, the concern here is with family membership in the cabinet. The larger the number of family members who have been ministers, the more prestigious and powerful is that family considered to be. However, the reverse is not necessarily correct; a family cannot be automatically regarded as politically weak because only one of its members became a minister. A large number of ministers from a particular family may indicate a high rate of intra-clan competitiveness and/or pervasive ambition in the family. Finally, a high ministerial count may reflect large family size and/or dynastic continuity in politics.

Table 30 lists the 20 families that have contributed more than one minister. Sixteen contributed two ministers each, among which were the As'ad and Karami father-son combinations, as well as the Franjiyyah brothers and the two Salims. Three families claimed three ministers each—the Lahhuds, the Sulhs, and the Shihabs, the latter including two Maronites and a distant Sunni cousin. One family, the Iddih, contributed four ministers in addition to President Emile Iddih, its founding member. Finally, there are the Khuris who have produced five ministers—four Maronites and one Orthodox, including President Bishara Khuri. Many of these families were politically active during the Ottoman and the mandate years and have continued to display political resilience

TABLE 30. *Lebanon: Ministerial Families*

FAMILY NAME	N OF MINISTERS
As'ad	
Ghusn	
Franjiyyah	
Hilu	
Hrawi	
Junblat	
Jumayyil	
Karami	2
Murr	
Naqqash	
Salim	
Shahin	
Skaff	
Taqla	
Trad	
Zayn	
Lahhud	
Shihab	3
Sulh	
Iddih	4
Khuri	5

and ambition. While certain of these clans, the Khuris in particular, are too extensive to be considered a closed kinship group, proximity to the clan patriarch's family would seem to increase an individual's political opportunity.

Cursus Honorum: Pathways to Power

The Lebanese ministerial elite has come from nine occupational backgrounds as indicated in table 31. Journalism and the military produced the fewest ministers; specifically, there were 3 journalists and 3 exofficers, each representing 2 percent of the total elite. The low proportion of journalists does not correctly reflect the incidence of journalism; the number of ministers who at one time were journalists was much higher. Two academicians became journalists, as did 10 lawyers (see chart 3, appendix) and 1 engineer, making a total of 16 (10 percent) ministers who worked in the journalism field. A number of well-known ministers were involved

TABLE 31. *Lebanon: Original Occupational Sources of Recruitment— Aggregate Count*

OCCUPATION	N	%
Law	74	46
Proprietorship	21	13
Engineering	21	13
Medicine	13	8
Business	10	6
Academia	9	5
Bureaucracy	5	3
Journalism	3	2
Military	3	2

in the "Fourth Estate," particularly Alfred Naqqash, Charles Hilu, Philippe Taqla, Kamal Junblat, and Georges Naqqash.

Because the Lebanese political culture does not emphasize the military arts, enterprising young Lebanese seem to find little to attract them to military life. Thus the military constituted only a small percentage of the cabinet elite. The three military men who reached the cabinet were Fu'ad Shihab, Jamil Lahhud, and Sulayman Nawfal.

The next largest occupational category (see chart 6, appendix) is bureaucracy with 5 ministers, 3 percent of the total. Of course many other ministers held bureaucratic posts at some period in their public life, but only 5 started as bureaucrats.

Academia came next with 9 ministers or 5 percent of the elite. As shown in chart 7 (see appendix), two academics entered the cabinet directly, while two others went to journalism and parliament first. The others took diverse paths to the cabinet. The low percentage of academicians is not surprising when one considers the position of teachers in Lebanese society, although this has slowly been changing in recent years.

The original occupational category of 10 (6 percent) ministers was business. Looking at chart 8 (see appendix) it seems that a prominent business career is a direct stepping stone to parliament and hence to the cabinet, for this pattern was evident for no less than 8 of the 10 businessmen. Some of these are renowned for their enterpreneurship and wealth, including Salha, Sahnawi, and Arab. Many other ministers had business interests and involvements but not as original occupations.

Medicine accounted for 13 or 8 percent. Half of the doctors went either directly or through the Chamber into the cabinet, while the rest followed other paths to the top. Since medical skill has little to do with political life, the 13 doctors constitute a relatively high percentage, indicating the high social prestige of the profession.

The next highest category of original occupation was engineering, which accounts for 21 ministers or 13 percent of the total (see chart 2 appendix). A significant number of engineers (9) advanced through the bureaucracy while some entered the cabinet from business. Another three entered the cabinet directly. The presence of so many engineers among the top elite is relatively high for a country like Lebanon where the economy is based on agriculture, finance, commerce, and tourism.

The proprietor category accounted for 21 or 13 percent of the ministers. The individuals classified as proprietors were landowners who did not possess any other trade, or even the training for it. The significant dimension here is the overwhelming predominance of the deputy-to-cabinet career pattern. A total of 17 proprietors proceeded directly through the Chamber to the cabinet (see table 32). The proprietors' direct path to the top testifies to the continuing political power of the rural zu'ama'. Another index of their strength is the fact that 15 of the 21, or two-thirds of the proprietors, served in the cabinet more than once; this in comparison to approximately one-third of the engineers and doctors and one-fourth of the academicians.

The foremost occupational source of recruitment was the legal

TABLE 32. *Lebanon: Deputy to Cabinet—Occupational Source*

OCCUPATION	N
Law	46
Proprietorship	21
Engineering	9
Medicine	6
Business	9
Academia	3
Bureaucracy	2
Journalism	3
Military	1

profession. Out of 159 ministers, 74 or 46.5 percent had been lawyers. In terms of ascent to the cabinet, 5 individuals went directly to the cabinet, while 25 others became deputies before assuming portfolios. Another 14 used the judiciary as a path to cabinet office. A significant number of lawyers combined their legal careers with interests in business and journalism.

Over half of the 74 lawyers returned to cabinet office at least once. While this figure is numerically significant, it is proportionately less than that of the proprietors. Nevertheless, because of their sheer numbers the lawyers have helped to establish group norms in both the cabinet and parliament and thus have had a telling impact on the political system.[72] The lawyer-ministers have included some of the foremost lawyers in Lebanon—i.e., Taqla, Taqi al-Din, Gaspard, Rizq, and Ma'luf.

Parliament as a Stepping Stone

Despite the secondary role that the Chamber plays vis-à-vis the executive branch, it is the major pathway into the cabinet. Out of 159 ministers, 106 or two-thirds had served as deputies before entering the cabinet. Thus, any serious aspirant to political power in Lebanon must consider his chances of being elected a deputy.

While cabinet office is preferable in social, political, and economic payoffs, a parliamentary seat retains substantial significance in the power structure. In at least one respect a deputyship is preferable to a ministry: once elected to parliament, a deputy can count on almost four years in office. Given the short life of Lebanese cabinets, a minister's tenure is brief and full of uncertainties.

If one views the parliament from a leadership perspective a number of prominent political families can be found. Among these are many well-known deputies who have not yet succeeded in getting into the cabinet. Examples include Dwayhi, Isa al-Khuri, Mukarzil, Fakhr, Burt, Awn, Firzli, Isbir, Fatfat, Sa'ad, Abu Fadl, Buwaiz, Harb, Jisr, and Qadri. During the next few years some of these deputies will doubtless become ministers.

If one were to construct a model of occupational paths to the cabinet, the Chamber emerges as the most frequent stepping stone. However, legislative service before the cabinet was less important for doctors, academicians, and engineers than for proprietors, lawyers, journalists, and businessmen (see table 32). Significantly, the lawyers, journalists, businessmen and proprietors with political ambitions are not inhibited by their professional careers from seeking legislative office. Not only does politics not detract from their professional careers, it can even promote them. In contrast, the involvement of a doctor, engineer, or academician in politics can detract from their professional endeavors. It is also possible for a doctor, engineer, or academician to be recruited directly into the cabinet by virtue of his professional expertise, i.e., for ministries of Health, Education, Public Works, and Power.

Disposition

Disposition constitutes the last phase of the elite circulation process. In terms of immediate disposition—that is, position held after leaving the cabinet—the Chamber stands out as by far the largest depository of Lebanese ministers. As shown in table 33, 79 ministers or almost 50 percent of the elite went back to the Chamber from whence most had come originally. Since 80 of the ministers had been deputies prior to entering the cabinet, they

TABLE 33. *Lebanon: Immediate Disposition*

OCCUPATION	N	%
Still Serving in Cabinet	16	10
Deputyship	79	50
Business	17	10.7
Bureaucracy	10	6.3
Academia	9	5.7
Law	8	5.0
Diplomacy	6	3.8
Engineering	4	2.5
Presidency	2	1.3
Medicine	2	1.3
Proprietorship	1	.6
Party	1	.6
Military	1	.6
Journalism	1	.6
Retirement	1	.6
Deceased	1	.6

Total 159

would remain deputies during cabinet tenure and revert to deputyship at leaving cabinet office. Of the remaining 50 percent, 10 percent were still ministers, 10.7 percent went to business, 6.3 percent entered the bureaucracy, 5.7 percent returned to college-level teaching, and 5 percent returned to their law practice. Smaller percentages of ministers went into diplomacy, engineering, medicine, and other occupations, as shown in table 33. Two ministers later became presidents of the Republic.

TABLE 34. *Lebanon: Ultimate Disposition*

OCCUPATION	N	%
Deceased	32	20.0
Business	24	15.1
Deputyship	24	15.1
Still in Cabinet	16	10.1
Law	13	8.2
Bureaucracy	12	7.5
Academia	10	6.3
Retirement	10	6.3
Medicine	4	2.5
Proprietorship	4	2.5
Engineering	3	1.9
Diplomacy	2	1.3
Party	2	1.3
Journalism	1	.6
Presidency	1	.6
Judiciary	1	.6
Total	159	

Ultimate disposition is considerably different as table 34 reveals. About 20 percent of the ministers had died as of January 1973—the cut-off date for determining ultimate disposition. Business and parliament claimed 15.1 percent each, 10.1 percent still served in the cabinet, 8.2 percent were practicing law, 7.5 percent had entered the bureaucracy, and 6.3 percent were back in academia, while an equal percentage had retired. Other occupations— the judiciary, medicine, engineering, journalism, diplomacy, proprietorship, and party—claimed smaller percentages. Purges or political imprisonment do not affect disposition in Lebanon, since they are foreign to the Lebanese democratic political culture.

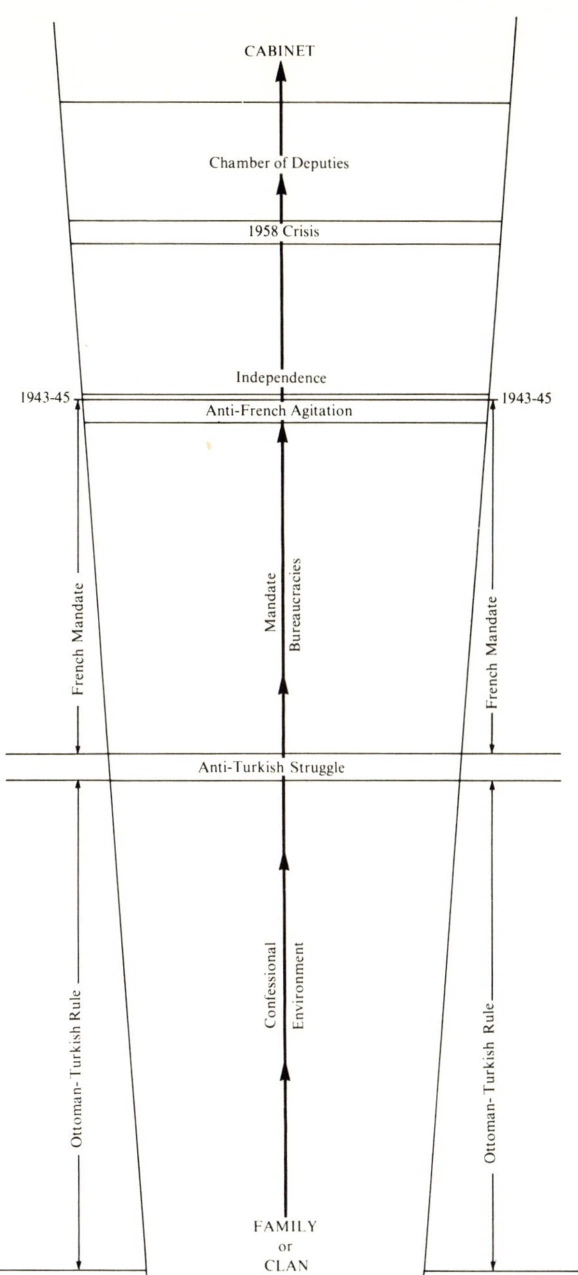

Figure 7   *Lebanon: Progression to Elitehood*

The Elite Under Stress

A retrospective glance at Lebanese politics clearly points to the centrality of crisis, both internal and external, in the life of the political elite. The leadership has been conditioned to the prevailing milieu of political uncertainty; indeed, the elite has not only learned to anticipate crisis, but frequently it has resolved or at least managed it.

In the first half of 1973 the Lebanese political system began to manifest certain pathological tendencies, unprecedented since the 1958 crisis, and the ability of the elite to manage conflict began to decline rapidly. One major outcome of this leadership crisis was a significant elite turnover, which included the demise of Prime Minister Salam's cabinet; a closely related development was the renewed prominence and independence of the army in Lebanese politics. Among the many crises that confronted the government, the most damaging were the Crontale missile controversy, the wide-ranging strikes, but most particularly the unending Israeli-Palestinian war of terrorism. Soon after the formation of Salam's last cabinet (May 1972), large-scale Israeli raids inside Lebanon became a monthly occurrence, invariably leading to a bloody confrontation between the guerrillas and the Lebanese Army. The last straw was the killing in Beirut of three Palestinian guerrilla leaders by Israeli agents (10 April 1973). Despite his resilience and political strength, Prime Minister Salam was forced to resign amid demonstrations protesting the army's failure to resist Israel.

The crisis milieu itself dictated the choice of the new premier, Dr. Amin Hafiz. A pro-Palestinian economist representing Tripoli in the Chamber, Hafiz was a new face at the top, in sharp contrast to his predecessor. His cabinet, which included six young recruits, ran the gamut of Lebanon's ideologies, leaders, sects, and interests; big business and rightist interests had strong representation, but there was also a leftist.

Despite these positive attributes, Prime Minister Hafiz's government lasted less than two months. Hafiz was unable to stop the ferocious fighting between the army and the Palestinians; he also was opposed by the combined parliamentary strength of Karami, Junblat, and Salam. In late June 1973 President Franjiyyah brought in a second prime minister in two months—Taqi al-Din al-

Sulh—the third member of the Sulh clan to hold that position. A former minister, Sulh lacked Dr. Hafiz's youth, but he brought to the premiership years of political experience. More important were the size and makeup of Sulh's cabinet. Composed of twenty-two ministers, this was Lebanon's largest cabinet—four more than the previous recordholders of May 1960 and May 1972. While during the fifties crises tended to produce small cabinets, in the sixties they had the opposite effect of substantially enlarging the cabinet. The twenty-two-man Sulh cabinet is a continuation of this upward trend and it represents the political system's response to Lebanon's crisis condition. By skillful recruitment, the Franjiyyah-Sulh administration coopted twenty-two politicians to represent over eleven different blocs and sectarian-ethnic communities.[73] Thus, the elite's unity was maximized, the opposition coalition weakened, and the cabinet crisis ended simultaneously with the conclusion of still another agreement between the army and the Palestinian guerrilla movements. As internal peace came, the army had gained strength, while guerrilla power declined. Despite its fractionalized mass base, the political system had been able to manage the crisis and move forward to face the new uncertainties of the October 1973 Arab-Israeli war.

3

Political Elites in a New Society: Israel

Israel simultaneously constitutes a new nation and an old people. Its experience in nation-building is unique in the world of developing states, particularly in the peculiar sequential juxtaposition of its phases of national development. Israeli nation-building began long before independence was achieved in 1948. The Yishuv's first settlers were already confirmed nationalists; that is, nation-building had long preceeded the settlement of the land. Here was a nation looking for a land to build a state.

In the West, Israel's political leadership is often symbolized by David Ben Gurion, or Moshe Dayan, or Golda Meir, none of whom is fully representative of the country's top elite. Behind them have been a large number of lesser known individuals, who collectively have shown a degree of elite effectiveness uncommon to most developing states.

This study does not attempt a comprehensive analysis of the Israeli political elite; rather it focuses almost exclusively on cabinet ministers, who constitute the most important sector of the total political elite however defined. This does not mean that all cabinet members are equally powerful, despite the one man, one vote, rule. It can be plausibly argued that a number of powerful leaders exist outside the cabinet and should be included in the political elite. Particularly important are the secretary-general of the Histadrut, the chief of staff of Tzahal (Israeli Defense Forces), and the secretary-general of the Mapai. Moreover, at various times in Israel's history such informal groups as the *havereynu* or the *sareynu* [1] were central to governmental decision-making. However, most of the individuals who served in the above positions have been included in the present study, since they became ministers at one point or another. [2]

The Forging of an Elite
The Milieu

Certain important socializational experiences often stand out in the lives of leaders, which have shaped their world views and influenced their subsequent behavior. It is necessary, therefore, to recreate the social-psychological-political milieu within which Israel's future leaders began to shape their political careers. Significantly, the elite shared the same socialization as a major portion of European Jews, who provided most of Israel's early settlers. This shared socialization pattern minimized the elite-mass cultural gap, one of the main factors responsible for Israeli strength.

The milieu relevant for most Israeli leaders was that of Europe at the turn of the century, which was characterized by the nationalisms of the competing imperialist nation-states. In view of their intolerance and exclusivism, these nationalisms did not foster conditions favorable to minorities such as the Jews. Those fifteen provinces of the Tzarist Empire known as the Pale of Settlement, which included parts of the Ukraine, Byelorussia, and Poland, constituted the epicenter of Jewish persecution.[3] To a lesser extent anti-Jewish manifestations also occurred in West Europe, particularly France, Austria, and Germany.

There were four types of Jewish response to the prevailing milieu. The first, and perhaps easiest, was emigration to the new dispersion in the Americas, especially the United States and Canada. Acculturation into the European national milieu was another option, although painful psychologically and spiritually; for example, there were the Marxes and the Mendelssohns who were converts to German Lutheranism. A third response was deep involvement in and often leadership of left-internationalist movements. Aimed at cross-national brotherhood and the weakening of the nation-state, this type of activity was related to the Jew's quest to break out of the European social-psychological ghetto. Most communist or socialist Jews, like Trotsky, had been acculturated fully into their societies; but there were others who fell back upon their Jewishness, especially after the great letdown by the Russian Revolution of 1917. With the Nazi massacres and the Stalinist excesses, the fourth option came into sharper focus. It was

Zionism—a Jewish variant of nationalism which had developed as a response to the various nationalisms of Europe.

Early Socialization

While official and unofficial persecution remained an external socializing factor, the Jewish community possessed its own internal socializational institutions, which had a formative influence upon the emerging elite. These included the family, the synagogue, religious schools, and various Jewish cultural and political groups devoted to the strengthening of a Jewish identity. While the precise number of those who attended a Heder or Torbuth is unknown, it is clear that a high percentage of the ministers (over 80 percent) had some Jewish schooling early in life. This type of learning experience helped reinforce the feelings of ethnicity imparted by the Jewish family; the family and the school acted in a complimentary manner to create a Jewish identity among the youth. It was in this milieu that *Galut* (diaspora) nationalism began to develop.

On the threshhold of adulthood another socializational agent entered the picture to reinforce the influences of the family, the school, and the oppressive milieu of the diaspora—a local branch of one of several Jewish organizations, some religious, others cultural and political. These groups included Gordonia (Socialist Zionist Youth), Po'ale Zion, Hoveve Zion, Tzi're Zion, Histadrut, Hashomer Hatza'ir, Dutch Zionist Organization, Mizrahi Youth, Hehalutz, Young Judea, Hapoel Hamizrahi, Betar, Zionist-Socialists of Russia, Zionist Labor Movement, and various other Zionist and religious organizations. Virtually all of these were ideologically committed to a return to Palestine, and over two-thirds of modern Israel's ministerial elite were involved in this type of group.[4]

In addition to being socialization agents, these organizations served as stepping stones for many a future Israeli leader to rise in the world Zionist movement and eventually assume leadership roles in the Yishuv itself. For example, Ben Gurion was active in the Po'ale Zion in Poland and the Hehalutz movement in the USA; Barzilai cofounded Hashomer Hatza'ir; Bar-Yehuda was secretary of the Zionist Labor Movement in Russia; Begin acted as head of Betar; Ben Aharon helped start Hashomer Hatza'ir in Rumania; Bernstein was president of the Dutch Zionist Organization; Dultzin headed the Zionist Federation of Mexico; Govrin was cofounder of the Hehalutz in the Ukraine; Gruenbaum headed the Polish Zionists; Joseph headed Young Judea in Canada; Josephthal led the Berlin Youth Aliya and Hehalutz in Germany; Luz founded Hehalutz in Bobruisk; Lavon was cofounder of Gordonia; Levin helped establish Agudat Israel in Poland; Maimon founded the Mizrahi movement in Vilna; Mintz was cofounder of Po'ale Agudat Israel; Kaplan was one of the founders of Tzi're Zion; Naphtali was chairman of the German League of Labor for Palestine; Nurock headed the Latvian Mizrahi; Rosen led the Kartell Judischer Verbinduugen and the Blau-Weiss in Germany; Shapira was a leading member of Hehalutz Hamizrahi; Serlin was chairman of the Academic Zionists; Shazar helped organize Hehalutz in Germany; Warhaftig became a vice president of Mizrahi in Poland. These leadership positions were extremely important as the hubs in a world-wide communications network [5] which dealt with a multitude of problems ranging from immigration to Palestine to collecting funds and lobbying for the Jewish cause in various capitals.

An Itinerant Elite

The early years of the Israeli elite are marked by an unusual amount of itinerancy. War, repression, and rootlessness combined to make these individuals what may be the world's most traveled top-leadership group; and in contrast to other leadership groups, intensive travel came early in life, long before acquiring leadership positions. These travels also provide important clues to socializational patterns.[6]

A number of patterns are discernible, the most common being travel within Europe, especially from Poland and Russia to Western Europe and finally to Palestine. A second pattern, peculiar to the older generation of leaders, included one early passage through Palestine before 1914 and a subsequent return for permanent settlement. In this category are found Ben Gurion, Kaplan, Rabbi Maimon, and former President Shazar; both Ben Gurion and Rabbi Maimon were deported by the Turkish rulers of Palestine and spent several years in the US before returning to British-occupied Pales-

TABLE 35 *. *Israel: Dates of Arrival ***

ALIYA	YEAR	NAME
	1906	Ben Gurion
	1906	Sharett
	1913	Maimon
2	1913	Remez
	1914	Eshkol
	1914	Galili
	1914	Zisling
	1920	Bentov
	1920	Luz
	1921	Meir
3	1921	Dinur
	1921	Joseph
	1922	Govrin
	1923	Kaplan
	1924	Carmel
	1924	Gvati
	1924	Namir
	1924	Shapiro
	1924	Shazar
	1925	Mintz
	1925	Pinkas
	1925	Shapira
	1925	Sharef
4	1926	Aranne
	1926	Bar-Yehuda
	1927	Sasson
	1928	Ben Aharon
	1929	Lavon
	1929	Sapir

tine. Certain others had unusual itineraries: Russian-born Warhaftig reached Palestine by way of Lithuania, Japan, and the US; Bar-Yehuda's, Begin's and Nurock's itineraries included Siberian jails; Premier Meir lived in Milwaukee, Wisconsin before moving to Palestine. Rabbi Toledano, a native of Tiberias, was deported by the Turks to Corsica during World War I and returned to Palestine after serving for twenty years in Sephardic communities throughout North Africa.

Even after settlement, these leaders were to travel far and wide, both before and after statehood, as heads of various diplomatic and rescue missions or on behalf of the Jewish Agency. Yet the painful memories of their early wandering seems to have had a powerful impact on their political attitudes and behavior—one that is crucial

ALIYA	YEAR	NAME
	1929	Yeshayahu
	1930	Almogi
	1930	Cohn
	1930	Hillel
	1931	Rosen
	1932	Hazani
	1932	Kol
	1933	Gruenbaum
	1933	Naphtali
	1933	Peled
	1933	Serlin
	1934	Barzilai
5	1934	Geri
	1934	Peres
	1935	Landau
	1935	Zadok
	1936	Bernstein
	1938	Josephthal
	1939	Bar-Lev
	1939	Rimalt
	1939	Shemtov
	1940	Burg
	1940	Levin
	1942	Begin
	1946	Eban
	1947	Nurock
6	1947	Warhaftig
	1956	Dultzin

* With the exception of the Fifth Aliya, the periodization of aliyot follows that found in S. N. Eisenstadt, *Israeli Society* (New York: Basic Books, 1967), p. 11.

** The listing includes all 64 ministers who served from 1948 through 1973.

in understanding the depth of their attachment to the land of Eretz Yisrael.

Aliyot and the Elite

In Israel's political culture the date of one's permanent settlement in Palestine carries special significance, for immigration made Israel's existence possible. One is struck by the fact that all major Israeli biographical works cite Aliya dates. Clearly an early date of settlement carries with it a certain prestige and the halo of the pioneer.

A number of significant findings emerge from a breakdown of ministers by their Aliyot dates. As table 35 indicates, most of the ministerial elite came in the twenties and thirties. Yet the real "founding fathers" of the Israeli state were settlers of the Second Aliya—between 1904 and 1913. Out of sixty-four ministers, four came during this period—Ben Gurion, Sharett, Remez, and Rabbi Maimon—along with others who subsequently held non-cabinet leadership posts—Ben Zvi, Katznelson, Gordon, Brenner, Sprinzak. Only if one considers the crucial roles of these leaders, does the full significance of the Second Aliya come into focus. The single most outstanding personality of the Second Aliya elite was Ben Gurion,[7] who first came to Palestine in 1906 at the age of twenty. In a sense Ben Gurion shares the honor of earliest settler with Moshe Sharett, whose family also entered Palestine in 1906 with their teenage son. Significantly these earliest of immigrants were destined to become Israel's first and second prime ministers. Not until 1913 did two additional future ministers arrive: the militant Mizrahi leader Rabbi Maimon, a veteran anti-British politician, and David Remez, a founder of Ahdut A'voda and Histadrut and chairman of Solel Boneh and Va'ad L'umi. All four members of the Second Aliya were destined to become signers of Israel's Declaration of Independence.

If the year 1914 is considered to fall within the Second Aliya, three more leaders would qualify for this early elite contingent. These include Israel's third prime minister, Levi Eshkol, as well as Haganah commander Israel Galili and Mapam leader Aaron Zisling, a signer of the Declaration of Independence. Of the seven Second Aliya leaders, only Galili continues to serve as minister.

The Third Aliya, beginning soon after World War I brought to Palestine seven additional future leaders during a brief four-year period. Not all of the Third Aliya seven were as prominent as the leaders of the Second Aliya; nevertheless, several still occupy top leadership roles in the cabinet, Histadrut and Mapai.

The most important personality of the Third Aliya was Golda Meir, the sole woman member of the elite and Israel's fourth prime minister; she too signed the Declaration of Independence along with the Mapam journalist Mord'khai Bentov. Equally prominent were Dov Joseph, veteran Mapai politician and governor of Jerusalem during the 1948 siege, and Kadish Luz, a Mapai member who was Knesset Speaker for some years. Also there were Rabbi Ben-Zion Dinur, a teacher and journalist, and Akiva

Govrin, a Mapai leader. The Third Aliya also included Eliezer Kaplan, Israel's first finance minister and supporter of Chaim Weizmann against Ben Gurion. Kaplan also became a signatory of the Declaration of Independence.

The leaders of the Fourth Aliya could not match the preeminence of the Third and especially the Second Aliya. However, what they lacked in prestige, they compensated for by their numbers; no less than twenty of Israel's future ministers settled in Palestine between 1924 and 1931. Like their predecessors, Fourth Aliya leaders came mostly from areas of the Tzarist Russian Empire, including Poland, Byelorussia, Lithuania, the Ukraine, and parts of the Balkans. However, there were important exceptions, for the Fourth Aliya elite became more heterogeneous in geographical origin with the arrival of Sephardic groups from the Arab countries. Among these future ministers were Eliahu Sasson of Damascus, Syria; Israel Yeshayahu (Sharabi) of San'a, Yemen; and Shlomo Hillel of Baghdad, Iraq. Sasson, a newspaperman, distinguished himself as a diplomat negotiating with the Arabs at Rhodes. Yeshayahu organized Operation Magic Carpet, which airlifted Yemenite Jews to Israel. Hillel, who immigrated in 1930 at the age of seven, was active in illegal immigration as well as in the diplomatic corps.

Moreover, the Fourth Aliya saw the beginnings of Jewish immigration from Germany. At the leadership level the arrivals included future ministers of justice, Hayim Cohn and Pinhas Rosen. Significantly, it was Rosen who cofounded the Association of Immigrants from Germany and its successor Aliya Hadasha, named after the Fifth Aliya, during which the bulk of German-born immigrants had arrived.

The remaining fifteen leaders who immigrated during the Fourth Aliya were of Russian-Central European origin. These included future President Zalman Shazar, Palmah officer Moshe Carmel, Agriculture Minister Hayim Gvati, Histadrut General Secretary Mord'khai Namir, Minister of Justice Ya'acov Shimshon Shapiro, Rabbis David Zvi Pinkas and Moshe Hayim Shapira of the Mizrahi movement as well as Binyamin Mintz of Agudat Israel. Both Pinkas and Shapira were signers of Israel's Declaration of Independence. Six additional future ministers came to Palestine during the Fourth Aliya. These included Haganah member and cabinet secretary, Ze'ev Sharef; Mapai secretary, and Histadrut leader, Zalman Aranne; Haganah leader, Bar-Yehuda; Histadrut secretary, Ben Aharon; Mapai party secretaries, Pinhas Lavon and Pinhas Sapir and Haganah leader, Joseph Almogi.

Each of the Aliyot represents a political generation [8] which was influenced by some key event or events. The Second Aliya endured the Russian pogroms, and World War I was the key element in the Third and Fourth Aliyot. The rise of Nazism and the extermination of European Jewry were the formative events of the Fifth Aliya.

In retrospect, ministers from the Fourth Aliya have left their mark on Israeli political life. Over half are still active in top governmental posts, some in the cabinet. While there were only two ministers in the December 1969 cabinet from the Third Aliya (Meir and Galili), the Fourth Aliya claimed six ministers—Almogi, Gvati, Hillel, Sapir, Shapiro, and Sharef. These included some of Israel's most powerful politicians. In terms of elite recruitment, the Fourth Aliya emerges as most crucial; the common perception that the Fourth Aliya "was humanly, ideologically and politically less significant than the previous ones" [9] is not entirely correct. As indicated by the data in table 35, the Fourth Aliya contributed more cabinet leaders than any other Aliya, both in absolute terms and in proportion to the total immigration during each Aliya.

Sixteen future leaders arrived during the Fifth Aliya (1932–1939)—the Aliya Hadasha (New Immigration). After the twenty leaders of the Fourth Aliya, this represents the largest group of future elite in absolute terms. Yet when the Fifth Aliya sixteen are considered in proportional terms with the massive 225,000 immigration of that period, it becomes obvious that these immigrants were not as heavily represented as those of earlier Aliyot. This may be attributable to two interrelated factors. First, arriving later in Palestine, they did not get the early political start as did the "founding fathers" of the earlier Aliyot. Second, in contrast to most earlier immigrants, the Aliya Hadasha consisted mostly of German Jews escaping from the impending Nazi holocaust. Despite their relatively massive influx, the German Jews were latecomers to Zionism and could not readily advance to top positions in a society dominated by the earlier settlers from Russia and Eastern Europe. Of the sixteen ministers who entered Palestine between 1932 and 1939, only four possessed "German" backgrounds—Peretz Naphtali, Peretz Bernstein, Giora Josephthal, and Hayim Bar-Lev. In Germany Naphtali had been prominent in the German Socialist Party and the trade-union movement, in addition to teaching economics and journalism. Bernstein was both a businessman and a journalist who came to Israel in 1936 and eventually became chairman of the General Zionist Party. Giora Josephthal reached Palestine in 1938 after heading Hehalutz in Germany. A refugee from Hitler's Germany, it was Josephthal who acted as cochairman of the German reparations committee. Finally, there was the Austrian-born Hayim Bar-Lev, one of Tzahal's top commanders. It was not until 1939 that he reached Palestine by way of Yugoslavia.

In addition to the foregoing four German-born ministers, twelve other future ministers arrived during the Fifth Aliya—most of them from Central and East European countries. But in contrast to the German-born who were underrepresented, the East European Jews who came during this period succeeded in achieving office in much larger numbers. Late arrival appears to have interfered less with the upward mobility of the non-German contingent, which included Michael Hazani of the National Religious Party and Moshe Kol, leader of the Independent Liberal Party and a signer of the Independence Declaration of 1948. Six others arrived during 1933–34—the first years of the Nazi era. These included Itzhak Gruenbaum, a veteran journalist and leader of the Jewish bloc in the Polish Sejm; as a General Zionist he signed Israel's Declaration of Independence. Another General Zionist leader was Yoseph Serlin, past secretary to Nahum Sokolow. There were also two Mapam leaders, Nathan Peled and Yisrael Barzilai, both active in the kibbutz movement. Two others were Ya'acov Geri, a South African businessman and Shimon Peres, the dynamic exdeputy defense minister and a cofounder of R'shimat Po'ale Yisrael (Rafi). The year 1935 saw the arrivals of future Haganah officer Hayim Zadok and Hayim Landau, who later emerged as a commander of Irgun Zvai L'umi. Rabbi Elimelekh Rimalt, a Galician working in Austria, had arrived during 1939.

Yet the immigration of ministers-to-be did not cease with the start of World War II. Rabbis Yoseph Burg of Mizrahi and Itzhak

Levin of Agudat Israel entered Palestine in 1940; both became signers of the Declaration of Independence. M'nahem Begin, who came in 1942, subsequently led the Irgun in its anti-British armed uprising.

Four future ministers reached Palestine in the post-World War II period. Abba Eban arrived in 1946. Rabbis Mord'khai Nurock and Zerah Warhaftig of the National Religious Party reached Palestine in 1947; the latter also signed the independence declaration. The last of the ministerial elite to arrive was Leon Dultzin, who came as late as 1956, after nearly three decades of Zionist activity in Mexico.

The foregoing breakdown of the cabinet elite by Aliyot does not include the Sabras—those ministers who were born in Palestine. The seven Sabra ministers were Y'gal Allon, Moshe Dayan, Yisrael Rokah, Yosef Saphir, B'khor Shalom Shitrit, Ya'acov Toledano, and Ezer Weizmann.

Class and Occupational Background

In view of the pioneering socialism of the settlers, no less than the egalitarianism of an immigrant society, inquiry into the class backgrounds of Israel's leaders may seem superfluous. Yet careful scrutiny will indicate the significance of elite class background not only within Israeli politics, but particularly in cross-national analysis between Israel and the Arab states.

In most polities, one is concerned with two aspects of class background: from what class did a leader originate and to what class did he belong immediately prior to top political office. However, the problem becomes complicated when one considers the itinerant backgrounds of Israeli leaders. Therefore it is necessary to determine a leader's class background in his country of birth, as a settler in Palestine, and prior to entering high governmental position.

With regard to the European-born leaders, one might expect to find middle-class backgrounds because of the *petit bourgeois* image of Jews in the European perception. Yet on the basis of our incomplete data, this is by no means true, at least not for Israeli ministers. It appears that the cabinet elite came from three more or less distinct classes. While few leaders originated in the upper class, one could discern a small contingent of about ten who belonged to upper-middle-class families, i.e., entrepreneurs, lawyers, and businessmen. These included Peretz Bernstein, Leon Dultzin, Ya'acov Geri, Giora Josephthal, Eliezer Kaplan, Peretz Naphtali, Yisrael Rokah, Pinhas Rosen, Yosef Saphir, and Ezer Weizmann.

Particularly noteworthy is the presence of late immigrants from Germany—Bernstein, Josephthal, Naphtali, and Rosen. Their upper-middle-class background may be reflective of the relatively high social-economic position of German Jewry in contrast to Polish or Russian Jews. Three others in this contingent, Saphir, Rokah, and Weizmann, were Sabras with unmistakable businessman-proprietor backgrounds. In view of the General Zionist support of free enterprise in contrast to Mapai's and Mapam's socialism, one may hypothesize a relationship between the class background of General Zionist ministers (Bernstein, Saphir, Rokah, Rosen, and Dultzin) and party identification. Yet it is also possible that many of these ministers joined parties other than the Mapai, because as latecomers they found their chances for advancement limited in an established party with an entrenched leadership under David Ben Gurion. In other words there may be a relationship between late arrival in Palestine and membership in such opposition parties as the Liberals (the General Zionists and the Progressives) and the Herut—since 1965 united as the Gahal. Of the twenty-two leaders who came to Palestine after 1932, eight belonged to opposition parties. Finally, late arrival may have pushed a number of latecomers into militant policies toward the Arabs. Noteworthy in this connection was the resignation of the Gahal ministers Landau, Rimalt, Dultzin, and Begin in protest of Secretary of State Rogers' peace initiative. This manifest hawkishness may have been related to their need to establish a legitimate claim to power by upstaging the government. In other words, the Gahal leaders' militancy may have been motivated by a desire to compensate for late arrival in Palestine.

The Gahal-big business tie remains strong; indeed, a number of party leaders are involved in a variety of large enterprises, either personally or through their families. General Weizmann is a case in point. He comes from a politically and economically prominent family with marriage ties to businessmen and politicians (e.g., Dayan). Nor is the Mapai insulated from the influences of Israel's economic elite; in addition to Finance Minister Sapir, General Bar-Lev is often regarded as representing business interests in the cabinet. Here the beginnings of a military-industrial complex may be discernible, one that enjoys close ties to the cabinet elite.

Over twenty ministers could be classified as middle class. This group included those whose families could afford to give them a university education in such professional fields as law or engineering. Also included in this middle-class contingent [10] were a number of prominent rabbis. Finally, the most difficult group to identify was that with a lower-middle or lower-class background, which accounted for about half of the ministerial elite. Although the data is insufficient for a definitive determination, one could plausibly hypothesize that most of the early settlers—the leaders from the Second, Third, and Fourth Aliyot—came from relatively modest economic backgrounds. Despite the pogroms in Russia, the well-to-do had little inclination to emigrate to the politically and economically hostile Ottoman-Turkish environment in Palestine. Also, the rich had the means to survive repression better than the less affluent; and even among the poorer it was the idealists who became *olim*—the immigrants to Palestine.

The New Class Base

Equally crucial to the process of elite socialization was the formative influence of the Palestinian environment. This included not only the political or physical threats from the Turks, the Arabs, and the British, but also the sorts of occupations the future elite undertook soon after arrival in Palestine. Table 36 presents a listing of those ministers who initially became agricultural workers, farmers, road workers, and watchmen—not very desirable jobs by Western standards; by fairly universal criteria these occupations imply a lower-class existence. Whatever their original class background, many of the olim began at the bottom once in Palestine. This applied particularly to the olim of the early Aliyot, since they were generally poorer than those who arrived later. Moreover, they had come to a generally poor and underdeveloped land.

Beginning with the Second Aliya the idea of self-labor among the olim created a strong impetus toward farming and agricultural labor generally. The newcomers organized the Po'ale Zion and Hapoel Hatza'ir parties which were ideologically committed to establishing ties to the soil by working it. This orientation led to conflict with established Jewish farmers, who preferred cheap Arab labor to Jewish labor,[11] a situation which prompted the young olim to set up such village settlements as Hityashvut Ha'Ovedat, D'ganya, Kinneret, and Merhavya.

TABLE 36. *Israel: Early Occupational Background*

MINISTER	OCCUPATION
Allon	Farmer; soldier
Aranne	Farmer; Road Worker
Bar-Yehuda	Road Worker
Barzilai	Farmer
Ben Gurion	Watchman; Agricultural Worker
Bentov	Worker
Dayan	Farmer; soldier
Eshkol	Watchman; Agricultural Worker
Galili	Farmer
Gvati	Farmer
Hazani	Farmer
Lavon	Farmer
Luz	Farmer; Worker
Meir	Agricultural Worker
Namir	Baker
Remez	Farmer
Sapir	Farmer
Shapiro	Agricultural and Construction Worker
Yeshayahu	Farmer; Weaver
Zisling	Farmer

Blended with the idea of self-labor were strong doses of socialist collectivism, which the settlers brought from Russia. The socialist component further reinforced the austere, lower-class culture which flourished in that unique socializational milieu—the kibbutz.[12] The physical and psychological association between Israel's future leadership and the kibbutzim has been extremely close. Over one-third of the ministers had had ties with the kibbutz and/or other types of agricultural settlements (table 37).[13] The ministers' involvement in kibbutzim ranged from membership to place of birth, as in the case of General Dayan (b. D'gania). A

TABLE 37. *Israel: Membership in Kibbutzim*

FOUNDED	KIBBUTZ	NAME
1910	D'gania B	Dayan, Eshkol,* Luz
1911	Merhavya	Meir, Shazar
1920	Kiryat Anavim	Eshkol *
1921	En Harod	Zisling
1922	Yagur	Bar Yehuda
1925	Givat Hash'losha	Shapiro *
1926	Gvat	Gvati
1926	Mishmar Ha'Emek	Bentov *
1929	Sarid	Peled
1930	Hulda	Lavon *
1930	Na'an	Galili,* Carmel
1932	Givat Hayim	Ben Aharon
1935	Sh'fayim	Sharef
1937	Ginnosar	Allon *
1939	Negba	Barzilai *
1941	Alumot	Peres
1945	Gal'ed	Josephthal *
1949	Ma'agan Mikhael	Hillel *
1952	S'de Boker	Ben Gurion

* denotes founder or cofounder of kibbutzim.

well-known exminister, Ben Gurion, retired to a kibbutz—S'de
Boker in the Negev. More important, ten, or approximately one-
sixth of the elite, founded or cofounded kibbutzim. As table 37
indicates, some of Israel's most outstanding leaders were
among the founding members of kibbutzim; e.g., Allon-Ginnosar;
Bentov-Mishmar Ha'Emek; Galili-Na'an; Barzilai-Negba; Shapiro-
Givat Hash'losha. Former Prime Minister Eshkol enjoyed the
distinction of having founded two kibbutzim-D'gania and Kiryat
Anavim. Even today a number of government ministers keep
residence on the kibbutz to maintain a tie to their old homestead.
Many kibbutz founders had worked in one of the early settlements
and later went on to establish a new moshav or kibbutz in some
other location.

A number of additional insights can be gleaned from tables 36
and 37 about elite-kibbutz relationships. About three-fourths of the

settlements in table 37 were founded before 1935 by the early settlers of the Yishuv—the olim of the Second, Third, and Fourth Aliyot. Only two of the table 37 ministers were not born in Tzarist areas—Hillel, an Iraqi, and Josephthal, a German. Thus, the kibbutz was simply a creation of the Russian-Polish olim; they created the kibbutz but in the process their lives were shaped by it. The kibbutz milieu helped toughen the elite and reinforced their identification with collective agricultural labor, which many had engaged in after coming to Palestine. There is something very meaningful and unique in identifying oneself as a farmer, as many Israeli ministers do even today in their official biographies. While it is true that most of the elite active in the kibbutz movement (table 37) had worked as farmers, watchmen, and laborers (table 36), those unacquainted with the Israeli ethos might find it peculiar that politicians proclaim with pride their humble origins.

In sum, the inhospitable Palestine environment, the socialist-Zionist ideology, and the kibbutz milieu, all combined to militate against the *embourgeoisement* of the elite, at least those of the Second, Third, and Fourth Aliyot. The kibbutzim played a similar role with regard to the Haganah and later the Tzahal—the Israeli Army. One might discern a relationship between the lack of *embourgeoisement* and the elite's unusual drive and fortitude in creating the foundations for a new society. Yet despite official warnings, today's Israeli society, especially since 1967, has raced headlong toward a bourgeois lifestyle. This Americanization of Israel and the corresponding dilution of the socialist ethos is bound to encourage an "end of ideology" situation and far-reaching changes in the future composition of the elite.

Common Experiences: Imprisonment

Arrests and imprisonment have been common experiences for many a nationalist leader. This was also true of many Israeli leaders with the difference that they experienced arrest and imprisonment under several flags, e.g., Russia, Turkey, Germany, and Britain. While the Russian and Turkish jailings mostly occurred before World War I, the German and British imprisonments took place during the thirties and the forties. The Germans held a substantial number of Jewish POWs captured in Greece and elsewhere, who had fought in British units. At least two Israeli ministers belong to this group—Almogi and Ben-Aharon. A much larger group of leaders were imprisoned by the British mandatory authorities as the tri-dimensional conflict in Palestine intensified. Over 25 percent, or sixteen, of all ministers had experienced imprisonment and of these, ten, or one-sixth of the total, were committed by the British to Latrun and Acre prisons during the forties on charges of subversive activity. These imprisonments constituted a shared experience to a considerable portion of the emerging leadership and as such symbolized joint sacrifice, defiance, and solidarity, and contributed to elite legitimacy which was so crucial to the development of the future state. The ten leaders who had been incarcerated at Latrun were Carmel, Dayan, Gruenbaum, Landau, Maimon, Remez, Rokah, Sharett, Joseph, and Pinhas Sapir— many of whom were among the most powerful of Israel's politicians. However, it was the late, fiery Rabbi Maimon who had the distinction of being jailed under three flags—the Russian, Turkish, and the British.

Common Experiences: Foreign Military Service

Of all the Israeli elite's learning experiences, service in foreign armies was certainly crucial in terms of defending the Yishuv and later the state of Israel. Indeed, there was a direct connection between foreign military service, the Haganah/Irgun, and the Tzahal.

During the First and Second World Wars, Jews served in the military forces of various nations depending on residence or citizenship; at the leadership level, at least sixteen of the sixty-four ministers had seen various types of military service, both in and out of Palestine. Because of the political circumstances in Europe and Palestine during World War I, Jews fought on both sides despite the fact that their deeper sympathies may have been with the Allies.

Ben Gurion, Eshkol, and Dov Joseph served in the British-sponsored Jewish Legion and Luz was in the Tzarist army, as was Dinur, who later became a Russian revolutionary. On the other hand, Sharett became an officer in the German-led Turkish army of the Levant and Pinhas Rosen served in the German army in

Europe. World War II saw a younger generation of leaders join the British army in Palestine to fight against Nazi Germany and her Vichy French ally which was acting as the mandatory power in Syria. This younger contingent included Allon, Almogi, Ben-Aharon, Dayan, Eban, Josephthal, and Ezer Weizmann. In addition Begin served in the Polish army and Shitrit had become an officer in the British-led Palestine police.

This early baptism of fire was to have a formative influence on elite behavior before and during Israel's war of independence. It prepared these leaders both psychologically and technologically for their future wars with the Arabs. Especially significant was service in British units during World War II; not only did the leaders learn the art of war-making first hand, but they got to know the British military-political apparatus from the inside—the kind of knowledge that was to prove useful in the Jewish resistance movement against the British mandatory authorities. In addition to actual military service some went on to study in British military schools, among them Generals Allon, Dayan, and Weizmann, all of whom played leading military roles against the Arabs. British training was especially crucial to Weizmann, who eventually helped create an air force second to none in the Middle East.

Common Experiences: Haganah/Palmah

The Haganah, perhaps more than any other single organization, affected the leadership of the Jewish state. Indeed, for many leaders the Haganah constituted the final test of certification before assuming high positions in the new government of independent Israel. One need not engage in a detailed analysis to note the striking continuity between foreign military service, Haganah work, and cabinet membership. A related dimension of continuity is discernible between the members of the kibbutz movement and the Haganah. Three top commanders of Haganah's elite corps, the Palmah, were kibbutz activists: Allon, Carmel, and Galili. Other Haganah members who came from a kibbutz background include Bar-Yehuda, Eshkol, Luz, Sharef, and Dayan.

In all, at least twenty-two ministers, or 29 percent, have served in Haganah posts, although not all of these engaged in combat missions. Ben Gurion was in overall command while Sharett, Eshkol, Sharef, and Sapir managed the financing and other supportive and administrative functions. In contrast, Allon, Bar-Lev, Carmel, Dayan, and Galili were commanders in the Palmah. Another key Palmah member who subsequently reached the cabinet was Bar-Yehuda, its coorganizer. Finally there were those serving in Haganah in various capacities: Almogi, Luz, Govrin, Namir, Shapiro, Peres, Saphir, Weizmann, and Zadok. In addition to the Haganah/Palmah contingent of twenty-two ministers, there were two who had been Irgun Zvai L'umi leaders: Begin and Landau. It was not until late in 1948 that the Irgun was incorporated into the Tzahal along with its rival, the Palmah.

The Haganah-Irgun rivalry nearly escalated into civil war when Ben Gurion ordered the Palmah to attack the Irgun ship Altalena which had brought arms into N'tanya harbor during June 1948. The confrontation was defused through the mediation efforts of Irgun's leader, M'nahem Begin, and three other opponents of Ben Gurion who eventually became ministers. Significantly two of the three were well-known rabbis, Yehuda Leib Maimon and Moshe Hayim Shapira. The third, Itzhak Gruenbaum, was a General Zionist, who along with Rabbi Maimom could be considered a senior statesman; as septuagenarian they were well suited to play a mediating role.

Common Experiences: The Great Event

In retrospect no single period stands out more in the national memory of Israel than the events of 1948; that is, the establishment and successful defense of the Israeli state. The external threat contributed to national unity and, in the long range, to national integration. So great was fear of the Arabs in the Jewish perception that it temporarily pushed into the background deep inter-elite differences, especially between Ben Gurion and Palmah and Irgun leaders. Although Ben Gurion proclaimed the Tzahal Israel's official army (31 May 1948), he still had considerable difficulty in bringing the Irgun and Palmah under his central authority.[14] Having achieved victory over the Egyptians, the Palmah commander, General Allon, wanted to preserve a degree of autonomy. Ben

Gurion rejected this and ordered the Palmah command to dissolve during the autumn of 1948. However, since the Palmah had acted as the Tzahal's elite force,[15] many of its top commanders led Israel's army in subsequent wars and campaigns.

The momentous events of 1948 left their mark on the elite in several respects. The elite had been tested and found capable of managing internal conflict, mobilizing for war, and defeating an enemy. Even more important, to the extent that the elite had brought the Zionist dream into reality, it had legitimized itself both in Israel and in the Jewish diaspora. Finally, achieving victory gave the leadership a certain cohesion as a ruling group. This made possible a high degree of systemic stability despite ideological and personal clashes which were to occur so frequently during subsequent years.

TABLE 38. *Israel: Minister Signatories of the Declaration of Independence*

Bentov	Ben Gurion
Bernstein	Warhaftig
Gruenbaum	Levin
Meir	Kaplan
Maimon	Rosen
Pinkas	Remez
Zisling	Shitrit
Kol	Shapira
Sharett	

The great event—achievement of statehood—was symbolized by the signing of a Declaration of Independence on 14 May 1948. The thirty-seven signatories of this key document were drawn from the top echelons of the Yishuv; of these, seventeen eventually became ministers. The background characteristics of the remaining twenty were little different from those of their ministerial colleagues. The ministerial group itself contained six rabbis, five of whom represented the religious parties, and Shitrit, who signed as the Sephardic representative. Ben Gurion, Remez, Sharett, Kaplan, and Meir signed for Mapai. Bentov and Zisling signed for Mapam, and Bernstein, Rosen, and Kol signed for the Progressive Party. Gruenbaum signed for the General Zionists.

Coalition Politics and Elite Behavior
Six Causal Factors

Since Israel's founding, elite behavior within the cabinet has been conditioned by a number of factors. Important among these are

1. The ghetto complex of the Yishuv reinforced by Arab threats.
2. The social background of the leadership.
3. The personality of David Ben Gurion.
4. The Western heritage in ideology, political style, and political culture.
5. A body politic fragmented along religious, ideological, and geographic lines.
6. An economy burdened by heavy defense and development demands and by the pressures of *embourgeoisement*.

In any analysis of Israeli mass or elite behavior, the collective memory of Jewish ghetto existence and the related themes of encirclement, massacre, persecution, and deportation should be regarded as supremely significant. It was precisely against the backdrop of the ghetto experience that Zionism put forth its promise of physical and spiritual salvation. After initial consideration of Africa, the Zionists focused on Palestine—a most inhospitable land both politically and economically. Had it not been for the intercession of American and German Zionists through Ambassadors Morgenthau and von Weigenheim, and Marshall Allenby's advance from Egypt, the 84,000 Jews of Palestine might have met the fate of the Armenians and other Christians in the Ottoman Empire—extermination and deportation.[16] Although the Turkish threat was gone after World War I, the Arab threat remained and intensified despite the eventual establishment of Israel as a state and success in defending herself against several Arab armies. In other words, the European ghetto had been transferred to Palestine with all of its negative implications. The persistence of the Arab threat and their refusal to recognize Israel's legitimacy in their midst has constituted at least a partial failure of the Zionist promise. Despite repeated victories, Israel has achieved only a partial negation of the holocaust. The feeling of physical and social encirclement persists, although in modified fashion. It is against this background that the elite's behavior should be viewed and explained.

It has been sufficiently demonstrated that save for the large influx of Oriental Jews, the Israeli elite—the sixty-four ministers—present a more or less clear reflection of society in terms of psychology, educational level, ideology, class background, and religious affiliation.[17] This similarity of the elite and the mass has constituted one of Israel's great strengths. Indeed, since elite perceptions have been little different from mass perceptions of reality regarding such things as encirclement, the Arab threat, and world public opinion, there has seemed to be a high degree of correspondence between elite and mass attitudes.

The elite is also characterized by a toughness and self-assurance acquired through years of labor, fighting, and winning against their adversaries. Like the masses they represent, the Israeli leadership is a "beginning of ideology" elite. Having forged a new identity based on a new value system, Zionism, they are new believers and as such often display a morally uncompromising attitude and behavior.

David Ben Gurion's psychology has not been the subject of close scrutiny, yet no man save Nasir has influenced Middle Eastern events as much. A loner, even within the cabinet or among the top Mapai elite (*havereynu*), he displayed fierce competitiveness and suspiciousness. His crisis-bound view of life, combined with his devotion to duty and great energy, seems to identify him as a typical active-negative leader.[18] Nevertheless it was his decisive leadership and the sheer weight of his personality [19] that made cohesive, coalition government possible.

Israel's Western heritage includes ideology—nationalism, socialism, and democracy—as well as style—parliamentary government patterned partly after the British system. Theoretically, the principle of collective responsibility is paramount in the operation of the cabinet system, as is coalition discipline.[20] In practice, however, both principles can be difficult to implement, especially at times of great interparty conflict. Central to Israel's political process is the idea of cabinet accountability to the Knesset and the people, an accountability that is enforced through elections, votes of confidence, and other rules of the game.

The fifth factor influencing elite behavior is Israel's fragmented popular base which is reflected in the country's multiparty system. In the absence of a majority party, it is necessary to rely on coalition governments. Given the wide religious and ideological differences between the parties and their leaders, collective responsibility and discipline have been difficult, at times, to maintain.

Finally elite behavior has been affected by the creeping *embourgeoisement*—the revolution of rising expectations among Israelis. Having identified these six key factors which shape elite behavior, it is now necessary to examine them in a chronological analysis of Israeli cabinet politics.[21]

The Early Ben Gurion Cabinets, 1948–53

With the progressive breakdown of order in Palestine and the British reluctance to impose the UN partition resolution by force, the Va'ad L'umi decided (March 1948) that Palestine Jewish Agency Executive members and the Va'ad L'umi Executive would join together as the National Council. This body, representing all Palestinian Jews, consisted of thirty-seven members with the affiliations shown in table 39. This was the body which later issued, over the signatures of its members, Israel's Declaration of Independence. A smaller body of thirteen (National Administration), chosen from the Council acted as its executive.

On 14 May 1948, the National Council met under Jewish Agency Chairman Ben Gurion and proclaimed the establishment of Israel. Thus, the National Council became the Provisional Council

TABLE 39.   *Israel: Membership of National Council*

PARTY	N
Mapai	10
General Zionist	6
Mizrahi and Hapoel Hamizrahi	5
Mapam	5
Agudat Israel and Po'ale Agudat Israel	3
Revisionist	3
Communist	1
World Zionist Organization	1
Aliya Hadasha (Progressive)	1
Yemenite	1
Sephardim	1

of State and the National Administration became the Provisional Government of Israel. Chaim Weizmann was elected president of the Provisional Council of State.

For all practical purposes the Provisional Government functioned as a cabinet. It consisted of thirteen members (table 40). This Provisional Government under Ben Gurion brought together the Yishuv's leading personalities and major political groupings except the communists on the left and the Revisionists on the right. It consisted of Ben Gurion, Kaplan, Remez, and Sharett, the top leaders of Mapai; Shitrit, the lawyer-rabbi-policeman who represented the Sephardim, was allied to Mapai; he was the cabinet's sole native-born member. Three other rabbis—Maimon, Levin, and Shapira, represented the United Religious Bloc. At seventy-three, the venerable Rabbi Maimon was the oldest member; he had been a passionate anti-British spokesman of Jewish rights in Palestine. Although Rabbi Levin did not serve in the cabinet for an extended period, Shapira was destined to be a near-permanent fixture, participating in many cabinets until his death in 1970. The Mapam leaders, Bentov and Zisling, represented the left wing of the kibbutz movement; Bentov would serve in many a cabinet until 1969. Gruenbaum, the cabinet's second oldest member at sixty-nine and a veteran Polish politician, represented the General Zionists, as did Bernstein, the German-born head of Dutch Zionism.

TABLE 40. *Israel: Membership of Provisional Government*

PARTY	MINISTERS	N	%
Mapai	Ben Gurion Kaplan Remez Sharett	4	31
General Zionist	Gruenbaum Bernstein	2	15
Mapam	Bentov Zisling	2	15
Mizrahi- Hapoel Hamizrahi	Maimon Shapira	2	15
Agudat Israel	Levin	1	8
Progressives	Rosen	1	8
Sephardim	Shitrit	1	8

On the ideological spectrum, the Mapai and Mapam represented the left, the General Zionists and the Progressives the center; and the religious parties and the Sephardim represented the rather nebulous traditionalist sector of the Israeli electorate. It was important for the cabinet to be as representative as possible, not only to cope with the existing emergency, but because it was the new state's very first governing body. As such it would set important precedents in terms of size, rules, and style for many years to come.

However, the Provisional Government lacked the legitimacy which elections can bestow. It was not until January 1949 that the first Knesset elections were held. Unable to win a majority (46 seats) for his party, Ben Gurion was obliged to organize Israel's first cabinet on the basis of a coalition of parties as was the Provisional Government. The new cabinet consisted of twelve ministers: Mapai (7), Religious Bloc (3), Progressives (1), Sephardim (1). The General Zionists declined to join the cabinet.

The March 1949 cabinet contained three important personalities not included in the Provisional Government: Meir, Shazar, and Joseph. Meir later became prime minister and Shazar became president, while Joseph continued to hold ministerial positions until the mid-sixties. In April 1949 a four-party coalition enacted an austerity plan to check rising prices caused by the influx of immigration. The government's second major problem was one that has plagued Israel's politics throughout her existence—the religious issue.

Ben Gurion's attempts to broaden his coalition failed mainly because of General Zionist opposition. By October, due to increasing economic difficulties, concessions were made to private enterprise and a new appeal sent to world Jewry for financial help. Also, Ben Gurion appointed Ya'acov Geri, a nonpartisan businessman, as minister of industry and commerce, to replace Dov Joseph, whose strict economic policies had been unpopular. This act induced the resignation of the three rabbis, not only because of the religious issue but because of their inability to acquire Geri's portfolio. As a result, Ben Gurion resigned, but he proposed a caretaker government of seven Mapai members—a proposal which the Knesset rejected on 18 October 1950. A day later President Weizmann asked Justice Minister Pinhas Rosen (Progressives) to form a government. After a week of consultations, Rosen declined in favor of Ben Gurion.

In an attempt to satisfy the Religious Bloc, Ben Gurion agreed to enforce both Sabbath restrictions and dietary laws on meat imports. This broke the impasse and another four-party coalition cabinet of thirteen came into office on 30 October 1950. Personnel changes included the appointment of Pinhas Lavon to fill the Mapai seat vacated by Shazar.

As precarious economic conditions continued to plague the new government, the General Zionists made gains in the municipal and rural elections of November 1950 which led to a call for new elections. The divisive issue of religion once again erupted in January 1951 as Rabbis Maimon, Shapira, and Levin threatened to resign unless the government would provide religious instruction to immigrants in camps (*ma'abarot*). The Mapai, on the other hand, insisted that the religious parties could not monopolize the education of immigrants, since each family was entitled to a free choice. The fundamental political issue was Mapai's desire to perpetuate its control over the immigrants' education to secure their votes. On 14 February 1951 the government fell over the issue of religious instruction, after which it assumed a caretaker role until Knesset elections. Soon, however, the religious issue once again came to the fore as Ben Gurion and the rabbi-ministers fought over the right of women to serve in the armed forces and settlements. A vote of the Knesset resolved the issue in favor of Ben Gurion, who stated that Israel would never be a theocratic state.

The Knesset elections of 30 July 1951 resulted in a slight Mapai loss and almost a tripling of General Zionist strength. Once again Ben Gurion was forced to form a coalition cabinet. His negotiations continued throughout the summer and early fall amidst food rationing, strikes, and immigrant demonstrations. Finally a new cabinet formed on 7 October 1951 brought together the Mapai (9), the Religious Bloc (3), and Agudat Israel (1); the General Zionists stayed in the opposition. Despite its inability to gain additional seats in the Knesset, the Mapai had ended up controlling two more cabinet positions than previously. The new cabinet brought in a host of new personalities—Dinur, Pinkas, Burg, Naphtali, and Eshkol. The most far-reaching change was the entrance into the cabinet of Eshkol, in place of Lavon as agriculture minister. Notable departures included Remez, who had died; Pinhas Rosen (Progressive), who declined to join the cabinet without the General Zionists; and Maimon, who had retired. Finally Ben Gurion named Hayim Cohn, the attorney-general and a non-partisan rabbi-lawyer as minister of justice. Occupationally the most striking feature of the new cabinet was the presence of seven rabbis—over half of the cabinet.

Early in 1952 another persistent issue began to plague the Israeli cabinet—the issue of German reparations and the more general problem of Israeli-German relations. In the midst of massive demonstrations against Ben Gurion's new policy of negotiations with the Germans, Herut leader M'nahem Begin threatened civil disobedience. Also during April, there were large-scale protests against Ben Gurion's economic policies. In August the government accepted Germany's reparation offer of $822 million—a much needed boost to the country's faltering economy. In September, Rabbi Levin of the Agudat Israel resigned in opposition to compulsory military service for women and was replaced by Rabbi Mord'khai Nurock. In view of these strains the cabinet could not long survive. Responding to president Ben Zvi's invitation, Ben Gurion formed a new cabinet of fourteen including the General Zionists (22 December 1952).

For the first time since the Provisional Government, the General Zionists (Bernstein, Rokah, Serlin, and Saphir) who clearly represented upper-middle-class interests took their place in Israel's ruling councils. The Sabra contingent of the cabinet also increased with the addition of Rokah and Saphir (in addition to Shitrit).The Religious Bloc received only two seats and the Progressive Party one with the return of Rosen to the cabinet as minister of justice. Additional personnel changes included Lavon's return as minister without portfolio to fill the cabinet seat of Kaplan, who had died.

The first major issue confronting the new government was the deterioration of Israeli-Soviet relations. Soon ideological problems began to rock the regime as the General Zionist ministers resigned to protest leftist activity in the schools. The cabinet crisis ended when Ben Gurion promised to curtail such activity. After weathering another crisis regarding national service for girls and sabotage plots by Herut, Ben Gurion unexpectedly went into a brief retirement at the kibbutz S'de Boker in the Negev. The Mapai Central Committee met to confirm Moshe Sharett as the party's candidate for prime minister.

The Sharett Interregnum, 1954–55

The unprecedented absence of Ben Gurion from the ruling coalition did not cause a serious break in continuity. Sharett's new government of January 1954 contained sixteen ministers who belonged to the same coalition of parties as did the previous cabinet. One of the few changes gave Lavon the Defense Ministry, which formerly had been Ben Gurion's bailiwick. Lavon's functions as minister of agriculture went to a new minister, Zalman Aranne.

The first thirteen months of Sharett's government were unusually peaceful, partly reflecting the temperament of the new prime minister. Then in February 1955 Lavon suddenly resigned and Ben Gurion returned from retirement to take back the Defense Ministry. What at first appeared to be a cabinet reshuffle subsequently became the "Lavon Affair." However, the immediate issue which brought about the cabinet's resignation was the "Kastner Affair," concerning a friend of Prime Minister Sharett who was accused of aiding the Nazis. When the General Zionists abstained in a vote of no confidence on the Kastner case, creating a breach of collective cabinet responsibility, Prime Minister Sharett forced the resignation of his cabinet. He organized a new cabinet on 29 June 1955 without General Zionist representation. This was a small caretaker cabinet of twelve ministers consisting of Mapai (9), Religious Bloc (2), and Progressive (1).

The elections for the Third Knesset which took place on 26 July reduced Mapai parliamentary strength by five seats to forty. On 15 August Sharett resigned as prime minister and Ben Gurion returned to form a government. His return constituted a turning point both in Israeli politics and in the Arab-Israeli conflict, for it signaled a new, militant phase in Israeli policy. After two months of negotiations, Ben Gurion announced his five-party coalition cabinet of sixteen members on 2 November 1955. It embraced a broad coalition of parties including Mapai (9), Mapam (2), Ahdut Avoda (2), Religious Bloc (2), and Progressives (1). While Mapai's loss of five Knesset seats had forced it into a broad coalition, Ben Gurion still held on to the nine cabinet seats by enlarging its size to incorporate the non-Mapai members of his coalition.

The Second Ben Gurion Era, 1955–63

New personalities in the November 1955 cabinet included Bentov and Barzilai of Mapam, Carmel and Bar-Yehuda of Ahdut Avoda, and Kadish Luz and Pinhas Sapir of Mapai. But the significant dimension in the November 1955 cabinet was its Haganah affiliation. In past cabinets only three ministers had played top Haganah roles—Ben Gurion, Sharett, and Eshkol—none of whom had been a fighting commander. In the new cabinet, however, at least eight of the seventeen ministers had been in the Haganah command and several had been actual field commanders. In view of this cabinet's policies, one might advance a hypothesis correlating Haganah affiliation with militancy on Arab issues.

On the home front the country's economic problems persisted. Even more serious was the fractionalized state of political life as the last Knesset election reflected. On the foreign front the conflict with the Arabs had assumed ominous dimensions. After a period of secret contacts with Nasir, spurred by Sharett's less militant Arab policy, the Israeli-Arab confrontation had intensified because of a number of fateful events.

An account of Arab-Israeli relations during the fifties falls outside the scope of this study; moreover, much of Egypt's and Israel's decision-making still remains shrouded in secrecy. Under the circumstances we can only present an analysis of the known facts and advance some hypotheses.

Central to any inquiry is the Lavon Affair—an abortive attempt by Israeli military intelligence to bomb the American and British embassies and offices in Egypt. Egyptian security apprehended the Israeli agents in July 1954, significantly a date coinciding with Anglo-Egyptian agreement on the British·withdrawal from the Suez, the Nasir-Nagib power struggle, and the secret contacts to arrange a meeting between Nasir and Sharett. While the precise aims of this Israeli conspiracy are unknown, the destruction of Anglo-American establishments by what would appear to be Egyptian saboteurs could have wrecked the Canal negotiations, the Nasir-Sharett contacts and/or the newly developing American-Egyptian relationship.[22] Whatever Israel's intentions, a number of the foregoing explanations appear plausible if one considers Israel's problems during this period. Military and economic security had eluded her; under the circumstances it seemed that solutions could only come from the Western countries, especially the United States. Hence it was imperative in the Israeli view to prevent an Anglo-American rapprochement with Egypt.

The events of 1955 were even more central than the Lavon Affair for analyzing elite behavior. When Turkey and Iraq announced their acceptance of the Baghdad Pact (February 1955), Nasir attacked it and received mass Arab praise for his defiance of the West. In mid-February, Ben Gurion returned from the Negev to take over the Defense Ministry from Lavon. Two weeks later, in response to fida'iyun infiltration, came the famous Gaza raid, which Sharett seems to have opposed.[23] Nasir and a number of writers [24] have contended that the large-scale raid revealed Egyptian weakness and forced the Egyptian president to buy arms from the Soviet Union, since inaction would have turned the Egyptian army against him. Indeed, if the aim of the Gaza raid was to cut Nasir down to size, it had the opposite effect. The Nasir of 1954 ("my brother Sharett") was not the Nasir of 1956—the leader of pan-Arabism. A great deal had transpired during the sixteen months after the Gaza raid.

In April 1955 Nasir attended the Conference of Non-Aligned States in Bandung, Indonesia, where he was treated as representative of the Arabs. By projecting him onto the world stage, Bandung made Nasir a pan-Arab leader of the first magnitude, a position Nasir reinforced by breaking the West's arms embargo with the Czech arms deal (September 1955). When Nasir suddenly nationalized the Suez Canal Company (26 July 1956) in response to the US-British withdrawal of financing for the Aswan Dam, the Egyptian leader acquired the halo of a charismatic in Arab eyes.

Israeli decision-making leading to the Suez War of 1956 went through a number of phases. The militancy which marked Ben Gurion's return to the Defense Ministry did not end with the Gaza raid; it appeared once again between September and November, when the Israeli army remilitarized the Al-Awja area on the Egyptian-Israeli border. A less militant phase ensued once Ben Gurion took over as prime minister and was maintained until 18 June when Sharett resigned as foreign minister as a result of policy disagreements with Ben Gurion. Golda Meir took over as foreign minister and her position as labor minister was given to Mord'khai

Namir, the secretary-general of Histadrut. On 19 June Ben Gurion justified Sharett's resignation by pointing to the need for greater coordination between the Ministries of Defense and Foreign Affairs. At the same time he warned against a preventive war but stated that there would be no Israeli evacuation from the demilitarized Egyptian border until Egypt changed what Ben Gurion considered to be an aggressive policy.

After Nasir nationalized the Canal Company, French diplomacy effected a rapprochement between Britain and Israel, thereby initiating the phase of "collusion," in which the three allies jointly planned an attack on Egypt to destroy Nasir. The collusion charge was repeatedly denied by all concerned until evidence from memoirs and documents confirmed it during the mid-sixties. It was in the midst of these developments that on 26 August Ben Gurion demanded free Israeli passage through the Suez Canal and the Straits of Tiran. On 17 October Ben Gurion called Nasir Israel's "first enemy," but a week later Israel pledged not to start a war. In spite of President Eisenhower's warning against war, Israel proceeded to attack Egypt alone, although with assistance from the French air force.

Despite a swift victory in the Sinai, the force of world public opinion at the UN and Eisenhower's wrath forced Ben Gurion to consider withdrawal from the occupied territories. Opposition came from Herut's M'nahem Begin as Ben Gurion defended the policy of withdrawal from Gaza and Aqaba in view of the UN guarantees. In sum, Israel's gains from victory included the neutralization of Egyptian power in the Sinai and the capture of much Soviet equipment, the opening of the Gulf of Aqaba to Israeli shipping, the demilitarization of the Gaza Strip and the placement of UNEF troops on the Egyptian side [25] of the border to prevent possible violations or commando raids. France remained Israel's main ally, while US-Israeli relations were strained since Eisenhower felt Ben Gurion had misled him.

Despite various disruptive incidents during 1957, it was an intra-cabinet conflict concerning West Germany which caused the government's resignation. On 17 December Ben Gurion cancelled what was planned as a secret military mission to Bonn because of leaks in the press. Two days later the Ahdut Avoda ministers Bar-Yehuda and Carmel were asked to resign for sabotaging Ben

Gurion's trip through the leaks, an obvious breech of collective responsibility. Faced with the ministers' refusal, Ben Gurion resigned to form a new government coalition.

His conditions for forming a new cabinet were that the coalition parties would agree to stay together until the end of the Knesset session, would accept collective responsibility, and would maintain secrecy in foreign affairs. On these bases he proceeded to form a five-party coalition cabinet on 7 January 1958, which contained the same ministers as before including Bar-Yehuda and Carmel.

The most important problem which faced the cabinet was the definition of a Jew. So disruptive was the "who is a Jew" [26] issue that it caused the resignations of the two ministers representing the National Religious Party—Rabbis Burg and Shapira. Much later they were replaced by the nonpartisan, Palestinian, Sephardic rabbi, Ya'acov Toledano. The cabinet's second main concern was the security dilemma resulting from the formation of the United Arab Republic (February 1958), joining Egypt and Syria and producing pro-Nasirite agitation in Lebanon and Jordan as well. Ben Gurion considered the acquisition of new arms as his cabinet's first priority. On 3 September 1958, in an unusual move, he appealed to American Jews to influence the American government on the question of arms for Israel.

By mid-1959 German-Israeli relations once again came to the fore as Ben Gurion threatened to resign because left-wing cabinet members criticized the sale of Israeli arms and ammunition to West Germany. The conflict between the Mapam and Ahdut Avoda ministers and Ben Gurion finally caused him to resign, bringing down the government. But because of his inability to form a new government, the old cabinet continued as caretaker until the elections and in this capacity had to deal with the violent riots of Oriental Jews.

Elections for the Fourth Knesset (4 November 1959) gave Mapai a substantial victory. Smaller gains were made by the Herut, the Progressives, and the Religious Bloc, while the leftist parties suffered losses as did the General Zionists. Once again on 15 December 1959 Ben Gurion put together a five-party government. Despite its parliamentary gains, the Mapai's ministerial representation remained the same as before—nine ministers or 56 percent. The National Religious Front and Mapam continued to have two posts each; reflecting its electoral losses, Ahdut Avoda received only one seat instead of two as in the previous cabinet. In addition there was one Progressive and one nonpartisan minister.

A number of new personalities appeared in the new coalition. The new Mapai ministers included Eban, Dayan, and Josephthal. Also significant were the returns of Rabbis Shapira and Burg, and that of Pinhas Rosen, the sole Progressive and Israel's first justice minister. The single Ahdut Avoda representative was Itzhak Ben-Aharon; Ben Gurion's persistent critics, Bar-Yehuda and Carmel, had been purged. Also there was Rabbi Toledano in a nonaligned capacity. Another rabbi, Binyamin Mintz (Agudat Israel), entered the cabinet in July of 1960 as minister of posts.

During the autumn of 1960, intra-elite relations were once again disrupted by Ben Gurion's reopening of the Lavon Affair. On 2 October Ben Gurion denied the existence of an inquiry on Lavon; two days later Lavon publicly attacked Ben Gurion amidst reports of a power struggle within the Mapai Party. In December a cabinet committee reported that a senior officer had forged a document implicating Lavon for the failure of the 1954 operation in Egypt. Also the Knesset met secretly to examine the circumstances of the resignation of General Laskov, the chief of staff. On 28 December Ben Gurion took a five-week leave of absence to reflect upon the Lavon discussion.

The end of the year did not bring the Lavon Affair to an end as Agriculture Minister Dayan claimed to possess evidence contradicting Lavon's testimony. On 10 January 1961 it was announced that ''a senior officer'' was discharged from the army because of responsibility for the Lavon episode. Refusing to join the majority of his cabinet in exonerating Lavon, Ben Gurion resigned in January 1961 inducing the fall of his government. Despite his renomination by Mapai, he failed to form a cabinet, and in late March the Knesset voted to dissolve itself as a result of the Lavon Affair.

The intra-elite fights within the Mapai had their impact on the Knesset elections of August 1961; the Mapai lost 5 seats, the Liberals won 3 and the Ahudt Avoda won 1 seat. Mapai's immobilism was again manifested when Ben Gurion could not form a government. Mapai then requested President Ben Zvi to ask Eshkol to form a government on behalf of Ben Gurion. The new cabinet (2

November 1961) was a narrow three-party coalition of the Mapai (11), the National Religious Party (3), and the Ahdut Avoda (2). Left out were Mapam, Progressives, and General Zionists. The two new Mapai ministers were Almogi, an ex-Haganah commander, and Sasson, a Syrian-born diplomat and Israel's first Oriental minister. Other new ministers were Zerah Warhaftig (Religious Bloc) and Gen. Y'gal Allon (Ahdut Avoda), the ex-Palmah commander.

The course of the new cabinet was marked by strikes, spy cases, religious disputes, and Eichmann's hanging. The government's weapons-procurement policy registered an impressive success in September 1962, when the United States agreed to sell Israel Hawk missiles. Meanwhile the arrest of Lieutenant-Colonel Beer, allegedly a communist agent, had shaken Israel's establishment, for Beer had been Ben Gurion's military advisor. Perhaps not by coincidence, another unnamed chief of Israeli security services resigned in March 1963.

Ben Gurion kept a generally low profile during the first half of 1963 with the exception of supporting continued military rule in the Arab areas of Israel. On 6 May he issued one of his periodic warnings of a planned Arab attack. Then, on 16 June Ben Gurion suddenly resigned as prime minister for ''personal reasons'' and as in 1954 he once again went into the desert to kibbutz S'de Boker.

The Eshkol Cabinets, 1963–69

The newly-elected third president of Israel, Zalman Shazar, asked Finance Minister Levi Eshkol to form the next government. Eshkol's selection had been a foregone conclusion, especially since his organizational abilities had met the severe test of forming the November 1961 cabinet on behalf of Ben Gurion. Moreover Eshkol had been an effective finance minister; he also enjoyed a reputation within the Mapai as a reconciler and peacemaker.

On 26 June 1963 Eshkol became the third person to act as prime minister of Israel. His cabinet, based on a narrow coalition of three parties, was called ''a government of continuity''—a term apparently designed to pacify the old master, Ben Gurion, and thereby prevent a second return to the helm. The fifteen seats of the cabinet were apportioned among the Mapai (10), the National Religious Party (3) and Ahdut Avoda (2). The personnel were virtually unchanged from Ben Gurion's last cabinet, except for the late addition of Akiva Govrin as Minister without portfolio. Meanwhile Ben Gurion announced that his retirement would be permanent, *except* in the case of a national crisis.

Eshkol's immediate problem was the widespread rioting of Orthodox students. In February 1964 the leadership was once again torn apart by none other than the Lavon Affair. Significantly, it was General Dayan, a Ben Gurion protege, who reopened the pandora's box by offering new testimony on the nature of the operation. Despite motions of no confidence by three opposition parties, the government carried the day. Considering the matter closed, Eshkol invited Lavon to rejoin the Mapai and the issue remained quiescent until 4 November, when yet another phase of the Lavon Affair was initiated by Dayan's resignation as minister of agriculture. Three days later Lavon and some of his supporters left the party and formed a new political organization, Min Hayesod. During December 1964 Ben Gurion requested the reopening of the Lavon Affair, which prompted Eshkol to threaten resignation if Ben Gurion's demand was not rejected. Eshkol soon resigned only to be asked by Mapai's Central Committee to form a new cabinet. On 22 December nearly the same government was brought into office as the cabinet officially closed the Lavon Affair despite Ben Gurion's vows to take the matter to the Mapai National Convention.

Whatever Ben Gurion's reasons for pursuing the Lavon episode, it was clear that he wanted to return to active politics. Despite his declared love of kibbutz life, he could not stay away from power for long. To this end in 1964 and 1965 he had started undermining Eshkol's hold on the Mapai and the cabinet, as he had done to Sharett ten years before. Ultimately, his attempt proved abortive, for Eshkol's hold on the Mapai and the cabinet was much firmer than Sharett's. Also, the Ben Gurion of 1965 was an old, bitter man who had alienated a large contingent of his party by his arbitrary and capricious behavior. Nevertheless in May he expressed his readiness to return if this was desired by the nation and by Mapai. Two days later, two of Ben Gurion's proteges left the government—Almogi and Shimon Peres. These resignations were followed by Ben Gurion's call to his followers to defect from Mapai and join him in establishing the Rafi (R'shimat Po'ale Yisrael).

The Sixth Knesset elections (September 1965) gave the joint Mapai-Ahdut Avoda alignment list (Ma'arakh) 45 seats, while Ben Gurion's Rafi won only 10 seats. In January 1966 Eshkol formed a four-party, eighteen-member coalition, comprised of Ma'arakh (12), National Religious Party (3), Mapam (2), and the Independent Liberal Party (1). It was Israel's largest cabinet to date; it was also unique in that six ministers were not Knesset members—the highest in any cabinet. The new ministers were Hayim Gvati, Ya'acov Shimshon Shapiro, Yisrael Galili—all a part of Ma'arakh—and Moshe Kol, an Independent Liberal. Galili's entrance into the cabinet was the delayed emergence of an old Third Aliya settler, who had been excluded from top positions because as acting commander of Haganah he had come into conflict with Ben Gurion. It was also significant that Mapam had returned to the Eshkol coalition after five years outside the government in opposition to Ben Gurion's policies.

The first year of Eshkol's government was generally quiet. Noteworthy, however, were the expansion of relations with the United States, which in scope and quality were unprecedented. While causal explanations fall outside this inquiry, it is clear that the new phase began after Lyndon Johnson acceded to the presidency and simultaneous with a progressive deterioration of US-Egyptian relations.

In November 1966 the cabinet succeeded in abolishing military government in the Arab areas—a policy Ben Gurion had repeatedly and vehemently opposed. The major domestic issue, however, was the economy, especially growing unemployment, which had led to demonstrations and rioting during March 1967. Meanwhile the Arab-Israeli conflict once again crept to center stage and eventually it subjected Israel's decision-making apparatus to strains and stresses unprecedented since the 1948 War of Independence.

Despite the ten-year respite on the Israeli-Egyptian front, the Palestinian guerrilla movement had experienced a revival which reached a crescendo in the fall of 1966. On 13 November Israeli forces responded by attacking the Jordanian village of Samu' reportedly a fida'iyun base. This action pressured King Husayn into promising that Jordanian territory would not be used for terrorist bases. Meanwhile Jordan and Saudi Arabia, both pro-US states, began to challenge Nasir's generally aloof attitude and called upon him to take action against Israel. In a sense the prelude to the 1956 War was repeating itself with the Palestinian fida'iyin acting as the primary catalysts of the conflict. It was not until 15 May that the UAR declared a state of alert and requested from the UN a withdrawal of UNEF units from the Egyptian-Israeli border. On 22 May Egypt declared the Straits of Aqaba closed to Israel and began sending large forces into the Sinai as Jordan and Egypt concluded a defensive treaty. This agreement, together with the Syrian-Egyptian treaty of November 1966, gave substance to Israel's fear of Arab encirclement. This paranoic fear, fed by Radio Cairo's propaganda, may have played a powerful role in limiting the options of Eshkol's cabinet. Even after almost a decade, some questions remain concerning the intentions and roles of the two superpowers as well as the combatants themselves.[27] The paucity of information on Egypt's intentions is matched by the obscurity of the Israeli decision-making process that culminated in the surprise attack on 5 June 1967. For a long time to come diplomatic historians are bound to inquire why Israel chose the ultimate of four basic options—a preemptive attack. Another option, diplomacy, was discarded after a brief two-week trial. A third possibility, to test the Egyptian blockade by dispatching an Israeli ship through the Tiran Straits, would have shifted the onus of armed aggression on the UAR, had the latter chosen to enforce the blockade. Finally, Israel could have attempted a limited armed action to open the straits by force.

Eshkol's reaction to Arab provocations seemed level-headed at the outset. After declaring that closing Aqaba constituted an act of aggression, Eshkol reaffirmed the cabinet's decision to continue "political action" to insure free passage through the Straits. However, there were mounting pressures from a panic-stricken population, to say nothing of militant politicians hoping to return former General Dayan, the victor of 1956, to power. While Eshkol's choice for a new defense minister was ex-General Allon, he finally agreed to Dayan's appointment on 1 June 1967. In addition to quieting popular clamor, Dayan's inclusion in the national unity cabinet neutralized intense criticism from the Rafi Party, of which

Dayan was a member. In another unity move, Gahal leader M'nahem Begin was brought in as minister without portfolio; so was his colleague, Yoseph Saphir, a former General Zionist leader. Begin's appointment was significant, since it finally conferred legitimacy on this militant Herut leader who had been in the opposition even before independence as the Irgun commander. Dayan and Begin greatly strengthened the cabinet's militant element, already high due to the inclusion of former Haganah men (nine or 41 percent). It was very much like the November 1955 cabinet (eight or 47 percent), which launched the 1956 Suez War.

Soon after Israel's facile defeat of the Arabs, cleavages began to appear in the cabinet of national unity. Certain leaders credited General Rabin, the chief of staff, with the June victory, rather than Minister of Defense Moshe Dayan, whose main role had been to boost morale. Nevertheless, attempts at interparty unity intensified as both the Ahdut Avoda and the Rafi parties voted to merge with the Mapai late in 1968 to form the Israel Labor Party. Another divisive issue was that Dayan supported and Sapir opposed the economic integration of occupied territories. On other issues such as annexation of a united Jerusalem into Israel and border changes in favor of Israel's security, there was substantial cabinet unity.

Intra-elite rivalry reemerged when Eshkol's sudden death in late February 1969 strengthened the hawkish contingent. On 3 March the Labor Party Leadership Committee voted to nominate Golda Meir as a compromise candidate for prime minister.

The Meir Cabinets, 1969–74

Prime Minister Meir's government of 11 March 1969 was virtually the same as Eshkol's last cabinet. Running on a platform of "continuity," the prime minister successfully prevented the possible defection of Rafi from her coalition. The Knesset elections of October 1969 gave the Labor-Mapam Alignment 56 seats, Gahal 26 seats, the religious parties 8 seats with the remainder distributed among the smaller parties.[28] On 11 December Prime Minister Meir formed a new cabinet of twenty-four ministers based on a five-party coalition. In size this cabinet was Israel's largest, expanded to accommodate four Gahal ministers in addition to Begin and

Saphir. These included Air Force General Ezer Weizmann—ex-President Chaim Weizmann's nephew; Elimelekh Rimalt, a rabbi from Austria; Leon Dultzin, Jewish Agency treasurer; and Hayim Landau, a former Irgun commander. In terms of background, ideology, and stated policy, the Gahal contingent could safely be termed hawkish on the Arab-Israeli conflict. Its presence also diluted the traditional socialist orientation of Israel's cabinets. For these reasons the left-wing Mapam party displayed considerable reluctance before joining the cabinet.

The cabinet's militant orientation in part reflected the continuing war on Israel's borders, especially along the Suez Canal. As long as the shooting continued, the cabinet remained substantially united in its Arab policy. With the coming of the peace initiative by US Secretary Rogers, the cabinet split wide open. When the Knesset voted to accept the US peace plan, the Gahal Party withdrew its six ministers from the cabinet (August 1970).

Despite Gahal's departure, the cabinet found it difficult to agree on a joint position for the Jarring talks. Bitter division existed on the US attitude on Egyptian violations involving new missile emplacements. Despite threats of leaving, Dayan remained in the Cabinet. After President Nixon promised virtually open-ended military and economic aid and the burial of the Rogers' Peace Plan, two of the major issues dividing the cabinet were temporarily laid to rest.

May 1971 witnessed extensive rioting in the Oriental Jews' ghettos—the first such major outbreak in recent years. The main complaint of the Orientals (Black Panthers) was that the government gave new Russian immigrants priority in housing, jobs, and other social benefits for which the Orientals had waited more than a decade. It was no mere coincidence that during the same month (November 1971) Finance Minister Pinhas Saphir declared his intention to cut the defense budget—a policy which placed him on a collision course with Dayan and the remaining hawks in the cabinet. The promotion of ex-Chief of Staff Lieutenant-General Bar-Lev generated misgivings among some party leaders about increased military influence at the top; nor did they approve of the cabinet or other top bureaucratic posts becoming a repository for gifted military officers. But others in Israel's hierarchy saw Bar-Lev as a potential anti-Dayan force who could take over as defense minister should Dayan leave the cabinet.

In the fall of 1972, a year before the Knesset elections, the debate on the disposition of the Arab occupied territories came to the fore when Sapir attacked Dayan's Arab policy as one of "creeping imperialism." In subsequent months Sapir's main opponent on economic policy, Histadrut Secretary Ben-Aharon, also took an anti-Dayan line.[29] A Fourth Aliya socialist, Ben-Aharon was the voice of the elite's conscience when he proposed [30] that Israel withdraw from the occupied territories without waiting for the Arabs to conclude a peace agreement. He felt that Israel should be built on Jewish labor and not on Arab labor from the occupied territories. Furthermore he thought that six years of occupation had eroded Israel's favorable image and moral capacity in the Western world and that Israel should recognize the Arab's religious and national aspirations by giving up the West Bank.

Implicit in Ben-Aharon's thinking was the old Zionist imperative of establishing a Jewish state in Palestine—not a binational state composed of a Jewish middle, upper-middle ruling class and an Arab proletariat. Deep down in Ben-Aharon's psyche was the old Zionist-socialist notion of sanctity of labor—and labor to the Histadrut leader meant the tilling of the land with sweat and blood.[31] But hawkish trends in public opinion and the forthcoming (October 1973) Knesset elections kept most politicians from supporting Ben-Aharon's views.

Meanwhile the in-fighting continued within the Ma'arakh as the nonpolitical event of electing a president was turned into a battle between the Dayan and Meir factions. In a last-minute maneuver the Meir faction put up Dr. Ephraim Katchalski (Katzir) to challenge Deputy Speaker Yitzhak Navon, a pro-Dayan politician. The party's 650-member Central Committee nominated Katchalski by a narrow margin (58), which permitted him to go on and win the Knesset vote (66–41) over the National Religious Party candidate. However, the battle indicated the considerable power of the minority Dayan faction as well as Golda Meir's determination to carry on as party leader and prime minister. Yet the fact that Meir opposed Dayan with the help of the cabinet doves did not mean a change of heart toward the Arabs, for she has been consistently a hard-liner in word and action. Her decision to stay in office postponed the ultimate struggle for succession to the leadership of Ma'arakh and to the premiership until the cataclysmic events of Yom Kippur 1973.

Israel's Presidents and Prime Ministers

While the presidency of Israel is a largely ceremonial office, the president holds the power of appointing a prime minister to form cabinets. Although it is taken for granted that the appointee will always be the leader of the largest party, the president may choose to play a more positive role, especially in the case of deadlocks.[32]

Israel's four presidents—Chaim Weizmann, Yitzhak Ben-Zvi, Zalman Shazar, and Ephraim Katzir—have come from strikingly similar backgrounds. All four were born in Russia's Pale of Settlement, which has particular meaning when one considers that about 70 percent of the cabinet elite, including every one of Israel's four prime ministers, were also born in the Russian Empire. Here is yet another indication of the special role Russian Jewry has had in establishing the Israeli state.

In educational background, Weizmann and Katzir were scientists. Both had distinguished themselves in their individual fields (chemistry and biophysics) and in war research, Weizmann for Britain and Katzir for the Haganah. In contrast, Ben-Zvi and Shazar had humanistic training, Ben-Zvi in law and journalism and Shazar in philosophy and journalism. While the scientists held doctorates, Ben-Zvi was unable to complete law studies in Istanbul because of World War I, and Shazar held a degree from the University of Berlin.

Of the four, President Katzir is closest to being a native Israeli, since he was brought to Palestine at the age of six. In sharp contrast, Weizmann, Ben-Zvi, and Shazar had more diversified and cosmopolitan backgrounds, which they gained in their world-wide travels and activities for the Zionist cause. In this sense these three had been politically active all their lives, while Katzir remained primarily a scientist.

Israel's prime ministers constitute a different breed—they are total politicians. Despite similar backgrounds in the Pale of Settlement, the prime ministers had lower formal educational levels than did the presidents. Only Sharett was a degree holder (BA), and he was the only prime minister brought to Palestine as a child. The longest tenured president was Ben-Zvi (1952–1963), and the longest tenured prime minister was Ben Gurion, who stayed in office over thirteen years. Finally, no prime minister has yet become president or vice versa, but President Shazar was a minister in Ben Gurion's cabinet of March 1949 before assuming the presidency.

Elite Profiles
Geographical Origins

Because of the unique history of the Jewish people and the discontinuous patterns of immigration to Palestine, a leader's country of origin assumes special significance. In Israeli politics, *Galut* background has played an important role especially at leadership levels.

Analysis of the elite's country background profiles reveals a number of important characteristics. The two most obvious findings which emerge from the *Galut* background map in table 41 are the overwhelming number of ministers who were born within the Russian imperial realm and the accompanying scarcity of Middle Eastern-Oriental-Sephardic types. Of course, these aggregations of

TABLE 41. *Israel: Countries of Origin*

COUNTRY	REGION	MINISTERS
Palestine		Allon
		Dayan
		Rokah
		Saphir
		Shitrit
		Toledano
		Weizmann
Germany		Bar-Lev
		Bernstein
		Burg
		Cohn
		Josephthal
		Naphtali
		Rosen
		Almogi
		Barzilai
		Ben Gurion
		Bentov
		Gruenbaum
		Hazani
Poland		Landau
		Levin

TABLE 41. *Israel: Countries of Origin (Continued)*

COUNTRY	REGION	MINISTERS
		Lavon
		Mintz
		Peres
		Sapir
		Serlin
		Zadok
	Russia	Aranne
		Shazar
		Carmel
		Dultzin
		Gvati
		Kaplan
		Kol
Tzarist Empire	Byelorussia	Luz
		Begin
		Remez
		Shapira
		Warhaftig
		Zisling
		Ben-Aharon
		Maimon
	Bukovina-Bessarabia	Rimalt
		Sharef
		Bar-Yehuda
		Dinur
		Eshkol
		Galili
	Ukraine	Govrin
		Meir
		Namir
		Peled
		Sharett
		Shapiro
	Lithuania	Geri
	Latvia	Nurock
Hungary		Pinkas
Bulgaria		Shemtov
South Africa		Eban
Canada		Joseph
Iraq		Hillel
Syria		Sasson
Yemen		Yeshayahu

power around geographical origins arise from a set of peculiar historical circumstances.

The contingent of ministers born within the Tzarist Empire numbered 43—over 67 percent of the total ministerial elite. This impressive presence was due to the fact that the olim of the Second, Third, and Fourth Aliyot were overwhelmingly Russian-born. They settled the land first and they still rule it despite the sharp and politically significant demographic changes which have occurred during the last quarter of a century.

The 43 Russian-born leaders came from the western provinces of the Tzarist Empire, most from within or close to the Pale of Settlement—the epicenter of Jewish pogroms and persecution. Despite numerous border and name changes which have occurred since the turn of the century, it is possible to pinpoint a number of specific areas where many Israeli leaders were born. Clearly Poland and the contiguous area of Byelorussia contributed the largest number of leaders. Among the 14 Polish-born were Ben Gurion, Bentov, Sapir, Gruenbaum, and Peres, to mention only a few. Byelorussia was close behind—it was the birth place of 11 leaders. Next highest was the Ukraine where 10 of the elite originated, among whom were four of Israel's foremost leaders—Sharett, Eshkol, Meir, and Galili. The fourth area of concentration was the Bukovina-Bessarabia region which had been annexed by Russia; it claimed 4 leaders. Another 5 were born in parts of the Russian Empire contiguous to the regions constituting the Pale of Settlement. Finally 2 others had come from Bulgaria and Hungary—both border regions of the Russian realm. Altogether, the Tzarist Russian contingent numbered 45—about 70 percent of the total cabinet elite.

The predominance of the Russian-born and their sons in the top elite accorded Israel the initial advantage of substantially homogeneous leadership. Despite differences in age and ideology, these individuals belonged to the same cultural and class base and had experienced similar socializational stimuli within the milieu of Tzarist Russia. Homogeneity gave the elite a common *Weltanschauung* and substantial inner cohesion, especially during Israel's early years.

The Fourth Aliya brought an increasing number of German-born Jews to Palestine; however only seven became ministers. Two reasons for this low presence were that the Germans arrived late, both to Zionism and to Palestine; only Hayim Cohn and Pinhas Rosen had arrived prior to 1932. The German environment had been far less threatening than the Tzarist milieu both politically and economically. Moreover, German Jewry had been far more assimilated and were probably more affluent and better educated than Russian Jewry. Therefore, until the advent of Nazism, the call of Zionism fell upon mostly deaf ears.[33]

Equally meager was the Sabra representation in the total cabinet elite. Only 7 of the 64 ministers (11 percent) were natives of the land. The Sabra's low presence, relative to their total numbers, seems to indicate that the older leaders were reluctant to turn over power to the native born. The 7 Sabra ministers do not constitute a homogeneous group. Three were celebrated generals—Y'gal Allon, Moshe Dayan, and Ezer Weizmann; 2 were Sephardic rabbis born in Tiberias—B'khor Shalom Shitrit and Ya'acov Toledano; the last 2 were businessmen-entrepreneurs—Yisrael Rokah and Yosef Saphir (see table 41).

The geographical areas least represented in terms of ministerial origins were the Middle East, Africa, and the Americas. The sole minister from the Western Hemisphere was Dov Joseph, a Canadian. Abba Eban was born in South Africa. As to the Middle East, a total of 3 ministers had been born in the Arab countries. These were Yisrael Yeshayahu of Yemen, Eliahu Sasson of Syria, and Shlomo Hillel of Iraq. Sasson was a Damascean journalist educated at St. Joseph University in Beirut—that renowned Jesuit institution which had exercised such an important impact on the Lebanese political elite. He came to Israel in 1927 and worked as a journalist; eventually he became an expert on the Arabs for the Jewish Agency and Israel's diplomatic service. Yeshayahu's life had been even more colorful; he had served as Imam Yahya's tailor in the hermetically isolated medieval kingdom of Yemen. After he came to Israel, Yeshayahu had organized Operation Magic Carpet to fly the Yemenite Jewish community to Israel. Hillel was brought to Palestine in 1930 as a child of seven. After being active in illegal immigration, he helped found Kibbutz Ma'agan Mikhail. Like Sasson, Hillel has served as an expert on Arab and Middle Eastern affairs both in Israel and in overseas posts. All these Middle Eastern-born (Oriental) ministers were Mapai members which made it possible for the party to attract Oriental voters. Moreover, one of the three has usually filled the Oriental seat in the cabinet.

The glaring paucity of Oriental ministers points to the most fundamental bifurcation in Israeli society—the social-psychological-economic gap between European and Oriental Jewry. Middle Eastern Jews came to Israel relatively late, mostly after 1948. While the European Jews came because of persecution and in response to Zionist ideology, the Middle Eastern Jews came because the Arab-Israeli conflict had unsettled life in the Arab countries. Their late arrival no less than their traditional orientation and lack of skills slowed their advancement in Israeli society. While government efforts and the Tzahal have accelerated social integration between the Western and Oriental Jews, progress in the economic and political spheres has been slow in coming.[34] Also the Oriental's negative view of political life, formed in their countries of origin ("politics is dirty"), has worked against their advancement in government.

Equally serious is the lack of Oriental representation in the governmental structure. The presence at the top of 3 ministers (4.7 percent) is regarded by Oriental Jewish leaders as mere tokenism. In the Knesset there are only 14, or 11.6 percent,[35] out of a total of 120;[36] none of Israel's 29 top generals came from Oriental backgrounds,[37] although the Oriental number is reported large in the lower ranks. This inadequate representation in elite positions becomes particularly ominous for the future when one considers that Oriental Jews constitute over half of Israel's population; and due to their high birth rate relative to the Ashkenazim, it is projected that by 1985, 72 percent of the population will be of Oriental origin.[38]

The Oriental-vs.-European unbalance is somewhat improved if the two Sephardic Sabra ministers are placed in the oriental column. The transfer of Rabbis Toledano and Shitrit raises the number of Middle Eastern-born ministers to 5, or almost 8 percent of the total elite. The problem with this approach is that it would steal 2 members from another politically underrepresented section of the Israeli population—the Sabra. As indicated in table 41, only 7, or 11 percent, of the cabinet elite was born in old Palestine. Besides the two Sephardic rabbis from Tiberias—Toledano and Shitrit—the Sabras included three generals and two civilians—all of Ashkenazi origin (Allon, Dayan, Rokah, Saphir, and Weizmann).

Age and Tenure

In recent years age has become an important variable in Israeli political life. This is primarily a result of the progressive aging in office of a generally old elite, while the average age of Israel's population has remained relatively young. As seen in table 42, independent Israel's very first cabinet was not young, as is the case with many new nations; rather it was relatively old—over 56 years. In subsequent cabinets average age fluctuated between a low of 55 years and an all-time high of 61 years for the March 1969 cabinet. The trend toward an increasing average age was reversed in the December 1969 cabinet when it dropped to 57 years.

TABLE 42. *Israel: Average Age—Over Time*

CABINET DATE		AVERAGE AGE
14 May	1948	56.5
3 March	1949	56.8
1 November	1950	55.9
7 October	1951	56.2
24 December	1952	56.1
25 January	1954	57.9
29 June	1955	60.3
2 November	1955	56.7
7 January	1958	60.4
16 December	1959	57.5
2 November	1961	56.9
16 June	1963	58.8
22 December	1964	59.1
10 January	1966	58.6
1 June	1967	59.6
11 March	1969	61.5
15 December	1969	57.5

Having settled in Palestine as young men, many Israeli leaders were already in their fifties at the time of independence. More precisely, over one-third of Israel's 64 ministers were born before 1900, including such well-known individuals as Ben Gurion, Eshkol, Meir, and Sharett. The conclusion that Israel's political culture tends towards rule by elders is reinforced by the findings on table 43. Taking key ministries (e.g. premier, deputy premier, defense, foreign affairs, finance, interior, and justice) it becomes apparent that in 12 of 17 cabinets the average age exceeded 60— perhaps reflecting, at least partly, a cultural tradition concerning the close relationship of authority, wisdom, and old age.

TABLE 43. *Israel: Average Age—Key Ministers*

CABINET DATE		AVERAGE AGE
14 May	1948	60.6
3 March	1949	57.0
1 November	1950	58.0
7 October	1951	53.8
24 December	1952	60.4
25 January	1954	58.8
29 June	1955	62.2
2 November	1955	63.6
7 January	1958	65.8
16 December	1959	65.4
2 November	1961	65.0
16 June	1963	60.5
22 December	1964	61.2
10 January	1966	60.6
1 June	1967	58.6
11 March	1969	60.0
15 December	1969	60.5

A great age differential exists between the cabinet elite, where sexagenarians predominate, and the population, 70 percent of which is younger than even the youngest cabinet minister.[39] This generational gap makes the leadership unrepresentative of the population and if maintained, it may have serious consequences for the political system.

Involvement in political life, defined broadly, came early to most members of the Israeli leadership, both in Mandatory Palestine and the Zionist context of the diaspora. But for those few who reached the cabinet, the ascent to the top came after a long and laborious wait; the average age of ministers at entering the cabinet was over 54 years. Once there the elite have accrued an average tenure of over 6 years. The average age at leaving the cabinet was about 63 years—again pointing to extended terms and late retirements. However, not all ministers had long tenures in office; there were 14 who served less than 24 months. One can also identify a contingent of 18 ministers whose tenures exceeded 100 months as table 44 shows. Not surprisingly the longest tenure has been Prime Minister Meir's—247 months or over 20 years. Close behind Meir were two rabbis—Shapira (242 months) and Burg (238 months) who have returned to the cabinet repeatedly as the leaders of the religious parties. Next in tenure was B'khor Shalom Shitrit, a Sabra (215 months) who for many years was the cabinet's sole Sephardi. Other long-tenured members include Sapir (208 months), Eshkol (201 months), and, of course, Ben Gurion (163 months). Several well-known ministers—Allon, Dayan, Eban—registered lower tenures; but some of these younger men may continue to remain in office and thus increase their lengths of tenure.

TABLE 44. *Israel: Long Tenure Ministers* *

NAME	TENURE IN MONTHS
Meir	247
Shapira	242
Burg	238
Shitrit	215
Sapir	208
Eshkol	201
Ben Gurion	163
Barzilai	151
Eban	151
Aranne	149
Rosen	143
Allon	139
Warhaftig	139
Dayan	131
Bentov	127
Joseph	111
Almogi	104
Carmel	103

* cut-off date, October 1973

Education: Level

It is fair to state that the educational level of the Israeli elite is low relative to the leaders of neighboring countries. Table 45 shows that more than 40 percent, or 26, of the ministers lacked or did not complete a college-level education. Another 5 percent of the elite probably lacked college degrees, although this could not be determined with certainty due to conflicting data. There is a high concentration of leaders at the Bachelor's level—38 percent—partly because holders of rabbinical degrees are included at this level. Finally, there were only 4 MA's (6.3 percent) and 8 doctorates (12.5 percent) for a total of 12 graduate degrees. There are a number of reasons which could explain the leaders' generally low educational level. It appears that the itinerancy of the elite worked against the completion of education. A large number of them enrolled successively in several institutions of higher learning and did not graduate—a reflection of the unstable milieu of the Jewish Central-European dispersion. Some of the earlier leaders with lower-middle and lower-class background simply could not afford to attend college. Significantly, the educational level of the upper-class latecomers, especially of the Fifth Aliya, was substantially higher than those of the earlier Aliyot. Once in Palestine opportunities for higher education were lacking; the early immigrants were too poor and there were no institutions of higher learning until the 1930s. Finally, there was the question of time; indeed, haste has characterized the Israeli leaders' style and actions for the last half century. So preoccupied have they been with the basic questions of settlement, survival, and sovereignty, that formal education became sidetracked, often permanently.

TABLE 45. *Israel: Educational Level*

LEVEL	N	%
BA/BS/License	24	37.5
MA/MS	4	6.3
PhD/MD	8	12.5
No Degree	26	40.6
Unknown	3	4.7

Several of the younger men whose education had been cut short by war later returned to school. For instance, after the Suez War of 1956, Allon, Dayan, and Bar-Lev returned to their studies at London, Hebrew, and Columbia universities respectively. But often education was interrupted when the potent smell of power came their way; a pattern common to many Israeli leaders is that of "having attended classes" or "taken courses" without graduating (e.g., Allon, Hillel, Almogi, Barzilai, Ben-Aharon, Carmel, Dultzin, and Peres). In addition to the quest for high positions of power,[40] another possible explanation may be that the elite's political culture did not emphasize academic degrees. A university education was not considered a major criterion for political advancement, as is common in many of the new states of Africa and Asia.

The paucity of academic degrees should not be taken to imply lack of intellectual ability or anti-intellectualism among the elite. In fact Israel's ministers can compete favorably with their equivalents in other countries. If literary production is considered a relevant index of intellectual prowess, then Israel's ministers score impressively. Over 78 percent of the 64 leaders have published a large number of articles and books, often in several languages. Several among them manifested considerable intellectual power, e.g., Bar-Lev, Eban, Naphtali, and Sharett. General Bar-Lev's graduate work at Columbia in the early 1960s is still remembered with admiration by his teachers and fellow students.

It is also possible to analyze education level over time, i.e., cabinet by cabinet, as shown in table 46. Overall, educational level has not changed radically since the founding of the state. At independence the educational index was 1.38, almost the same as

TABLE 46. *Israel: Educational Level—By Cabinet*

CABINET DATE		NO DEGREE N	%	BA N	%	MA N	%	PHD N	%	EDUCATIONAL INDEX	TOTAL
14 May	1948	4	31	8	62	1	8	—	--	1.38	13
3 March	1949	3	25	8	67	—	—	1	8	1.67	12
1 November	1950	3	23	8	62	1	8	1	8	1.78	13
7 October	1951	3	20	8	53	1	7	3	20	2.06	15
24 December	1952	6	38	6	38	2	12	2	13	1.62	16
25 January	1954	6	35	7	41	2	12	2	12	1.65	17
29 June	1955	3	25	6	50	1	8	2	17	1.92	12
2 November	1955	8	47	8	47	—	—	1	6	1.17	17
7 January	1958	8	47	8	47	—	—	1	6	1.17	17
16 December	1959	6	35	8	47	—	—	3	18	1.65	17
2 November	1961	8	47	4	24	—	—	5	29	1.65	17
16 June	1963	7	44	5	31	—	—	4	25	1.63	16
22 December	1964	8	47	5	29	—	—	4	24	1.53	17
10 January	1966	10	48	8	38	—	—	3	14	1.33	21
1 June	1967	12	55	6	27	1	5	3	14	1.23	22
11 March	1969	12	55	6	27	1	5	3	14	1.23	22
15 December	1969	15	55	5	19	2	7	5	19	1.33	27

the most recent cabinet (1.39). Between the March 1949 cabinet and the January 1954 cabinet there was a discernible rise, peaking at 2.06 in October 1951. Generally the educational level has ranged between 1.17 and 2.06, for the most part below the BA level.

Although the overall index has varied minimally over time, there have been changes in the distribution of degrees. While BA's have substantially decreased, doctorates have more than doubled. The most noteworthy development is the considerable increase in the proportion of ministers who hold no degrees. Although the December 1969 cabinet had an educational index close to that of the first cabinet, the level distribution within the cabinet has shifted to the two extremes: a higher proportion of Ph D's (19 percent) and a higher proportion of no degrees (55 percent). This trend could be seen as early as June 1967, where there were 55 percent degreeless ministers and 14 percent doctorates. The increase in doctorates may reflect the rising educational level of a country that already had a high literacy rate at the time of independence. However, the trend toward an increasing proportion of degreeless ministers indicates an elite-mass educational gap and is further evidence of the political tenacity of first- and second-generation leaders.

Education: Specialization

There were a large number of ministers for whom educational specialization was not indicated primarily because their schooling was interrupted too early to permit sufficient field concentration. However, among the degree holders the patterns of specialization are apparent. As indicated in table 47, the fields of religion and law claimed the largest number of ministers with 14 and 13 respectively; 3 of the 14 rabbis were also trained in law and therefore are counted in that category as well. It has been common for many male members of Jewish families to attend religious school to study the Talmud and most of Israel's ministers have been no exception. But the 14 ministers in question graduated from rabbinical colleges and actually served in religious-educational capacities. Economics/Business claimed 4 ministers, among them a general

TABLE 47. *Israel: Educational Specialization*

SPECIALIZATION	N	%
Religious Studies	14	21.9
Law	13	20.3
Military Science	3	4.7
Engineering	3	4.7
Economics/Business	4	6.3
History	2	3.1
Philosophy	1	1.6
Oriental Studies	1	1.6
Agriculture	2	3.1

who also specialized in military science as did 2 others. Three ministers studied engineering and 2 specialized in history and agriculture. Oriental studies and philosophy claimed 1 minister each. Specializations that did not lead to a degree have not been included.

Religion and law were the only specializations traced over time because other fields were not represented in significant numbers. Table 48 indicates that rabbinical studies had an overall decline.

TABLE 48. *Israel: Educational Specialization by Cabinet— Rabbis and Lawyers*

CABINET	RABBIS		LAWYERS		BOTH		TOTAL *
	N	%	N	%	N	%	
May 1948	3	23	3	23	1	8	13
March 1949	3	25	2	17	1	8	12
November 1950	3	23	4	31	1	8	13
October 1951	6	40	1	7	2	13	15
December 1952	3	19	3	19	1	6	16
January 1954	3	18	3	18	1	6	17
June 1955	3	25	2	17	1	8	12
November 1955	2	12	2	12	1	6	17
January 1958	3	18	2	12	1	6	17
December 1959	4	24	3	18	1	6	17
November 1961	2	12	2	12	2	12	17
June 1963	2	13	1	6	2	13	16
December 1964	2	12	2	12	2	12	17
January 1966	2	10	3	15	2	10	20
June 1967	2	9	3	14	1	5	22
March 1969	2	9	3	14	1	5	22
December 1969	4	15	2	7	1	4	27

* Total includes all individuals who have served during the tenure of the cabinet.

The highest concentration occurs in the October 1951 cabinet—over half the members were rabbis. With the exception of the November 1961 cabinet, there has been a declining trend in the rabbinical proportion of the cabinet. In the June 1967 and March 1969 cabinets the rabbinical presence had reached an all-time low of 14 percent. Law also registered an overall decline, after reaching a high of 31 percent in November 1950.

Place of Education

The Israeli elite studied at an unusually large number of schools located in fourteen different countries—a clear index of their cosmopolitan background. Table 49 presents a detailed breakdown by country of all the schools the 64 ministers were known to have attended regardless of length or completion of study. A considerable number of ministers went to more than one school. As one would expect, the Tzarist Empire (Russia and Poland) led in the number of schools attended and the number of degrees awarded. Of particular importance were Warsaw University (5) and Warsaw Rabbinical Seminary (3 degrees). Although not highly developed at the time, Palestinian institutions were attended by 16 individuals, 4 of whom received degrees from Hebrew University and 3 from the rabbinical seminaries of Tiberias and Jerusalem. Germany gave a total of 10 degrees, 4 of which were from Berlin University.

TABLE 49. *Israel: Place of Study*

COUNTRY	REGION	SCHOOL	ATTENDEES
		Estonia University	1
		Kharkov University	1
		Kharkov Agricultural University	1
		Moscow University	1
Tzarist	Russia 9	Odessa University	2
Empire		Petrograd University	1
18		Rabbinical Seminary, Lithuania	1
		Rabbinical Seminary, Slobodka	1
		Lvov University	1
	Poland 8	Rabbinical Seminary, Warsaw	3
		Warsaw University	5
		Warsaw Polytechnic	1

TABLE 49. *Israel: Place of Study (Continued)*

COUNTRY	REGION	SCHOOL	ATTENDEES
Palestine and Israel 16		Haifa Technical	1
		Hebrew University	9
		Hebrew Teachers Seminary	1
		Kedourie Agricultural School	1
		Mekvah Agricultural School	1
		Nahalal Agricultural School	1
		Rabbinical Seminary, Jerusalem	1
		Rabbinical Seminary, Tiberias	2
		School of Economics and Law, Tel Aviv	1
		Technion	1
Germany 10		Berlin University	7
		Dresden University	1
		Frankfurt University	1
		Freiburg University	2
		Hamburg University	1
		Heidelburg University	1
		Leipzig University	1
		Munich University	2
		Hildesheimer Rabbinical Seminary	3
		Rabbinical Seminary, Lubeck	1
Great Britain 6		Cambridge University	1
		London University	1
		London School of Economics	1
		Oxford University	1
		RAF Staff College	1
		Senior Officers School	1
Switzerland 3		Basel University	1
		Berne University	1
		Federal Polytech, Zurich	1
		University of Lausanne	1
Austria 2		Rabbinical Seminary, Vienna	1
		University of Vienna	1
United States 2		Columbia University	1
		Harvard University	1
		New School for Social Research	1
France 2		Institute of Political Science	1
		Sorbonne	1
Turkey 3		Istanbul University	3
Miscellaneous 4	Canada 1	McGill University	1
		Laval University	1
	Lebanon 1	St. Joseph University	1
	Mexico 1	National University of Mexico	1
	South Africa 1	Witwatersrand University	1

Four rabbis graduated from German schools, 3 of them from the well-known Heldesheimer Rabbinical Seminary of Berlin. Britain ranked next largest with 6 individuals attending such various schools as London University, London School of Economics, Cambridge University, and military schools. Countries which had educated one or two students were Austria, France, Switzerland, Turkey, the United States, Canada, Mexico, South Africa, and Lebanon.

Cursus Honorum: Pathways to Power

The determination of occupational background is fairly difficult in the case of Israeli leaders because they led highly mobile lives and held many and various jobs, especially during the early period of their lives. However, correct determination of occupational background is essential for inferring a leader's class base as well as for determining class mobility and career patterns. For Israeli leaders the crucial starting point is original occupation, which often consisted of several simultaneous jobs held for varying lengths of time.

The elite's ten original occupational sources of recruitment are found in table 50. The largest category, 20 or 31.3 percent, is that of worker/farmer, which includes all types of laborers doing un-skilled work. Most of the worker/farmer contingent were the young settlers of the Second and Third Aliyot, including some of Israel's best-known leaders. All of these are now either dead or retired

TABLE 50. *Israel: Original Occupational Source—Aggregate Count*

OCCUPATION	N	%
Worker/Farmer	20	31.3
Rabbinate	14	21.9
Lawyer	8	12.5
Zionist Bureaucracy	6	9.4
Haganah	5	7.8
Business	4	6.3
Engineering	3	4.4
Journalism	3	4.4
Academia	1	1.6

from active politics—Ben Gurion, Remez, Bentov, Eshkol, and Zisling. While many of them worked at various public or private occupations on their way to the cabinet, as young men they engaged in physical labor, for the most part in various settlements and kibbutzim.

As shown in chart 10 (see appendix), while the occupational paths of the 20 differed somewhat, there were important areas of similarity. Such aspects as foreign military service and imprisonment have been analyzed under other headings. Additional similarities include party leadership positions and/or roles in the various Zionist and Yishuv bureaucracies, e.g., labor councils, Zionist organizations, Histadrut, or Jewish Agency. Significantly, 11 of the 18 had held Histadrut positions and 8 had Haganah experience. All 20 had been members of Knesset.

The second largest original occupation was the rabbinate (chart 11, appendix), which accounted for 14 individuals, or over 21 percent of the total leadership. After their training and ordination, the 14 rabbis functioned in some religious-educational capacity prior to engaging in other occupations such as law and politics.

This surprisingly large clerical presence in the cabinet probably springs from the large role that Judaism and its institutions have played in Jewish life in the diaspora. Lacking a Jewish political existence, the religious establishment served as the preserver of Jewish values and culture. This resulted in a unique blending of ethnic culture and religion which has had few parallels in world history, except the Armenians and to a lesser extent the Poles and the Irish. It is against this historical background that the large rabbinical presence in Israel's elite has to be analyzed. The 14 rabbi-ministers represent a tradition of community leadership which found natural reinforcement in Israeli political life where many Jewish religious traditions had come under attack, especially from the socialist secularists of Israel's powerful labor parties. Supported by the Orthodox parties, the rabbis have played the role of "defenders of the faith."

Some of the rabbi-ministers came early to Palestine: Rabbi Maimon came in the Second Aliya and Rabbi Dinur in the Third Aliya. Another five came after 1925—Mintz, Pinkas, Shapira, Cohn, and Hazani. Three rabbi-ministers came at the start of the Second World War—Rimalt, Burg, and Levin—and Warhaftig and Nurock came last in 1947. Throughout Israeli history the rabbi-ministers have exercised considerable influence on cabinet decision-making, much more than other Israeli leaders care to admit. Most of this influence has been possible because of their leadership of religious parties. Chart 11 indicates that of the 14 rabbis, 9 were religious party leaders, 1 was a Gahal-Liberal and 1 was a Mapai member. Another Mapai minister, Shitrit, represented the Sephardim, along with the nonpartisan Rabbi Toledano. Finally, there was Cohn, another nonpartisan, who later entered the High Court.

It is to be noted in chart 11 that three of the rabbis also had law degrees: Shitrit, Cohn, and Warhaftig—but law was not their original occupation. Given the primacy of law in Judaism, such an interest is natural; for Shitrit law was also relevant to his police work before independence and later as Israel's first minister of police. Finally as party leaders, 12 of the 14 rabbi-ministers served in the Knesset; Cohn and Toledano—both nonpartisan—were the exceptions.

The third largest source of recruitment was the legal profession with 8, or 12.5 percent of the elite (see table 50). Six other ministers acquired law degrees in mid-career as a secondary or supplementary field. This relatively large lawyer presence may be partly due to the Judaic concern with law (*Halacha*). Moreover, as Westerners, these men regarded law as a *sine qua non* for political life. This was, in turn, reinforced by the Ottoman-Islamic legalistic tradition of Turkish Palestine as well as by the British legal influence during the mandate. In other words, the legalistic influence was present both in Poland and Palestine—the two countries where most of the law degrees were acquired.

Of the 8 ministers who began as lawyers all served in the Knesset except Geri, a nonpartisan businessman (see chart 12, appendix). Also about half had been active in various Yishuv bureaucracies and 3 had held party posts. The best known members of this group were Pinhas Rosen, Israel's minister of justice for over a decade; Dov Joseph, a justice minister who also served in a number of other cabinet posts; Begin, the former Irgun leader who led the militant wing of the Gahal; and Zadok, a Mapai leader who also served in the Jewish Settlement Police.

The next largest group is composed of 6 ministers whose first occupation had been service in Zionist organizations and bureaucracies in and out of Palestine (see chart 13, appendix). This group included Prime Minister Golda Meir, who made her way to the top through the Histadrut, the Jewish Agency, the diplomatic corps, and, of course, the Mapai Party. Besides their early low-level bureaucratic role, Bar-Yehuda and Sharef functioned as laborers. Later these two ministers joined the Haganah along with Govrin. All had served as members of Knesset and most had held posts in the Histadrut.

The fifth occupational category, the Haganah, accounts for 5, or 7.8 percent, of the ministers. Considering Haganah membership as an occupation may seem unusual until one realizes that Haganah involvement was often more than a full-time job, although Allon and Dayan seem to have farmed intermittently. Moreover, for these 5 ministers Haganah was truly their first job. Allon and Dayan joined at the unusually young age of 13, Weizmann at 15, and Almogi and Bar-Lev before their 18th birthdays. It is noteworthy that 4 ended up in the Tzahal (see chart 14, appendix), although only Bar-Lev, Dayan, and Weizmann remained there for a long period. While Allon, Almogi, and Dayan are seasoned politicians with Knesset experience, Bar-Lev and Weizmann are newcomers to politics and lack legislative experience.

The next recruitment group was business with 4, or 6.3 percent, of the ministers. This relatively small number may reflect the unattractiveness of Palestine for Jewish businessmen, not to mention the early elite's kibbutz-based socialist ethos, which could not readily accommodate enterpreneurial types until recently. Of the 4 businessmen, the careers of Bernstein and Naphtali show great similarity (see chart 15, appendix). Both were born in Germany and advanced through various Zionist bureaucracies on their way to the Knesset and the cabinet. Like Bernstein, Dultzin became prominent in the Jewish Agency and rapidly advanced to the cabinet through the Gahal party, despite having arrived later than any other cabinet member (1956). Saphir, in contrast, was a Palestinian-born businessman and large-scale cultivator. All but Dultzin served in the Knesset and all but Saphir were prominent in various bureaucratic posts.

Engineering was one of the smaller sources of elite recruitment. Only 3 ministers came from engineering—an incredibly low figure when one considers the elite's commitment to technological development. Indeed, there exists a general paucity of ministers with scientific or technological training; however scientific-technical expertise abounds at the sub-ministerial level. This seems to indicate that the party-based cabinet elite has not encouraged the rise of highly trained specialists. Indeed, the 3 engineers in chart 16 (appendix) rose not because of technical expertise but through membership in the main political parties.

As original occupation, journalism also claimed only 3 ministers (chart 17, appendix). Yet 7 others subsequently took up careers in journalism, bringing the total to 10. This constitutes about one-sixth of the cabinet elite—an indication of the Zionist concern with the propagation of the message both in Palestine and in the diaspora. One might even group the 10 journalists and the 7 lawyers (one man being both) as a single facet of the nationalist struggle—that of arguing and presenting the nationalist cause. Zalman Shazar, who had been editor of *Davar*, became president of Israel. The other two journalists were Eliahu Sasson, a Syrian-born publisher of Arabic and Hebrew newspapers in Damascus, and Itzhak Gruenbaum, a member of the Polish Sejm.

The remaining two occupational sources are military service in foreign armies and teaching (see chart 18, appendix). The sole teacher was Abba Eban. Although two ministers started in foreign military service, the total number of ministers who served in foreign armies in mid-career was much greater.

Overall, the single most important gateway to the cabinet is the Knesset—Israel's unicameral legislature. For a number of reasons, only 8, or 12.5 percent, of the cabinet elite have not been MK's. Geri and Toledano were nonpolitical types; Bar-Lev and Weizmann entered the cabinet directly from the Tzahal where they had made their political reputations; however, this does not preclude the possiblity of their seeking Knesset seats in the future. Gruenbaum was defeated in the first Knesset election and retired from politics. As a former attorney-general and High Court justice, Rabbi Cohn remained above the Knesset's partisan politics. Finally, Gvati became a MK after entering the cabinet, and Jewish Agency treasurer, Dultzin, a late immigrant, is relatively new to political life.

Disposition

The last phase of the elite circulation process is disposition: what happens to elites after cabinet office. Table 51 presents an aggregate breakdown of disposition of Israeli ministers after cabinet office. Nineteen of the 64 leaders, or almost 30 percent, were still serving as ministers in 1973. A larger contingent of 24 (37.5 percent) remained in the Knesset. Only 7.8 percent had retired. Other post-cabinet positions included Jewish Agency (2), judiciary (1), business (1), and party (1). Finally, 11, or 17.2 percent, died in office or directly after leaving. As in many parliamentary regimes, the Knesset was the major depository of the cabinet elite.

Table 51. *Israel: Immediate Disposition*

DISPOSITION	N	%
Still Serving in cabinet	19	29.7
Knesset	14	21.9
Knesset and Bureaucrary	2	3.1
Knesset and Party	6	9.4
Knesset and Diplomacy	1	1.6
Knesset and Business	1	1.6
Deceased	11	17.2
Retired	5	7.8
Jewish Agency	2	3.1
Business	1	1.6
Judiciary	1	1.6
Party	1	1.6
Total	64	

In terms of ultimate disposition, as of 1973 (table 52), 20, or 31 percent, had died and an almost equal number (19) were still in the cabinet. The Knesset was a repository for 9 (14.1 percent) ministers and 12 (18.8 percent) had retired from politics. Jewish Agency, party, business, and judiciary claimed one minister each. In sum 69 percent of the surviving elite is still politically active—an index of the leaders' propensity to stay in politics as long as possible.

With disposition, the last phase of the elite circulation process culminates. A diagrammatical model of the leaders' progression to elitehood is presented in figure 8. It includes the major elements of the socialization process since childhood, a process consisting of

TABLE 52. *Israel: Ultimate Disposition*

DISPOSITION	N	%
Deceased	20	31.3
Still Serving in Cabinet	19	29.7
Knesset	4	6.3
Knesset and Party	3	4.7
Knesset and Histadrut	1	1.6
Knesset and Business	1	1.6
Retired	12	18.8
Jewish Agency	1	1.6
Business	1	1.6
Judiciary	1	1.6
Party	1	1.6
Total	64	

three phases: the diaspora, Palestine, and Israel. Figure 8 is a generalized representation of the life history of the standard Israeli cabinet leader and ties together the social, ethnic, and educational background characteristics, covered earlier, with the analysis of cursus honorum.

The Elite at Bay: The October War

The decision-making of the Israeli elite after the Six-Day War can best be characterized as one of procrastination; this is particularly true of the disposition of occupied territory. Several factors can be identified to explain the lethargic pace of a once dynamic elite.

Ben Gurion's departure removed the forceful hand who made coalition politics in Israel a going concern. He acted as the catalyst and energizer of the political system and was the lynchpin that kept the coalition partners together under a degree of cabinet discipline. Lacking their predecessor's leadership attributes, Eshkol and Meir automatically came to rely on consensual politics. Forcefulness was replaced by a slow-moving process which tended to procrastinate until consensus had been achieved. As a result crucial decisions on the occupied Arab lands were postponed and into the decisional vacuum moved Dayan's military bureaucracy, which busily began creating "facts" of Jewish settlement and economic integration.

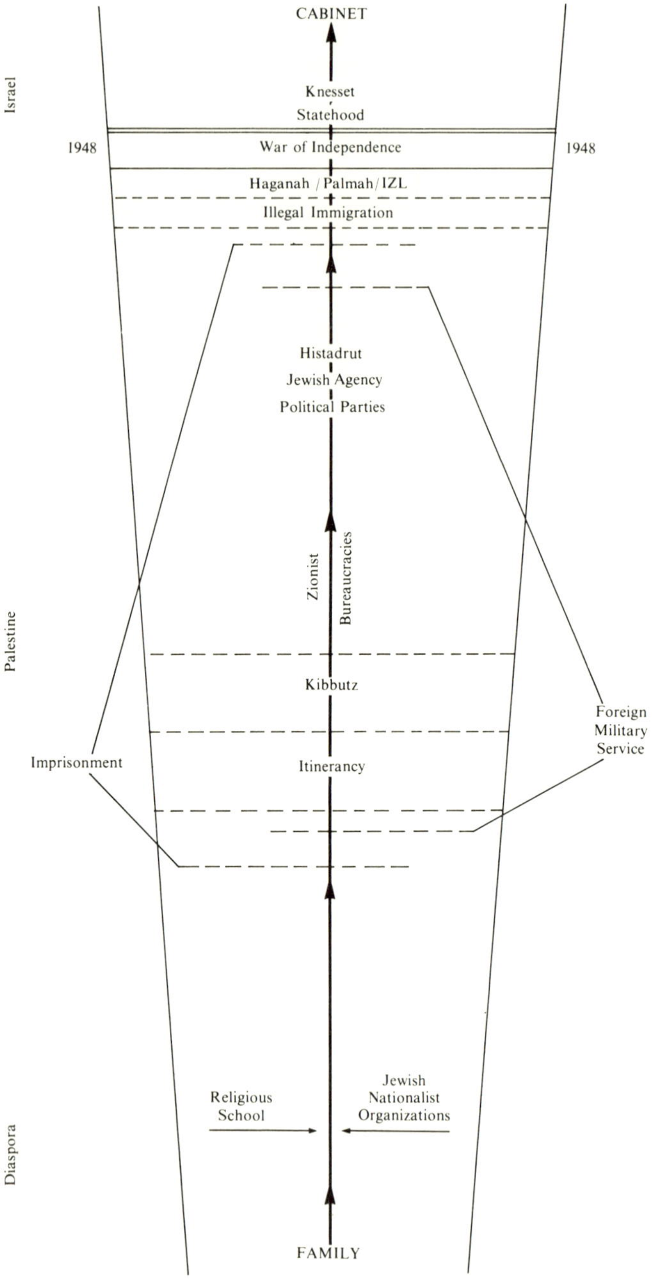

Israel
Palestine
Diaspora
Figure 8 Israel: Progression to Elitehood
CABINET
Knesset
Statehood
1948
War of Independence
1948
Haganah / Palmah / IZL
Illegal Immigration
Histadrut
Jewish Agency
Political Parties
Zionist Bureaucracies
Kibbutz
Imprisonment
Foreign Military Service
Itinerancy
Religious School
Jewish Nationalist Organizations
FAMILY

Perhaps equally significant in explaining the elite's drift and indecisiveness was the ongoing struggle of power for the succession to the premiership. Many ministers were reluctant to support one or the other of the proposals on the Arab territories since behind each scheme stood an aspirant to the premiership (e.g., Allon, Dayan), whose chances would be affected by the cabinet's decisions. As soon as Israel's Arab policy became intermingled with its succession problem, domestic considerations affecting the inter-elite struggle clouded the rational choice among hard options on Arab policy.

There were also more positive reasons for the postponement of the territorial settlement. The occupied Arab lands seemed to provide more security, new sources of manpower and markets, not to mention the valuable oil of the Sinai. Meanwhile the Arabs were not willing to talk peace, at least not in terms of the victor's peace which Israel wished to dictate. Neither could they collectively mount a credible military challenge to the thrice-victorious Tzahal. Finally, the widely anticipated pressure from the two superpowers did not materialize as it had in the aftermath of the 1956 Suez War. Unwilling to compromise her detente with the US, the Soviet Union refused to be involved militarily on the Arab side to eject Israel forcibly. Save for a few half-hearted attempts, there was little US pressure for a territorial settlement until after October 1973. These factors, coupled with the availability of American money and weaponry and an expanding economy, reinforced the cabinet's propensity to sit tight, at least until after the Knesset elections scheduled for October 1973.

Against this background the joint Egyptian-Syrian attack on Yom Kippur not only constituted a rude awakening for Israel, but it destroyed several of the tenets on which her foreign policy had rested since the 1967 War. While the Arabs did not win the October War, they proved Israel's vulnerability in protracted conflicts in terms of manpower, arms, economic production, and war financing. In addition to her heavy reliance on American arms and economic aid, Israel's small society could not provide the human cannon fodder necessary for a long conflict with such populous Arab opponents as Egypt, with a population of 35 milliion. Also the October War substantially altered the widely held belief that the Arab armies could not match Israel in motivation, technology, and organization. Finally, the Arabs were able to unite to induce joint action by the superpowers and, through effective diplomacy, to isolate Israel at the United Nations. In both endeavors the oil weapon played an important part. Yet even before the use of oil, few states were prepared to support continued occupation of Arab land; by 1973 Israel had lost the sympathy that she enjoyed during the 1967 War.

The upshot was the discrediting of the cabinet elite, which had been caught off guard by the Arab's attack. The leadership's inability to win a quick victory and the substantial losses in men and equipment prompted vociferous criticism and a credibility gap regarding the truth of the government's statements and statistics.[41] Dayan and some generals were stripped of their heroism, except for General Arik Sharon who led the Tzahal's breakthrough to the West Bank of the Canal, and others like Generals Eytan, Hoffi, Bren, Peled, Lanner, and Bar-Lev. During the campaign for the delayed Knesset election of 31 December 1973 Sharon joined Begin to lead the militant Likud coalition, which captured 39 seats, a gain of 7. Meanwhile the ruling Ma'arakh strength dropped to 54, a loss of 6 seats. In order to continue in power, Prime Minister Meir had to include the religious parties. However, the price of their participation in the cabinet—the continuation of the rabbinates' traditional prerogatives in Israeli life and annexation of the West Bank—was heavy enough to cause repeated delays in the formation of a new government. Nor was it easy to quiet the mass protests directed against the ruling elite around Golda Meir. The first post-electoral cabinet was finally constituted on 6 March 1974 bringing together the Ma'arakh, the National Religious Party, and the Independent Liberals in a narrow coalition. It included 7 new ministers (Ya'ariv, Rabin, Rabinowitz, Uzzani, Rosen, Raphael, and Hausner). Yet the key men around Prime Minister Meir remained in their positions despite mounting public clamor for a substantial changeover at the top. This, coupled with persistent intra-elite dissension led to Golda Meir's sudden resignation ("I've had enough") on 10 April 1974 from the premiership.

The search for a new premier focused on politicians who had not been tainted by the mistakes of the October 1973 War. Once a strong candidate, General Dayan was put out of the running by the war. Clearly, as in 1969, the man of the hour was Pinhas Sapir, Israel's most powerful politician and economic boss. But Sapir declined the premiership and lent his support to former General Yitzhak Rabin who went on to defeat a strong challenge by the Rafi chief, Shimon Peres, a Dayan associate.

Fathers to Sons

The formation of the Rabin government (4 June 1974) marked the most significant generational change in the Israeli elite since the early days of the Yishuv. In terms of average age, Rabin's cabinet was Israel's youngest—8 years younger than Golda Meir's cabinet of March 1974 and 5 years younger than the December 1969 cabinet. More important than age was the change in the personalities which had dominated Israel's politics since the fifties. Not only was Meir replaced by a leader 26 years her junior but her famous "kitchen cabinet" was also dissolved. Of her inner circle only Galili survived despite protests from outgoing Mapai leaders. The powerful Pinhas Sapir preferred to leave the cabinet to head the Jewish Agency—a move which may restore power to that organization and conceivably revive its rivalry with the cabinet. Other notable departures included Eban, who had a long-standing rivalry with Rabin, Gvati, who was retired, and Dayan, who had been blamed by many for the October War. The rabbi-ministers of the previous cabinet were absent because of the opposition of the Religious Bloc to the government.

In effect Rabin's accession to the prime ministry meant the demise of the so-called heir apparents—Allon, Dayan, Sapir, and Eban. Unlike them, Rabin was untainted by the mistakes leading to October 1973. He also had the advantage of being unallied to any of the warring factions in addition to being the major hero of the Six-Day War. His background as a Sabra and a highly successful ambassador to the United States, also contributed to his appeal as a personality who could restore public confidence in the ruling elite and in the political system as a whole.

The cabinet was based on a narrow coalition that included Ma'arakh, Independent Liberals, and the Civil Rights Movement of Shulamit Aloni, the cabinet's new and only female member.

Despite its narrow base, the various factions of the Labour Alignment were well represented—Rabinowitz and Ofer represented the "Gush" Party Bloc; Allon and Galili, Ahdut Avoda; Shemtov and Rosen for Mapam; Peres represented Rafi; Yadlin, the kibbutzim; Uzzani, the moshavim; and Hillel, the Orientals. The military and the business establishment was represented by Bar-Lev. Clearly Peres and Allon received two of the most important positions as defense and foreign minister respectively. A total of six ministers had held rank in the Tzahal, including Rabin, Allon, Galili, Ya'ariv, Bar-Lev, and Hausner—a possible measure of military influence in the cabinet. In October, the National Religious Party joined the government prompting Aloni's departure. Nevertheless, the epicenter of power consisted of Rabin, Allon, Bar-Lev, Ya'ariv and Zadok. Strikingly, everyone except Zadok was a Sabra in Rabin's kitchen cabinet and for the first time in Israel's history, about one-third of the total cabinet consisted of Sabras. While the "fathers" of the Fourth and Fifth Aliya still held control over Mapai, Histadrut, Hityashvut, and the Jewish Agency, in the cabinet the "sons" had come into their own.

4

Political Elites in a Charismatic
Setting: Egypt

The most outstanding feature of Egypt's contemporary scene has been the personality of Gamal Abd al-Nasir. From 1954 until his sudden death in September 1970 Nasir was unquestionably Egypt's and the Arab world's greatest leader in modern times. His charismatic hold on the Egyptian and Arab masses was a fact of life in the Middle East, despite defeats by Israel.

Yet however important, the Nasir factor cannot by itself explain the political process of revolutionary Egypt. Rather, Nasir represented a whole generation of young Egyptians who reached maturity during the bleak interwar years and who provided the military and civilian political leadership of the Revolution of July 1952. It is this elite, composed of all cabinet-rank individuals—prime ministers, deputy prime ministers, ministers, and deputy ministers, as well as presidents and vice presidents—which will constitute the focus of analysis.

Prelude to Revolution
The Burden of History

Few countries in the world have had a civilization as ancient and as glorious as Egypt's; yet in no land is the past such a burden upon the builders of the present. To understand the social-psychological milieu which produced the Nasirite leadership, it is necessary to emphasize a number of historical realities which have left a deep imprint upon the Egyptian political elite.[1] The first and most basic reality is the almost continuous subjugation of the Valley of the Nile to foreign occupation since the collapse of the pharaohs. To contemplate a servitude of over 2,500 years is a mind-boggling experience; yet unless the social-psychological-political impact of foreign rule is properly evaluated, it is difficult to explain modern-day Egyptian politics and elite behavior, not to mention its problems in waging war against Israel. Indeed, one primary reason for the initial success of the Nasirite revolution was its "Egyptianness." The Nasirite elite were the first native group to rule Egypt since the last pharaoh—a fact which bestowed considerable legitimacy on them.

One cannot emphasize sufficiently the significance of indigenousness to a people ruled successively by Greeks, Romans, Arabs, Kurds, various Turkish rulers, including the Ottoman Turks, and finally the British. The stage of foreign rule preceding the Revolution had been a unique three-layered variant of imperialism consisting of the Ottoman Turks, non-Egyptian Khedival descendants of Muhammad Ali, and the British, who had gotten there last but managed to do most of the ruling. Originally, the British had come to suppress an army revolt led by Arabi Pasha in 1882 against the Khedive and the Turkish-Circassian military elite; but they remained until the mid-fifties.

The Arab conquest had the most lasting impact on Egyptian society, for it Islamized Egypt, except the Coptic Christians, who now number about 15 percent of the population. On the heels of Islamization came Arabization (*isti'rab*)—a process which began when Arabic became the language of the Egyptian people and Arabic literature, traditions, and culture were disseminated in Egyptian society. More complicated, however, was the question of Egyptian versus Arab identity—a problem which even Nasir and his Revolution could not fully resolve.

A Milieu of Multidimensional Crisis

Egypt entered the modern age with two burdens of history. First there was the psycho-sociological disorientation of a population in perpetual servitude. The second involved the deep identity crisis centered on the question—"what is an Egyptian?" Was he to identify with Africa, Islam, or the Arabs; or was he to identify with pharaonic Egypt? The Arabi revolt of 1882 signaled the beginnings of an indigenous Egyptian identification—Egyptian nationalism—which in the subsequent decades developed ties to the ancient Egyptian past. Yet this was not the only doctrine seeking acceptance; Pan-Islamism was another. Under Shaykh Jamal al-Din al-Afghani and his disciples, Pan-Islamism stood for a reformed and modernized Islam to unite the Islamic countries against Western imperialism. During the thirties and the forties the Muslim Brotherhood rose as a powerful manifestation of Pan-Islamism. Finally, an Arabist trend began to be felt in Egypt, particularly during the forties, not to mention the appearance of socialism. Thus, the Nasirite elite was born and socialized in an atmosphere filled with these competing ideologies.[2]

These value systems reflected the inability of Egypt's intellectuals to develop a single comprehensive nationalist ideology. Despite the intensity of the European intellectual and political challenge, a synthesis of thought did not occur; nor did Egypt possess a strong enlightened leadership that could forge a synthesis. Thus, the ideological cleavages, coupled with palace misrule and British intervention, produced a state of continuous crisis. The nationalist Wafd Party pursued the dual aims of ridding the country of British power and limiting the monarchy's autocratic rule. Yet despite electoral victories, it was repeatedly prevented from effective rulership by the palace. Into this triangular struggle came the Muslim Brotherhood—a revivalist mass movement which attracted thousands of frustrated Egyptians who had lost hope in the government's ability to deal with the existing crisis environment.

The period from the end of World War II to the 1952 Revolution was one of protracted violence, where a decrease in traditional and legal legitimacy led to increasing reliance on force as a means of control. The political assassinations that plagued Egypt during this period were an unmistakable sign of deepening crisis.

Having briefly sketched the main features of the crisis situation, we shall now turn to examining the socializational experiences of the Nasirite elite within that environment (see figure 9).

Early Socialization

The influence of the family is difficult to assess in the case of the Nasirite elite because reliable information is lacking. However, it is clear that most of them came from large, extended families,

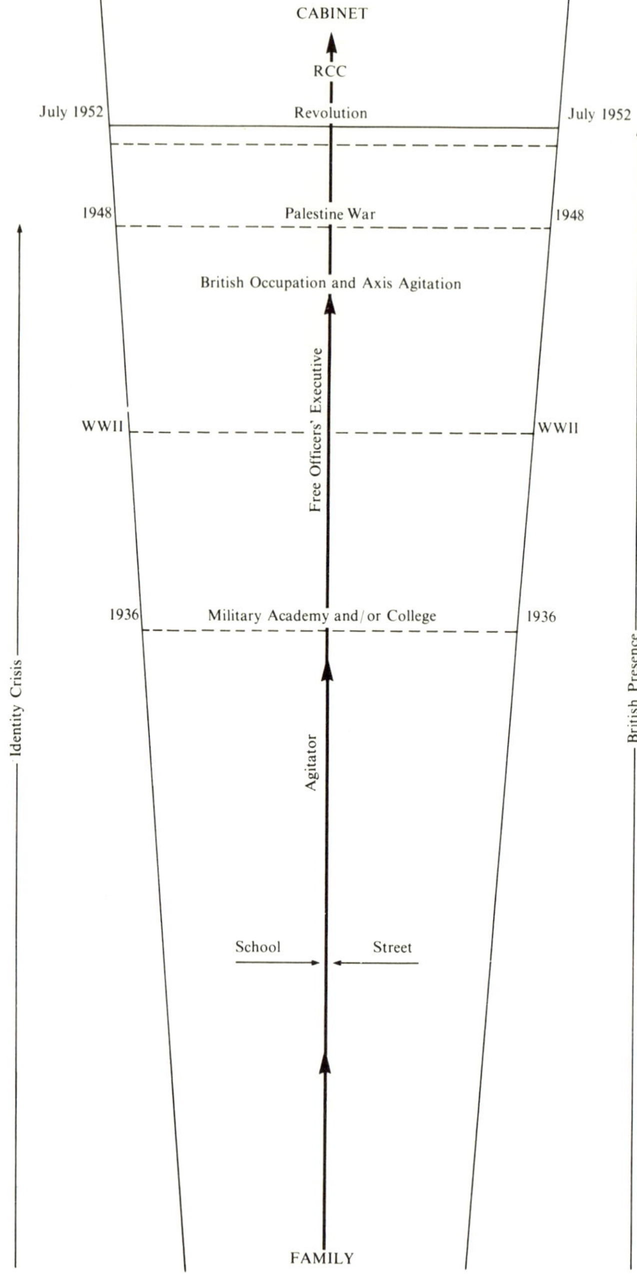

Figure 9 *Egypt: Progression to Elitehood*

172

mostly of peasant origin, but in the process of urbanizing. They had been brought to the city as very small children or were born there soon after the family's arrival. Life in the city and the process of urbanization itself constituted a traumatic experience for the child and family as well. The fact that these families were in the process of moving from village to the city points to an unstable social situation as well as marginality—a social background variable to be discussed subsequently.

While children of large families may not recive sufficient attention, two other socialization agents usually take up the slack—the school and the street. It is significant that a large portion of the future elite did not attend *Kuttabs* or religious schools, but rather went to secular institutions partly modeled after European schools. Perhaps even more important, these schools were centers of nationalist agitation. For instance, Nasir attended the Nahda School which Vatikiotis maintains was always at the forefront of political demonstrations.[3]

In the Middle Eastern milieu of the interwar period, student demonstrations were commonplace. Closing down the school and taking to the street was part and parcel of every student's socialization process. Fragmentary evidence indicates that these events were the crucible in which Egypt's future political elite were tempered. Thus political consciousness came at an early age in the midst of rioting and police repression;[4] the beatings and jailings that the students experienced probably had a greater impact on the students' personalities than formal schooling.

During the turbulent thirties the politicized students of Egypt joined a variety of groups expounding diverse programs and ideologies. At one time or another Nasir and his colleagues were attracted to these organizations, but did not find a permanent niche. Nasir himself went in and out of several political movements—Misr al-Fatat, the Wafd, and the Brethren. Sadat was first involved with the Misr al-Fatat and subsequently developed connections to the Brethren. Others involved with the Brethren included Abd al-Hakim Amir and Kamal al-Din Husayn, while Hasan Ibrahim had been a Fatat member. On the left of the political spectrum, Gamal Salim belonged to the Egyptian Socialist Party and Khalid Muhyi al-Din was a communist.[5]

Formative Events

In retrospect it is possible to identify a number of turning points in the lives of the Nasirite elite. First there was the Anglo-Egyptian treaty of 1936, which they regarded as a betrayal of Egypt. However, the same treaty did make possible the expansion of the Egyptian army, for Britain desired to strengthen her ally against an Italian threat from Ethiopia.[6] This enabled the Nahhas government to do away with class discrimination in choosing candidates for the Military Academy—a policy which permitted the entrance of middle- and lower-middle-class cadets, among them Nasir and his colleagues. The army was one of the few avenues of advancement available in Egypt and now it had been opened to nonaristocratic native Egyptians.

Documentary evidence presented by Vatikiotis[7] shows that eleven of the founding members of what became the Free Officers Executive entered the Military Academy in or just after 1937. One can discern another contingent of fourteen second-string Free Officers who entered between 1937 and 1943. It was at the academy that this particular generation of young men forged their early ties, which were strengthened as they were posted together in various parts of Egypt and the Sudan. At Mankabad in 1938 Nasir found two of his closest co-conspirators—Anwar al-Sadat and Zakariyya Muhyi al-Din.[8] Subsequently Nasir requested to be sent to the Sudan where he was reunited with another schoolmate—Abd al-Hakim Amir.

Socializationally the year 1941 was important; Field Marshall Rommel's armies approached Egypt amidst strong pro-German popular sentiment. So much were the British hated that many an Egyptian nationalist hoped for a German victory. During the German advance a number of Free Officers were involved in pro-German agitation and even spying; they included Anwar al-Sadat, Hasan Ibrahim, Husayn Zu al-Fiqar Sabri, and Abd al-Mun'im Abd al-Ra'uf. After an abortive attempt to fly General Aziz al-Masri toward the German lines, the group was arrested—all except Abd al-Nasir, who had been reluctant to involve himself in the plot.

The next major event that burnt into the collective memory of all young Egyptian patriots occurred on 4 February 1942, when Sir Miles Lampson, the British High Commissioner, surrounded the king's palace and forced him to appoint Nahhas Pasha as prime minister of a pro-British government. In nationalist eyes, the British had humiliated the Egyptian people. As a result not only did anti-British feeling intensify but two of the mainstays of the political structure—the king and the Wafd—were discredited.

Yet no collective experience was more traumatic for the Egyptians than the Palestine debacle; especially for the young officers who fought there. Ill-trained and badly equipped, the army had been committed to battle against a formidable foe to distract popular attention from the palace and the sorry state of domestic affairs. Particularly relevant was Nasir's entrapment with several of his colleagues (Amir, Z. Muhyi al-Din, Ukasha, S. Salim) in the Faluja enclave. Not only did Faluja give the Nasirities another common experience, it also provided an opportunity to meet the enemy for the first time, both in battle and in negotiations. Furthermore, the entrapment once again dramatically focused the attention of the officers on the corrupt political order in Cairo. The young officers returned home deeply shaken. As crisis after crisis convulsed Egypt after 1949, the newly organized Free Officers began to plan an eventual takeover.

A number of distinguishing qualities accorded the Free Officers' group certain advantages vis-à-vis competing conspiratorial organizations and the existing power structure. These were unity, leadership, information, and tactical mobility. The unity that existed among the inner core of eleven officers was reinforced by past ties of school and combat as well as by their shared revulsion against the status quo. The group was effectively led by the chairman of the Executive Committee, Abd al-Nasir, and utilized the cell system. Thus a good deal of power was concentrated in the hands of a few, who also controlled certain key army units. Also through strategically placed contacts they were able to gather intelligence about the plans of other secret societies, the high command, the palace, and the key embassies. At the hub of this communications network [9] was Nasir himself. Moreover, the Free Officers were able to move quickly and boldly to preempt the actions of competing groups and the palace. (Indeed, after witnessing their strength in the Officers' Club elections, the king was preparing to crush them). Their boldness in being the first group to act guaranteed them success. Considering the weak state of the power structure, conceivably another officers' group could have effected the coup, if it had moved first. Many existing historical accounts fail to mention that the two other major officers' groups had been on the decline during 1950–51, while the Free Officers were gaining momentum.[10] Because of their continuous terroristic involvement, Captain Mustafa Kamal Sidqi's band of twenty-three officers had come under constant surveillance and harassment by the authorities that resulted in the group's partial breakup. The Brotherhood, on the other hand, had dissipated its energies in the guerrilla campaign against the British in the Canal Zone. Government action against the Brethren was especially harsh, since of all the conspiratorial groups this was the largest and most powerful both outside and inside the army.

The Revolutionary Command Council

The coup d'etat of 23 July 1952 was an unprecedented occurrence in Egypt. Unlike Iraq and Syria, Egypt had no tradition of coup d'etat politics. While other Arab states had successive coups, Egypt had only one, which later became a revolution. To the great majority of Egyptians, the revolution was to be the major socializational event of their lives. This was particularly true of the Free Officers who had succeeded in taking power and retiring the last ruler of the Muhammad Ali dynasty. Their two most immediate problems were the lack of a detailed program and the appearance of intra-elite cleavages. After reconstituting itself as the Revolutionary Command Council (RCC), the top leadership of the Free Officers asked Ali Mahir to form a civilian government which was soon dismissed because it failed to implement agrarian reform.

Even after a lapse of twenty years it is not easy to establish the precise membership of the Free Officers group. It is, however, possible to identify a core leadership contingent around Nasir and then discern two other groups of second- and third-level Free Officers, many of whom gradually emerged in cabinet posts.

The original core was the Free Officers Executive, which as the RCC continued to function after 23 July 1952. It consisted of the eleven officers listed on the upper part of table 53. Those listed below the line had been associated with the Nasirite core for limited periods, and left the officers' group to engage in conspiracies against the RCC. The leftists Shawqi and Sadiq and the Muslim Brother Abd al'Ra'uf belonged to this category as well as Abd al-Mun'im Amin, a pro-Western officer.[11] Two others, Ahmad Anwar and Lutfi Wahid, fell out of the Nasirite contingent during the first year of the revolution. The only inner-core member who temporarily separated from the pro-Nasir majority was the leftist Khalid Muhyi al-Din. The remaining RCC members stood behind Abd al-Nasir in his successful confrontation with General Nagib during 1954.

TABLE 53. *Egypt: Free Officers Executive*

Gamal Abd al-Nasir
Abd al-Hakim Amir
Salah Salim
Gamal Salim
Kamal al-Din Husayn
Hasan Ibrahim
Abd al-Latif al-Baghdadi
Anwar al-Sadat
Khalid Muhyi al-Din
Zakariyya Muhyi al-Din
Husayn Shafi'i

Abd al-Mun'im Amin
Ahmad Shawqi
Yusif Sadiq
Abd al-Mun'im Abd al-Ra'uf
Ahmad Anwar
Lutfi Wahid

The eleven-member RCC core constituted only the visible head of the select group of pro-Nasir Free Officers who spread through the governmental machinery in order to supervise and control. In the early sixties another contingent of Free Officers emerged in top positions. Although not a part of the original core, these officers had been close to it. Table 54 shows this second elite contingent, which included some of the most powerful men in Nasirite Egypt, among them former premiers Ali Sabri and Sidqi Sulayman. After years of apprenticeship at the periphery, these fourteen officers were eventually given key functions ranging from internal security, to war, to the construction of the High Dam.

TABLE 54. *Egypt: Second-Level Free Officers*

Kamal Rif'at
Ali Sabri
Husayn Zu al-Fiqar Sabri
Sarwat Ukasha
Abbas Rudwan
Mahmud Riyad
Abd al-Mun'im Abu al-Nur
Sidqi Sulayman
Mahmud Yunis
Abd al-Qadir Hatim
Amin Huwaydi
Sha'rawi Guma'a
Muhammad Fawzi
Abd al-Wahhab Bishri

Still a third Free Officer contingent can be identified as shown in Table 55. Though relatively unknown, these twenty third-string Free Officers were nevertheless important. Most of them were several years younger than the inner-core members, but nevertheless had come under Nasirite influence at the Military Academy or the Staff Staff College where Nasir and his colleagues were teachers.

TABLE 55. *Egypt: Third-Level Free Officers*

Hamdi Ashur
Ahmad Tu'aymah
Ahmad Hamdi Ubayd
Ahmad Tawfiq Bakri
Muhammad Fa'iq
Samir Hilmi
Salah Hidayat
Tal'at Khayri
Nur al-Din Qurra
Abd al-Fattah Tawfiq
Fathi Rizq
Hasan Tuhami
Sami Sharaf
Kamal Badir
Muhammad Sa'ad Zayid
Hilmi Muhammad Sayyid
Muhammad Ibrahim Salim
Muhammad Sadiq
Hasan Sabri Khuli
Muhammad Ahmad Muhammad

In terms of background variables, there is substantial similarity between these three groups, which together constituted the principal portion of what became the Free Officers Association. All fifty-one graduated from the Military Academy after 1937 and most had gone on to the Staff College or such other fields as engineering, journalism, physics, political science, etc. Since virtually all belong to the same political generation, there are certain similarities in their political behavior—a topic to be discussed with reference to the conditioning effect of charismatic politics.

Charisma and Elite Behavior

The analysis of elite behavior in charismatic milieux inevitably focuses on the relationship between the charismatic leader and the elite contingent that surrounds him. Here the spiritual nature of the charismatic bond needs to be emphasized. The leader-follower relationships, based on the leders's ability to induce normative changes in his subjects' value system, is uncharacteristic of traditional and legal-rational situations. Clearly, the leader's chief lieutenants are affected by the spiritual relationship in various degrees, depending on the circumstances of their association with the leader and his movement. If association took place before the leader's manifestation of charisma, the relationship is most likely not charismatic but collegial. On the other hand, joining the leader's retinue as a result of the charismatic bond makes one a disciple rather than a colleague. Whatever the case, these subordinate leaders function in a charismatic milieu; their behavior is conditioned by charisma and conversely they influence the charismatic leader's behavior.

Despite the usual secrecy that surrounded Nasir, a considerable amount of information has come out since his death regarding his relations with subordinate leaders. Using social distance [12] as criterion, one can identify two distinct groups of officials. Closest to him were his army friends, the core of the Free Officers group, who later held positions in the RCC and the government. The other contingent consisted of second- and third-string Free Officers as well as a large number of pro-Nasirite civilian leaders, who filled ministerial and other high posts in the power structure. Not only did Nasir interact differently with the two groups but also this interaction changed over time due to his acquisition of charisma, peculiarities of personality, and the force of events. A detailed explication of these factors is necessary for an understanding of the behavior of the Egyptian elite until 1970.

Nasir's relations with the first group went through three distinct phases. During the initial phase, as the revolution was planned and executed, Nasir's position vis-à-vis his RCC colleagues was *primus inter pares*—first among equals. During the long years of conspiracy, power had gravitated toward him almost naturally by virtue of his gifted personality and capacity for work. He had been the main organizer and anchorman of the Free Officers movement, and only he and Amir knew the secret cells of the Free Officers' conspiratorial network.[13] Nevertheless, Nasir possessed only one vote within the RCC and the Free Officers Executive and in a number of known instances he was outvoted by his colleagues. Although his friends showed unmistakeable deference toward Nasir's person, their long years as classmates, soldiers, and revolutionaries, no less than marriage and family ties, had the effect of minimizing the social distance between them. Clearly the relationship was not one of dominance.

The close ties among the top Nasirite military elite produced an uncommon collegiality in political decision-making which transcended the 1952 revolution and the Nasir-Nagib power struggle of 1954. The sole defector from the Nasirite inner core was the pro-Nagib Khalid Muhyi al-Din, who subsequently was permitted to return to the fold as a journalist and an ASU party official. The others—Amir, Baghdadi, Sadat, Husayn, Ibrahim, Shafi'i, Z. Muhyi al-Din, and the two Salims—were placed in charge of whole sectors of national endeavor; each possessed real power.

However the events of 1955 and 1956 came to modify Nasir's relationship with his colleagues. A highly unusual conjction of events inadvertently propelled the Egyptian president to a position of universal visibility unprecedented in Egyptian-Arab history since the rise of Salah al-Din. The Nasir who had successfully defied the West by rejecting the Baghdad Pact, going to Bandung, getting arms from the Soviet Union, was not the Gamal of collegial days. These events, coupled with the nationalization of the canal company and the ability to survive the Anglo-French-Israeli onslaught, made Nasir a powerful charismatic figure who could move the Arab multitudes with his message of Pan-Arabism directed against Israel, Britain, the US, and their clients in the Middle East. By symbolizing the Arab's collective quest for greatness, Nasir could relate to his mass constituency (*gemeinde*) in a uniquely spiritual manner, something that his fellow officers and other Arab rulers could not hope to accomplish. While his personal charisma had legitimized the revolution, it had also set him above and apart from his old companions. Although the men of the RCC admired him and deferred often to his wishes, they were not the subservient, awestruck disciples of the charismatic's newly acquired mass gemeinde. In the end, despite the charismatic environment many of the core Free Officers were unable to achieve the psychological transition from colleague to disciples or henchmen. Indeed, charisma was detrimental to collective decision-making, effective teamwork, and creativity. Ironically, Weber's conception of charisma as a creative force did not apply to the individuals close to the leader; instead charisma induced conformity at the top. Also having established the charismatic bond and experienced mass adulation, Nasir may have tried to treat his comrades as errand boys who were not indispensable anymore. The comrades' reactions could not but include bitterness and jealousy toward a colleague who had been raised above the group by the force of charisma. A number of these observations can be validated when one examines the progressive atrophy of the RCC core.

Late in 1954 General Nagib had been ejected from the RCC and the presidency for policy and personality clashes with Nasir and his colleagues; nor could the young officers tolerate Nagib's mass popularity. The Salam brothers, Gamal and Salah, were next to be ejected in the late fifities after intermittently serving the regime. The early sixties revealed a number of new problems which contributed to the atrophy of the RCC core contingent. Collective decision-making had declined as Nasir increasingly relied upon himself to decide on major issues. Simultaneously, he was reluctant to delegate real authority to his colleagues [14]—a practice which multiplied his own decision-making load thereby sacrificing effectiveness and eventually his health. Furthermore, Nasir's suspiciousness and tendency to interfere in petty bureaucratic routine had the effect of increasing the existing intra-elite cleavages. The major exception was his close friend, Marshal Amir, who had been given real authority over the army and as governor of Syria but had failed in both—the Suez War of 1956 and the Syrian secession of 1961. Rebounding from the blow of Syria's break-away, Nasir decided to promulgate the doctrine of Arab Socialism which through extensive nationalizations dispossessed Egypt's capitalist and landowning classes between 1961 and 1964. These socialistic measures did not have the blessing of three RCC members—Baghdadi, Husayn, and Ibrahim.[15] Furthermore, Baghdadi and Muhyi al-Din had opposed an Egyptian policy of Pan-Arab over-involvement, particularly in the Yemeni War [16]—a policy which had been supported by Marshal Amir and his army generals. The last attempt to revive RCC collegiality in decision-making came within the framework of the Presidential Council established in 1962. Both Nasir and his RCC colleagues wanted to reduce Amir's control of the army, which had been made into an exclusive satrapy of the marshal.[17] Not only did Nasir need to re-establish personal control over the military, but he was concerned about the declining professional competence of the armed forces. Despite Amir's vehement objections, the first steps were taken to restore presidential power over the military. In the end, however, Nasir did not see through what had been started, since he feared a coup by Amir and his army commanders which could lead to civil war. Once again the majority faction within the RCC had lost. In March 1964, the Presidential Council was dissolved and Marshal Amir became Nasir's chosen successor as first vice president. The other RCC members remained vice presidents, as Ali Sabri, a second-string Free Officer, was made prime minister against the collective wishes of the RCC men. As a result, in early 1964, Vice Presidents Abd al-Latif Baghdadi and Kamal al-Din Husayn resigned from the government and were soon followed by Hasan Ibrahim. By 1965, there were only four RCC men left in the high councils of the Egyptian government—Zakariyya Muhyi al-Din, Anwar al-Sadat, Husayn al-Shafi'i, and Amir himself. Of these only Amir and Muhyi al-Din had continuous access to Nasir, who had increasingly isolated himself from colleagues whose advice and criticism he could not tolerate any more. Perhaps the only exception was a civilian, Muhammad Hasanayn Haykal, who eventually became the president's close confidant and mouthpiece to the world.

Thus beginning in the early sixties a second contingent (see tables 54 and 55) of Free Officers emerged from the bureaucracies (which they had invaded after the revolution) to take over the void left at the top by the departing RCC men. These officers had been on the periphery of the RCC's main core since the revolution and as such their relationship with Nasir was characterized by greater social distance and a much greater degree of deference than the RCC-Nasir relationships. While it contained many loyal devotees of the charismatic leader, it also included opportunist henchmen and sycophants, who magnified the shortcomings and the dysfunctional behavior of the leader. There were those who had served Nasir well, e.g., Sulayman (High Dam), Riyad (Foreign Affairs), Hatim (Culture), Abu al-Nur (Local Government), and Rif'at (ASU), to mention a few. But there were also others who feigned devotion and loyalty to the leader to further their own careers. Two of these yes men—Ali Sabri and Sami Sharaf—managed to ''protect'' the president from outspoken colleagues and advisors. Significantly both were military intelligence men whose skills were placed at the service of an increasingly suspicious Nasir, especially vis-à-vis Amir's army cirle, American intelligence, and the Muslim Brotherhood. Sharaf took over as Nasir's cabinet secretary in 1961 and proceeded to dominate the presidency and through his own intelligence apparatus made himself one of Egypt's five most powerful men until thrown into jail for joining Ali Sabri in the abortive May 1971 coup against Sadat.

The protective wall around Nasir was briefly pierced when Zakariyya Muhyi al-Din became prime minister. While Muhyi al-Din's appointment improved US-Egyptian relations and assured some additional wheat supplies, it did little to end Nasir's isolation or correct the mismanagement of Ali Sabri. Nor could Muhyi al-Din counter Amir's influence on Nasir concerning Yemen; indeed, Nasir refused to heed Muhyi al-Din's repeated pleas to withdraw from the Yemen, if only for the sake of shoring up the country's sagging economy.[18] In September 1966, Muhyi al-Din left the premiership in deep disillusionment and was once again kicked upstairs as vice president without real power. High Dam Minister Sidqi Sulayman was appointed prime minister in keeping with Nasir's desire to have in the premiership a technician who could quietly and quickly implement his decisions. Meanwhile Nasir had already drifted into an anti-Western policy despite

Muhyi al-Din's advice—a policy which was based on his dislike of President Johnson and the cut-off of wheat shipments and which was destined to have tragic consequences for Egypt and the Arab world.

During the fateful events of late May 1967, once again two of Nasir's old cronies—Baghdadi and Ibrahim—resurfaced to warn Nasir about the closing of Aqaba, overreliance on Soviet promises and the necessity of maintaining a Soviet-American balance in Egyptian foreign policy. These and similar polite warnings by several civilian ministers were dismissed by Nasir who regarded Israeli threats as bluffs. He furthermore gave the United States his promise not to begin the shooting and in turn believed in American assurances that Israel would not attack.

The easy defeat of the Egyptian Army in June 1967 was a manifestation of the leadership crisis that had prevailed at the top since the early sixties. The military's claim to a privileged position crumbled in the face of a mass outpouring of criticism. Nasir himself resigned after appointing Muhyi al-Din as his successor. So vehement were public remonstrances that Nasir had to take back his resignation. Despite the enormity of the defeat the charismatic bond still held. What followed was a period of wide-ranging public debate, student and worker unrest, and the institution of reforms in both the military and civilian sectors. Marshal Amir, along with Generals Badran, Nasr, Mahmud, and their coterie of about fifty officers, was arrested and charged with conspiracy to overthrow the government. In September 1967 Amir was reported to have killed himself by poisoning. In March 1968 Vice President Muhyi al-Din also resigned his position as Nasir's successor over differences in policy. Not until December 1969 did Nasir appoint a new vice president, Anwar al-Sadat, who had been Speaker of the National Assembly. Indeed, by 1970 only two of the eleven original Free Officers remained around Nasir. These were Sadat and Husayn al-Shafi'i, neither of whom seemed to have posed a threat to the president. The trauma of the 1967 War apparently brought a degree of openness to Nasir's interactions with his lieutenants and a relaxation in the political system as a whole.

Elite Profiles
Who is Who: Military vs. Civilian

After three experiments with all-civilian cabinets under Ali Mahir (July 1952) and General Nagib (September and December 1952), leading RCC members came forth to assume key cabinet posts in June 1953. What followed was a massive infusion of officers into key bureaucratic positions. It is true that some of the politically unreliable bureaucrats of the old regime did have to be replaced by persons who combined political loyalty and administrative expertise—qualities that were readily found mostly in military officers. While detailed information on the military's overall presence in the government is unavailable, overwhelming predominance is evident at the highest and intermediary levels.

TABLE 56. *Egypt: Aggregate Breakdown—Military versus Civilian*

	MILITARY			CIVILIAN	
	Officer	Officer-Technocrat	Total		Total
N	37	23	60	126	186
%	20.0	12.5	32.0	67.7	100

In purely quantitative terms, table 56 reflects the degree of the military's presence at the very top of the power structure.[19] Out of an aggregate of 186 cabinet-rank leaders,[20] 60, or 32 percent, had been military officers of various types in contrast to 126, or 67.7 percent, who had a civilian background. However, one should not be misled by the two-to-one civilian majority. While it clearly illustrates the regime's reliance on civilians, especially in technical areas, it is not to be regarded as a valid index of their relative power. Most of these civilians were the tools of the RCC and subsequently of Nasir himself. Since the civilians lacked an independent power base, none of the 126 emerged as a political leader in his own right in the Nasirite period, not even during the postwar turmoil of 1967–1969. Coupled with Nasir's persistence in placing ex-officers in key ministries, this made the military the virtual master of the system. Only after Nasir's death did two civilians become prime minister—Mahmud Fawzi and Aziz Sidqi.

To be sure, one peculiarity of recent Egyptian political life has been the appalling lack of backbone among the civilian leadership. Though men of great intelligence, efficiency, and expertise, they were also singularly depoliticized, devoid of political and ideological consciousness, and therefore unable or unwilling to present a counterweight to the military. In the various power contests at the top, the civilians, or at least some of them, tended to side with different factions headed by former officers; yet as far as one can discern, no civilian has actually *led* a factional power struggle. The few who have dared to stand up to the military have been purged; the vast majority, more interested in high office than principles, have complied with the military's wishes.

The best index of the officers' position within the leadership is their control of strategic posts. All of Egypt's presidents—Nagib, Nasir, and Sadat—were once officers, as were all of the vice presidents. The five premiers during the Nasirite period—Nagib, Nasir, Sabri, Muhyi al-Din, and Sulayman—were also ex-officers. In addition, several key ministries—Defense, Local Administration, Military Production, and the Ministry of State (for Intelligence)—have been headed by officers from the very outset. Certain other ministries alternated between ex-officers and civilians, i.e., Foreign Affairs, Tourism, Industry, Power, High Dam, Information, Scientific Research, Communications, Agrarian Reform, Supply, Youth, Labor, Education, Social Affairs, Planning, Waqfs, Culture, and National Guidance. The highly sensitive Interior Ministry became the preserve of ex-officers such as Muyhi al-Din and Guma'a, with the single exception of Abd al-Azim Fahmi, a police officer. Even the Ministry of Public Health experienced a quasi-military intrusion; Muhammad Nassar and Abd al-Wahhab Shukri have both been long identified with the armed forces as military physicians. The Ministry of National Guidance, the state's supreme propaganda agency, had been headed by former officers since 1958.

Ministries with uninterrupted civilian leadership include Justice, Public Works, Housing and Utilities, Irrigation, Commerce, Agriculture, Treasury, and Higher Education. These are highly technical areas, generally unsuitable for individuals of military backgrounds. Yet, in the final analysis, various means were devised to assure military control over these "civilian" ministries as well.

Basically, there have been three control strategies since the military's direct involvement in government beginning in 1953. The first and crudest strategy was outright takeover of key ministries by leading RCC members, who employed civilians in second-level slots as sources of expert advice. In later years, as vice presidents and deputy premiers in charge of clusters of ministries, or "sectors," the leading officers continued to exercise direct supervisory functions over the subordinate ministries, which civilians often headed. Baghdadi, Shafi'i, Muhyi al-Din, Husayn, Rif'at, Abbas Rudwan, Abu al-Nur, and Hatim, all headed such superministries. The second strategy was to maintain a military presence in the civilian-led ministries by placing officers in the number two positions. Depending on the organizational make-up of the particular ministry, the military appointment could come at the deputy minister (a cabinet post) or undersecretary (below cabinet) level. Such were the roles of Husayn Zu al-Fiqar Sabri (until 1964) and Mahmud Riyad (1964–1967), both of whom successively served as deputies to Foreign Minister Mahmud Fawzi, a civilian. Qurra's position as undersecretary to Supply Minister Ramzi Stino is an example of military presence at that level.

The military's most ingenious method of control was through the appointment of a new breed of officers identified here as officer-technocrats (off-techs). Most of these men began to appear in leading positions in the late fifties and soon achieved cabinet or higher status, often displacing civilians and other nontechnical military men.

Virtually all of the 23 (12.5 percent) officer-technocrats have been military men who went on to receive nonmilitary degrees in diverse fields—engineering, physics, medicine, political science, law, history, and journalism. The best known was General Muhammad Nagib, an officer with a law degree. Other well-known off-techs include former Premier Sidqi Sulayman and Ministers Abd al-Wahhab Bishri, Sarwat Ukasha, Salah Hidayat, Abd al-Qadir Hatim, Mahmud Yunis, Hilmi Muhammad Sayyid, and Muhammad Sa'ad al-Din Zayid.[21]

In essence, the rise of the officer-technocrats was the military's answer to its civilian critics. For now the military had its *own* trained experts to cope with the new and diverse complexities of an industrializing society. Through these men the military could

TABLE 57. *Egypt: Age and Background Characteristics by Cabinet*

| CABINET | AVERAGE AGE | BACKGROUND | | | | | | | | RELIGION | | | | TOTAL |
| | | Officer | | Officer-Technocrat | | Total Military | | Civilian | | Muslim | | Copt | | |
		N	%	N	%	N	%	N	%	N	%	N	%	
7 September 1952	50.4	—	—	1	6.3	1	6.3	15	93.8	15	93.8	1	6.3	16
8 December 1952	49	—	—	1	5.9	1	5.9	16	94.1	16	94.1	1	5.9	17
18 June 1953	44.7	4	21	1	5.3	5	26.3	14	73.6	18	94.7	1	5.3	19
4 October 1953	42.6	7	31.8	2	9.1	9	40.9	13	59	21	95.5	1	4.5	22
17 April 1954	40.9	9	37.4	2	8.3	11	45.8	13	54.1	23	95.8	1	4.2	24
1 September 1954	43.5	10	43.4	2	8.7	12	52.1	11	47.7	22	95.7	1	4.3	23
30 June 1956	43.1	7	31.8	1	4.5	8	36.3	14	63.6	21	95.5	1	4.5	22
5 March 1958	44.3	7	33.3	1	4.8	8	38.1	13	61.9	20	95.2	1	4.8	21
Presidents and Vice Presidents		3	100	—	—	3	100							3
Central Cabinet		5	50	1	10	6	60	4	40					10
Regional Cabinet		2	19.8	—	—	2	19.8	9	89.1					11
7 October 1958	44.9	11	33.3	5	15.2	16	48.5	17	51.5	32	97	1	3	33
Presidents and Vice Presidents		3	100	—	—	3	100	—	—					3
Central Cabinet		9	52.9	1	5.9	10	58.8	7	41.2					17
Regional Cabinet		2	12.5	4	25	6	37.5	10	62.5					16
17 August 1961	47.8	11	35.4	5	16.1	16	51.5	15	48.3	30	96.8	1	3.2	31
Presidents and Vice Presidents		6	100	—	—	6	100	—	—					6
19 October 1961	45.9	10	34.4	5	17.2	15	51.6	14	48.2	28	96.6	1	3.4	29
Presidents and Vice Presidents		5	100	—	—	5	100	—	—					5
29 September 1962	47.7	12	33.2	5	13.9	17	47.1	19	52.6	35	97.2	1	2.8	36
Presidents and Vice Presidents		6	100	—	—	6	100	—	—					6

Presidential Council		10	83	—	—	10	83	2	16.3					12
Executive Council		2	8.3	5	20.8	7	29.1	17	70.7					24
24 March 1964	49.9	10	22.7	6	13.6	16	36.3	28	63.6	41	93.2	3	6.8	44
Presidents and Vice Presidents		5	100	—	—	5	100	—	—					5
Prime Ministers and Deputy Prime Ministers		3	24.9	2	16.6	5	41.5	7	58.1					12
Ministers		2	7.4	4	14.8	6	22.2	21	77.7					27
2 October 1965	51.1	13	31.6	6	14.6	19	46.2	22	53.5	38	92.7	3	7.3	41
Presidents and Vice Presidents		5	100	—	—	5	100	—	—					5
Prime Ministers and Deputy Prime Ministers		2	22.2	2	22.2	4	44.4	5	55.5					9
Ministers and Deputy Ministers		6	22.2	4	14.8	10	37	17	62.9					27
10 September 1966	50.5	13	34.2	8	21	21	55.2	17	44.7	35	92.1	3	7.9	38
Presidents and Vice Presidents		4	100	—	—	4	100	—	—					4
Deputy Prime Ministers		1	20	3	60	4	80	1	20					5
Minister's and Deputy Ministers		8	27.5	5	17.2	13	44.7	16	55					29
19 June 1967	50.1	11	37.8	8	27.5	19	65.4	10	34.4	28	96.6	1	3.4	29
Presidents, Vice Presidents and Deputy Prime Ministers		4	80	1	20	5	100	—	—					5
Ministers		7	29.1	7	29.1	14	58.2	10	41.6					24
20 March 1968	50.2	8	24.2	5	15.2	13	39.4	20	60.6	31	93.9	2	6.1	33
28 October 1968	50.3	7	22.6	6	19.4	13	41.9	18	58.1	29	93.6	2	6.4	31
21 October 1970	51.9	8	22.2	5	15.2	13	39.4	20	60.6	32	96.7	1	3.0	33
18 November 1970	51.1	6	18.2	5	15.2	11	33.3	22	66.7	32	96.7	1	3.0	33
14 May 1971	52.7	4	11.1	7	19.4	11	30.6	25	69.4	35	97.2	1	2.8	36
20 September 1971	54.9	7	19.4	6	16.7	13	36.1	23	63.9	35	97.2	1	2.8	36
17 January 1972	54.2	5	13.0	3	8.8	8	23.5	26	76.5	33	97.1	1	2.9	34

extend its scope of effective control, simultaneously reducing its reliance on the civilian experts. Given the views and needs of the leadership, the off-techs were bound to succeed; they combined and enjoyed the best of two worlds.

The analysis of elite backgrounds is a useful technique that can be employed to study systemic evolution. For example, the changing proportions of officers and civilians may be particularly important to gain insights into the workings of military dictatorships. Table 57 contains data concerning certain elite background characteristics. Particularly significant is the cabinet-by-cabinet breakdown of the number and proportion of officers, officer-technocrats, and civilians. The general pattern that emerges quantitatively illustrates the increasing militarization that took place during the early fifties and the recent trend toward civilianization.

On 7 September 1952 General Nagib became prime minister at the head of an all-civilian cabinet, replacing the previous RCC-installed civilian government of Ali Mahir. In both the September 1952 cabinet and the reshuffled December 1952 cabinet Nagib was the sole officer—classified as off-tech in table 57. The picture began to change when four additional officers entered the June 1953 cabinet—Nasir, Baghdadi, Amir, and Salah Salim. Their deep distrust of the civilian elite, combined with Nagib's growing popularity, had brought forth these four main architects of the July 1952 coup. The June 1953 cabinet began an upward trend in the military's presence at the top for the next two and a half years. During the Nagib-Nasir power struggles in 1953 and 1954, the military component continued to increase from 26.3 percent in June 1953 to 40.9 percent in the reshuffled October 1953 government. A further increase to 45.8 percent in the April 1954 cabinet reflected Nasir's consolidation of power against Nagib and his civilian supporters. Between June 1953 and April 1954 Nasir succeeded in packing the cabinet with his fellow officers and retiring pro-Nagib civilians. The September 1954 reshuffle was the first cabinet in which officers (52.1 percent) exceeded the civilians.

Early 1956 saw the first attempts at civilianization, subsequently interrupted by the Suez War. The military suffered a loss of four posts in the June 1956 cabinet, thus dropping its total to a low of 36.3 percent. With the formation of the United Arab Republic the military component once again began to increase.[22] Taking the aggregate of the multilevel leadership (president, vice presidents, central and regional ministers), the military registered less than a 2 percent increase in the March 1958 government; in the October 1958 cabinet, however, the total of officers went up by over 10 percentage points to 48.5 percent. In both cabinets the president and all vice presidents were ex-officers. At the Central Cabinet level, the military predominated with 60 percent (in March 1958) and 58.8 percent (in October 1958). Only in the regional cabinet did officer representation reach a low of 19.8 percent (in March), however it climbed to 37.5 percent in October 1958. With the abolition of the regional cabinet system in August 1961, the military component rose from 48.5 percent to 51.5 percent, a level that was maintained in the first post-secession cabinet (October 1961). The maintenance of an officers' majority seems to have reflected the regime's reliance on the coercive force of the military to help keep the UAR united in August 1961 and to prevent a Syrian-style countercoup in Egypt in October 1961. One should also note the increase of off-techs in cabinet posts since October 1958. By September 1966 the off-techs claimed 21 percent of the posts; by June 1967 it had reached an all-time high of 27.5 percent.

Having recovered from the shock of Syria's breakaway, a new phase of partial civilianization was started in 1962, which culminated in the founding of the Arab Socialist Union. The regime's new commitment to etatism and rapid industrialization could not be achieved without a greater reliance on civilian expertise; hence the progressive decline of the military component to 47.1 percent in September 1962 and 36.3 percent in March 1964. Not since June 1956 had the military's presence been that low.

The disproportionately greater power of the military elite, despite its decreasing numerical strength (1962 and 1964), bears repeating. For example, in the September 1962 two-level cabinet, the Presidential Council (supreme policy-making agency) was 83 percent military in contrast to only 29.1 percent military representation on the Executive Council. Also, in the multilevel cabinet of March 1964, Egypt's largest cabinet (44), the military scored 41.5 percent at the deputy prime minister level, but only 22.2 percent at the ministerial level.

A multitude of economic and political problems converged in

the mid-sixties—the Yemeni War, the economy, internal unrest—to produce a protracted crisis situation culminating in the 1967 War. The immediate effect of this turmoil was to produce a ten-point upswing in the military component of the Muhyi al-Din government, a trend which reached the unprecedented high of 55.2 percent in Sidqi Sulayman's cabinet of September 1966. In the aftermath of the June War, the military presence in Nasir's 19 June 1967 cabinet reached an all-time high of 65.4 percent. This peak came at a time of great internal instability accentuated by Marshall Amir's attempted coup. It may be that in Nasir's perception a military-dominated leadership could more effectively control internal unrest and neutralize further insurrectionist activity in the demoralized military establishment.

Popular reaction against the military after the 1967 defeat, coupled with the student-worker riots of February 1968, prompted Nasir to begin a far-reaching reorganization of political life, the first manifestation of which was the March 1968 cabinet. The number of civilians doubled, with a concomitant decrease of 6 officers, in a cabinet of 33 members. The sharp military drop from 65.4 percent (June 1967) to 39.4 percent (March 1968) signaled the start of a new demilitarizing stage. Under Sadat's presidency, there has been a generally decreasing military presence except the September 1971 cabinet. In the January 1972 cabinet, under Aziz Sidqi, the military presence reached the lowest level in twenty years. While there was an increase to over 30 percent in Sadat's war cabinet of March 1973, in his April 1974 cabinet the military component was once again down to a mere 22 percent. The trend toward increasing civilianization is expected to continue if all other factors remain constant. However, if developments since 1952 are a guide, internal and/or external crises are likely to increase the military presence at the top.

Age and Tenure

Although political involvement may have come early in adult life, the attainment of first political office came somewhat later, at an average age of 40 (see table 58). This would have been higher were it not for the intrusion of the young officers whose first politi-

TABLE 58. *Egypt: Age*

	YEARS
Average age at first political office	40.1
Average age at first cabinet office	49.4
Average age at leaving cabinet office	51.5

cal office was a cabinet post. Moreover, the relative youth of the officers and certain of their civilian recruits kept the average age at first cabinet office just over 49. The average would have been still lower had it not been for Nagib and older civilians such as Yusif, Tarraf, Fawzi, and Sharabasi and for second-and third-level Free Officers who waited their turn until reaching the cabinet. On the other hand, despite the political longevity of the foregoing civilians, the average age at leaving cabinet office was a relatively low 51.5 years, reflecting the briefness of tenure at the top for many officials. As seen in table 59, the overall average tenure in office was 3 years 1 month. Yet significantly, the average tenure of officers and officer-technocrats was almost two years longer than that of the civilian leaders—4 years 5 months and 2 years 11 months, respectively. This fact reflects not only the military's durability and entrenchment but also its leading position with respect to the civilians.

TABLE 59. *Egypt: Tenure*

	YEARS	MONTHS
Average tenure of cabinet members	3	1
Average tenure of military officers	4	5
Average tenure of civilians	2	11

An analysis of average age data for each cabinet bears few surprises (see table 57). Age sharply declines between Nagib's all-civilian cabinets of 1952 and the June 1953 cabinet, because the young RCC officers, including Nasir, entered at that point. With the influx of additional officers during October 1953 and April 1954 the average age level dropped to an all-time low of 40.9 from the previous high of 50.4. Since that time there has been an almost uninterrupted rise in average age as many of the permanent figures aged in office and new recruits were brought in mostly from older age brackets. The trend toward generally older cabinets continued until October 1965 when the average age of 51.1 years surpassed even the previous high of Nagib's first cabinet. Average age then remained virtually constant at about 50 years until October 1970, after which age continued to rise to an all-time high of 54.9 in September 1971.

Educational Specialization

Educational backgrounds of the elite can reveal important clues about the leadership's sense of priorities, the direction of socio-political change, and the political system itself. Because the modernizing countries are attempting to develop rapidly, the type and level of the elite's education has assumed greater importance than it has in modernized societies. One might even hypothesize that educational background is a more significant variable in the study of developing countries than it would be for developed systems. In Egypt, education has traditionally been a politically significant dimension, and it has been even more so since the revolution.

Table 60 presents an aggregate breakdown of educational specialization by fields. As in table 57, the total military is divided into two main categories according to their educational specialization. The officer category contains 37 individuals whose primary field of formal study was military science, in which they held at least one degree. While several of these pure military types also pursued nonmilitary studies, none of them actually completed the requirements for academic degrees. In contrast, the officer-technocrats went beyond a military education to obtain academic degrees in nonmilitary fields. There were a total of 23 off-techs, 11 of whom specialized in engineering in preparation for highly successful careers in the cabinet. Of the remaining 12, 4 became political scientists, 2 graduated as medical doctors, 2 held law degrees, 2 were journalists, and 1 was a historian. Finally, 1 became an atomic physicist.

Among the 126 civilian leaders, there were 26 engineers—the largest single specialization category. When the 26 civilian engineers are added to the 11 engineer off-techs, the total engineering category numbers 37—equalling the pure military category. Engineers represent 20 percent of the total leadership and as such

TABLE 60. *Egypt: Educational Specialization by Fields—Aggregate Count*

	N	%	N	%	N	%
Military					60	32.3
Officers			37	19.8		
Officer-Technocrats			23	12.4		
Military-Political Science	4	2.2				
Military-History	1	0.5				
Military-Engineering	11	5.9				
Military-Physics	1	0.5				
Military-Law	2	1.1				
Military-Journalism	2	1.1				
Military-Medicine	2	1.1				
Civilians					126	66.4
Law	24	12.9				
Law-Political Economy	7	3.8				
Law-Religion	1	0.5				
Criminology	3	1.6				
Engineering	26	14.0				
Sociology	1	0.5				
Political Science	1	0.5				
Educational Psychology	6	3.3				
Chemistry	4	2.2				
Agriculture	11	5.9				
Economics-Business	14	7.5				
Islamic-Arabic Studies	4	2.2				
Medicine	8	4.3				
Fine Arts	1	0.5				
Geography	5	2.7				
Mathematics	1	0.5				
No College Education	3	1.6				
No Data	8	4.3				
Total					186	

reflect the regime's singular commitment to rapid industrialization.

The stress on general economic development is further reflected by the relatively high number of agronomists (11), chemists (4), and economists (14 plus 7). The 11 agronomists are indicative of Egypt's serious food problem. Among the social sciences, the more traditional field of geography (5) is overrepresented in contrast to sociology (1). Law claims a high proportion, especially when the 2 military lawyers are added to 24 civilian lawyers. But the fact that the number of lawyers falls short of the military or engineer categories clearly indicates their secondary role in Egypt, in contrast to such countries as Lebanon and the United States. Finally, the presence of educational psychologists shows special concern with the educational process, while the 3 criminologists may indicate excessive systemic preoccupation with police work.

A number of additional insights emerge from examining changes of educational specialization over time (see table 61). Although those with a purely military education became a permanent fixture after June 1953, simultaneously there has been an increase of off-techs, which reached a peak in the June 1967 cabinet. The technological specializations of agriculture and engineering climbed progressively until August 1961; after 1964 several scientists (chemistry, physics, botany) made their debut. The percentages of the smaller categories of medicine and social science fluctuate without clear trends.

The two fields of specialization that registered a decline since September 1952 were humanities and law. After a high of 18.8 percent in September 1952, the humanities (literature, Islamic studies, fine arts, linguistics) declined, then disappeared between March 1964 and January 1972 when two humanists again appeared. Taking the Law and Law/College columns together, the lawyers achieved preponderance in the December 1952 and June 1953 cabinets, then they registered a precipitous decline in 1958; by October 1968, however, their proportion began to increase. The decline of lawyers and humanists since the revolution and the concurrent increase of officers, off-techs, engineers, and scientists reflected basic changes in Egyptian politics. A heavily lawyer-oriented system before the revolution, Egypt continued to rely on lawyer-politicians in the early years of the revolution. With the advent of planned, accelerated socio-economic development that required technical specialists, the lawyer's utility gradually declined. As generalists the lawyers and humanists lacked the specialized training to cope with the new technological environment. Politically, the military-revolutionary milieu also proved inhospitable to the lawyer. Not only was he too closely identified with the pre-revolutionary political culture, but also his traditional "brokerage" functions were in less demand in the new society. The rather legalistic, competitive politics and economics of the old regime had been replaced by more ideological and revolutionary politics, and the lawyer became the odd man out. Under Sadat, the lawyers are more in evidence but not to the extent that they were before the revolution.

TABLE 61. *Egypt: Educational Specialization*

| | | PROFESSIONAL SCHOOLS | | | | | | COMBINATIONS: PROFESSIONAL AND COLLEGE | | | | | | COLLEGE ** | | | | | | | |
| | TOTAL MEMBER- | Military | | Law | | Medi- cine | | Military/ College | | Military/ Law | | Law and College | | Tech- nology | | Human- ities | | Social Sciences | | Economics | | Pure Science | |
CABINET *	SHIP	N	%	N	%	N	%	N	%	N	%	N	%	N	%	N	%	N	%	N	%	N	%
1. 7 September 1952	16	—	—	4	25.0	1	6.3	—	—	1	6.3	—	—	1	6.3	3	18.8	1	6.3	3	18.8	—	—
2. 8 December 1952	17	—	—	6	35.3	1	5.9	—	—	1	5.9	—	—	2	11.8	2	11.8	2	11.8	2	11.8	—	—
3. 18 June 1953	19	4	21.1	7	36.8	1	5.3	—	—	1	5.3	—	—	3	15.8	1	5.3	1	5.3	1	5.3	—	—
4. 4 October 1953	22	7	31.8	5	22.8	1	4.6	1	4.6	1	4.6	—	—	3	13.6	1	4.6	1	4.6	2	9.1	—	—
5. 17 April 1954	24	9	37.5	4	16.7	1	4.2	1	4.2	1	4.2	1	4.2	3	12.5	1	4.2	1	4.2	2	8.3	—	—
6. 1 September 1954	23	10	43.5	4	17.4	1	4.4	1	4.4	1	4.4	1	4.4	3	13.0	1	4.4	—	—	1	4.4	—	—
7. 30 June 1956	22	7	31.8	4	18.2	1	4.6	1	4.6	—	—	1	4.6	5	22.7	1	4.6	1	4.6	1	4.6	—	—
8. 5 March 1958	21	7	33.3	3	14.3	1	4.8	1	4.8	—	—	1	4.8	5	23.8	1	4.8	1	4.8	1	4.8	—	—
9. 7 October 1958	33	11	33.3	2	6.1	2	6.1	3	9.1	—	—	1	3.1	8	24.2	1	3.1	2	6.1	2	6.1	—	—
10. 17 August 1961	31	11	35.5	2	6.5	1	3.2	4	12.9	1	3.2	—	—	8	25.8	—	—	3	9.7	1	3.2	—	—
11. 19 October 1961	29	10	34.5	2	6.9	1	3.5	4	13.8	1	3.5	1	3.5	6	20.7	—	—	3	10.3	1	3.5	—	—
12. 29 September 1962	36	12	33.3	2	5.6	2	5.6	4	11.1	1	2.8	1	2.8	6	16.7	1	2.8	4	11.1	2	5.6	—	—
13. 24 March 1964	44	10	22.7	2	4.6	2	4.6	5	11.4	1	2.3	3	6.8	10	22.7	—	—	5	11.4	3	6.8	2	4.0
14. 2 October 1965	41	13	31.7	2	4.9	1	2.4	6	14.6	—	—	3	7.3	9	22.0	—	—	2	4.9	2	4.9	2	4.5
15. 10 September 1966	38	13	34.2	2	5.3	1	2.6	8	21.1	—	—	2	5.3	7	18.4	—	—	2	5.3	1	2.6	1	2.9
16. 19 June 1967	29	11	37.9	2	6.7	1	3.5	8	27.6	—	—	2	6.7	3	10.3	—	—	—	—	2	6.7	—	—
17. 20 March 1968	33	8	24.2	2	6.1	1	3.0	5	15.2	—	—	4	12.1	7	21.2	—	—	3	9.1	2	6.1	1	3.0
18. 28 October 1968	31	7	21.9	1	3.1	2	6.3	5	15.6	—	—	3	9.4	7	21.9	—	—	3	9.4	2	6.3	1	3.0
19. 21 October 1970 ***	33	8	24.2	3	9.1	2	6.1	5	15.2	—	—	1	3.0	8	24.2	—	—	2	6.1	2	6.1	1	3.1
20. 18 November 1970	33	6	18.2	5	15.2	3	9.1	5	15.2	—	—	2	6.1	6	18.2	—	—	2	6.1	2	6.1	1	3.0
21. 14 May 1971 ***	36	4	11.1	5	13.9	3	8.3	7	19.4	—	—	3	8.3	8	22.2	—	—	2	5.6	2	5.6	1	2.0
22. 21 September 1971 ***	36	9	25.0	2	5.6	—	—	6	16.7	—	—	3	8.3	6	16.7	—	—	2	5.6	2	5.6	1	2.8
23. 19 January 1972 ***	34	5	13.0	4	11.8	2	5.9	3	8.8	—	—	2	5.9	7	20.6	2	5.9	1	2.9	3	8.8	—	—

* Educational information on two cabinet officers is unavailable, as seen in cabinets number 1, 2, and 3. One cabinet officer had no college education; see cabinets number 12, 13, 14, and 15.

** The various college specializations are grouped into five fields. Technology includes engineering and agriculture. Pure sciences—botany, chemistry and physics. Humanities—literature, Islamic studies, fine arts, linguistics, philosophy, and journalism. Social sciences—political science, geography, history, sociology, educational psychology, education, and criminology. Economics—business, commerce, finance, and political economy.

*** This denotes cabinets on which educational information was unavailable for some ministers.

Educational Level

In cross-national studies of leaders it is striking to note the relatively high level of education that the political elite in certain developing countries possess. Preliminary investigations seem to show that the general educational level of cabinet leaders in a number of developing countries actually exceeds that of corresponding Western elites.[23] While the identification of the causal factors of this phenomenon fall outside the scope of this study, it seems that countries committed to rapid modernization feel a greater actual and psychological need for highly trained experts at the top. To a large extent this has been true for modern Egypt. As table 62 shows, only 3 out of 186 leaders lacked a college education. A more impressive fact is the unusually high number of those holding doctorates—over 46 percent. In other words there were almost as many doctorates as the BA's and MA's combined.

TABLE 62. *Egypt: Educational Level—Aggregate Count*

LEVEL	N	%
BA/BS	53	28.5
MA/MS	44	23.7
PhD/MD	86	46.2
No Information/No College Education	3	1.6
Total	186	

Data reflecting the fluctuations of educational level since 1952 are found in table 63. After a high of 31 percent in September 1952, the BA's decline sharply, displaced by doctorates in December 1952 and the entrance of military officers with MA's during 1953. The December 1952 cabinet marked an all-time high (over 70 percent) for doctorates. The year 1953 saw a progressive decline in doctorates as officers entered the cabinet. The low point for doctorates (30.4 percent) came in the September 1954 cabinet. This trend reversed sharply with the limited demilitarization of June 1956 and rose to over 42 percent in the joint UAR cabinets of 1958. After several fluctuations in the early sixties, the doctorates reached a high of 47.7 percent in the layered 1964 cabinet where they displaced officers with MA degrees. However, under the consolidated Muhyi al-Din cabinet, the doctorates dropped to 36.5

TABLE 63. *Egypt: Educational Level—*
*By Each Cabinet *

CABINET	TOTAL NUMBER	BACHELOR N	BACHELOR %	MASTER N	MASTER %	DOCTORATE N	DOCTORATE %	INDEX
1. 7 September 1952	16 **	5	31.3	2	12.5	8	50	3.2
2. 8 December 1952	17	4	23.5	1	5.9	12	70.6	3.5
3. 18 June 1953	19	3	15.8	5	26.3	11	57.9	3.4
4. 4 October 1953	22	3	13.6	8	36.4	11	50	3.4
5. 17 April 1954	24	5	20.8	10	41.6	9	37.5	3.2
6. 1 September 1954	23	6	26.1	10	43.4	7	30.4	3.0
7. 30 June 1956	22	5	22.7	8	36.4	9	40.9	3.2
8. 5 March 1958	21	5	23.8	7	33.3	9	42.9	3.2
9. 7 October 1958	33	8	24.2	11	33.3	14	42.4	3.5
10. 17 August 1961	31	8	25.8	10	32.2	13	41.9	3.2
11. 19 October 1961	29	6	20.6	10	34.4	13	44.7	3.2
12. 29 September 1962	36 ***	7	19.4	13	36	15	41.6	3.1
13. 24 March 1964	44 ***	10	22.7	12	27.2	21	47.7	3.2
14. 2 October 1965	41 ***	10	24.3	15	36.5	15	36.5	3.1
15. 10 September 1966	38 ***	11	28.9	14	36.8	12	31.6	2.9
16. 19 June 1967	29	7	24.1	13	44.7	9	31	3.1
17. 20 March 1968	33	7	21.2	9	27.3	17	51.5	3.2
18. 28 October 1968	31	7	21.8	8	25	16	53	3.5
19. 21 October 1970	33 ***	8	24.2	8	24.2	16	48.5	3.3
20. 18 November 1970	33 ***	8	24.2	8	24.2	16	48.5	3.3
21. 14 May 1971	36 ***	10	27.8	7	19.4	18	50.0	2.9
22. 21 September 1971	36 ***	7	19.4	4	11.1	14	38.9	2.3
23. 19 January 1972	34 ***	5	13.0	6	17.7	22	64.7	3.4

* The bachelor's level includes all BA and BS degrees, military academy, and licensates in law. The master's level includes all MA and MS degrees, staff college, and graduate diplomas from institutes. The doctorate level includes all PhD degrees and MD's.
** No information is available on one cabinet member.
*** One cabinet member serving in each of these cabinets did not have a college education.

percent while MA's went up almost 10 percentage points and the BA's 2 points. In the two cabinets preceeding and following the 1967 War, the doctorates again dropped (31.6 percent) as a large number of officers were brought in. Not until the March 1968 cabinet was this downward trend reversed. Responding to popular anti-military sentiments expressed in the February riots, Nasir brought into the cabinet 8 civilians holding doctorates. This brought the BA's down 3 points and MA's down 17 points while the doctorates rose to 51.5 percent. The upward trend in doctorates continued in the October 1968 reshuffle, reaching 53 percent, but still far short of the December 1952 cabinet. Under Sadat, the proportion of doctorates has fluctuated widely from 38.9 percent

(September 1971) to a high of 64.7 percent (January 1972). The overall educational index fluctuated between a high of 3.5 for the December 1952, October 1958, and October 1968 cabinets and a low of 2.3 for the September 1971 cabinet. While no major trend is discernible, it is clear that the educational index of Egyptian ministers is substantially higher than those of the Lebanese and the Israelis.

The desire for social respect and political mobility has resulted in a headlong quest for doctorates in the last decade that Haykal has characterized as a mockery. He described the situation as one in which "those with doctorates wanted political office, and those in political office wanted doctorates." [24] There are already signs pointing to an excess of PhD's in certain specializations. If this trend continues it could eventually put Egypt's PhD's, along with many of her lawyers, into the ranks of the unemployed.

Place of Study

Despite France's great cultural influence on Egypt, a larger number of leaders went to Britain and the United States to study. Ideologically, however, French influence, particularly that of the French left, seems to be greater than that of the US and Britain. Typically Britain and the US attracted those seeking technical specializations, while France attracted students of law and/or political economy.[25] Possibly because of the language problem, only 4 future leaders studied in Germany, while Italy and Austria claimed 1 each. As far as it is known only 1 of the 186 studied at a Soviet institution, the Frunze Military Academy. Almost surely this will increase in the next decade.

The largest share of higher education has been borne by Egyptian universities, especially at the bachelors and masters level and increasingly at the doctorate. In view of the high cost of foreign education, the ever more diverse offerings at Egypt's five universities, and the well-known reluctance of the foreign-educated to return to Egypt, one can anticipate a sharp decrease in the number of those studying abroad. Despite the obvious benefits, any significant curtailment of foreign study will tend to push the country's higher education into intellectual isolation and stagnation. The

TABLE 64. *Egypt: Educational Institution and Country—Number of Degrees* *

FRANCE		EGYPT		BRITAIN		UNITED STATES		MISCELLANEOUS	
17		292		28		21		7	
Montpelier	1	Ain Shams	1	Birmingham	3	Chicago	1	Germany	4
Paris	16	Azhar	3	Cambridge	4	Columbia	3	Rome	1
		Cairo	102	Durham	1	Harvard	4	Vienna	1
		Military Academy	50	Edinburgh	4	Illinois	1	Russia	1
		Staff College	39	Leeds	1	M.I.T.	1		
		Alexandria University	2	Liverpool	3	Ohio	1		
		Police Academy	2	London	6	Oregon	1		
		Textiles Institute	1	London School		Stanford	1		
				of Economics	1	Syracuse	1		
				Manchester	3	University of			
				Oxford	1	California	5		
				Military School	1	University of Penn	1		
						Wisconsin 1			

* This breakdown of the number of degrees (bachelors, masters, and doctorates) represents only those which were positively identified. In certain cases, it was impossible to identify the institution granting the degree.

foreign education of 62 [26] out of the 186 leaders can be taken as an index of their foreign exposure; this number will inevitably decrease as educationally home-grown leaders replace them. The result will be a narrowing of the elite's world view—a development already observable among the officers and officer-technocrats, most of whom are locally educated.

Cursus Honorum or Pathways to Power

To determine the different avenues potential leaders take to reach the top requires systematic data on the career patterns of each leader. The crucial starting point for a leader's march to the top is original occupation. A total of ten occupational sources are identified on table 65 and illustrated in the diagrammatical representations of charts 19 through 28 (see appendix). The largest group is, of course, the military with some 60 persons, or 32.3 percent of the entire elite (see chart 19, appendix). Virtually all of these men, including the officer-technocrats, were associated with the coup of July 1952. However, their paths to the cabinet differed considerably depending on their original positions in the Free Officers movement and their personal relationship with Nasir, to mention two of the more important determinants. With Nagib and Nasir leading the way in 1952 and 1953, eventually 16 of the officers entered the cabinet directly from the armed forces. Most of

TABLE 65. *Egypt: Occupational Sources of Recruitment— Aggregate Count*

OCCUPATION	N	%
Military	60	32.3
Academia	41	22.0
Engineering	25	13.4
Law	23	12.4
Bureaucracy	15	8.1
Business-Professional	7	3.8
Police	2	1.1
Diplomacy	4	2.2
Medicine	4	2.2
Journalism	1	0.5
Unknown	4	2.2
Total	186	

these were leading members of the Free Officers and the RCC. A second contingent of lesser known officers went from the military into various bureaucracies—ministerial, presidential, provincial, managerial—for the express purpose of establishing the regime's control over them. Of the 21 officers who entered the bureaucracy directly, 9 went to the cabinet without holding intervening posts.

The diplomatic corps possessed a special attraction for the officers; 7 went directly from the military into ambassadorial and related foreign posts, 2 more reached there after holding a bureaucratic job. While at least 5 officers were deputies at various times before assuming cabinet office, 2 officers went directly into the National Assembly. Finally, there were those military men who passed through the intelligence services. The lack of data on this aspect of political life makes it difficult to differentiate between intelligence activity in the military context and that pursued in the presidential bureaucracy. One suspects that the two often overlapped organizationally. Whatever the case, 7 officers were involved in intelligence work as their first job and another 6 served in intelligence at some time prior to entering cabinet positions—making a total of 13. These findings point to the prominent position of former intelligence men in the government, as well as the regime's obsessive concern with its own security. Taken together with other information, the high proportion of former intelligence operatives manifests the military elite's conspiratorial mentality and paranoia, which was periodically reinforced by Israeli and Western attempts to overthrow the regime.

Less visible than the cabinet, the leaders of the party, or the army, the presidential bureaucracy was always a primary center of power in the political system by virtue of its closeness to Nasir himself. It is significant that as a path to cabinet office the presidential bureaucracy has been used exclusively by those with military backgrounds. Only 1 civilian—Aziz Sidqi—retired to the presidential bureaucracy between cabinet offices. All 17 who passed through the presidency on the way to cabinet office were former officers. Representing over 28 percent of the 60 ex-officers in the cabinet, the presidential bureaucracy has provided a main channel of upward movement for the military elite.

In addition to fulfilling control and supervisory functions, the officers in the various bureaucracies familiarized themselves with the administrative skills they sorely lacked. In this sense the bureaucracies provided the RCC and other officers with what J. C. Hurewitz calls their "political apprenticeship" [27] before cabinet office; a total of 28 served in bureaucracies before entering the cabinet, 14 of whom were officer-technocrats. Finally, at least 24 out of 60 officers have been associated with party organization or legislative work (ASU, National Union, and National Assembly), some on a full-time basis.

The second largest occupational source of elite recruitment is academia (see chart 20, appendix). This classification includes university professors, deans and rectors of colleges and universities, and heads of other top-level academic institutes. Lower-level teachers and military instructors were excluded from this classification.

There have been no less than 41 academics, constituting 22 percent of the total cabinet membership since September 1952. Their numerical position, second only to the military (see table 65), indicates the regime's reliance on competent civilian experts. While relatively scarce in the early years of military rule, the number of recruitable academics greatly increased during the early sixties as a growing number returned from Western institutions. The potentialities of the academic road to the top generated not only a rush to acquire PhD's but also, as Haykal pointed out, "every PhD wanted to enter the cabinet." However, many of the PhD's lacked visibility; they could not be recruited unless noticed by the men at the top. Most academic recruits have come from the upper reaches of the university hierarchy—rectors, deans, department chairmen, institute heads, and full professors.

Chart 20 shows the different pathways academics have taken to reach the cabinet. About 19 went directly into the cabinet from positions in academia. The remaining 22 took the bureaucratic route; 13 went to the ministerial bureaucracy, 3 joined the public-sector organisms, and 3 became diplomats.

The third largest source of leaders was the engineering profession (25), representing 13.4 percent of total cabinet members (see chart 21, appendix). None of the engineers went directly to the cabinet, in contrast to a large portion of the academics. For 16 the first step was either the ministerial or the public sector bureaucracies. The remaining 9 entered academia; from there 2 went di-

directly to cabinet while 6 others had to enter the various bureaucracies first. Thus for 16 of the 19 professional engineers the bureaucracies were stepping stones to the top.

Law constituted the fourth largest category with 23 members, or 12.4 percent of the total. As one would expect, a large number (11) served in the judiciary at some point prior to cabinet office (see chart 22, appendix). Others used diplomatic service, party organization, academia, ministerial bureaucracy, or a combination of these as stepping stones to the top. Again the relative scarcity of lawyers may reflect the incongruity of the legal profession with a military revolutionary milieu.

With 15 members (8.1 percent), the ministerial bureaucracy is the fifth largest recruitment source. These are the professional bureaucrats who worked up the ladder to the undersecretary positions and went from there into the cabinet. As long-time servants in the bureaucratic apparatus, these ministers knew, more than anyone else, the intricacies of bureaucratic life—a type of knowledge that proved useful for the ruling officers. Since 16 of the engineer category entered the bureaucracy prior to the cabinet and remained there for long periods of time, one might also count them as bureaucrat, which would swell the bureaucratic component to 26, or 19 percent, of the total (see charts 21 and 23, appendix).

The remaining occupational categories of medicine, journalism, business-professional, police, and diplomatic corps accounted for 9.8 percent of the total leadership. The business-professional group of 7 consisted mostly of businessmen who had been active in the early years of the revolution (see chart 28, appendix). Despite the advent of socialism, several of these men continued to serve the regime well into the seventies.

Overall, the number of leaders going from original occupation directly to cabinet was very high—44 or approximately 23.7 percent. Of the remaining, 98 passed through one or more of the bureaucracies prior to cabinet office. Thus for over 50 percent of the elite, bureaucracy was one of the main occupational gateways to the top.

Table 66 presents a breakdown by cabinet of elite recruitment sources. The fluctuating proportions of the military found in column 1 are exactly the same as those found in column 4 on Table 57 which shows background characteristics. The ministerial bu-

TABLE 66. *Egypt: Original Occupational Sources of Recruitment by Cabinet*

CABINET	MILITARY		BUREAUCRACY		BUSINESS-PROFESSIONAL		LAW		ACADEMIA		DIPLOMACY		ENGINEERING		POLICE		TOTAL
	N	%	N	%	N	%	N	%	N	%	N	%	N	%	N	%	
7 September 1952	1	6.3	3	18.8	3	18.8	4	25	3	18.8	2	12.5	—	—	—	—	16
8 December 1952	1	5.9	3	17.7	1	5.9	5	29.4	4	23.5	2	11.8	1	5.9	—	—	17
18 June 1953	5	26.3	2	10.5	1	5.3	5	26.3	3	15.8	1	5.3	2	10.5	—	—	19
4 October 1953	9	40.9	1	4.6	2	9.1	4	18.2	3	136	1	4.6	2	9.1	—	—	22
17 April 1954	11	45.8	1	4.2	2	8.3	4	16.7	2	12.5	1	4.2	2	8.3	—	—	24
1 September 1954	12	52.2	1	4.4	1	4.4	4	17.4	3	8.7	1	4.4	2	8.7	—	—	23
30 June 1956	8	36.4	1	4.6	2	9.1	4	18.2	4	13.6	1	4.6	3	13.6	—	—	22
5 March 1958	8	38.1	—	—	2	9.5	3	14.3	7	19.1	1	4.8	3	14.3	—	—	21
7 October 1958	16	48.5	1	3	2	6.1	2	6.1	7	21.2	1	3	4	12.1	—	—	33
17 August 1961	16	51.6	1	3.2	2	6.5	1	3.2	5	16.1	1	3.2	5	16.1	—	—	31
19 October 1961	15	51.6	1	3.5	1	3.5	1	3.5	6	20.7	1	3.5	4	13.8	—	—	29
29 September 1962	17	47.2	3	8.3	2	5.6	1	2.8	7	19.4	1	2.8	4	11.1	1	2.8	36
24 March 1964	16	36.4	2	4.6	2	4.6	3	6.8	10	22.7	1	2.3	9	20.5	1	2.3	44
2 October 1965	19	46.3	2	4.9	1	2.4	2	4.9	7	17.1	1	2.4	8	19.5	1	2.4	41
10 September 1966	21	55.3	2	5.3	1	2.6	2	5.3	3	7.9	1	2.6	7	18.4	1	2.6	38
19 June 1967	19	65.5	—	—	2	6.9	1	3.5	4	13.8	1	3.5	2	6.9	—	—	29
20 March 1968	13	39.4	2	6.1	2	6.1	2	6.1	9	27.3	1	3.0	4	12.1	—	—	33
28 October 1968	13	41.9	2	6.5	1	3.2	2	6.5	9	29	—	—	4	12.9	—	—	31
21 October 1970 *	13	39.4	1	3.0	1	3.0	1	3.0	8	24.2	2	6.1	5	15.2	—	—	33
18 November 1970	11	33.3	3	9.1	1	3.0	3	9.1	8	24.2	2	6.1	3	9.1	—	—	33
14 May 1971	11	30.7	3	8.3	1	2.8	3	8.3	11	30.7	2	5.6	2	5.6	—	—	36
20 September 1971	15	41.7	4	11.1	1	2.8	1	2.8	9	25.0	2	5.6	3	38.3	—	—	36
19 January 1972 *	8	23.5	4	11.8	—	—	3	8.8	10	29.4	1	2.9	4	11.8	—	—	34

* Denotes that information on 1 and 3 individuals, respectively, is not available.

reaucracy registered a decrease as a recruitment source from October 1953 to September 1962 when an upturn took place. After a drop in December 1952, the business-professional group fluctuated between 1 or 2 members until the seventies. The legal profession registered a high 29.4 percent in December 1952, after which it began a fluctuating decline to an all-time low of 2.8 percent in September 1962; there were additional fluctuations after the upturn of March 1964, but the percentage of lawyers has remained below 10 percent in recent years. This reinforces earlier conclusions about the general decline of the legal profession in the political system. After a brief appearance from 1962 to 1966 the police category disappears, as does the diplomatic service.

The two categories that have shown gains since 1952 were academia and engineering. From 18.8 percent in September 1952, the academic component increased to a high of 23.5 percent by the end of the year. The successive declines that began in October 1953 and reached a low of 8.7 percent in September 1954 were a result of the growing military presence in the cabinet. In 1956 the proportion of academics began an upward trend which reached 21.2 percent in October 1958. After several fluctuations, there was a sharp drop in 1965 and an all-time low in the Muhyi al-Din cabinet of September 1966. Since the June War, the proportion of academics successively increased, reaching 30.7 percent, an all-time high, in May 1971.

Engineering as an original source of recruitment increased through March 1958 and after fluctuations reached a high of 20.5 percent in March 1964. Finally, after sharp declines in June 1967 and May 1971, the engineering component reached an all-time high of 38.3 percent in September 1971.

Disposition

A breakdown of post-cabinet disposition of the Egyptian political elite is presented in table 67. Taking January 1970 as cut-off date for the pre-Sadat period, 31, or 23.7 percent of the total, were still in cabinet office. Of the rest, the largest group (22) had retired from both cabinet and political office. The second largest group

TABLE 67.   *Egypt: Immediate Disposition* *

	N	%
Still Serving in Office	31	23.7
Diplomacy	11	8.4
Bureaucracy-United Nations	3	2.3
Bureaucracy-Organizational	13	9.9
Bureaucracy-Ministerial	2	1.6
Bureaucracy-Presidential	2	1.6
Law	3	2.3
Judiciary	1	0.8
Academia	12	9.2
Party	10	7.6
National Assembly	3	2.3
Retired	22	16.8
Purge	7	5.3
Deceased	1	0.8
Unknown	10	7.6

* The table includes only the 131 ministers of the Nasirite period (1952–1970).

(13) went to the bureaucracies of the various public organizations, usually as chairmen or as other top officials.

Another major depository of the ministerial elite was academia—consisting of a group of 12 ministers that had been originally recruited from the universities. The party has provided still another repository. Acquiring a party post after cabinet office is generally considered a demotion, with the possible exception of the ASU Supreme Executive.

The postcabinet status of 10 ministers could not be ascertained. There were 7 clear-cut cases of purge, where the cabinet member was known to have fallen out with the leadership and been dismissed from the cabinet. However, the actual number of those purged was certainly larger, since the real reasons for an individual's retirement were often not made public. Thus, many placed in the retired category may have actually been purged.

A particularly attractive and desirable postcabinet position was the diplomatic corps where 11 ministers settled. The presidential and the ministerial bureaucracies each claimed 2 ministers and private legal practice claimed another 3. Three others received high posts in the United Nations, 3 became deputies, 1 entered the judiciary, and 1 died soon after leaving the cabinet.

Comparing disposition to original occupational category reveals a number of interesting findings. For example, although the military enjoyed many privileges, it suffered the highest number purged—probably exceeding the 7 indicated on table 67. In terms of ultimate disposition (table 68), as of January 1969, at least 9 of the 11 purged were former officers. Other postcabinet positions taken by officers included diplomatic corps (4) and party posts (6). Indeed the party possessed a certain attraction for the military generally; at various times during their political careers 21 of the ex-officer ministers had been involved in ASU activity. In addition, 9 of the officers at some point were elected as assembly deputies. While 9 of the 30 academics returned to the universities after cabinet office, as far as known, not a single officer returned to active military service.

TABLE 68. *Egypt: Ultimate Disposition* *

	N	%
Still Serving in Office	31	23.7
Diplomacy	5	3.8
Bureaucracy-United Nations	4	3.1
Bureaucracy-Organizational	9	6.9
Bureaucracy-Ministerial	1	0.8
Bureaucracy-Presidential	2	1.6
Law	2	1.6
Academia	11	8.9
Party	12	9.2
Retired	27	20.6
Purge	11	8.4
Deceased	6	4.6
Unknown	10	7.6

* The table includes only the 131 ministers of the Nasirite period (1952–1970).

In terms of ultimate disposition, 27 ministers retired, 12 became party officials, 11 went to academia, 6 died, 5 went into diplomatic service, 2 reverted to law, and a total of 16 were serving in the various bureaucracies (table 68). The total picture shows a greater degree of elite stability than is characteristic of other revolutionary situations. In a great many cases outright purge was apparently replaced by demotion to a lesser post. It seems that unless a cabinet officer directly challenged the leadership, he was guaranteed government positions until retirement. Obviously the net effect of such a policy would be circulation of the same leaders in the top eche-

TABLE 69.   *Egypt: Positions Held Between Cabinet Offices*

	FIRST INTER-CABINET POST	SECOND INTER-CABINET POST
National Assembly	1	
National Assembly-party		1
Party	2	
Diplomatic Corps	1	
Military	1	
Bureaucracy-Organizational	5	1
Bureaucracy-Presidential	1	
Retired	2	

lons of government, party, public enterprises, and academia, thereby restricting the infusion of new blood. While the available data does not indicate a closed system, Haykal's lament on the need for new leadership has considerable relevance.

For the 13 ministers who held cabinet positions more than once, the bureaucracies and the party provided between-cabinet jobs, as table 69 shows. Two others retired between their first and second cabinet jobs, one returned to the military and another took a diplomatic post. A large majority (66.4 percent) occupied only a single post. Another 19.1 percent occupied two different cabinet posts. As table 70 shows, there were 7 ministers who held as many as four different cabinet positions, and 2 who occupied five different posts. The last two groups included some of the top RCC members as well as certain of their long-time civilian collaborators.

Of the 13 ministers who held ministerial positions more than once, 7 were originally officers—another measure of the military's influence in the system. Of the rest, 3 were academics, 1 was an engineer, 1 a businessman, and 1 a lawyer. There was no circula-

TABLE 70.   *Egypt: Number of Different Ministerial Positions Held*

N OF POSTS	N OF OFFICIALS	%
1	87	66.4
2	25	19.1
3	10	7.6
4	7	5.3
5	2	1.5

tion between the military and the academic groups, since the officers could teach only in military colleges and not in any of the major universities. On the other hand there was considerable circulation between academia and the bureaucracies; as many as 17 academics had held bureaucratic posts either before or after cabinet office. Finally, 32 percent of the ministers held high party posts concurrently with ministerial positions, an indication of the extensive linkage between the top echelons of the ASU and the government. It also reflects the degree to which the ASU relied on the government, which corroborates some of the criticism made in the press during the late sixties.

Regional Affiliation and Religion

The study of regional affiliation—a leader's identification with an area by virtue of residence, occupation, or birth—does not yield any great surprises. As table 71 indicates, about one-fourth of the 122 leaders on whom data was available came from the Cairo region. Given the traditional centrality of the capital and its dominance in all aspects of Egyptian life, one would expect Caireens to constitute a large portion of the Egyptian elite. The second largest urban center, Alexandria, accounted for about 11 percent, with Daqahliyyah, Asyut, Shariqyyah, Gharbiyyah, and Manufiyyah each contributing about 6 percent. It should be noted that in a highly centralized political system such as Egypt's, regional identification does not play an important role. The significant finding is the predominance of Cairo, thereby illustrating one of the leadership's concerns—how to limit the number of over-eager Caireens in government and party leadership posts and simultaneously prepare provincial leaders to assume a larger share of political responsibility and activity.

As an important political variable, religion applies mainly to the Coptic Christian minority in this predominantly Muslim society. While it is somewhat difficult to ascertain the size of the Coptic community, it is safe to assume that it is above 5 million, about one-sixth of the total population. After historically enjoying a disproportionately large presence in Egyptian political life, the Coptic influence had been somewhat reduced by the time of the revolu-

TABLE 71. *Egypt: Regional Affiliation* *

PROVINCE	NUMBER	PERCENTAGE
Alexandria	20	10.8
Assyut	6	3.2
Aswan	1	0.5
Bani Suayf	2	1.1
Buhayrah	2	1.1
Cairo	35	18.8
Daqahliyyah	14	7.5
Dumyat	4	2.2
Fayyum	2	1.1
Gharbiyyah	8	4.4
Giza	3	1.6
Isma'iliyyah	1	0.5
Kafr al-Shaykh	2	1.1
Manufiyyah	6	3.2
Minyah	2	1.1
Port Said	1	0.5
Qalyubiyyah	3	1.6
Red Sea	1	0.5
Sharqiyyah	6	3.2
Sudan	4	2.2
Suhag	2	1.1
Total	122	
Unknowns	64	34.4

* Regional affiliation—a general category that denotes an individual's identification with an area by virtue of residence, occupation, and/or birth.

tion. Since September 1952 the revolutionary regime has maintained the practice of appointing at least one Coptic minister per cabinet; when multilevel cabinets were instituted after March 1964, two additional Coptic members were brought in as deputy ministers (see table 57). This practice continued until the June 1967 cabinet. Since the 1967 War the government has attempted to strengthen the Copts' sense of identification with the regime as a part of a general program to broaden the national consensus during a time of external peril. It is also possible that the government's more amicable attitude was partially prompted by the desire to acquire world Christian support against Israel. Two manifestations of renewed official attention were the prominent role the regime assumed in the building and consecration ceremonies of the new Saint Mark's Cathedral in mid-1968 and the favorable press coverage of the apparition of Virgin Mary in the same year. At the leadership level, the Coptic ex-minister Dr. Kamal Ramzi Stino was elected as one of the eight members of the ASU Supreme Executive Committee. President Sadat has had to redouble the government's efforts to reassure the Coptic community in the wake of Coptic-Muslim disturbances beginning in 1971.

Ideology

Ideological identification among cabinet and higher-level Egyptian leaders presents a number of major difficulties, particularly since the regime has undergone several ideological changes. Also there is a paucity of information on the ideological orientations of a considerable number of leaders. At the most general level both the officer and civilian components of the elite had a primary commitment to Egyptian nationalism. One can further discern leftist and rightist tendencies among the elite from their close association with the Brethren, the Wafd, the Left, Misr al-Fatat, or the Ruwwad. After the 1954 power struggles and Nasir's emergence, official identification with any of the above groups and ideologies was rejected in favor of commitment to pure Egyptian nationalism and after 1955 to Pan-Arabism. Those sympathizing with the outlawed political groups and their ideologies were either purged or reoriented themselves in keeping with the new political line. With the leftward evolution of the system in the late fifties and the official adoption of socialism in 1961, the elite ostensibly identified itself with the new ideological framework. There is no way of knowing the extent of each leader's commitment to the new faith; however, an attempt has been made to discern the ideological orientation of individual leaders through content analyses of their pronouncements, bits of circumstantial evidence derived from their policies, and press commentaries.[28] The major shortcoming of this approach was that a number of leaders made few ideologically oriented pronouncements. This contingent was labeled "tacit leftist," since they operate within the general limits of the official ideology without manifesting strong leftist or rightist doctrinal views.

After the suppression of the Brethren and the rest of the Egyptian political right, only the left-of-center range of the ideological spectrum remained operational. Since by definition there could be no right, the common identification of ex-Premier Muhyi al-Din as a rightist in the Western press is incorrect. He is here labeled ''conservative-leftist,'' as are others who advocate a conservative to moderate and flexible approach to socialism internally, coupled with a generally more accommodating attitude toward the West.

The third ideological grouping one may label ''vocal leftist.'' These are reputed to be more doctrinaire socialists; their rhetoric contains a heavy dose of socialist terminology. To be sure they are less evident in the cabinet than in the ASU and the press and one should remember that being vocal in socialist jargon does not automatically mean a deep commitment to socialist ideology. Also it is possible that some committed leftists exist in the large tacit-left grouping, but it is difficult to identify them positively because they have refrained from making ideological pronouncements. A number of these were purged from the government following Ali Sabri's abortive coup d'etat in May 1971.

Since by definition this ideological classification applies only to cabinet leaders since the breakup of the UAR, there are only a total of 94 ministers considered here. Of these, 70 belonged to the tacit left, 16 were conservative leftists, and 8 vocal leftists. The tacit left is by far the largest category; it includes many of the officer-technocrats, engineers, and professionals. The 2-to-1 numerical strength of the conservative left over the vocal left may be a valid index of leftist weakness in the cabinet. Further evidence of the left's weakness could be found in the dismissal of communists from both the cabinet and the ASU in 1973.

The Class Base

In discussing the impact of childhood environment on socialization, it was observed that many among the elite were born during the urbanization process, either just prior to the family's leaving the village or just after settling in the big city.[29] The fundamental variable is not where the child was born but the fact that he was born in the midst of an urbanizing environment.

The crisis which urbanization commonly generates is well documented cross-nationally. This study proposes to view urbanization in the Egyptian milieu as a breaking away from one class in the attempt to attach oneself to another; that is, the abandonment of the rural, lower-middle-, middle-class life in quest of a relatively more modern and more affluent urban lower-middle, middle-class existence. While some families were able to gain the desired upward mobility, many more simply became the city lower-class—the urban proletariat.

The children of newly urbanizing families were born in a milieu of crisis—ambivalent class consciousness, mixed loyalties, alienation, and marginality. These families were aspiring for upward mobility, and since only a few achieved it, the unsuccessful were left bitter and frustrated. It is within this context that class background should be analyzed.

In terms of both definition and data collection, studying the socioeconomic backgrounds of leaders presents major difficulties, especially in the Egyptian context. The notion of middle-class predominance in the elite may be somewhat exaggerated. Certain of the leaders came from families who could be classified as upper class by virtue of their wealth and social prestige. A well-known example is the late Field Marshall Amir, whose family's wealth (landowners) and social prestige could not possibly be labeled as middle class. Other upper-class leaders include Ukasha and the Sabri brothers. At the other extreme are a small number who came from poor rural and urban families. While the whole question of socio-economic background as it relates to Egypt needs thorough reexamination and reformulation, what is presented here are some tentative conclusions based on incomplete data. Approximately 32 percent of the leaders came from upper/upper-middle-class families; 45 percent had middle-class backgrounds and about 10 percent came from lower-class origins. Class backgrounds on 15 percent of the leaders could not be determined.

A great deal has been written about the rural middle-class background of the Egyptian military; of particular note are the studies of Eliezer Beeri [30] and Leonard Binder. [31] However, the full sociopolitical significance of the military's rural middle-class connection remains somewhat obscure. The relevant question in the present context is whether class loyalties persist among the top leadership, especially the former officers. Often one is given the impression by Egyptians that the rural connection has greatly withered and is not too significant politically, although verification of this by field research has not as yet been done.

Political Opportunity

On the basis of the foregoing analysis, one may identify a number of prerequisite conditions or operating standards for admission into the political elite. First, political opportunity depends on the frequency with which cabinet positions become vacant. In contrast to the United States, where cabinet positions are usually filled every four or eight years, the Egyptian system shows no such regularity. Instead, cabinet changes or reshuffles have coincided with internal or external developments, e.g., the Nagib-Nasir contest, the formation and dissolution of the UAR, economic problems, the June War, and internal instability (student riot of February 1968). But the lack of regular turnover did not appreciably reduce the frequency of vacancies in the past. However, since changeover has mostly depended on the occurrence of instability and crisis, the future availability of cabinet positions may also depend on these factors.

The other factor that affects opportunity is size of the cabinet. In Egypt cabinet size grew from 16 members to 24 between September 1952 and April 1954. In the next four years it declined to 21, but the second UAR cabinet reached a high of 33. The March 1964 multilevel cabinet of 44 members marked the peak in cabinet size; since then, the size has decreased through successive reorganization schemes. In the last two years, cabinet size has remained around 34 (see table 61). It is not likely to become much smaller.

A cluster of social, economic, and political factors affect the political opportunity of aspiring individuals. In Egypt, as in all political systems, political reliability constitutes the most important prerequisite for cabinet appointment. Political reliability used to mean loyalty to the person of Nasir and firm adherence to the revolution's goals as he delimited them. For civilian aspirants, a lack of political-ideological coloration has usually been a requisite. In the fifties, most civilians recruited were specialists, not politicians. The few who were politicians before the revolution—Tarraf, F.

Rudwan—soon became manifestly unpolitical as servants of the new order. The practice of recruiting apolitical civilian experts continued in the sixties. More recently, in addition to political reliability and expertise, other political considerations have emerged. One is the cabinet member's role as the representative of various interest groups—economic, functional, religious, social. This has applied to the Coptic leaders since pre-revolutionary days and the ex-officer ministers are seen as representatives of the military establishment. Because of a restive student constituency, the role of popular professors in the cabinet is no less important. Nasir, for instance, selected several prominent professors for his March 1968 cabinet. Other constituency-determined appointments included the ministers of agriculture (S. Mar'i) and labor (A. Salamah; K. Rif'at). While he may have been given a cabinet post by virtue of being an ex-Free Officer, Rif'at's appointment as minister of labor may also have been prompted by his close association with workers.

There are also socio-economic standards of eligibility. Though most individuals of the landowning and capitalist-entrepreneurial classes have been excluded since the early sixties, wealth has not constituted an impediment to high office in certain cases (Amir, Zaki). Nevertheless, considering the leftward drift of the political system until Nasir's death, one would have expected most future recruits to come from the middle class and perhaps from the activist elements of the urban and rural lower-middle classes—i.e., peasants and workers; however this does not seem to have been the case. In view of the changes since June 1967, previous membership in the military, even as a former Free Officer, may not determine eligibility, as it did previously.

A number of new admission standards may be emerging under Sadat. After the ASU purge of 1971, political reliability remains a major criterion along with a more centrist ideological orientation than was the case under Nasir. If the regime continues to move in a pro-Western and nonsocialist direction, it is possible that a larger number of upper-middle-class and upper-class businessmen and lawyers may enter the cabinet. Finally with the aging of the present leadership and the ferment among the students, youth may become a requisite for eligibility.

Political Cost

The rewards and deprivations that accompany entrance to and exit from cabinet positions are commonly referred to as political cost. As this cost is intimately tied to a society's values, cross-national analysis must consider the different value systems of the societies to be compared. To evaluate political cost comparatively one needs information on such variables as income, social prestige, political power, and personal risk, as they relate to the particular political system. For example, in the United States, acquiring a cabinet position often means a considerable loss of income, whereas cabinet office in Egypt usually means a higher income, since most cabinet officials come from lower salaried positions. Conversely, leaving the cabinet would certainly mean a loss of income in Egypt, while in the United States the result is often a large net-income gain from lucrative nongovernmental positions. In both countries, a cabinet member derives great social prestige from his office, although as in Lebanon and Israel, he probably has greater status in Egypt than in the United States. Unless expressly fired, an American secretary's loss of office is not nearly so serious a blow to his prestige as it can be to the Egyptian, except for those retiring. It appears that the only way for a minister to leave the cabinet without losing prestige would be promotion to the presidency, vice presidency, or some other high position.

Finally, political cost involves an element of personal and/or political risk. In contrast to West European countries or Lebanon, Egyptian cabinet officials cannot easily move into a variety of nongovernmental positions outside the state's influence. The contrast is even greater for ministers purged for opposing the leader's policy. In Israel, Lebanon, and the United States, such opposition may bring dismissal or resignation; a politically vulnerable president or prime minister may even tolerate a recalcitrant cabinet member. However, in Egypt, explicit opposition would usually result in purge—a process that entails high personal as well as political risks. The only known case of Nasir temporarily tolerating opposition is that of Marshall Amir until his dismissal after the June War and subsequent house arrest and death.

The Transfer of Power

Despite the great shock of President Nasir's death, the transfer of power was swift and orderly. The elite did not lose its cohesiveness, at least not initially. In accordance with Egypt's provisional constitution, Vice President Anwar al-Sadat became acting president until elections could be held. His long association with Nasir, no less than his position as vice president, were instrumental in according Sadat the initial legitimacy that new rulers usually lack. The legitimacy transfer was completed when over six million Egyptians elected Sadat with 85 percent of the vote on 15 October 1970. Although this fell short of Nasir's usual 99.5 percent tally, it still constituted a strong endorsement for his successor.

The new president's twin themes were to maintain revolutionary continuity and to pursue the struggle against Israel. Initially, Sadat did little that would signal a departure from Nasirite precedents. His first cabinet (October 1970) consisted mostly of carryovers from Nasir's last government with the major exception of Muhammad Hasanayn Haykal, who resigned as minister of National Guidance and returned to the full-time editorship of *Al-Ahram*. An unexpected development was the appointment of ex-Foreign Minister Dr. Mahmud Fawzi as premier and presidential advisor. This, coupled with Abd al-Muhsin Abu al-Nur's appointment as ASU secretary general, indicated that Sadat was reluctant to keep supreme control of both party (secretary general) and government (premier), as was Nasir's practice. Sadat's action represented a substantial redistribution of power; it also meant a major delegation of responsibility to a collective leadership which included not only Sadat and Fawzi but the remaining five members of the ASU Supreme Executive, two of whom—Ali Sabri and Husayn al-Shafi'i—were also vice presidents. All of this seemed natural, since Sadat could not became a Nasir overnight; he had to share power with other lieutenants of Nasir. In such a context, Sadat was no more than first among equals. Even after his election as ASU president by the National Congress on 12 November 1970, Sadat's position in the party remained tenuous, as later developments indicated.

The choice of Dr. Fawzi, Egypt's first civilian premier since September 1952, indicated special governmental concern with domestic problems. Fawzi viewed the internal front as reinforcing the fighting front; clearly the new government had a duty to assure domestic stability before the inevitable diplomatic and/or military showdown with Israel. The cabinet decreed a reduction in prices of basic consumer items including tea, sugar, paraffin, radios, refrigerators, pullovers, and blankets. On 18 November 1970, Dr. Fawzi formed a new cabinet for the stated purpose of increasing internal effectiveness and cooperation at a time of external peril. The premier emphasized the need for reforms in health, education, and politics—what he called the "evolution toward democracy."

In structure, the November 1970 cabinet resembled the layered cabinets Abd al-Nasir had often employed in the sixties. This system grouped various ministries into sectors headed by four deputy prime ministers. All service ministries were gathered in one sector; agricultural production, foreign affairs, and general industrial development formed the other three sectors. Within these sectors, the separate ministries would operate on a day-to-day basis under their own minister, while the deputy prime minister would be left free to concentrate on general policy affecting the whole sector.

The Passing of an Elite

Less than a year after Nasir's death his successors were in great disagreement and disarray. Despite his popular election, Sadat was not master of his house. As *primus inter pares* he had to share substantial power with his colleagues in the ASU Supreme Executive Committee. In April 1971, Ali Sabri and his majority faction in the SEC challenged Sadat's federation scheme with Libya and Syria; finally the power struggle had been joined. On his side Sabri had the ASU's political apparatus and almost all the major personalities of the regime including War Minister General Muhammad Fawzi and Interior Minister Sha'rawi Guma'a. Witnessing the strength of his opposition in the ASU, Sadat moved decisively to marshall support from a number of sources—the military, the security services, and the masses. Sabri's resignation on 2 May, just two days before Secretary of State Roger's arrival, may have been designed to provoke a governmental crisis that would lead to Sadat's resignation or subject him to ASU control. Eventually the other members of the Sabri faction did tender their resignations (13 May), but their undecisiveness, timidity, and lack of army and popular support all combined to assure their downfall. Sadat moved quickly to consolidate his power by appointing trusted aides to key posts.

A total of 91 officials were brought to trial in August and September 1971; most received jail sentences and a few were acquitted. In addition to high treason, the defendants were charged with rigging elections and running a police state. New elections were ordered for the ASU and the National Assembly, secret police tapes were publicly burned, and Sadat pledged an atmosphere of "full liberty and democracy." On 1 September 1971, after an endorsement referendum, Egypt joined Libya and Syria in the Federation of Arab Republics and Sadat renamed his country the Egyptian Arab Republic. However, due to policy and personality differences between Sadat and Qaddafi, the Federation was stillborn.

After his spectacular victory in May 1971, Sadat was no longer first among equals. While very successful in preserving his power, he had also increased his responsibilities, especially in dealing with Israel. In the very process of power struggle, however, Sadat had substantially changed the composition of the leadership—an elite which had had wide influence in Egypt and the Arab world. For the most part the core of this elite had included second- and third-string Free Officers and officer-technocrats, all of whom had served in the presidency under Nasir. Sabri himself, ambitious, intelligent, unscrupulous, was the first of these men to emerge from the shadows of the presidential bureaucracy after the mid-fifties and assume top positions. Others included Abd al-Muhsin Abu al-Nur, Sha'rawi Guma'a, Sami Sharaf, Muhammad Fa'iq, Hilmi al-Sa'id, Sa'ad al-Din Zayid, Ahmad Kamil, Amin al-Huwaydi, and Kamal Badir. These men had wielded substantial power— economic, political, organizational, military—from their privileged sanctuaries at the presidency. Most of them were willing to serve Nasir and no one else. As the power brokers of the Nasirite era, it was difficult for them to accommodate themselves to the new situation under Sadat. It was no mere accident that all ten of these exofficers figured in the anti-Sadat clique, along with such key ASU civilian *apparatchiki* as Dia' al-Din Dawud, Kamal Hinnawi, Labib Shuqayr, and Ali Sayyid Ali. However, the purge of these key bureaucrats was not a purposeful liquidation of the Nasirite faithful; they were removed because they opposed the new president—one who was determined to exercise his executive powers to the fullest, with or without ASU approval. Another group of lesser known officials from Nasir's presidential staff continue to work in the high reaches of Sadat's government. These include Hafiz Isma'il, Hasan Tuhami, Muhammad Ibrahim Hasan Salim, Mamduh Salim, Muhammad Ahmad Muhammad, Muhammad al-La'ithi Nasif, Hasan Sabri al-Khuli, and Ahmad Muhammad Iffat.

Sadat Ascendant

By mid-1971 Sadat had become the master of his house; yet his success against his internal enemies was not matched by diplomatic or military prowess against Israel. So debilitating was the Israeli presence in the Sinai that the Egyptian leadership found it often impossible to concentrate on the internal tasks of nation-building and economic development. Sadat's power position remained tenuous as he skipped from one initiative to another hoping to generate pressure on the great powers and force Israel out of the Sinai. Within the Arab sphere he was able to garner Saudi economic and diplomatic support and Syria's agreement to open a second front against Israel. Domestically, Sadat played a waiting game, balancing competing interests and keeping potential enemies off balance by selective purges. These moves included ideological zigzagging, purging the press and the ASU of leftist intellectuals, and retiring Defense Minister General Sadiq, who had helped him liquidate the Sabri faction in May 1971. Like his charismatic predecessor,[32] Sadat attempted to create constant movement and fluidity; only he needed movement more than Nasir, since he had not gathered sufficient legitimacy for an unquestioned claim to power. The large-scale student demonstrations of January 1972 and January 1973 and unrest among the workers were surface manifestations of powerlessness, identity crisis, and alienation at the mass level. Sadat's dynamic, created by promulgation of new programs, changes of cabinets and prime ministers, and repeated threats to go to war, began to lose momentum only to be revived temporarily when Soviet forces departed from Egypt in mid-1972. Unable to get a Soviet guarantee of military support for a canal crossing and faced with anti-Soviet manifestations in the officer corps, Sadat seems to have decided to send the Soviets home amid manifestations of Egyptian nationalism. While this act increased his standing at home and in Saudi Arabia, it also weakened Egypt's defense without a prior US and Israeli promise to vacate the Sinai. Indeed, little was heard from Washington or Jerusalem, for neither country wished to make unpopular decisions before their elections scheduled for 1972 and 1973 respectively.

A number of developments converged to make 1973 a favorable year for Sadat and the Egyptian elite. While the Watergate scandal seemed to reduce the chances of American presidential pressure on Israel, the great world fuel crisis suddenly highlighted the importance of Arab oil and forced a more vigorous and balanced US foreign policy toward the Arab-Israeli conflict. The virtuoso implementation of this policy by Secretary of State Henry Kissinger, a political scientist of German-Jewish background, gave it a certain legitimacy and acceptability both in Congress and among American supporters of Israel. Simultaneously one could detect the clear signs of rapprochement in the Arab orbit. Egypt's close ties with Syria and Saudi Arabia were reinforced by normalization of relations with Jordan, and King Husayn freed Palestinian guerrillas jailed since 1970. Most other Arab states, except Libya, coalesced behind Egypt and Syria in an unprecedented show of Arab unity. Not only would King Faysal underwrite the costs of war, but as the world's leading oil producer, he would consent to use oil as a weapon. Meanwhile, Egyptian and Arab diplomacy were isolating Israel at the United Nations, as an increasing number of African states severed diplomatic relations with Israel; nor was there pro-Israeli sentiment among the large European states, at least, not with respect to Israel's hold on the occupied territories. Finally, Sadat may have induced the Soviet Union to pledge limited involvement in the conflict; at the least this would have included supplying military hardware and at most a Soviet military intervention in case of Egyptian reverses.

The Egyptian-Syrian attack of 6 October 1973 caught the thinned-out Israeli Army by surprise. Moving with extreme caution and incredible secrecy, Sadat was able to dictate the time and place of battle—something Israel had decided in previous wars. Moreover, in the initial stages of the conflict, the Syrian and Egyptian armies achieved moderate success in recapturing territory and inflicting losses in men and equipment. Despite their subsequent retreat before Israel's slow-moving reaction force, the Arab armies were far from being annihilated, and no quick Israeli victory was in sight. Given their large populations, oil wealth, and Soviet weapon supplies, the Arabs could afford to fight much longer than Israel, which as a small state could not afford a high level of human attrition and economic dislocation. Egypt considered the destruction of the Bar-Lev line and the entrenchment in the Sinai as victories of the first magnitude when compared with the facile defeats of yesteryear. The significance of these accomplishments transcended their function as morale boosters; to a collectivity burdened by a historical legacy of subjugation, the limited victories in the Sinai were "great events" and as such will have important, long-range socializational consequences. In the short term, these victories, combined with subsequent Israeli withdrawal into the Sinai, have given Sadat and the Egyptian elite a new legitimacy, which could be sustained by inducing further Israeli withdrawal from occupied territory.

5

Three Elites in Comparison

The cross-national analysis which follows consists of two parts. First, specific observations will be made from the data in the preceeding chapters and general hypotheses will be advanced which may be relevant to other political systems as well. This will be followed by an analytic commentary on each leadership group cast within a comparative framework. Due to their uniqueness to each polity, certain important features of the leadership groups will be left out. However these peculiar features have already been analyzed at length in the separate chapters.

Presented in Table 72 are the major areas in which any two of the three leadership groups manifested strong similarity. These comparative groupings coincide with the following cross-national observations gleaned from the data.

Recruitment Bases

1) The Egyptian army's Free Officers Association and the Yishuv's Haganah apparatus and to a lesser extent, the Irgun, have been primary agencies of elite socialization and recruitment in the two states.

In analyzing the process of elite formation, one can often identify major events and related groups or organizations that have had a formative influence. The Egyptian Revolution of 1952 was such an event and the Free Officers Association was the organization that effected the takeover of power. In Israel the great event was the struggle leading to independence in 1948 and the key organization was the Haganah and to a lesser extent the Irgun Zvai L'umi.

In both countries these great events marked the culmination of the socialization process of the two emerging elites. Moreover, the successful participation of the two leadership groups in these events created the necessary cohesion and impetus for their subsequent leadership roles. Each elite group had a common historical memory.

TABLE 72. *Similarities Among the Three Elites*

ISRAEL-LEBANON	EGYPT-ISRAEL	LEBANON-EGYPT
recruitment base by occupation and specialization	recruitment base by organizations	secularization
educational level	role of the military	class base/aspirational model
political risk	role of ideology	weakness of parties
political cost	socialization/integration	place of study
institutionalization		representativeness by class
		representativeness by minorities
		age and tenure

In the Egyptian case, no less than 60 out of a total of 186 cabinet ministers who served between September 1952 and January 1972 were Free Officers. They constituted over 32 percent of the top elite. The leading members of the Free Officers group the Free Officers Executive, contained 11 members that included Nasir and his closest associates, some of whom still rule Egypt.

TABLE 73. *Core Elite Recruitment Groups*

COUNTRY	GROUP	N	RATIO	%
Israel	Haganah (and Palmah)	22	24/64	37.5
	Irgun	2		
Egypt	Free Officers Association	60	60/186	32.0

The Haganah was the para-military defense arm of the Yishuv that was used against the British and the Arabs; it subsequently became the Israeli Defense Forces. The Irgun was a more militant group, which competed with the Haganah until their reconciliation. Of the 64 ministers who served in the Israeli cabinet between 1948 and 1973, 22 belonged to the Haganah apparatus and

2 were Irgun leaders, making a combined component of 24, or 37.5 percent of all ministers. This group includes many leading personalities of Israeli political life—Sharett, Dayan, Allon, Carmel, Eshkol, Galili, Bar-Lev, Sharef, and Ezer Weizmann of the Haganah, and Begin and Landau of Irgun.

Both in terms of recruitment and leadership preparation, the Free Officers Association and the Haganah-Palmah-Irgun were roughly equivalent, since they had similar functions in Egypt and Israel respectively. While the Lebanese elite also shared certain common historical memories (e.g., Turkish and French rule), it lacked a core contingent as in Egypt and Israel.

> 2) The religious establishment and men of religion exercise a greater influence on Israeli politics than on Egyptian or Lebanese politics.

A larger number of Israeli ministers possessed religious educational and occupational backgrounds than either Lebanese or Egyptian ministers, as can be seen in tables 74 and 75. Of the 159 Lebanese ministers only one could be classified as a clergyman— Abd al-Hamid Karami of Tripoli was a mufti before becoming a politician. In Egypt, a strongly Islamic state, there were 3 ministers out of 186 who were Al-Azhar shaykhs and as such could be considered clergymen, although some others may have been exposed to religious education in village schools. In Israel, no less than 14 rabbis had become cabinet ministers, or one-fifth of the total elite. This finding is one index of the substantial power that Israel's conservative religious establishment wields through the religious parties, which play an important part within the context of Israel's coalition cabinets. Moreover, a large number of the remaining ministers have had some religious education. If these are taken as indices of political secularization, Israel will register very low, while Egypt and Lebanon will register very high. While the religious establishments of Egypt and Lebanon are by no means negligible, they nonetheless fall far short of possessing the political influence that Israeli religious parties exercise. Although religion is crucial to Lebanese politics, the separate religious institutions and hierarchies play only a muted, behind-the-scenes role, which is seldom politically decisive. Not even the country's most powerful cleric, the Maronite patriarch, can cause cabinets to rise or fall; few Lebanese politicians are politically bound to any of the religious heads of the several denominations. While Islam continues to possess great popular influence in Egypt, the religious establishment has functioned as a bureaucratic arm of the government since the suppression of the Muslim Brotherhood and the entrenchment of the Nasirite regime in 1955.

TABLE 74. *Educational Background*

SPECIALIZATION	LEBANON %	ISRAEL %	EGYPT %
Law	47	22	17
Religion	0.6	22	3
Engineering	14	5	20
Military	2	5	32
Economics/Business	3	6	8
Medicine	8	2	4

TABLE 75. *Occupational Background*

OCCUPATION	LEBANON %	ISRAEL %	EGYPT %
Law	47	13	12
Religion	—	22	3
Engineering	13	4	13
Academia	6	2	22
Labor/Farming	—	31	—
Business	6	6	5
Military	2	17	32

3) The military plays a larger role in Egyptian and Israeli politics than in Lebanese politics, for in terms of occupational and educational backgrounds there was a larger military presence in the cabinet elites of Egypt and Israel than in that of Lebanon (see tables 74 and 75).

Determining the extent of military presence and influence in the Egyptian elite is a relatively simple task (see Chapter 4). The takeover of July 1952 was an all-military affair and after initial reluctance the Free Officers moved into key governmental positions. At the cabinet level the officers have constituted one-third of the total ministerial elite and they have usually been at the helm of the more important ministries.

More complicated is the determination of military presence in the Israeli political elite. This problem stems from the difficulty of determining the military status of ministers who were involved in underground resistance movements prior to independence. Here it is necessary to note that not all members of the Haganah were engaged in combat activities; a number of ministers (e.g., Eshkol and Sharett) were engaged in administrative support functions such as finance, foreign affairs, and supply. These individuals are not numbered among the military; rather the military category includes former Haganah/Irgun commanders who entered political life after leaving the armed forces voluntarily or being retired by Ben Gurion.

On this basis the Israeli military contingent consists of 8 ministers or 13 percent of the total elite. While this percentage is less than half of Egypt's military contingent of ministers, it is still high for a democracy such as Israel, especially when compared with Lebanon's 2 percent. Clearly one major cause of this substantial military presence in Israeli cabinets centers on the defense imperative of this "garrison state" and the need to reward with cabinet posts the top commanders of the armed forces.

Lebanon contrasts sharply with Egypt and Israel both in terms of the military's influence on politics as well as the extent of military presence in the cabinet elite. Lebanon's small army of less than 20,000 is kept primarily for quelling internal disorders. Thus, despite Lebanon's very real security problem with respect to her two neighbors, Israel and Syria, the country cannot maintain a large army because of internal factors and instead relies on diplomacy to defend herself. Of course in times of internal or external crisis the Lebanese army does assume a larger political role; and the army contributed one president to the republic—General Fuad Shihab. Yet this enlarged influence occurs intermittently and for short periods; civilian supremacy is reasserted as soon as the crisis passes.

Political Culture and Education

4) In terms of certain occupational and educational elite background characteristics, Lebanon represents a more Western-type (e.g., US), pragmatic political culture than either Egypt or Israel, which are more ideologically oriented. Over half of Leb-

anon's ministers were lawyers in contrast to less than 25 percent for Israel and Egypt (see tables 74 and 75).

A political system's heavy dependence on the legal profession is often considered a hallmark of Western, democratic political cultures. The prevalence of lawyer-politicians in the top ruling and legislative bodies of the US and West European countries may indicate a systemic dependence on the bargaining and brokerage functions of lawyers—a feature less prevalent among the more ideological polities of the Third World. In this context, Lebanon represents a Western lawyer-oriented model brought in by the French and their universities, which educated many early Lebanese leaders. During the French mandate ''legalistic'' Western-style, parliamentary politics became firmly established and survived the stresses of achieving independence. Lebanon was spared the cataclysms that overturned Western democratic-type regimes in many other Middle Eastern countries.

In this respect, Egypt's political development was substantially similar to Lebanon's. Western political norms and styles, especially French and British, had entered Egypt long before independence. These included the centrality of the legal profession to politics, as indicated by the early establishment of a law faculty as well as the general prevalence of lawyers in government.[1] As in Lebanon, a legal career was regarded as a means toward status satisfaction. During the fifties Egypt even began to export a large number of lawyers to the Arab countries. However, with the entrenchment of the revolution, the need for the lawyer's brokerage functions seems to have declined or been assumed by others. At the cabinet level, the lawyer-politicians were mostly replaced by military officers and civilian technicians and administrators with doctorates whose style of rule was based less on bargaining—the lawyers' forte—and more on technical expertise. Nor was the lawyer particularly well suited to perform the ideology-building functions of a revolutionary elite.

Israel presents a unique case; it is modeled after the Western parliamentary systems, but as a new state it is in the ''beginning-of-ideology'' phase unlike the ''end-of-ideology'' Western democracies. Thus, despite their similarities as democracies, Israel and Lebanon would fall at opposite ends of the spectrum on the question of the role of ideology. Indeed, Lebanon is more an "end-of-ideology" state and therefore nearer to the Western model than Israel.

As a "beginning-of-ideology" state, Israel has had an activist, settler elite who were more interested in farming and achieving independence than pursuing academic degrees. In this aspect the typical Israeli politician has been unlike those of the West. Yet with the passing of the founding leadership, one may anticipate an increase of the lawyer component at the top. This trend may be accompanied by a less ideological phase of political development.

> 5) A higher correlation between educational specialization and cabinet post exists in Egypt than Israel or Lebanon. Egyptian ministers have a higher level of education than Lebanese or Israeli ministers.
>   a) Egypt relies on specialists in cabinet positions while Israel and Lebanon do not.
>   b) There is a greater reliance on academia as a source of recruitment in Egypt than in Israel and Lebanon.
>   c) In all of the above observations Egypt seems to act like non-Western developing states, while Israel and Lebanon follow the practice of Western nations.

The foregoing observations group Israel and Lebanon in contradistinction to Egypt. The central finding is that the Egyptian ministerial elite has included many highly educated specialists in contrast to the Israeli and Lebanese elites. The relatively higher level of specialized education of the Egyptians was often a factor in their recruitment into the cabinet. For example, Egyptian ministers had five times as many doctorates as the Israelis and three times as many as the Lebanese. Once the military elite had consolidated its position in key bureaucracies, it began to recruit highly trained but mostly apolitical civilians, especially those with the expertise to run the more technical ministries that the military officers could not efficiently operate themselves. The recruitment of these civilians accorded the military elite an easy way to civilianize the regime without having to rely on the civilian politicians of prerevolutionary Egypt; it also placed a premium upon those holding doctorates and other advanced degrees. Clearly the main sources of such men were Egypt's institutions of higher learning.

Most of these academics were sufficiently apolitical not to threaten the supremacy of the revolutionary officers. Indeed, virtually none of the civilians emerged as a serious contender for power even in the period after Nasir's death.

TABLE 76. *Educational Level*

LEVEL	ISRAEL %	EGYPT %	LEBANON %
BA/BS/License	38.0	29.0	54.0
MA/MS/Certificate/Diploma	8.0	23.0	11.0
PhD/MD/LLD	12.5	49.0	17.0
No College/No Information	44.0	4.0	8.0

In sharp contrast to Egypt, Israel and Lebanon possessed cabinets of politicians; that is, leaders of parties, parliamentary factions and/or sectarian groupings were recruited into cabinet positions. Educational specializations and level as such have rarely been criteria for recruitment into the Israeli cabinet. As for Lebanon, except for a few "technical" governments, most cabinets have consisted of politicians representing the major sectarian groups and factions, and education was seldom a criterion. In both countries, however, highly educated experts are utilized in sub-cabinet positions. Also, many veteran Israeli and Lebanese politicians who lacked college degrees or formal specialized training eventually made themselves experts in various subjects through self-education and practical experience gained in the field before reaching the cabinet. This is particularly true of Israeli leaders whose overall levels of formal education were even below that of the Lebanese, but who had often mastered difficult areas of specialized knowledge by prodigious homework.

On the basis of these preliminary findings it can be tentatively hypothesized that the cabinets in non-Western states will probably show a higher correlation between type of cabinet job and educational specialization and a generally higher level of education than in most Western-type polities such as Lebanon, Israel, most West European countries, and the United States. While a great deal of additional documentation is necessary, it appears that in many new Third World states, cabinets are usually composed of specialists, while in Western countries, full-time politicians, especially lawyers, hold sway.

The fundamental debate about placing specialists or generalists in ministerial positions falls outside the scope of the present inquiry. Yet the incidence of many generalist politicians in Israeli and Lebanese cabinets permits the following observation: [2]

6) There appears to be more professionalism in political careers and reliance on negotiation, bargaining, and adjudication in Israel and Lebanon, than there is in Egypt.

Tenure, Age, and Political Culture

7) Tenure, age, and other recruitment patterns indicate aspects of the political cultures of the three countries particularly in terms of political stability and political cost. There is a positive relationship between the degree of authoritarianism in a regime and the levels of political cost and political risk.
   a) High rates of elite circulation are indicative of political crisis.
   b) The relatively brief tenures in office in Egypt and Lebanon indicate higher political cost and relative systemic instability in comparison to Israel.
   c) Overall political risk is higher in Egypt than in Lebanon and Israel.

TABLE 77. *Average Tenure: Aggregate Count*

	EGYPT	ISRAEL	LEBANON
		months	
Average tenure of ministers	37	72	30

As indicated in table 77, the Lebanese ministers have the shortest average tenure with 30 months, followed by the Egyptians with 37 months and the Israelis with 72 months. Thus the Egyptians' average tenure is somewhat higher than that of the Lebanese and the average tenure of the Israelis is twice that of their Arab counterparts. The low Lebanese tenure is partially due to the very high rate of cabinet turnover—45 since independence in 1943—as well as to the high political cost that cabinet jobs carry especially for newcomers. While about a dozen personalities continue to reappear, 62 ministers out of 159 (40 percent) served in only one cabinet. Moreover, in a period of about thirty years, 159 ministers served in the cabinet—an average of 5.3 ministers per year. The Lebanese cabinet therefore is a high-cost, low-stability type. Egypt experienced a slower turnover of cabinets (23 between 1952 and 1972) but a higher circulation rate and political risk; in twenty years no less than 186 ministers have come and gone (an average of 9.3 ministers per year), a rate exceeding that of Lebanon. Also, in Egypt political risk has sometimes meant jail, while in Lebanon it merely meant loss of office. In as much as they were specialists and bureaucrats, the Egyptian ministers kept away from open competitive politics typical of democracies. As long as they were efficient, honest, and loyal to Nasir, they could generally retain power.

Both political cost and risk have been lower in Israel where average tenure is 72 months (over 6 years). Like the Lebanese cabinet, the Israeli represents a coalition of parties, personalities, and interests; yet the Israeli ministerial coalition is far more stable than its Lebanese counterpart. Israeli cabinets change infrequently—17 since 1948—and the party leaders who become ministers incur very low political cost—substantially lower than the specialist ministers of Egypt. Only 64 Israeli ministers served during the twenty years since independence (an average of 2.7 ministers per year), the lowest circulation rate of the three countries. It follows that the high tenure of Israeli ministers and low cabinet and personel turnovers indicate a high-stability, low-political-cost system. It also means a lower level of competition for cabinet posts. It might be more precise to state that certain institutional devices in Israel dampen competition, or at least prevent it from radically affecting the leadership composition. These dampening devices include the Israeli party system and the working of Israeli electoral politics.

> 8) There is a positive relationship between the political power of a party and the length of tenure and level of age of cabinet officials. In Israel, the primacy of the Mapai Party tends to lengthen the tenure and increase the age of ministers, while the absence of such a party is one reason for a shorter tenure and younger age of Egyptian and Lebanese ministers.

The primacy [3] of the Labor Party (Mapai) since 1948 as the senior coalition partner in the government has reduced the opportunities for new men to enter the ruling elite. Not only have Israeli cabinets changed infrequently, but the top leaders of the Mapai, a relatively stable party, return repeatedly as ministers, thus assuring lengthy tenures.

Comparing the total tenures of the Mapai and non-Mapai cabinet members illustrates the relative longevity of Mapai ministers. While non-Mapai ministers served in the cabinet an average of 63 months, the Mapai ministers' tenure was an average of 85 months.

Table 78 shows that the average age of Egyptians and Lebanese at entering cabinet office is about 49 and 47 respectively. This is substantially lower than the Israeli ministers whose average entrance age is 54. The Israelis' much higher average age is partly due to their long years of service in political parties and other government posts before being brought into the cabinet. Moreover, virtually all Israeli ministers had grown old during the long years of the mandate. By the time independence came many of Israel's early cabinet ministers were already in their fifties and sixties. Because of relatively slow circulation in the Israeli cabinet, those who entered it tended to stay there longer than their Egyptian and Lebanese counterparts (see table 78). In other words, more Israelis grew old while in the cabinet than Egyptians or Lebanese; hence the comparatively high average age of Israeli ministers (63) at leaving cabinet office. The average age of Egyptian ministers at leaving cabinet office was 52 and that of the Lebanese was 53.

TABLE 78. *Average Age: Aggregate Count*

	EGYPT	ISRAEL	LEBANON
Age at Entering Cabinet	49	54	47
Age at Leaving Cabinet	52	63	53

Egypt's relatively low entrance-age figure (49) indicates the general youth of the revolutionary officers and their original civilian recruits for the cabinet. While many of these early officers and civilians aged in cabinet office, the high level of elite circulation that Nasir maintained assured the introduction of younger ministers, thus keeping the average age generally low. Indicative of their short tenure is the fact that Egyptian ministers left cabinet office relatively early: at the average age of 52.

Similarly the Lebanese minister's average cabinet entrance age was low because of a very high rate of circulation—one even higher than Egypt's. As table 78 indicates, short average tenure caused a relatively early average age of departure for the Lebanese ministers: 53 years. While this is slightly above Egypt's figure, it is far below that of Israeli ministers (63).

These conclusions are reinforced by an analysis of age over time in all three elite groups. As table 57 indicates, the Egyptian minister's average age dropped (40 years) from 1952 to 1954 as more and more young military officers joined the cabinet. From 1954 on successive Egyptian cabinets registered progressively higher age levels until 1965, after which average age remained at 50 until 1968.

In the Israeli case, average age in the 1948 cabinet was 56.6 (see table 42). In subsequent years it has fluctuated between the mid-fifties and 61. In 1969 it was 58. In contrast to Egypt and Israel, in Lebanon there is no clear trend in average age because of frequent fluctuations. Every time an upward trend begins, it is soon broken by the influx of younger men. The average age of cabinets has ranged from a low of 37 in September 1943 to a high of 63 in October 1968 (see table 11).

Place of Study

9) In terms of formal education, Egypt and Lebanon were more influenced by Britain, America, and France (or Western Europe) than the Israeli elite, whose educational training took place mostly in Germany, Central Europe, and Russia.

As table 79 indicates, a large number of Egyptian and Lebanese leaders were educated in the US, France, Britain, and other West European countries. While more Lebanese went to French universities, the Egyptian preference was for Anglo-American schools. In contrast, relatively few Israeli ministers were educated in West European schools. Rather, a very large number of them were educated in Central and East European countries—e.g., Russia, Ukraine, Poland, Germany, and Lithuania. Thus, the Lebanese and Egyptian elites have been exposed to greater US-West European intellectual influences than the Israelis, whose intellectual development took place mostly in Germany and Russia. In view of this reality it is ironic that Israelis are generally regarded as more "Western" than the Arab elites.

TABLE 79. *Country of Study—Number of Degrees*

	BRITAIN/ UNITED STATES	WEST EUROPE (France, Italy, Austria, Switzerland)	CENTRAL AND EASTERN EUROPE (Germany, Russia, Poland, Balkans, Ukraine, Lithuania)	HOME	MISCEL- LANEOUS
Egypt	49	19	5	292	—
Israel *	11	7	28	16	3
Lebanon	20	37	2	70	9

* In Israel's case the data represents the number of ministers who studied in the various countries, not the degrees attained.

Representativeness by Class and Sect

10) In terms of class representativeness, the Israeli elite is more representative than the Egyptian, which in turn is more representative than the Lebanese.

Are the three elite groups representative of the class backgrounds and sectarian/ethnic composition of their respective bodies politic? The question is especially important from the point of view of democratic theory, which assumes a fair degree of representation to be both morally desirable and politically necessary to promote stability. Of course these assumptions do not obtain in authoritarian and traditional polities where the political culture presumes the existence of a ruling elite belonging to a single party, race, or hereditary autocracy. In the modern context, however, even totalitarian elites realize that certain types of representation are imperative to maintain stability and internal peace (e.g., the representation of the various nationalities in high state and party organs of the Soviet Union).

In essence, no ruling group can be representative in terms of class. Indeed, one might hypothesize that by the time of their recruitment into the cabinet most ministers have become urban dwellers and members of at least the middle class. Nevertheless, the class background of an individual's parents or grandparents should be considered analytically important.

Of the three groups, the Israeli leadership is most representative of its country's class base. While there are recent signs of creeping capitalism, the early socialist ethos of the immigrants and the leadership, no less than the paucity of wealth in a poor land, precluded the rise of a wealthy elite. Moreover, the Jews answering the call of aliyah were overwhelmingly poor or impoverished. The result was a lower-middle to middle-class population and elite. With the exception of the poorer sectors of Arab-Israelis and Sephardic-Oriental groups, Israel's cabinet elite shares a class base with the rest of the country's population. The lack of a large class gap between the elite and the mass is one strength of the Israeli political system.

In comparison, the Egyptian political elite is less representative of the Egyptian masses. When the capitalist and landowning classes were liquidated after 1961, the class structure of Egypt changed substantially. The redistribution of wealth was meant to increase the urban and rural middle class (*al-tabaqah mutawassitah*)—the very class that the middle and upper-middle-class Nasirite leadership favored. But the bulk of landless peasants and the urban lower class remain unrepresented at the top in significant numbers.

The Lebanese elite is not representative of large segments of the Lebanese people, especially the rural and urban poor—the lower and lower-middle-classes. This is because a fifth of the Lebanese elite have aristocratic (zu'ama') backgrounds and over half of the total come from wealthy families. Thus, in terms of class base, the Lebanese elite is even less representative than the Egyptian.

> 11) In terms of sectarian/ethnic representation, the Lebanese elite
>   is the most nearly representative, followed by Egypt, and fi-
>   nally by Israel.

As table 80 indicates, the Lebanese elite is most representative of the sectarian/ethnic minorities in that country. It might be even safe to hypothesize that no country can approximate the Lebanese representation of minorities in the cabinet, for the Lebanese political system is based on strict confessional representation.

The Egyptian elite is much less representative than the Lebanese in the sectarian aspect. The main religious minority in Egypt, the

TABLE 80. *Cabinet Representation by Sectarian/ Ethnic Affiliation*

COUNTRY	GROUP	%
Egypt	Copt	5
	Muslim	95
Israel	Ashkenazim	89
	Sephardim	11
Lebanon	Armenian	1
	Catholic	11
	Druze	12
	Maronite	26
	Orthodox	12
	Shi'ite	14
	Sunni	24

Copts, are a group of monophysite Christians estimated to constitute one-sixth of Egypt's population, but they have provided only 5 percent of cabinet membership between 1952 and 1968. While every Egyptian cabinet includes at least one Copt, the aggregate tenure of all Coptic ministers between 1952 and 1972 is much below the percentage of the Coptic population (15 percent). Therefore, Muslims were represented in excess of their number (see table 80). Least representative of its minorities is Israel. As shown in table 80, Ashkenazi ministers far surpass the Sephardim (Oriental) in aggregate cabinet tenure. The Sephardim, which constitute at least 50 percent of Israel's population, have had only 11 percent of the total tenure of all ministers between 1948 and 1969. While the Sephardim are underrepresented, the Arab minority of Israel— just under one-half million—has had no cabinet representation at all. However, there are Arab deputies in the Knesset as well as Arab deputy ministers just below the cabinet level.

Systemic Institutionalization

12) The Israeli and Lebanese elites possess institutionalized bases of recruitment, legitimacy, and support, while institutionalization has proceeded more slowly in Egypt where the political system remains in flux.

For Israeli and Lebanese leaders ascent to elite status represents the end of a well-defined and routinized cursus honorum in which competitive legislative and partisan politics were central. Indeed, relatively few Lebanese and still fewer Israelis reached the cabinet without the baptism of the electoral process. This differs markedly from the Egyptians most of whom have reached elite position by express presidential appointment or approval and by virtue of their technical skills and/or apolitical status. As such, few possessed constituencies or other forms of organizational support. While leaders compete within the ASU, the scope of competition is circumscribed. The president controls ascent to the top more than is the case with Lebanon and far more than the prime ministers in Israel. Under Sadat the Egyptian political system continues to be in flux particularly with regard to the institutionalization of a party system and a cursus honorum for the Egyptian elite. While at present Lebanese and Israeli elites are predominantly professional politicians, the Egyptians are either technocrats or fledgling politicians. Institutionalization is also reflected in the disposition end of the circulation process—a large percentage of Lebanese and Israeli cabinet ministers returned to the legislature after cabinet office, while in Egypt disposition is far more fragmented and uninstitutionalized.

Integration

13) In terms of socialization the Israeli elite is more integrated than the Egyptian, while the Lebanese elite is the least integrated.

Above all, common, lengthy, and intense socializational experiences—persecution, itinerancy, imprisonment, war—helped to integrate the Israeli elite. This relationship between experiences and integration may explain the ease with which the elite unites in the face of external danger. Despite substantial policy conflicts on the Arab and religious issues and wide differences in country of origin, common socialization has homogenized them in terms of *Weltanschauung*, aspirations, and general goals.

Socialization as a factor in elite integration is also important to the Egyptians. Their common experiences included British imperialism, royal misrule, chaotic party government, as well as revolutionary involvement and the humilation of defeats by Israel. Yet the revolution itself, in terms of planning and execution, was almost completely a military affair directed by Nasir and his colleagues, with little civilian participation. Thus, the revolution was far more important to the military third of the elite in terms of an integrative experience than to the civilian two-thirds who were brought in after the 1952 Revolution. This military-civilian distinction somewhat detracts from the Egyptian elite's socializational homogeneity, more so than the Coptic-Muslim dimension.

In contrast to Israel and Egypt, the Lebanese elite is least integrated or homogeneous. The struggles for independence against the Ottoman Turks (World War I) and the French (World War II) are still an important part of the Lebanese collective historical memory, but their integrative force has declined with the passage of time. Confessional bases of ministerial recruitment make this elite the most heterogeneous of the three; nevertheless, over the years a degree of elite integration has occurred.

Crisis Management and Social Priorities

14) In times of crisis all three political systems turn to crisis-managers. In Egypt and Israel, the crisis-managers are usually military men; in Lebanon although crises occasionally call forth military men, such situations are generally handled by nonpolitical senior statesmen.

While in Lebanon the incidence of crisis tends to coincide with an increase in the number of extra-parliamentary senior statesmen in the cabinet, in Egypt and Israel crisis tends to coincide with an increase in the military component in the Egyptian and Israeli cabinets.[4] These constitute systemic responses to environmental challenges which the three countries have experienced in the last quarter century. In each political system the type of systemic response is determined by the character of each society. Thus, the role of crisis-manager is filled by different groups in different societies. It should be noted that in Egypt and Israel the group (the military) functioning in this capacity is at least partially determined by the unavailability of senior statesmen. In Egypt the revolution had discredited most politicians who could have fulfilled the role

of crisis-manager. In Israel, there were no apolitical senior statesmen.

> 15) In the three political systems, recruitment patterns will reveal
> fundamental societal values, priorities, and aspirations.

In Egypt, security (internal and external) and modernization are
fundamental concerns; these priorities and aspirations have been
reflected in elite recruitment—the soldier was paramount to the
quest for security and the technocrat (off-techs and civilian specialists) were needed to direct modernization. For Israel, security
and identity were foremost concerns; hence the recruitment of
paramilitary men and rabbis. While development was also a main
Israeli concern, fewer technocrats appeared at the top, since second-level technocrats were generally capable of managing the
modernization effort. In Lebanon, where values centered on confessional compromise and enterpreneurial endeavor, lawyers and
businessmen (financiers, industrialists, and proprietors) predominate. The imperatives of confessional cooperation placed a premium on the bargaining and brokerage skills of Lebanon's lawyers
and businessmen,

Testing Some Classic Theories

> 16) Elites and elite groups constitute the hubs of communications
> networks (Arensberg, Deutsch, Rustow), particularly during
> formative periods. This is especially true in Lebanon and Israel
> and to an extent in Egypt.

Substantial evidence has been presented showing the centrality
of Lebanese elites and elite families to the political, economic, and
cultural realms of Lebanese life. Figures 1 through 6 provide a
wealth of information about the linkage role of leaders who are sit-
uated in the midst of complex communications networks. The
same is true of Israel where the elite has extensive national and
transnational ties. These include a communications grid which ties
them to transnational Jewish elites and organizations (e.g., WZO,
Jewish Agency, Alliance Israélite) as well as domestic elites and

organizations (Histadrut, parties, the religious establishment, Haganah). In the Egyptian case, the ties and networks of the early period are not documented in detail. However, the Free Officers and Nasir maintained careful contacts not only inside the army but also with the palace, the British and American embassies, and such political groups as the Wafd and the Muslim Brotherhood.

> 17) a) The elite is endowed with certain personal attributes not common among the general population (Pareto).
> b) Members of the elite usually possess attributes which are highly esteemed by their society (Mosca).

These are restatements of two classic hypotheses in elite theory. Although Pareto's original version contained a causal statement making rulership dependent on one's possession of attributes, our data is insufficient to make such an ambitious determination. All that the data indicates is that the three elites possessed personal gifts which set them apart from most of their subjects and that these attributes were esteemed in their respective societies. For example, Israel's founding fathers around Ben Gurion and the Revolutionary Command Council officers around Nasir had been regarded as possessing exceptional gifts—e.g., heroism, fearlessness, dedication, intelligence—by most members of their societies. On the other hand, if education is considered an elite attribute, then the Egyptian and to a lesser extent the Lebanese elites are set apart from the bulk of their populations because of their high educational level—an attribute highly regarded in both polities. Because of the relatively low educational level of Israeli leaders, the opposite obtained; i.e., despite the widespread respect for them, they were not esteemed by the sophisticated and growing intelligentsia which centered around the country's main universities. Interestingly, the military third of the Egyptian elite was similarly snubbed by the more highly educated civilian elites and by the intellectuals around the main newspapers and the universities. In each country, moreover, prestige became associated with possession of the specific attribute which symbolized each elite group. In Lebanon businessmen and financiers have been highly regarded; in Israel prestige has gone to Haganah/IDF fighters and/or kibbutzniks; in Egypt military position brought status.

> 18) A positive relationship exists between the position of a group
> in the economic process and its position in the political process
> (Lasswell).

The foregoing is Lasswell's restatement of the famous Marxian hypothesis. Specifically, it means that the dominant political position of a ruling elite is dependent on its position in the economic substructure.

While our data is insufficient to show causality in each case, a number of tentative observations are possible. In Lebanon, the Marxist hypothesis may be relevant as a description of reality, in view of the centrality of the business establishment and its large role in politics. In Egypt and Israel this is less certain. The Nasirite elite were not primarily moved by economic considerations in deposing their king, although they did promulgate agrarian and educational policies that would aid the rural and urban middle classes from which a considerable number of the officers had come. It is however difficult to define with assurance and precision what class the officers and their civilian recruits belonged to and what their positions were in the production process and why that position determined their political position as the ruling elite. Similarly, it is not easy to define the Israeli elite's position in the economic process and its relationship to their quest for power.

Quantitative Techniques

A word needs to be said about the utility of various quantitative techniques in the comparative analysis of elite backgrounds. A variety of quantitative approaches might be used to test the above hypotheses using the data presented in the preceding chapters, as well as suggest new ones. The most obvious technique that suggests itself is factor analysis.[5] While there is wide disagreement about the wisdom of using factor analysis to discern causal linkages, it can be fruitfully utilized in delineating patterns of elite recruitment cross-nationally. A second technique is path analysis. This involves using regression or path coefficients in establishing causal linkages between the background characteristics of leaders and their political mobility.[6] One can also develop different circulation indices of the rate of elite mobility in and out of leadership groups.[7] Finally, one can use the elite mobility data as presented in the cursus honorum charts, to calculate probabilities by using Markov chains and other stochastic models.[8]

The Three Elites in Perspective

Against the backdrops of each country's historical experience, it is possible to make further observations about each leadership group. A number of strengths and weaknesses become apparent, in addition to several internal contradictions, especially when one contrasts elite backgrounds with elite performances.

Lebanon

To devise a delicately balanced sectarian system of political existence is the product of the Lebanese genius. In this sense, their system of inter-sectarian equilibrium is *sui generis* and the Lebanese elite are to be credited both for its invention and implementation.

The major weakness of the system is its inability to deal with external threats, especially those which have a connection to one of the country's main sectarian communities. This was the nature of Syria's threat in 1958, which affected the Sunnis mainly, but not exclusively. More to the point is the internal crisis created by Israel's attacks on Lebanon and on Palestinian guerrillas located in refugee centers throughout Lebanon. Any major government attempt to suppress the Palestinians usually alienates sections of the Lebanese public, especially the Sunni community which has kinship and religious ties to the Palestinians.

Another problem is the unrepresentativeness and insensitivity of the elite to the country's lower and lower-middle class. Their keen sensitivity to sectarian rights and privileges is not matched by enlightened concern for the Lebanese poor. Since Lebanon's emergence as a great financial center, affluence and poverty have existed there side by side, reflecting a general lack of social consciousness among the elite. Unless more is done to ameliorate the economic conditions of the poor, neither confessionalism nor democracy can be preserved for long.

Even if the Lebanese elite possessed the will to enact a social welfare program, it could still find it difficult to implement. Indeed, the very nature of Lebanon's decentralized and pluralistic confessional system works against elite effectiveness, as does the propensity of many a leader to accept the pecuniary benefits of the *wasitah* (connections) system.

Israel

Israel's experience in nation-building and certain features of its political system are unique in the contemporary world of developing states. Its political elite is no exception; a number of important background characteristics (Chapter 3) help set Israel's leaders apart from their Arab counterparts. The distinction becomes even more apparent in the area of leadership performance or elite effectiveness, for the Israelis have outdone the Arab leaders both in the foreign and domestic areas of rulership. Of course, the Israelis have had a lot of help—financial, military, and political—in fulfilling their successful leadership roles; yet these factors by themselves are insufficient to insure success in a hostile environment. The establishment of a nation-state in a few short decades upon successive crests of victories was unprecedented and can be seen as a measure of elite effectiveness. Despite their virtuoso performance, however, the Israeli elite faces a number of contradictions and ironies which continue to cause concern after a quarter century of independence.

The elite established a state in its own image—Zionist, socialist, Western—yet relatively few of their compatriots from the Pale of Settlement followed them to Palestine. Those who eventually came in large numbers were not from Russia, but from Germany. Significantly the German Jews who came to Palestine were prompted less by ideological commitment than by the deadly reality of Hitlerite extermination. Even after Israel became independent, the Ashkenazi dispersion remained mostly unmoved by Ben-Gurion's invitations to immigrate. Galut nationalism in the West brought strong political and financial support but little immigration. Instead, the new arrivals were Oriental-Sephardic Jews from the Middle Eastern and North African countries—culturally, religiously, and racially very different from the Ashkenazi (European) founders of the state. And most Orientals came not for strong ideological reasons but because of Arab persecution resulting from the very attempt to establish a Jewish state in Palestine. The influx of Oriental Jews soon after Israel's establishment presented the elite with one of its two major internal problems.

The Zionist elite had resolved to establish a Jewish national home in Palestine after considering a number of African locations. One reason given for choosing Eretz Israel was because it was there that the Jews' ". . . spiritual, religious, and political identity was shaped." [9] In other words Palestine was chosen for the "ingathering," because the Jews wanted to reclaim their ancient identity as a Middle Eastern people. But once in Palestine, the Western founders of the Jewish state proceeded to establish a Western state—based on socialist and nationalist principles—which were largely alien to the Middle Eastern milieu of the period. Despite the significant synthesis of Middle Eastern and Western culture that has occurred partly as a result of the Oriental Jews' influx, Israel has remained a Western cultural island—a reality reinforced by the creeping Americanization of Israeli society. It is even more ironic that a state established as a protest against the West, where the Jews had suffered and perished so often, should evolve into a Western state, thus becoming an extension of Western civilization—the very culture which had decreed the Jews' liquidation. The umbilical cord between Israel and the West could not be severed, certainly not by an elite mostly born and bred in Europe. On the contrary, ties to the West and the US have been strengthened, particularly for reasons of Israeli national security.

However, the Israeli elite has been most ineffective in its quest for peace with the Arab states. Despite numerous utterances since 1948 of non-belligerency toward their threatening Arab neighbors, the elite has consistently adopted an offensive strategy which has culminated in three major and many minor Israeli victories. Fought in the name of security, these wars have humbled the Arabs but have not achieved peace. The price of maintaining the political, psychological, and military status quo, has been substantial, especially since the Six-Day War. Most visible has been the growing influence of the military (Tzahal) establishment—a development that may have a detrimental impact on Israeli democracy in the long run. Perhaps more serious is the elite's inability to formulate an internally consistant and rational policy toward the Arabs, including the disposition of occupied Arab land. Beset by internal power struggles and a tough war in October 1973, the elite has been divided over making concessions to the Arab side. Given the elite's generally uncompromising stance, similar attitudes have developed in the media as well as at the mass level. This has forced even relatively moderate politicians to adopt more militant public postures. There is also evidence of an elite-mass credibility gap, especially on military matters, since the October 1973 War. The absence of such a gap had once set the Israeli elite apart from the Arab leaders.

Egypt

Egypt's present ruling elite has to sustain itself in a country faced with major economic, political, and social problems compounded by a continuing Israeli presence in the Sinai. Despite the success of the October 1973 War, long-range elite effectiveness will be substantially dependent upon its ability to induce an Israeli withdrawal.

Domestically, it is significant that the elite has continued to hold power so long after the disaster of June 1967. One basic reason for the elite's phenomenal longevity is the well-known Egyptian propensity not to challenge the prevailing ruling order. This is especially true for this regime which has managed, despite constant military threat, to maintain a tolerable level of existence. Another factor contributing to elite strength has been the virtual absence of any organized counter-elite; both the Islamic right and the communist left have been too weak to overthrow a regime which still derives a large part of its power from the military establishment. Finally, despite the purges of May 1971, the composition of the present elite is not too different from that surrounding President Nasir, and as such still enjoys the charismatic legitimacy derived from this association. It also has residual legitimacy that flows from the "Egyptianness" of the ruling group in contrast to the foreign rule of Britain and the Ottoman-Turkish Muhammad Ali dynasty.

Until the death of Nasir it was almost inconceivable to consider the Egyptian elite separately from the leader himself. Indeed, Nasir's charismatic personality overshadowed the less visible presence of his colleagues and aides. While Nasir infused the elite with a sense of discipline and purpose, he had also stifled free initiative and spontaneity among his top cadres. The sudden removal of Nasir may permit the Egyptian elite to come into its own if other conditions are propitious. Until that time, however, the elite continues to face a number of fundamental problems and inconsistancies in the areas of national identity, ideological development, revolutionary goals, and the class base.

Despite the legitimizing role of Nasir's charisma in the evolution from Egyptian nationalism to Arabism, residual attachments to nationalism persist. After the June 1967 War, proponents of Egyptianism surfaced to blame Egypt's defeat on her Arabism. The ensuing debate reopened the long dormant issue on the nature of the ''Egyptian personality.'' Were the Egyptians Arab or pharaonic? [10] A full-scale reversion to Egyptianism could have wrecked the whole structure of legitimacy which the Nasirite elite had built for itself since its commitment to Arabism in 1955; it could also seriously complicate Egypt's relations with the Arab states and impair her position of primacy. Perhaps more detrimental to the nation's psychological well-being would have been the critical identity crisis that a retreat from Arabism would surely trigger. It was clear that the elite could not afford a sudden ideological shift, yet the leadership felt that official censorship of Egyptian nationalist writers would be detrimental to the semblance of national unity they wished to promote vis-à-vis the Israelis in the Sinai. As a result a shift of emphasis has taken place in the nation's media, which presents a more balanced view of the Egyptian past and includes a reformulation of the ''Egyptian personality'' that gives due place to Egypt's pharaonic heritage, along with its Islamic and Arabic components.[11] In sum the elite has managed as best as it could a very ticklish political problem; yet the long-range problem of dealing with the identity crisis still persists.

Closely related to the identity problem is the elite's ambiguous attitudes toward the West, the Soviet Union, and the revolution itself. In retrospect it appears that despite the progressive alienation of Egyptians from the West, their admiration and enchantment with the West's middle-class model of socioeconomic development persisted even during the anti-Western phases of the Nasirite era. This development was only natural. The worldwide manifestation of the West's military and industrial might had awed and humbled the Afro-Asians, among them the Egyptians. Hence the aspiration among the Egyptian elite for Westernization—the crude imitation of the Western model. It should also be remembered that the families of the Nasirite elite had been recently urbanized by leaving the rural middle class and joining the urban middle class in their quest for Westernization. But the desirability of emulating the West came into question primarily because of the Western pro-Israeli stance. The subsequent adoption of socialist-etatism was at variance with the elite's middle and upper-middle-class origin and its Western middle-class values and aspirations which had persisted in what had become a love-hate relationship between the Arabs and the West. Unwilling to shed their fixation on a middle-class revolution and constrained by their class connections and Islam, the Egyptian elite could not fully internalize the values of their adopted socialist model. Much less could they pursue the militant goals of a more comprehensive socialist revolution based on participation of the urban lower class and the peasants, who constitute over 80 percent of Egypt's population. The present leadership under Sadat cannot be expected to lead such a revolution; rather it is anxious not only to use American pressure to induce an Israeli withdrawal but to dilute its socialistic program by reintroducing a modified Western model in the context of friendly relations with the United States.

Projective Hypotheses

19) The process of *embourgeoisement,* common to all three elite groups is in an advanced stage in Lebanon. Although Israel and Egypt are not as advanced, there is little in either their policies or their class bases to retard or reverse embourgeoisement—a near universal phenomenon that accompanies modernization.

20) With the obsolescence of the key recruitment groups—
Haganah and the Free Officers—the importance of the military
as a recruitment source may decrease in Israel and Egypt. The
prospects of peace in the Middle East may also decrease the
importance of the military as a recruitment source.
21) The departures of Nasir and Ben Gurion removed the charismatic dimension and its concomitant ideological militancy
from the two political systems. These developments, coupled
with rule by unheroic technocrats in both countries, may have
a mellowing effect and result in a decline in their mutual
animosity.
22) The perceptible increase in Egyptian elite effectiveness and the
concomitant decrease in Israeli elite effectiveness (both as
manifested in the October 1973 War) may create an "effectiveness balance" between the two elites. This balance, along
with other environmental restraints, may contribute to an
Egyptian-Israeli peace in the future.

The foregoing hypotheses relate changes in elite composition
and effectiveness to the possibilities of peace and war in the Arab-
Israeli conflict. Any projection of elite effectiveness in and between the three polities is bound to be affected by the October
1973 War. If the final outcome of Dr. Kissinger's shuttle diplomacy is a general Arab-Israeli settlement, then the nature of that
settlement may also influence elite effectiveness. In the Lebanese
case, the coming of peace would surely contribute to elite effectiveness, particularly if it contains an accommodation on the Palestinian question. In the cases of Israel and Egypt, the role of the
war as a contributory factor to elite effectiveness is far more important than it is for Lebanon. Taking the war as a starting point,
one might attempt an effectiveness projection for these two elites.
On balance the war profited the Egyptians and harmed the
Israelis despite the latter's last-minute success in crossing to the
west bank of the Canal. Both elite groups were affected in terms of
reputation, prestige, and self-image. The Egyptians succeeded in
surprising Israel, thereby dictating the time, place, nature, and
scope of the war. More significantly, they managed to draw blood
by inflicting relatively heavy casualties and ended up holding two
strips along the east bank of the Canal. Since these achievements
were unprecedented in modern Egyptian or Arab history, their fa-

vorable impact on the prestige, reputation, and legitimacy of Sadat and his colleagues was inestimable. Not only did the war affect the international and inter-Arab standing of Egypt's rulers, but it affected the Egyptians' view of themselves. After centuries of humiliation and defeat they had succeeded in holding an enemy at bay. In Daniel Lerner's words, the defeat and humiliation under British rule had "scarred the Egyptian elite and confused its perception" [12]—a process only deepened by the successive Israeli victories since 1948. It is precisely this psychological dimension that was changed by Egypt's limited success in the October War. The elite has now gained greater legitimacy at home and more self-confidence, especially in its future military and diplomatic dealings with Israel. In this respect it is an ascendant elite.

The October War was disadvantageous to the Israeli elite. Its reputation, both international and domestic, was compromised. Having repeatedly defeated their weak Arab enemies, Israel's elite progressively overcommitted itself in word and deed to convince the Israeli people that the occupation could be maintained indefinitely and at relatively low cost in lives and money. But pursuing such an ambitious military policy was incongruent with the country's limited resources and small population; nor did the elite correctly appraise the Arab's ability to mount a credible military threat. Three easy victories had so colored the Israeli perception of their Arab foe that they discounted the possibility of genuine social change in the Arab world. For example, there is little evidence to indicate that the Israeli leadership had sufficiently considered the Egyptian army's advances in training and weapons, the emergence of an effective officer corps, much less the psychological benefits that would accrue from achieving a surprise attack or possessing a cause to fight for—the liberation of occupied territory.

In an earlier analysis of Egyptian and Israeli capabilities, this writer observed that despite manifestly inadequate performance in past wars, the Egyptian soldier's fighting abilities under offensive conditions were simply unknown,[13] especially if he had the benefit of air cover. The October War provided enough evidence to show that they performed better than anyone had expected, including the Egyptians themselves. Can it be that this prowess in fighting performance was evidence of genuine social change in Egypt and in the army itself? Clearly it is too early to find a conclusive answer.

It is entirely possible that Israel's lengthy presence in the Sinai and the Arab's repeated defeats may have transformed Egypt sufficiently for her to face the Israelis as military equals. Ironically, the Israelis' past military success may have inadvertently helped to induce changes in Egyptian character and culture which may become detrimental to future Israeli interests.

Therefore the Egyptian leadership seems ascendant vis-à-vis Israel's when one couples their newly manifested effectiveness in war with our earlier findings on the Egyptians' superior education. Yet these positive attributes do not automatically erase the latent effectiveness of the Israeli leadership. Despite its educational deficiencies and serious errors in judging the Arab social psychology, the Israeli elite has been highly effective, especially in postwar diplomacy with the Arabs. It is significant that the intra-elite conflict and the attendant cabinet crisis of January–March 1974 did not prevent the elite from making hard and unpopular decisions regarding limited territorial concessions to effect a disengagement of forces. The handing over of power to younger, native-born Israeli leaders may have facilitated their acceptance of a new Arab reality. In terms of capabilities and resources, the Egyptian and Israeli elites may have gained a clearer perception of each other than they have had at any previous time—a development which eventually could reach the lower strata of the two societies.

Enduring peace in the Middle East may well depend on whether the two elites perceive each other as equals in effectiveness. If they do, the two polities will achieve a balance of power which could bring long-term peace to a region which has endured conflict and misery for countless generations.

Lebanon

Abbreviations Key

Acad	—academia
Bur	—bureaucracy
Bus	—business
Cab	—cabinet
Dep	—deputy
Dipl	—diplomacy
Eng	—engineering
Jour	—journalism
Jud	—judiciary
Law	—law
Med	—medicine
Mil	—military
Pres	—president of republic
Prop	—proprietor
Py	—party
Ret	—retired

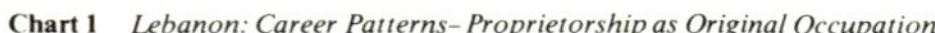

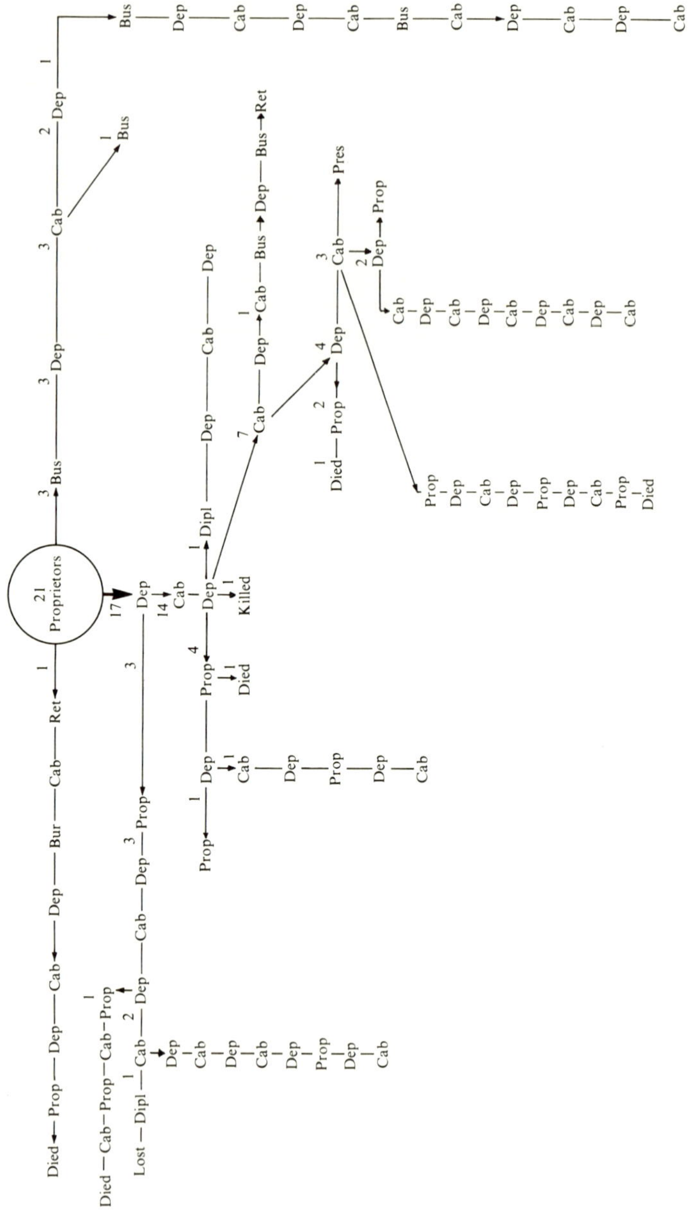

Chart 1   *Lebanon: Career Patterns – Proprietorship as Original Occupation*

Chart 2   *Lebanon: Career Patterns–Engineering as Original Occupation*

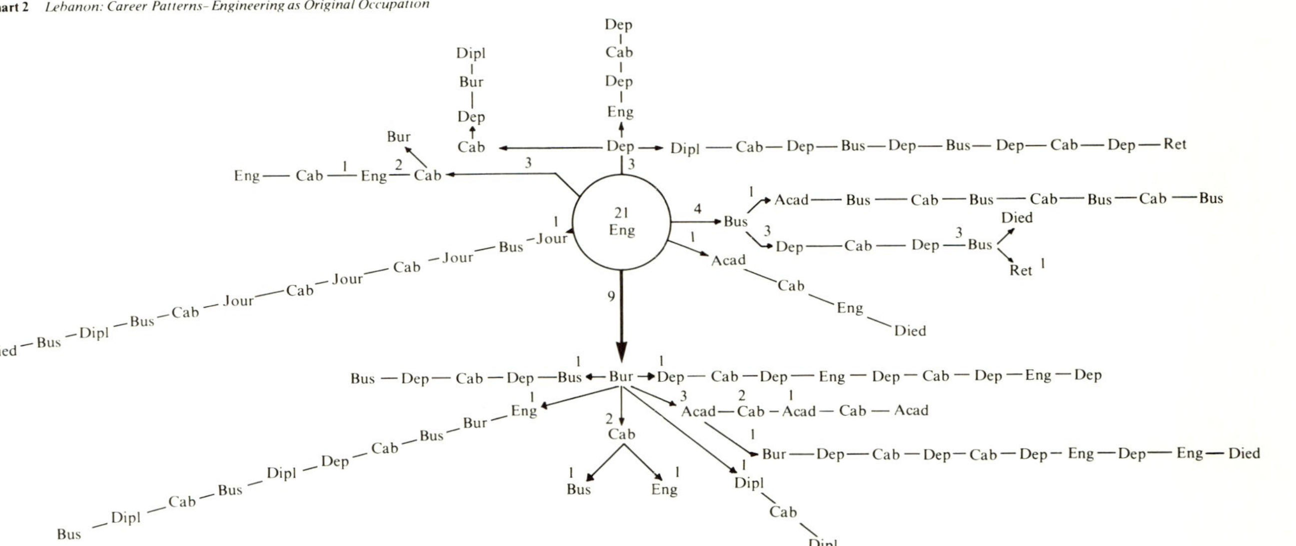

Chart 3 *Lebanon: Career Patterns–Law as Original Occupation*

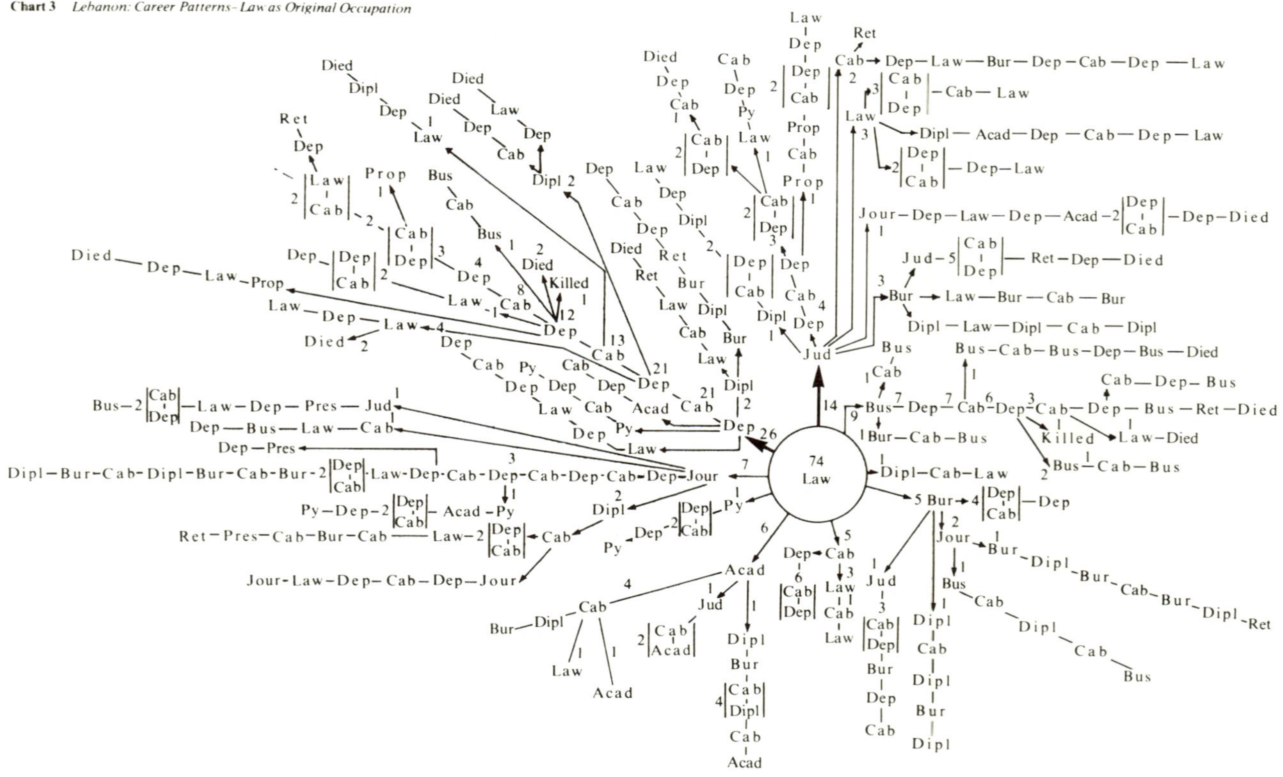

Chart 4   *Lebanon: Career Patterns- Military as Original Occupation*

Ret — Dep — Cab — Dep — Bur ← 1 [3 Military] 2 → Cab → Mil — Cab — Mil — Pres — Ret

Cab → 1 Bus

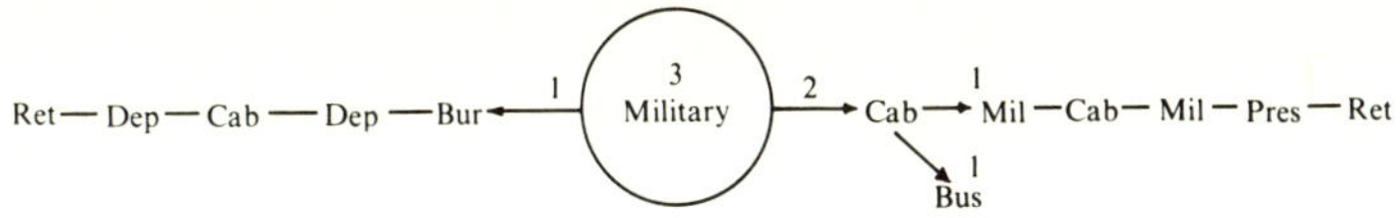

Chart 5   *Lebanon: Career Patterns— Journalism as Original Occupation*

Died — Jour — Cab — Jour — Cab — Py — Jour ← 1 Dep → Cab — Dep — Jour — Died

2 ↑ [3 Journalism] ↓

Acad

Bus

Bur

Py

Dep

Jour

Dep

Cab

Dep

Ret

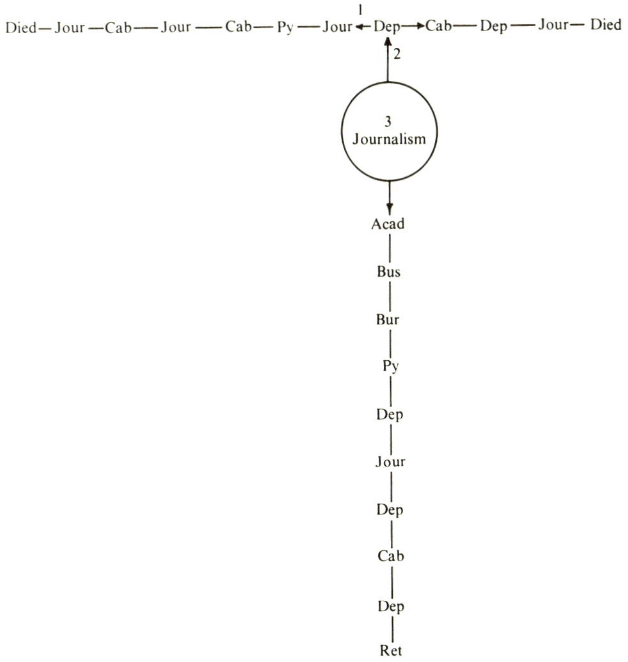

Chart 6   *Lebanon: Career Patterns–Bureaucracy as Original Occupation*

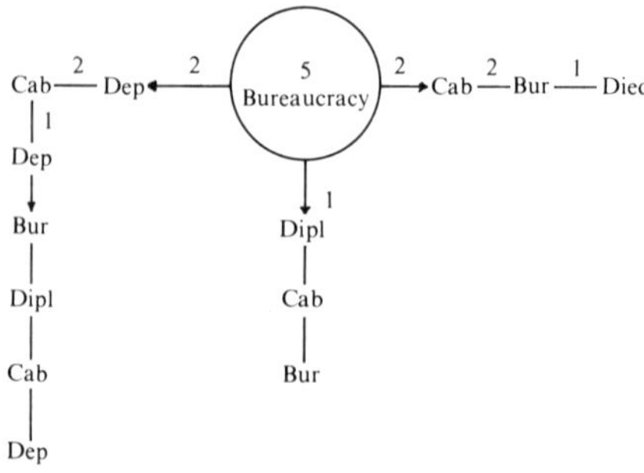

Chart 7   *Lebanon: Career Patterns–Academia as Original Occupation*

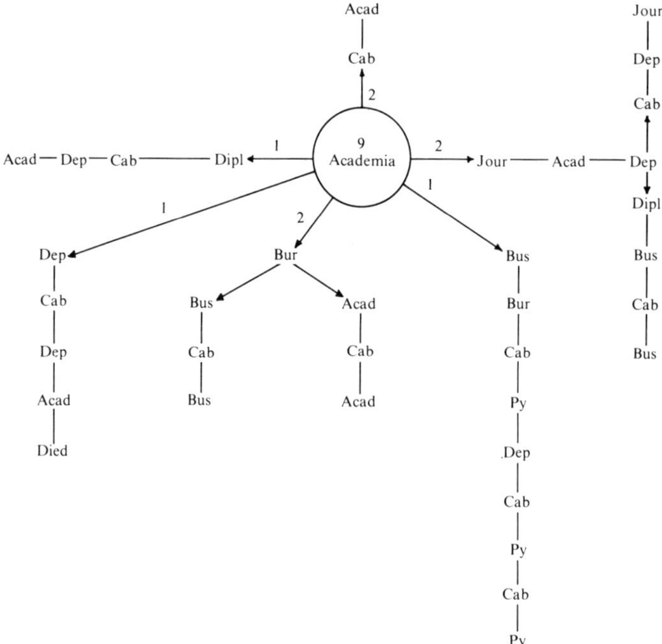

Chart 8   *Lebanon: Career Patterns- Business as Original Occupation*

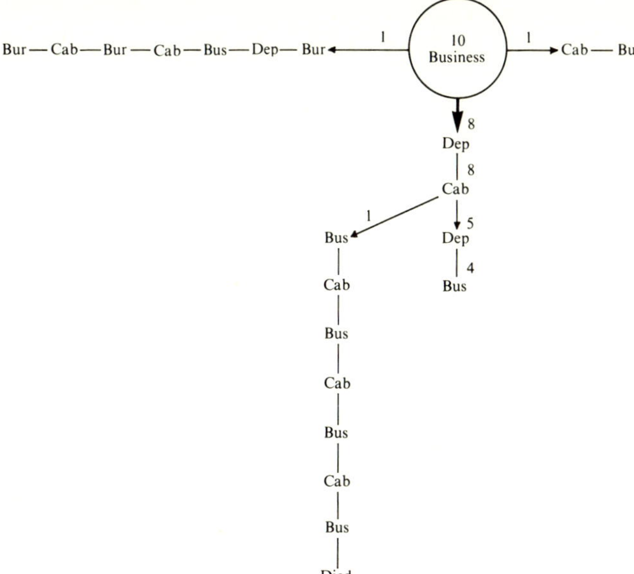

Chart 9   *Lebanon: Career Patterns- Medicine as Original Occupation*

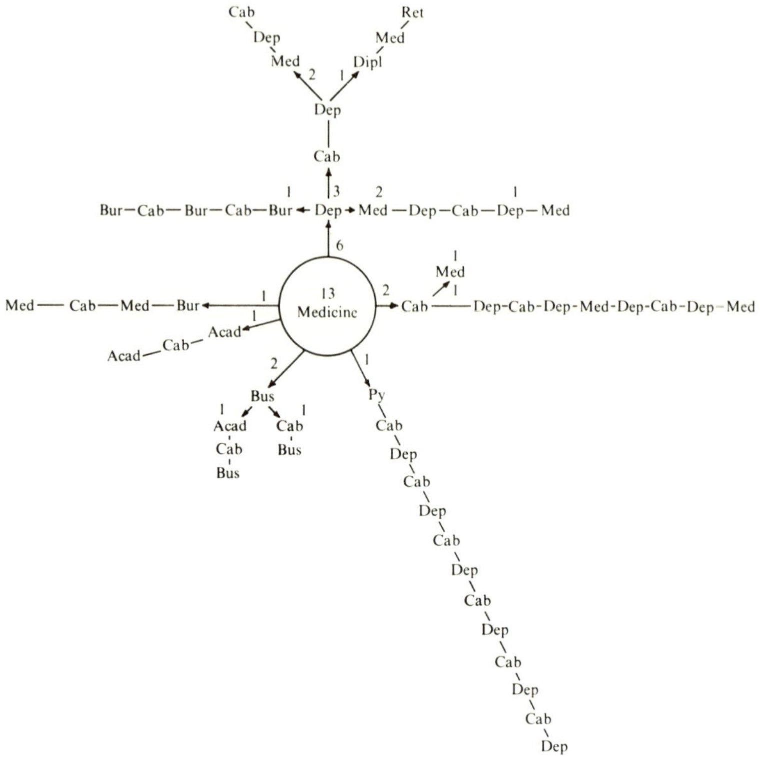

Cab   Ret
Dep   Med
Med   Dipl
2 1
Dep
Cab
1 3 2   1
Bur—Cab—Bur—Cab—Bur ← Dep → Med —Dep—Cab—Dep—Med
6
1
Med
13   2 1
Med — Cab—Med—Bur ← Medicine → Cab ——Dep-Cab-Dep-Med-Dep-Cab-Dep-Med
1
Acad
Acad—Cab
Acad—Cab
2   1
Bus   Py
1   1   Cab
Acad Cab   Dep
Cab   Bus   Cab
Bus   Dep
Cab
Dep
Cab
Dep
Cab
Dep
Cab
Dep

Israel

Abbreviations Key

Acad   —academia
Bur   —bureaucracy
Bus   —business
Cab   —cabinet
Dipl   —diplomacy
For Mil —foreign military service
Hist   —Histadrut
Jour   —journalism
MK   —member of Knesset
IDF   —Israeli Defense Force
J A   —Jewish Agency
Jud   —judiciary
Py   —party position
Ret   —retired
ZB   —Zionist bureaucracy in and out of Palestine
Wkr   —worker/farmer

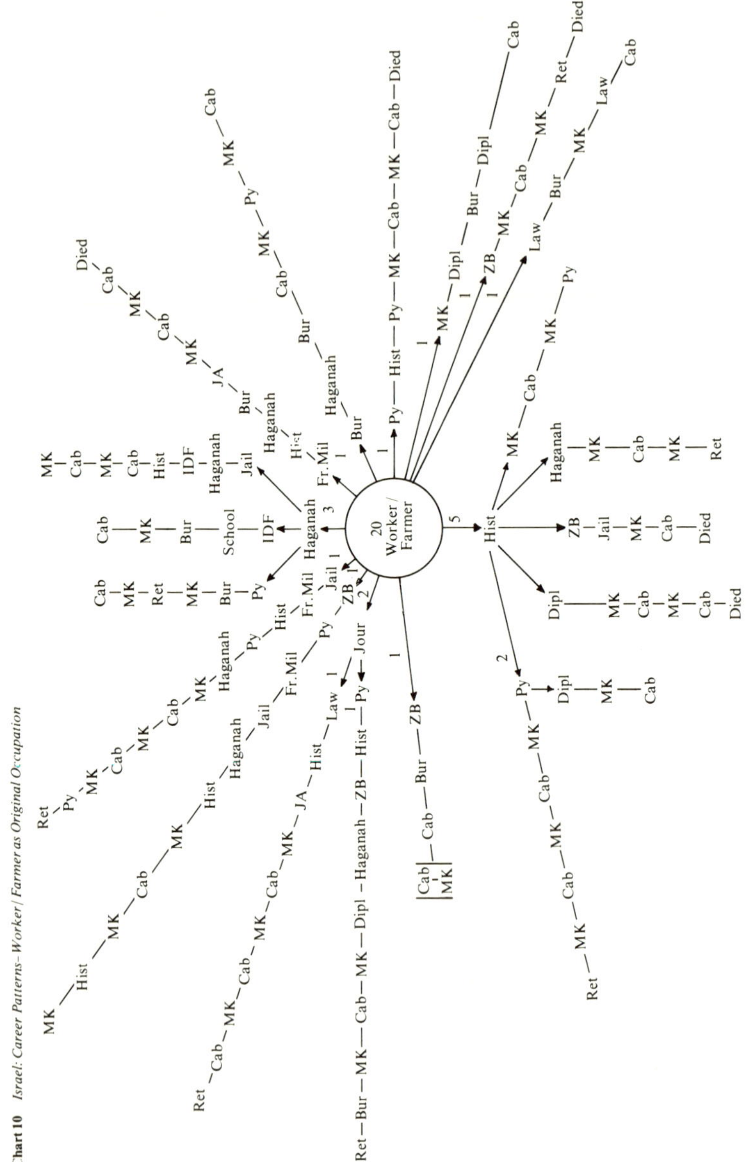

Chart 10   *Israel: Career Patterns—Worker/Farmer as Original Occupation*

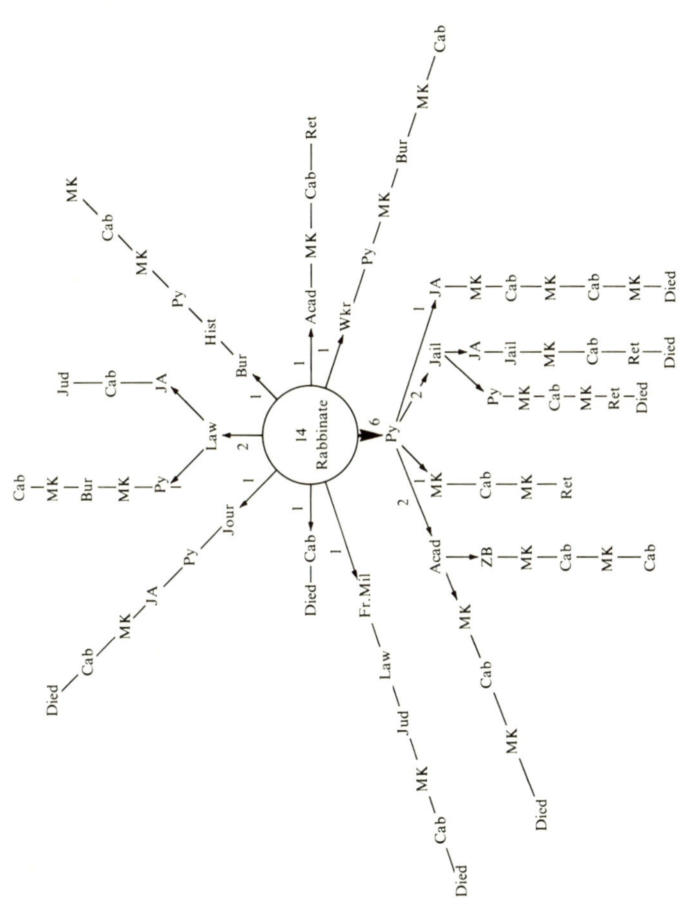

Chart 11   *Israel: Career Patterns– Rabbinate as Original Occupation*

Chart 12   *Israel: Career Patterns–Law as Original Occupation*

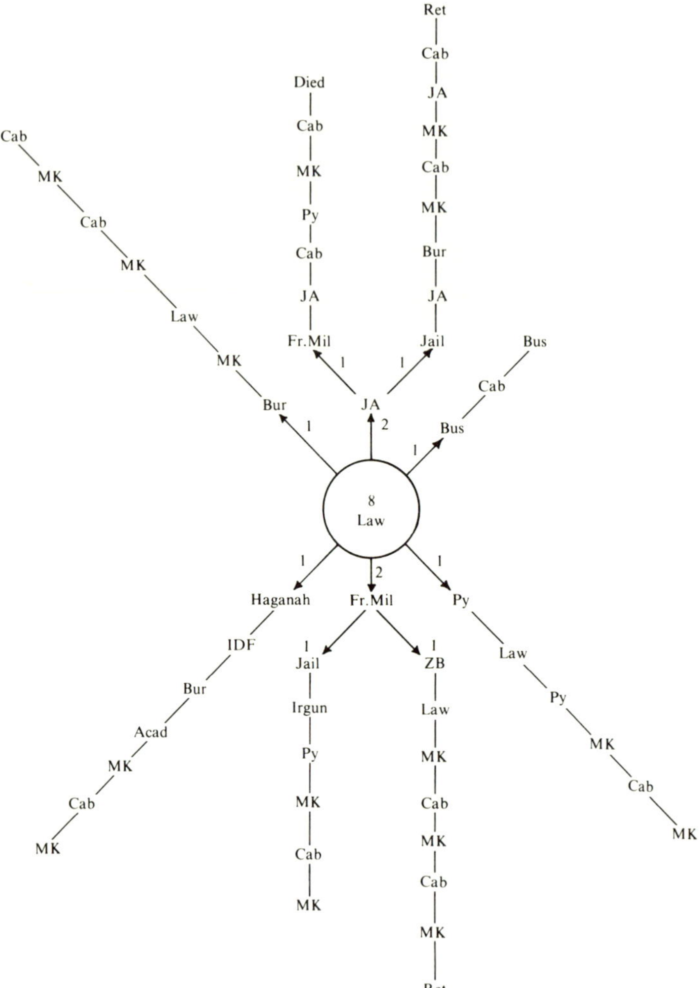

Chart 13 *Israel: Career Patterns–Zionist Bureaucracies as Original Occupation*

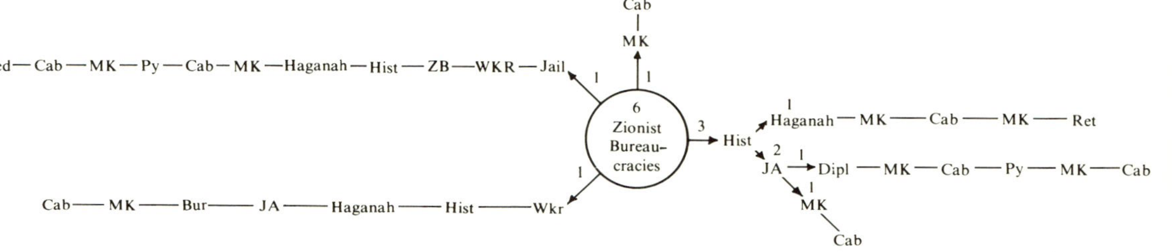

Chart 14 *Israel: Career Patterns–Haganah as Original Occupation*

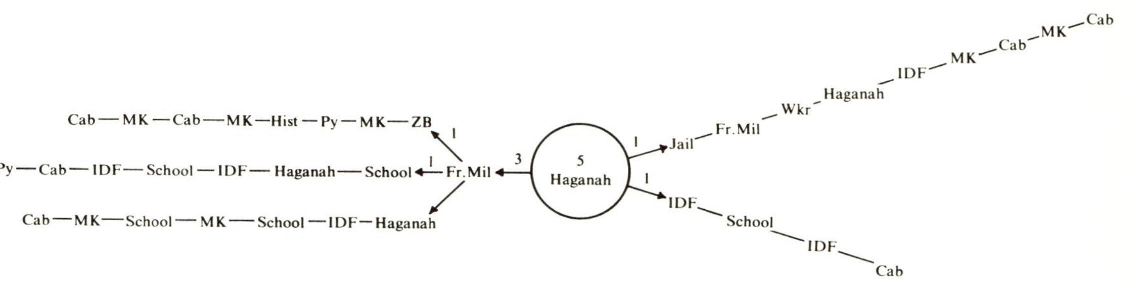

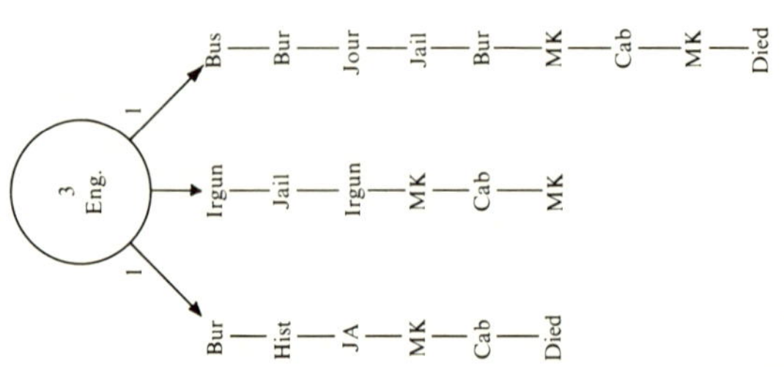

Chart 16   *Israel: Career Patterns – Engineering as Original Occupation*

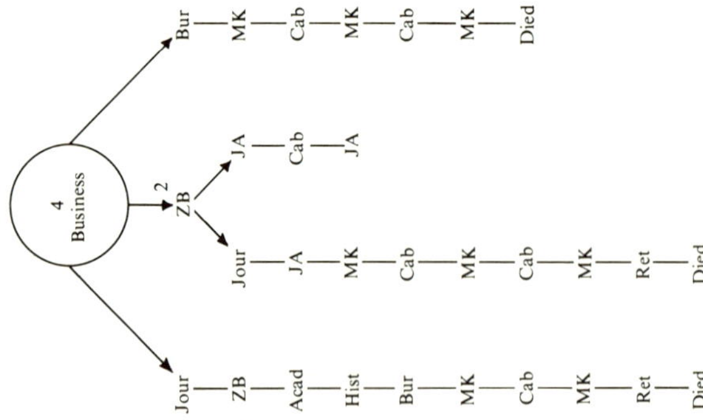

Chart 15   *Israel: Career Patterns – Business as Original Occupation*

Chart 18 *Israel: Career Patterns–Academia and Foreign Military Service as Original Occupations*

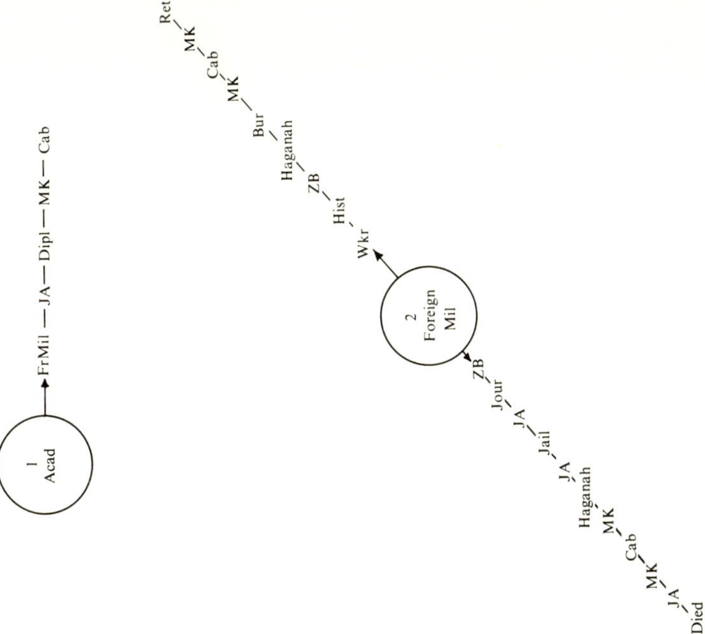

Chart 17 *Israel: Career Patterns–Journalism as Original Occupation*

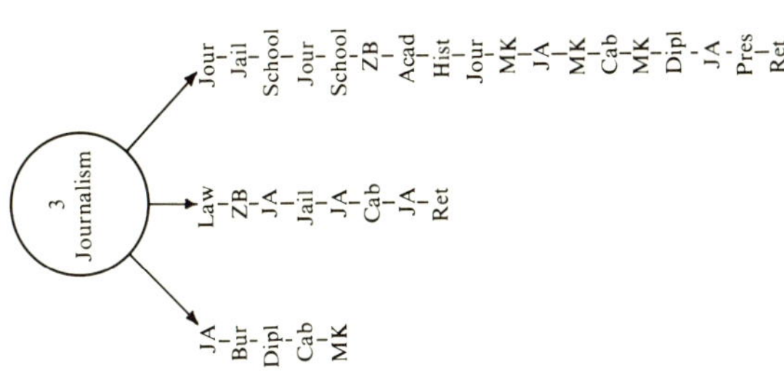

Egypt

Abbreviations

Acad	—academia
B_{Gov}	—governors of provinces
B_{Min}	—ministerial bureaucracy
B_{Org}	—bureaucracies of the public organizations
B_{Pres}	—presidency
B_{UN}	—United Nations posts
Cab	—cabinet
Dipl	—diplomatic corps
Int	—intelligence
Jud	—judiciary
Law	—legal practice
NA	—National Assembly
Py	—party
Rel	—religion
Ret	—retired

Chart 19 *Egypt: Career Patterns–Military as Original Occupation*

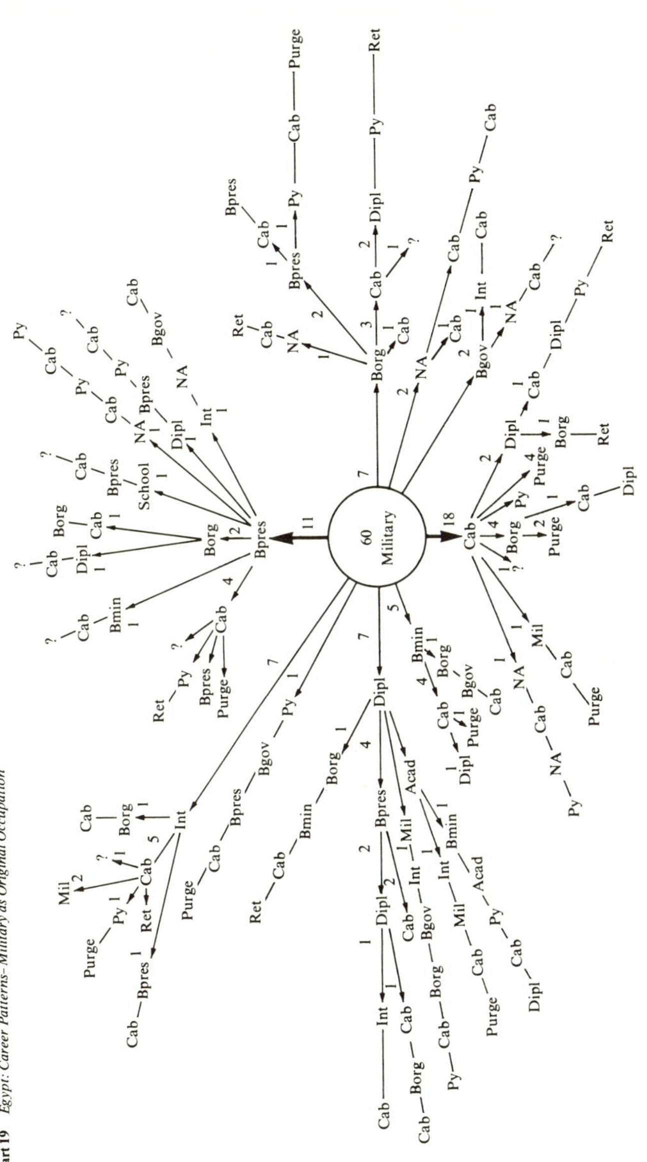

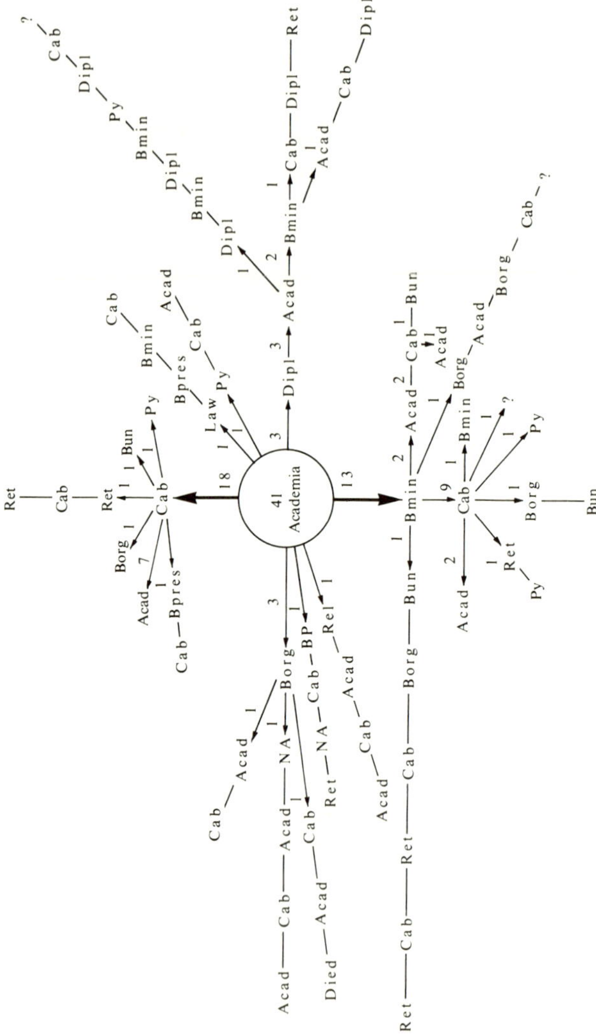

Chart 20   *Egypt: Career Patterns–Academia as Original Occupation*

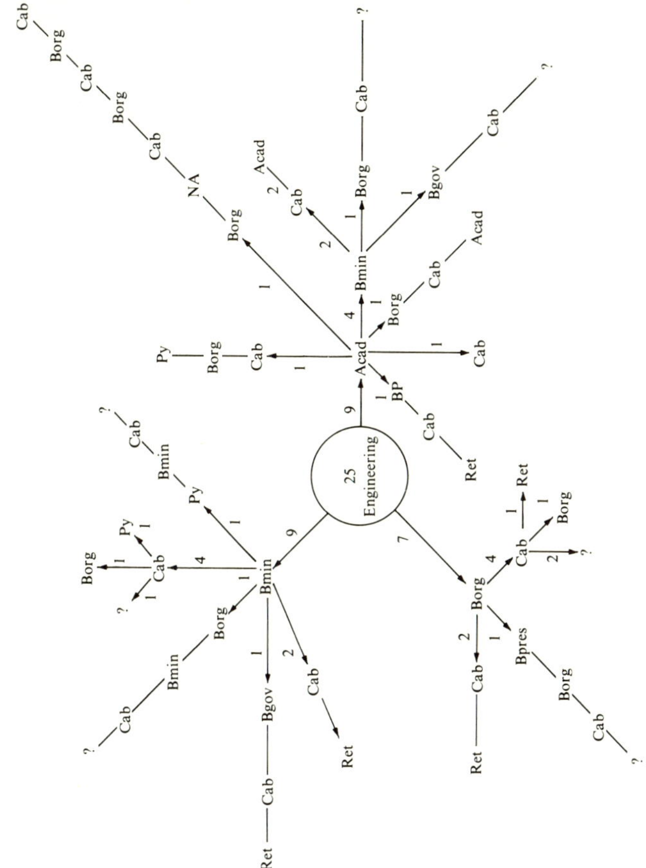

Chart 21 *Egypt: Career Patterns–Engineering as Original Occupation*

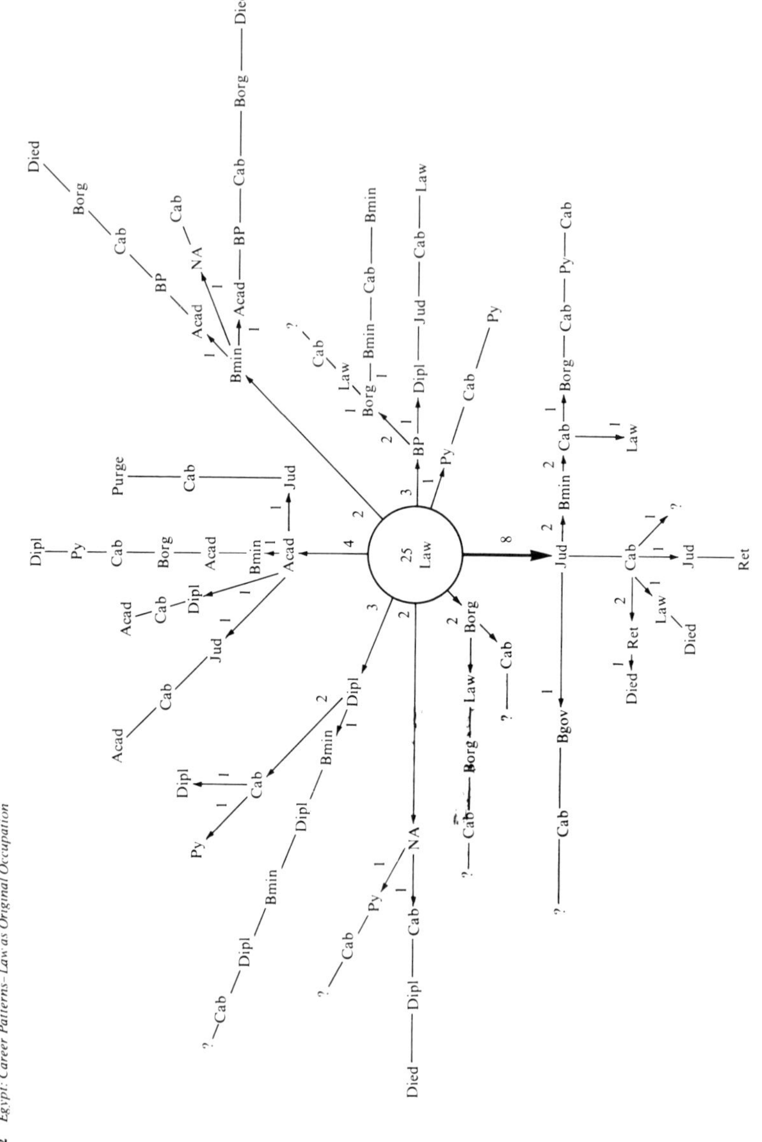

25
Law
Died
Borg
Cab
BP
NA
Acad
Bmin
BP
Cab
Borg
Died
Cab
Law
Borg
Bmin
Cab
Law
BP
Py
Cab
Purge
Cab
Jud
Dipl
Py
Cab
Borg
Acad
Bmin
Acad
Acad
Cab
Dipl
Acad
Cab
Jud
Acad
Cab
Dipl
Cab
Py
Dipl
Bmin
Dipl
Cab
Dipl
Bmin
Dipl
?
Cab
Py
Cab
NA
Died
Dipl
Cab
?
Cab
Borg
Law
Borg
?
Cab
Cab
Bgov
?
Jud
Bmin
Cab
Borg
Cab
Py
Cab
Law
Cab
Died
Ret
Law
Died
Jud
Ret
?

Chart 22   Egypt: Career Patterns–Law as Original Occupation

Chart 23   *Egypt: Career Patterns–Ministerial Bureaucracy as Original Occupation*

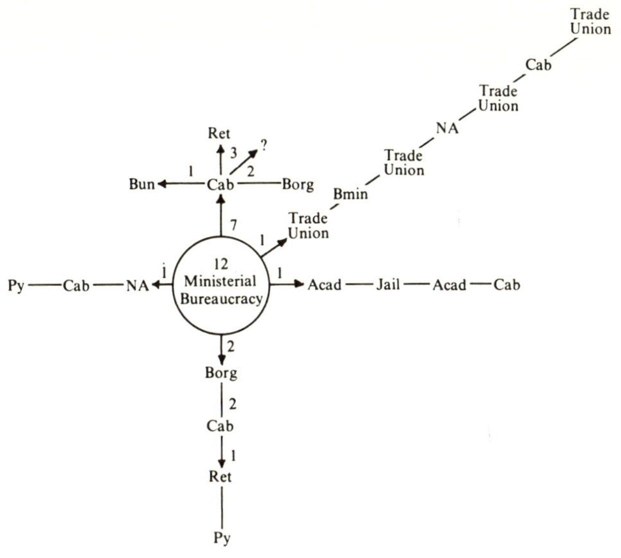

Chart 24   *Egypt: Career Patterns–Business-Professional as Original Occupation*

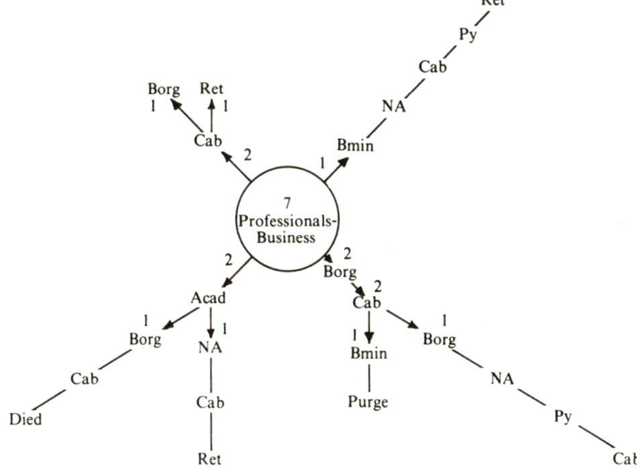

Chart 25 *Egypt: Career Patterns–Police as Original Occupation*

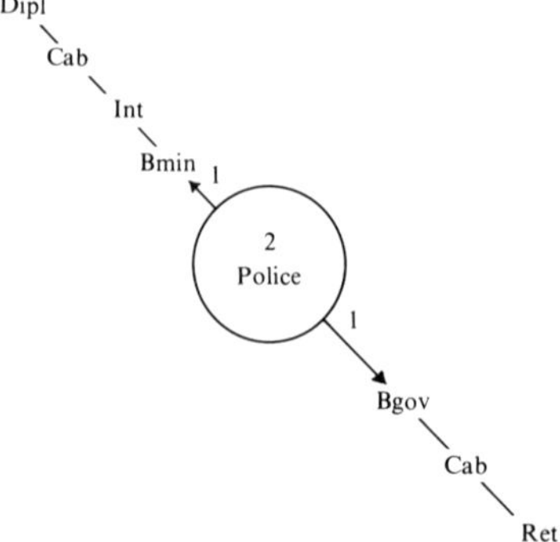

Chart 26 *Egypt: Career Patterns—Diplomatic Corps as Original Occupation*

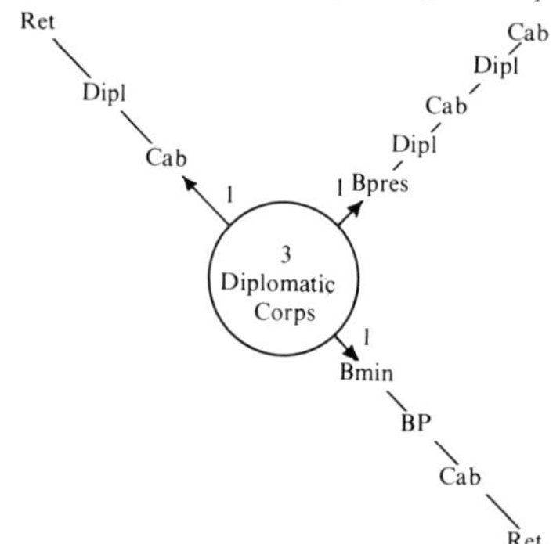

Chart 27   *Egypt: Career Patterns–Medicine as Original Occupation*

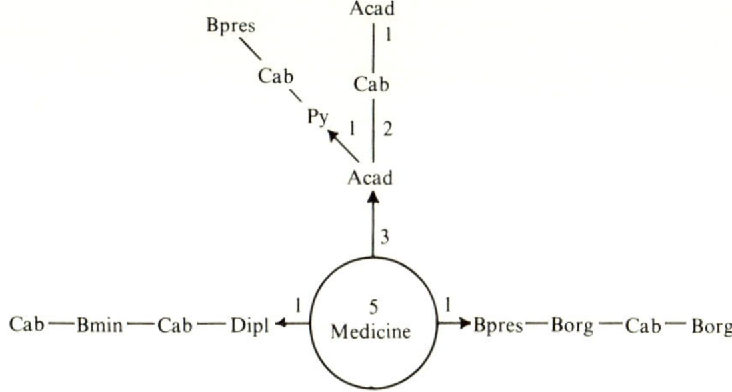

Chart 28   *Egypt: Career Patterns–Journalism as Original Occupation*

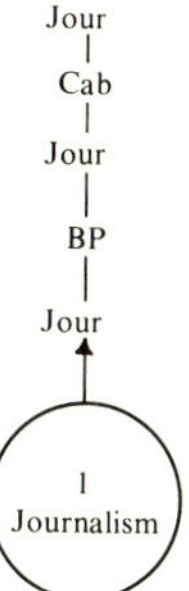

APPENDIX B

Lebanon: List of Ministers

Abbud, Muhammad
Abdallah, Husayn
Abi al-Lama', Ra'if
Abi Shahlah, Habib
Abu Hamad, Khalil
Abu Haydar, Najib
Abu Jawdih, Khalil
Abu Khatir, Yusif
Akkari, Nazim
Alam al-Din, Najib
Ali, Sulayman
Ammun, Fu'ad
Aql, Georges
Arab, Ali
Arslan, Majid
As'ad, Ahmad
As'ad, Kamil
A'war, Bashir
Aziz, Jean
Babikian, Khachig
Barbir, Nasib
Baydun, Rashid
Bayhum, Amin
Bazzi, Ali
Bitar, Emil
Bizri, Fu'ad
Bizri, Nazih
Bulus, Philippe
Bustani, Emil
Butrus, Fu'ad
Cham'un, Camille

Cozma, Farid
Daghir, Pierre
Dana, Usman
Da'uq, Ahmad
Dumit, Michel
Fadl, Muhammad
Far'awn, Henri
Fayyad, Bulus
Franjiyyah, Hamid
Franjiyyah, Sulayman
Gaspard, Edmond
Ghusn, Fu'ad
Ghusn, Nicolas
Hakim, Georges
Hamdan, Munir
Haydar, Salim
Hibri, Khalil
Hilu, Charles
Hilu, Pierre
Himadih, Sabri
Himadih, Sa'id
Hrawi, Georges
Hrawi, Yusif
Hunayn, Eduard
Husayni, Ahmad
Iddih, Henri
Iddih, Michel
Iddih, Pierre
Iddih, Raymond
Jarudi, Sa'ib
Jumayyil, Maurice

Jumayyil, Pierre
Junblat, Kamal
Junblat, Khalid
Karam, Georges
Karami, Abd al-Hamid
Karami, Rashid
Kayruz, Habib
Khalil, Kazim
Khatib, Anwar
Khazin, Clovis
Khuri, Elias
Khuri, Fu'ad
Khuri, Kamal
Khuri, Khalil
Khuri, Michel
Kibbih, Jamil
Kni'u, Muhammad
Lahhud, Emil
Lahhud, Jamil
Lahhud, Salim
Mahmassani, Subhi
Majdalani, Nassim
Makkawi, Jamil
Malik, Charles
Mallat, Wajdi
Ma'luf, Nasri
Mansur, Husayn
Mashnuq, Abdallah
Mu'awwad, Rene
Mubarak, Musa
Mughabghab, Na'im
Mugdad, Hasan
Mukhaybar, Albert
Munla, Sa'adi
Murr, Gabriel
Murr, Michel
Musharrafiyyah, Hasan
M'ushi, Badri
Mutran, Habib
Naffa', Fu'ad
Nahhas, Gibran
Na'im, Wadi'

Naja, Rafiq
Najjar, Fu'ad
Najjar, Joseph
Naqqash, Alfred
Naqqash, Georges
Nawfal, Sulayman
Nsuli, Muhyi al-Din
Nun, Eduard
Rizq, Fu'ad
Sa'adah, Georges
Saba, Ilyas
Sabbah, Anwar
Sabra, Muhammad
Safi al-Din, Muhammad
Sahnawi, Antoine
Salam, Sa'ib
Salha, Najib
Salim, Nicolas
Salim, Yusif
Salman, Salah
Sarraf, Ya'qub
Sassin, Michel
Sawmah, Edward
Sawdah, Joseph
Shadir, Joseph
Shahin, Ghalib
Shahin, Rafiq
Sharaf al-Din, Ja'far
Shihab, Fu'ad
Shihab, Jamil
Shihab, Khalid
Skaff, Jean
Skaff, Joseph
Stifan, Antoine
Sulh, Riyad
Sulh, Sami
Sulh, Taqi al-Din
Talhuq, Jamil
Taqi al-Din, Bahij
Taqla, Philippe
Taqla, Salim
Tarabay, Henri

Trad, Basil
Trad, Farid
Twayni, Ghassan
Tyyan, Emile
Usayran, Adil
Usman, Bashir
Uwayni, Husayn

Wahid, Rida
Wazzan, Shafiq
Yafi, Abdallah
Zayn, Abd al-Latif
Zayn, Sulayman
Zuwayn, Maurice

Israel: List of Ministers

Allon, Y'gal
Almogi, Joseph
Aranne, Zalman
Bar-Lev, Hayim
Bar Yehuda, Israel
Barzilai, Israel
Begin, M'nahem
Ben Aharon, Yitzhak
Ben Gurion, David
Bentov, Mord'khai
Bernstein, Peretz
Burg, Joseph
Carmel, Moshe
Cohn, Hayim
Dayan, Moshe
Dinur, Ben Zion
Dultzin, Leon
Eban, Abba
Eshkol, Levi
Galili, Israel
Geri, Ya'acov
Govrin, Akiva
Gruenbaum, Itzhak
Gvati, Hayim
Hazani, Mikhail
Hillel, Shlomo
Joseph, Dov
Josephthal, Giora
Kaplan, Eliezer
Kol, Moshe
Landau, Hayim
Lavon, Pinhas

Levin, Itzhak Meir
Luz, Kadish
Maimon, Yehuda-Leib
Meir, Golda
Mintz, Binyamin
Namir, Mord'khai
Naphtali, Peretz
Nurock, Mord'khai
Peled, Nathan
Peres, Shimon
Pinkas, David Zvi
Remez, David
Rimalt, Elimelech
Rokah, Yisrael
Rosen, Pinhas
Sapir, Pinhas
Saphir, Yoseph
Sasson, Eliahu
Serlin, Joseph
Shapira, Moshe Hayim
Shapiro, Yaacov Shimshon
Sharef, Ze'ev
Sharett, Moshe
Shazar, Zalman
Shemtov, Victor
Shitrit, B'khor Shalom
Toledano, Ya'acov Moshe
Warhaftig, Zerah
Weizmann, Ezer
Yeshayahu, Israel
Zadok, Hayim
Zisling, Aaron

Egypt: List of Ministers

Abd al-Fattah, Hasan
Abd al-Fattah, Tawfiq
Abd al-Hay, Sulayman
Abd al-Karim, Muhammad Ali
Abdallah, Ismail Sabri
Abd al-Majid, Ahmad Ismail
Abd al-Malik, Jindi
Abd al-Nasir, Gamal
Abd al-Raziq, Ali
Abd al-Salam, Mahmud
Abu al-Izz, Muhammad
Abu al-Nur, Abd al-Muhsin
Abu Ghazi, Badr al-Din
Abu Nusayr, Muhammad
Abu Zayd, Hikmat
Abu Zayd, Husayn
Ahmad, Muhammad Bakr
Ahmad, Muhammad Mursi
Ahmad, Mustafa Ahmad
Ali, Abd al-Aziz
Amarah, Abd al-Mun'im
Amir, Abd al-Hakim
Ammar, Abbas Mustafa
Antun, Farid
Arafa, Musa
Ashur, Hamdi Muhammad
Badawi, Bahjat Hilmi
Badawi, Hafiz
Badawi, Hasan Fahmi
Badir, Kamal Henri
Badran, Shams al-Din
Badran, Usman Adli
Baghdadi, Abd al-Latif
Baghdadi, Hasan
Baghdadi, Hasan Ahmad
Bahi, Muhammad
Bakri, Ahmad Tawfiq
Baquri, Ahmad Hasan
Bishri, Abd al-Wahhab
Bultiya, Abd al-Latif
Burullusi, Abd al-Wahhab

Darwish, Ahmad
Dawud, Dia' al-Din
Dif, Nazih Ahmad
Fahmi, Abd al-Azim
Fahmi, Murad Mustafa
Fa'iq, Muhammad
Faraj, Ahmad Ali
Fawzi, Mahmud
Fawzi, Muhammad
Gaballah, Sayyid
Galal, Fu'ad Muhammad
Ghalib, Muhammad Murad
Ghanim, Ismail
Ghanim, Muhammad Hafiz
Gharib, Salah al-Din
Giritli, Ali
Guma'a, Sha'rawi
Hafiz, Muhammad Ali
Hafiz, Sulayman
Hafiz, Yusif
Hamdi, Mahmud
Hammuda, Badawi Ibrahim
Hanna, William Salim
Hashad, Muhammad
Hashim, Ahmad Najib
Hashim, Zaki
Hasuna, Muhammad Isam
  al-Din
Hatim, Abd al-Qadir
Haykal, Muhammad Hasanayn
Hidayat, Salah al-Din
Hijazi, Abd al-Aziz
Hilmi, Samir
Himaydah, Hasan
Husayn, Kamal al-Din
Husni, Ahmad
Huwaydi, Amin
Huzayyin, Sulayman
Ibrahim, Hasan
Ibrahim, Ibrahim Najib
Ibrahim, Muhammad

Iffat, Ahmad Muhammad
Imari, Abd al-Galil
Ismail, Ahmad
Ismail, Muhammad Hafiz
Ismail, Muhammad Kamal
Jabali, Mustafa
Kamil, Abd al-Aziz
Kamil, Amin Hilmi
Khalifa, Ahmad Muhammad
Khalil, Mustafa
Khallaf, Husayn
Khatib, Muhammad Fathallah
Khawaja, Muhammad
Khayri, Muhammad
Khishin, Shafiq
Khuli, Hasan Sabri
Mazkur, Ibrahim
Mahfuz, Mahmud Muhammad
Mahmud, Abd al-Halim
Mansur, Muhammad Sabri
Mar'i, Hasan
Mar'i, Sayyid
Marziban, Muhammad Abdallah
Mazin, Ahmad
Mubarak, Husni
Muhammad, Abd al-Aziz
Muhammad ali al-Sayyid
Muhammad, Awad Muhammad
Muhammad, Muhammad Ahmad
Muhandis, Muhammad
  al-Nabawi
Muharram, Ahmad
Muhyi al-Din, Zakariyya
Mulla, Yahya
Murad, Muhammad Hilmi
Mursi, Fu'ad
Mustafa, Hasan
Najib, Muhammad
Nasif, Muhammad al-Laithi
Nassar, Muhammad Mahmud
Nasr, Muhammad Abd al-Raziq
Nuh, Ahmad

Qabbani, Ismail
Qaysuni, Ibrahim Zaki
Qinnawi, Ibrahim
Quni, Muhammad Awad
Qurra, Muhammad Nur al-Din
Ratib, Aysha
Rif'at, Kamal
Riyad, Mahmud
Riyad, Muhammad
Rizq, Fathi
Rudwan, Abbas
Rudwan, Fathi
Sa'ad, Abd al-Malik
Sa'ad, Aziz Yusif
Sabri, Ali
Sabri, Husayn Zu al-Fiqar
Sadat, Anwar
Sadiq, Muhammad Ahmad
Sa'id, Husayn Muhammad
Salah al-Din, Hasan
Salama, Anwar
Salama, Muhammad
Salama, Muhammad Izzat
Salih, Ali Zayn Abdin
Salim, Abd al-Aziz
Salim, Gamal
Salim, Mamduh
Salim, Muhammad Ibrahim
Salim, Salah
Sallam, Abdu
Sayyid, Abd al-Aziz
Sayyid, Hilmi
Shafi'i, Husayn
Shakir, Amin Mustafa
Sharabasi, Ahmad
Sharaf, Sami
Sharif, Abd al-Hamid
Sharkawi, Fathi
Shinnawi, Abd al-Khaliq
Shukri, Abd al-Wahhab
Shuqayr, Muhammad Labib
Sidqi, Abd al-Raziq

Sidqi, Aziz
Stinu, Kamal Ramzi
Sulayman, Sidqi
Sultan, Ahmad
Tarraf, Nur al-Din
Tayi', Ahmad Faraj
Tuhami, Hasan
Tu'aymah, Ahmad Abdallah
Tulbah, Mustafa Kamal
Turki, Ahmad Riyad
Ubayd, Ahmad

Ukasha, Sarwat
Wakil, Shams al-Din
Wali, Ali
Yasin, Aziz Ahmad
Yunis, Mahmud
Yusif, Sayyid Muhammad
Zaki, Hasan Abbas
Zandu, Ahmad
Zayid, Muhammad Sa'ad al-Din
Zayyat, Abd al-Salam
Zayyat, Muhammad Hasan

Notes

Chapter 1. The Comparative Study of Political Elites

1. Edinger discusses the reasons for scarcity of research on leadership in Lewis Joachim Edinger, "Political Science and Political Biography: Reflections on the Study of Leadership (I)," *Journal of Politics* 26, no. 2 (May 1964): 428–430. Commenting on the underdeveloped status of elite studies, Seligman contends that the study of the American executive has progressed little in the last thirty years, see Lester G. Seligman, "Political Elites Reconsidered," *Comparative Politics* 6, no. 2 (January 1974): 313. For data compiled on American cabinet secretaries, high-level bureaucrats, and White House personnel, see David T. Stanley, Dean E. Mann, and Jameson W. Doig, *Men Who Govern* (Washington, D.C.: Brookings Institution, 1967); John Jay Corson and R. Shale Paul, *Men Near the Top* (Baltimore: Johns Hopkins Press, 1966); Dean E. Mann and Jameson W. Doig, *The Assistant Secretaries* (Washington, D.C.: Brookings Institution, 1965); Richard F. Fenno, *The President's Cabinet* (Cambridge, Mass.: Harvard University Press, 1959); Alex B. Lacy, Jr., "The White House Staff Bureaucracy," *Transaction* 6, no. 3 (January 1969): 50–55; George William Domhoff, *Who Rules America?* (Englewood Cliffs: Prentice-Hall, 1967). For extensive bibliographies on elites see Lewis Joachim Edinger, *Political Leadership in Industrialized Societies* (New York: John Wiley, 1967) and William B. Quandt. *The Comparative Study of Political Elites* (Beverly Hills, Calif.: Sage Publications, 1970).

2. Harold Dwight Lasswell and Daniel Lerner, eds., *World Revolutionary Elites* (Cambridge, Mass.: M.I.T. Press, 1965) and Harold Dwight Lasswell, Daniel Lerner, and C. Easton Rothwell, *The Comparative Study of Elites* (Stanford, Calif.: Stanford University Press, 1952).

3. Edinger, *Political Leadership in Industrialized Societies.*

4. Robert Barry Farrell, ed., *Political Leadership in Eastern Europe and the Soviet Union* (Chicago: Aldine Publishing Co., 1970). Also see the paper by Carl Beck, "Aggregate Career Characteristics of Eastern European Political Leaders" (Paper delivered to International Studies Program, Pittsburgh, 1968).

5. Quandt, *The Comparative Study.*

6. Dwaine Marvick, *Political Decision-Makers* (New York: Free Press of Glencoe, 1961).

7. Rupert Wilkinson, ed., *Governing Elites* (New York: Oxford University Press, 1969).

8. Seymour Martin Lipset and Aldo Solari, eds., *Elites in Latin America* (New York: Oxford University Press, 1967).

9. Zbigniew Brzezinski and Samuel P. Huntington, *Political Power: USA/USSR* (New York: Viking Press, 1964). Another two-country elite study is Thom Kerstiens, *The New Elite in Asia and Africa: A Comparative Study of Indonesia and Ghana* (New York: Frederick A. Praeger, 1966). On the comparative analysis of legislative elites see John C. Wahlke, Heinz Eulau, William Buchanan, and LeRoy C. Ferguson, *The Legislative System* (New York: John Wiley, 1962).

10. C. C. Moskos Jr. and W. Bell, "Attitudes Towards Democracy Among Leaders in Four Emerging Nations," *British Journal of Sociology* 15, no. 4 (December 1964): 317–337.

11. Daniel Lerner and Morton Gorden, *Euratlantica: Changing Perspectives of the European Elites* (Cambridge, Mass.: M.I.T. Press, 1969).

12. Karl Wolfgang Deutsch, Roy C. Macridis, and Richard L. Merritt, *France, Germany and the Western Alliance: A Study of Elite Attitudes on European Integration and World Politics* (New York: Charles Scribner's Sons, 1967).

13. E. Victor Wolfenstein, *The Revolutionary Personality* (Princeton: Princeton University Press, 1971) and *Personality and Politics* (Belmont, Calif.: Dickenson Publishing Co., 1969).

14. James David Barber, *The Presidential Character* (Englewood Cliffs: Prentice-Hall, 1972).

15. Dankwart A. Rustow, ed., *Philosophers and Kings* (New York: George Braziller, 1970). Also noteworthy is a monograph comparing presidents, see Erwin C. Hargrove, *Presidential Leadership: Personality and Political Style* (New York: Macmillan & Co., 1966).

16. This is often called Robert Michels's "iron rule of oligarchy," see Geraint Parry, *Political Elites* (New York: Frederick A. Praeger, 1969), p. 42.

17. For a cogent discussion, see Frederick W. Frey, "The Determination and Location of Elites: A Critical Analysis" (Paper delivered at Sixty-sixth Annual Meeting of the American Political Sciences Association, Los Angeles, California, 8–12 September 1970). Also see Robert Putnam, "Studying Elite Political Culture," *American Political Science Review* 65, no. 3 (September 1971): 651–681.

18. Seligman finds this centrality of elites to be a distinguishing feature of the twentieth century. See Lester G. Seligman, "The Study of Political Leadership," *American Political Science Review* 44, no. 4 (December 1950): 904–915.

19. Especially relevant in this connection is the quotation from Montesquieu in Dankwart A. Rustow, *A World of Nations* (Washington, D.C.: Brookings Institution, 1967), p. 135, "At the birth of societies, it is the leaders of the commonwealth who create the institutions; afterwards, it is the institutions that shape the leaders."

20. On differing views about the determination of the elite see, Robert Alan Dahl, *Who Governs?* (New Haven: Yale University Press, 1961); Peter Bachrach, *The Theory of Democratic Elitism* (Boston: Little Brown & Co., 1967); Gaetano Mosca, *The Ruling Class,* trans. by Hannah D. Kahn (New York: McGraw-Hill Co., 1939); Charles Wright Mills, *The Power Elite* (New York: Oxford University Press, 1956); Richard L. Merritt, *Systematic Approaches to Comparative Poli-*

tics (Chicago: Rand McNally & Co., 1970), pp. 104–139; Robert Putnam, "Studying Elite Political Culture"; Frederick W. Frey, "The Determination and Location of Elites."

21. For a general discussion of Lebanon see Michael Craig Hudson, *The Precarious Republic* (New York: Random House, 1968). On the situation in Egypt see Richard Hrair Dekmejian, *Egypt Under Nasir* (Albany, N.Y.: State University of New York Press, 1971; University of London Press, 1972). On Israel see Joseph Badi, *The Government of the State of Israel* (New York: Twayne Publishers, 1963), pp. 266 and 173–216; also Yehoshua Freudenheim, *Government in Israel,* trans. by Meir Silverstone and Chaim Ivor Goldwater (Dobbs Ferry, N.Y.: Oceana Publications, 1967), pp. 169–70; Ervin Birnbaum, *The Politics of Compromise: State and Religion in Israel* (Rutherford: Fairleigh Dickinson University Press, 1970). On Lebanon also see Ralph E. Crow, "Religious Sectarianism in the Lebanese Political System," *Journal of Politics* 24, no. 3 (August 1962): 504–508.

22. Elite studies using approaches which have been useful to the author include: Raymond Aron, "Social Structure and the Ruling Class," *British Journal of Sociology* 1, no. 1 (March 1950): 1–16; Donald R. Matthews, *The Social Background of Political Decision-Makers* (Garden City, N.Y.: Doubleday & Co., 1954); Carl Beck and James M. Malloy, "Political Elites: A Mode of Analysis," (Geneva, 1964); Lewis Joachim Edinger and Donald D. Searing, "Social Background in Elite Analysis," *American Political Science Review* 61, no. 2 (June 1967): 429–445; Morris Janowitz, "The Systematic Analysis of Political Biography," *World Politics* 6, no. 3 (April 1954): 405–412; Lester G. Seligman, "Elite Recruitment and Political Development," *Journal of Politics* 26, no. 3 (August 1964): 612–624; W. L. Guttsman, *The British Political Elite* (London: MacGibbon and Kee, 1963); Frederick W. Frey, *The Turkish Political Elite* (Cambridge, Mass.: M.I.T. Press, 1965); M. P. Gehlen and M. McBride, "The Soviet Central Committee: An Elite Analysis," *American Political Science Review* 62, no. 4 (December 1968): 1232–1241; Manfred Halpern, *The Politics of Social Change in the Middle East and North Africa* (Princeton: Princeton University Press, 1963); Robert Vance Presthus, *Men at the Top* (New York: Oxford University Press, 1964); William B. Quandt, *Revolution and Political Leadership* (Cambridge, Mass.: M.I.T. Press, 1969); Austin Ranney, *Pathways to Parliament* (Madison: University of Wisconsin Press, 1965); Joseph A. Schlesinger, *Ambition and Politics* (Chicago: Rand McNally & Co., 1966); José Luis de Imaz, *Los Que Mandan,* trans. by Carlos A. Astiz (Albany, N.Y.: State University of New York Press, 1971); Karl Mannheim, *Man and Society in an Age of Reconstruction* (New York: Harcourt, Brace and World, 1967), pp. 82–86; T. B. Bottomore, *Elites and Society* (London: C. A. Watts, 1964); Marvick, *Political Decision-makers;* Parry, *Political Elites;* and Lasswell and Lerner, *World Revolutionary Elites;* and Dankwart Rustow, "Who's Who, When and How," *World Politics* 18, no. 4 (1966): 690–717.

23. Although often the distinction between deductive and inductive approaches may be artificial, see Ted Robert Gurr, *Politimetrics* (Englewood Cliffs: Prentice-Hall, 1972), p. 7

24. Parry, *Political Elites,* p. 102; Guttsman, *The British Political Elite,* p.

32. For a review of the traditional literature on elites, see Renzo Sereno, *The Rulers* (Leiden: E. J. Brill, 1962).

25. Seligman, "Elite Recruitment," pp. 612–613.

26. Seliqman, "Elite Recruitment," pp. 612–613; also Quandt, *The Comparative Study,* pp. 195–197.

27. Dekmejian, *Egypt Under Nasir,* pp. 2–16. However, the strictly representative character of an elite may not be necessary for its legitimation if representativeness is not important in a particular political culture. In such instances the elite may rather be drawn from those who are believed most capable of ruling. See, Parry, *Political Elites,* p. 105; Bottomore, *Elites and Society,* pp. 32–33; Guttsman, *The British Political Elite,* pp. 67–69. With the modernization process, however, the quest for representation has become universal.

28. Edinger and Searing, "Social Background," p. 445; Donald B. Searing, "The Comparative Study of Elite Socialization, *Comparative Political Studies* 14, no. 4 (January 1969): 471–500; Schlesinger, *Ambition and Politics,* pp. 13–15.

29. Wilkinson, *Governing Elites,* pp. 215–224.

Chapter 2. Elites in a Sectarian Democracy: Lebanon

1. The sources of data include: *Majmu'ah al-Bayanat al-Wizariyyah al-Lubnaniyyah* [Collection of Lebanese Ministerial Pronouncements] (Beirut, n.p., 1965); *Al-Intikhabat Khamsin Sanat wa Sanat* [Fifty-One Years of Elections] (Beirut: Al-Nahar, 1972); *Who's Who in Lebanon, 1963–4, 1965–6, 1967–8, 1970–1; Arab Report and Record; Al-Nahar; Daily Star; Al-Hayat; Keesing's Contemporary Archives; Facts on File; Whitaker's Almanac; Middle East and North Africa.*

2. Arnold Hottinger, "Zu'ama' in Historical Perspective," in *Politics in Lebanon* by Leonard Binder, ed. (New York: John Wiley & Sons, 1966), pp. 86–105.

3. For an in-depth study see Peter Gubser, "The Zu'ama' of Zahlah: The Current Situation in a Lebanese Town," *Middle East Journal* 27, no. 2 (Spring 1973): 173–189. Also see Evelyn Aleene Early, "The Emergence of an Urban Za'im: A Social Network Analysis" (paper delivered at Middle East Studies Association Conference, Milwaukee, Wisconsin, 8–10 November 1973). On the class structure of Lebanon see Fuad I. Khuri, "The Changing Class Structure in Lebanon," *Middle East Journal* 23, no. 1 (Winter 1969): 29–44.

4. This is the opposite of Hottinger's assertion, Hottinger, "Zu'ama'," p. 86.

5. Historical analysis of this period is based on the following: Kamal Suleiman Salibi, *The Modern History of Lebanon* (New York: Frederick A. Praeger, 1965); Antun Dahir al-Aqiqi, *Lebanon in the Last Years of Feudalism, 1840–1868,* trans, and ed. by Malcolm H. Kerr (Beirut: American University of Beirut, 1959); William Roe Polk, *The Opening of South Lebanon 1788–1840* (Cambridge, Mass.: Harvard University Press, 1963); Iliya F. Harik, *Politics and Change in a Traditional Society: Lebanon, 1711–1845* (Princeton: Princeton Uni-

versity Press, 1968); Albert Habib Hourani, *Syria and Lebanon* (New York: Oxford University Press, 1946); Leonard Binder, ed., *Politics in Lebanon* (New York: John Wiley & Sons, 1966); *Ri'asa' ma Qabl al-Istiqlal* [Presidents Before Independence] (Beirut: Political Library, 1970); Basim al-Jisr, *Ri'asah wa Siyasah wa al-Lubnan al-Jadid* [The Presidency, Politics, and the New Lebanon] (Beirut: Al-Hayat, 1964); Husayn Ghadban Abu Shaqra and Yusif Khattar Abu Shaqra, *Al-Harakat fi Lubnan ila Ahd al-Mutasarrifiyyah* [Movements in Lebanon During the Mutasarrifite Period] (Beirut, n.d.); Amir Haydar Ahmad Shihab, *Lubnan fi Ahd al-Umara al-Shihabiyyin* [Lebanon in the Period of the Shihabi Amirs] (Beirut: Lebanese University, 1969), 3 volumes; Shaykh Ahmad Ibn Muhammad al-Khalidi, *Lubnan fi Ahd al-Amir Fakhr al-Din al-Ma'ani al-Thani* [Lebanon During the Time of Amir Fakhr al-Din al-Ma'ani, the Second] (Beirut: Catholic Press, 1936); Hamdi Badawi al-Tahiri, *Siyasah al-Hukm fi Lubnan* [The Politics of Governance in Lebanon] (Cairo: Dar al-Qawmiyyah, 1966); Gibran Jurayj, *Haqa'iq an al-Istiqlal Ayyam Rashayya* [Facts about Independence and Rashayya Days] (Beirut: Dar al-Fann, n.d.).

6. The list includes only those political families whose members have reached cabinet office since 1943.

7. Stephen Hemsley Longrigg, *Syria and Lebanon Under French Mandate* (London: Oxford University Press, 1958), p. 51. Also Zeine N. Zeine, *The Emergence of Arab Nationalism,* 3d ed., (Delmar, N.Y.: Caravan Books, 1973). It has been alleged by various individuals that some of the nationalist leaders were initially supporters of Jemal Pasha's conspiracy against the Ottoman Empire and the Young Turk ruling oligarchy. This plan would have brought about a secession of the Arab provinces of the Ottoman Empire under Jemal's leadership. It is alleged that eventually the conspiracy was aborted and Jemal liquidated his Arab supporters. However, to date, there is no sufficient documentation to support this theory.

8. Salim Butrus Usabiyus, *Dalil Marahil Lubnan Abr al-Tarikh* [Directory of the Historical Stages of Lebanon] (Beirut: n.p., 1955), p. 5.

9. On certain of these Lebanese patriots see, Hottinger, ''Zu'ama','' p. 93.

10. Michael Craig Hudson, *The Precarious Republic* (New York: Random House, 1968), pp. 131–132, and Hottinger, ''Zu'ama','' p. 87. Note that table includes only landed families who have contributed ministers. Other large landed families include the Jisrs, Dwayhis, Muqaddams, to mention a few.

11. Salibi, *The Modern History,* p. 10.

12. Leila M. T. Meo, *Lebanon, Improbable Nation* (Bloomington, Indiana: Indiana University Press, 1965), pp. 151, 135, 173.

13. See Hottinger, ''Zu'ama','' p. 92, and Salibi, *The Modern History,* p. 174.

14. One such emerging Sunni is Amin Hafiz, a Tripoli deputy who was appointed prime minister during the fighting between the Lebanese army and the Palestinians in the spring of 1973. Another Sunni Leader, Taqi al-Din Sulh, succeeded Hafiz as prime minister.

15. Salibi, *The Modern History,* p. 170. The ensuing historical analysis is based on Meo, *Lebanon;* Hudson, *The Precarious Republic;* and Muhammad

Jamil Bayhum, *Lubnan Bayna Mushriqin wa Maghribin, 1920–1969* [Lebanon Between Easterners and Westerners, 1920–1969] (Beirut: n.p., 1969); Malcolm H. Kerr, "Political Decision-Making in a Confessional Democracy," in Binder, *Politics in Lebanon,* pp. 187–212; Eli Salim, "Cabinet Politics in Lebanon," *Middle East Journal* 21, no. 4 (Autumn 1967): 488–502; Kamal Salibi, "Lebanon Under Fuad Chehad: 1958–1964," *Middle Eastern Studies* 2, no. 3 (April 1966): 211–226; Malcolm H. Kerr, "Lebanese Views on the 1958 Crisis," *Middle East Journal* 15, no. 1 (Winter 1961): 211–217; and Malcolm H. Kerr, "The 1960 Lebanese Parliamentary Elections," *Middle Eastern Affairs* 11, no. 9 (October 1960): 266–275.

16. Also Bahij Taqi al-Din and Bashir al-A'war.

17. Rashid Baydun, Muhammad Safi al-Din, Husayn al-Abdallah, Ahmad al-Husayni, and Muhammad al-Fadl.

18. For a detailed analysis, see Hudson, *The Precarious Republic,* pp. 145–151.

19. The Catholics included Salim and Philippe Taqla, Henri Far'awn (and M. Chiha), Yusif Salim and Sulayman Nawfal.

20. Other Maronite cabinet leaders under Khuri included Wadi' Na'im, Yusif Hrawi, Elias al-Khuri, Ra'if Abi al-Lama', Khalil Abu Jawdih, Edward Nun, Michel Dumit, Musa Mubarak, and Antoine Stifan.

21. For a comprehensive list of cabinets, see *Who's Who in Lebanon, 1970–71.*

22. The new ministers were Hamid Franjiyyah (M), Emile Lahhud (M), Sami al-Sulh (Su), Sa'adi Munla (Su), Gabriel Murr (O); and Yusif Salim (C).

23. These were Constitutionalists Emile Lahhud, Philippe Taqla, Arslan, and Husayni, and Independents such as Munla, Yusif Hrawi, Sa'ib Salam, and Gabriel Murr.

24. Hudson, *The Precarious Republic,* p. 152.

25. Including Rashid Karami, Rashid Baydun, Sulayman al-Ali, Philippe Taqla, and others.

26. Khalid Shihab, Musa Mubarak, Salim Haydar, and George Hakim.

27. Hudson, *The Precarious Republic,* pp. 154–5.

28. Carryovers in the September 1954 cabinet were Arslan, Naqqash, Murr, Karami, Zuwayn, Mughabghab, Haydar, al-Nsuli, and Hilu.

29. The interministerial conflicts causing the fall of the cabinet included a dispute over the ambassadorial appointment to Paris. The real and deeper reason was the deepening sectarian conflict.

30. Besides Arslan and Khalil, the recruits included Jamil Makkawi, Jamil Shihab, Nazih al-Bizri, Joseph Skaff, Salim Lahhud, Fu'ad Ghusn, and Georges Aql.

31. Also included were Emile al-Bustani, Muhammad Sabra, Georges Karam, and Georges Hakim.

32. For fuller accounts see, Meo, *Lebanon,* pp. 97–101 and Hudson, *The Precarious Republic,* pp. 288–9.

33. Meo, *Lebanon.*

34. These were Muhammad Sabra, Nasri Ma'luf, and Charles Malik.

35. He was replaced by Emile Tyyan.

36. Meo, *Lebanon,* p. 133.

37. *Ibid.,* pp. 135–6.

38. Included Arslan, Khalil, Salim Lahhud, Joseph Skaff, Makkawi, Cozma, and Malik.

39. Meo, *Lebanon,* p. 154.

40. This large cabinet also included Malik, Skaff, Cozma, Khalil, A'war, Usman, Arslan, Hibri, Mukhaybar, Khazin, and Baydun.

41. Meo, *Lebanon,* p. 174.

42. These included Muhammad Safi al-Din, Joseph Sawda, Rafiq Naja, Farid Trad, and Fu'ad Najjar.

43. However, Sami al-Sulh was successful in getting elected to the Chamber in 1964.

44. Hudson, *The Precarious Republic,* p. 332. The new ministers were Philippe Taqla, Ali Bazzi, Fu'ad Butrus, Maurice Zuwayn, and Fu'ad Najjar.

45. Others were Naqqash, Nahhas, Baydun, Najjar, Gaspard, and Muqdad.

46. The few who won included Arslan, Skaff, Bustani, and Usayran.

47. Hudson, *The Precarious Republic,* pp. 303–4.

48. These were Junblat, Taqla, Jumayyil, and Franjiyyah. Others were Mashnuq, Ali, Safi al-Din, and Bulus.

49. Butrus, Bulus, Naja, Dana, J. Skaff, Taqla—later Bizri replaced Hunayn.

50. Taqla resigned in April 1964 and his place was taken by another Catholic, Joseph Najjar.

51. These neutrals were Amin Bayhum, Muhammad Kni'u, Rida Wahid, Fu'ad Najjar, and Gibran Nahhas.

52. Both Raymond Iddih and Camille Cham'un were defeated.

53. The cabinet included Uwayni, Taqla, Zuwayn, Hunayn, Jumayyil, Taqi al-Din, Dana, G. Shahin, Sarraf, and T. Sulh.

54. Others included Sulayman Zayn, Joseph Najjar, Muhammad Kni'u, Rafiq Naja. Subsequent additions were Michel Khuri, Rida Wahid, and Pierre Daghir.

55. The government included Junblat, Jumayyil, K. al-As'ad, Hunayn, Mahmassani, J. Lahhud, Usman, and F. Butrus.

56. Michel Iddih, Michel Khuri, Sulayman Zayn, Fu'ad Rizq, Sa'id Himadih, Badri M'ushi, Fu'ad Bizri, and Nassib Barbir.

57. These were Yafi, Franjiyyah, Hunayn, Aziz, Dana, Khatib, and Junblat. The only loser was Fu'ad Butrus.

58. Far'awn resigned protesting electoral irregularities; Joseph Najjar took his place.

59. Khalil Khuri, Yusif Salim, Habib Kayruz, and Muhammad Safi al-Din.

60. The ministers were Majdalani, Kayruz, Zayn, Mu'awwad, Taqi al-Din, Arslan, Safi al-Din, Wazzan, Usayran, Dana, Abu Khatir, Murr, Salim, Khuri, and Babikian.

61. The remaining ministers were Mutran, Majdalani, Franjiyyah, Zayn, Usayran, Ghusn, Abu Khatir, Shahin, Khatib, Dana, and Babikian.

62. Other ex-Cham'unites included Joseph Skaff, Nazih Bizri, and Sulayman al-Ali.

63. Except Hunayn (August 1972) and his replacement by Henri Iddih who was later dismissed for insubordination.

64. Hudson, *The Precarious Republic*, p. 240.

65. The same drop in the proportion of landowners in the Chamber was noted by Hudson, *The Precarious Republic*, pp. 241–244.

66. Salibi, *The Modern History*, p. 132.

67. This point is confirmed in regard to deputies by Michael Hudson, *The Precarious Republic*, pp. 244–245.

68. The overrepresentation of the Sunnis and Greek Orthodox is also manifested at ambassadorial and high administrative levels. Similarly the Shi'ites at these levels are grossly underrepresented. See Ralph E. Crow, "Religious Sectarianism in the Lebanese Political System," *Journal of Politics* 24, no. 3 (August 1962): 519

69. The fifteen ministers whose birthplaces are unknown might include one or more born in Bint Jbayl.

70. There has not been a census in Lebanon since 1932.

71. The findings on competitiveness for cabinet office differs from those of Michael Hudson regarding parliamentary elections. By using electoral margins Hudson finds Mount Lebanon most competitive, followed by South Lebanon, Biqa', North Lebanon, and Beirut. See Hudson, *The Precarious Republic*, pp. 228–9.

72. Also applicable here is reference-group theory which emphasizes the psychological relationship between an individual and the groups with which he identifies. Such reference groups are thought to affect one's values and behavior. See Robert M. Price, "A Theoretical Approach to Military Rule in New States," *World Politics* 23, no. 3 (April 1971): 399–430. However, one may always find exceptions, i.e., soldiers and lawyers who do not behave according to their group behavioral norms.

73. These included Center Bloc, National Awakening Movement, National Struggle Party, Salam Bloc, National Liberal Party, As'ad Bloc, National Bloc, Kata'ib, Dashnaks, Skaff Bloc, and Ba'ath.

Chapter 3. Elites in a New Society: Israel

1. Peter Y. Medding, *Mapai in Israel: Political Organization and Government in a New Society* (London: Cambridge University Press, 1972), pp. 122–129.

2. Biographical sources utilized for quantitative analysis included: *Israeli Government Yearbook, 1950–1972; Who's Who in Israel, 1952, 1964–5, 1966–7, 1972; Zionist Yearbook, 1969–70, 1970–71, 1972; Who's Who in World Jewry, 1965; Encyclopedia of Zionism and Israel, Vol. I and II; Whitaker's Almanac; Statesman's Yearbook; Keesing's Contemporary Archives; Facts on File;* "Chronology" of *Middle East Journal; Jerusalem Post; Haaretz; Maariv; Statistical Abstract of Israel,* 1972 (Jerusalem, 1972); David Knaani, *Entzeklopedia le-Mada'ei Ha-Hevrah,* Vols. I, II, III, IV (Jerusalem, n.d.); Mikha'il Ben Tzvi, *Reshei' Ha-Rishu'yot Ha-Mikomiyot bi-Yisrael* (Heads of Local Councils in Israel) (Tel Aviv, 1971); Yehudah Slutzki, *Toldot Ha-Haganah* (History of the Haganah) (Tel Aviv: AmOved, 1972); Nathan Yoni, *Kar'a Batsameret* (Cleav-

ages in the Leadership) (Tel Aviv: Artzi, 1969); Nachman Tamir, ed., *Anshe Ha-Aliyah Ha-Sheniyah* (The People of the Second Aliyah) (Tel Aviv: Histadrut, 1970, 1971, 1972). Biographical data was standardized in accordance with the *Encyclopedia of Zionism and Israel.*

3. For a concise account of the anti-Jewish milieu, see Terence Prittie, *Eshkol: the Man and the Nation* (New York: Pitman Publishing Corp., 1969, pp. 3–15; Gershon Winer, *The Founding Fathers of Israel* (New York: Bloch Publishing Co., 1971).

4. Of course, those born in Palestine and other Middle Eastern lands were not involved in these groups, nor did the few who were brought to Palestine as children.

5. The relationship between communications and leadership is explored by Dankwart A. Rustow, *A World of Nations* (Washington, D.C.: Brookings Institution, 1967), pp. 162–164.

6. For data on the great frequency of foreign travel and residence of Jewish Executive members, see Taysir Nashif, "A Quantitative Comparative Study of the Jewish and Palestine Arab Elites (1920–48)" (Ph.D. diss., SUNY-Binghamton, 1974).

7. Also Yitzhak Ben Zvi, later president of Israel.

8. For the concept of political generation, see William B. Quandt, *Revolution and Political Leadership* (Cambridge, Mass.: M.I.T. Press, 1969), p. 20.

9. V. D. Segre, *Israel: A Society in Transition* (London: Oxford University Press, 1971), p. 61. It should be noted that the author's periodization does not always agree with Segre's.

10. Govrin, Shapira, Mintz, Levin, Joseph, Eban, Shapiro, Maimon, Rimalt, Shazar, Serlin, Shitrit, Warhaftig, Zadok, Yeshayahu, Sasson, Namir, Toledano, Luz, Kol, Pinkas, and Nurock.

11. See Ben Gurion's view of early Jewish farmers whom he labeled "effendis" in a derogatory sense. David Ben Gurion, *Israel: Years of Challenge* (New York: Holt, Rinehart, and Winston, 1963), p. 7.

12. On kibbutz ideology, see Alan Arian, *Ideological Change in Israel* (Cleveland: Press of Case Western Reserve University, 1968), pp. 58–170.

13. On the disproportionate influence of kibbutz members in Israeli life, see Albert I. Rabin, "Personality Study in Israeli Kibbutzim," in *Studying Personality Cross-Culturally* by Bert Kaplan, ed. (Evanston, Ill.: Row, Peterson, 1961), pp. 519–29; Lewis S. Feuer, "Leadership and Democracy in the Collective Settlements of Israel," in *Studies in Leadership* by Alvin Ward Gouldner, ed. (New York: Russell and Russell Inc., 1965), pp. 363–385. For an in-depth analysis of the types of agricultural settlements, see, Dorothy Willner, *Nation-Building and Community in Israel* (Princeton: Princeton University Press, 1969).

14. Amos Perlmutter, *Military and Politics in Israel* (New York: Frederick A. Praeger, 1969), pp. 52–53.

15. *Ibid.*

16. Klaus J. Herrmann, "Political Response to the Balfour Declaration in Imperial Germany: German Judaism," *Middle East Journal* 19, no. 3 (Summer 1965): 311

17. In terms of representativeness at independence, the major unrepresented

group was the Israeli Arab. Also the Germans were underrepresented as stated before.

18. For the concept of the active-negative leader, see James David Barber, *The Presidential Character* (Englewood Cliffs: Prentice-Hall, 1972).

19. For an incisive account of Ben Gurion's role in coalition politics, see Jacob Coleman Hurewitz, *Middle East Politics: The Military Dimension* (New York: Frederick A. Praeger, 1969), pp. 370–373.

20. Asher Zidon, *Knesset: The Parliament of Israel,* trans. by Aryeh Rubinstein and Gertrude Hirschler (New York: Herzl Press, 1968), pp. 259–60; State of Israel, *Taknon Ha-Knesset* (Regulations of the Knesset) (Jerusalem, November 1965).

21. For much of the sequence of events the "Chronology" of the *Middle East Journal* was relied upon.

22. Uri Avneri, *Israel Without Zionists* (New York: Macmillan & Co., 1968), pp. 115–118. On the controversy surrounding the Lavon Affair, see Hurewitz, *Middle East Politics,* pp. 374–376 and *The New York Times,* 29 March 1964, p. 4.

23. Segre, *Israel,* p. 168.

24. Kennett Love, *Suez: The Twice-Fought War* (New York: McGraw-Hill, 1969) presents an appraisal of the consequences of the Gaza action.

25. Israel would not accept a UNEF force on her side of the border.

26. For a discussion of this issue, see Ervin Birnbaum, *The Politics of Compromise: State and Religion in Israel* (Rutherford: Fairleigh Dickinson University Press, 1970), pp. 178–89 and Zidon, *Knesset,* p. 313. An analysis of the continuing role of the Israeli religious parties is found in Stephen Oren, "Continuity and Change in Israel's Religious Parties," *Middle East Journal* 27, no. 1 (Winter 1973): 36–54.

27. For a discussion of Egyptian motives and strategy, see Richard Hrair Dekmejian, *Egypt Under Nasir* (Albany, State University of New York Press, 1971; University of London Press Ltd., 1972), pp. 240–243.

28. On the 1969 Knesset elections and campaign issues, see Don Peretz, "Israel's 1969 Election Issues—The Visible and the Invisible," *Middle East Journal* 24, no. 1 (Winter 1970): 31–46.

29. *The New York Times,* 14 February 1973.

30. *Ibid.*

31. *The New York Times,* 29 March 1973.

32. Two such instances were President Weizmann's appointment of Pinhas Rosen and President Ben-Zvi's appointment of Eshkol, although the two circumstances differed considerably.

33. For an analysis of the German-Jewish environment, see, Ben Halpern and Shalom Wurm, eds., *The Responsible Attitude: Life and Opinions of Giora Josephthal* (New York: Schocken Books, 1966), pp. 49–54.

34. For cogent analyses of this problem, see, Oded Remba, "Income Inequality in Israel: Ethnic Aspect," in *Israel: Social Structure and Change* by Michael Curtis and Mordechai Chertoff, eds. (New Brunswick: Transaction Books, 1973), pp. 199–214; also Shlomo Avineri, "Israel: Two Nations?" in *Israel: Social Structure and Change* by Michael Curtis and Mordechai Chertoff, pp. 281–305.

35. Zidon, *Knesset,* p. 339.

36. Further statistics on the prominence of European Jews in the Knesset are in Amos Elon, *The Israelis: Founders and Sons* (New York: Holt, Rinehart, and Winston, 1971), pp. 306–307.

37. According to biographical portraits, the generals are either European-born or sons of European immigrants, see Moshe Ben Shaul, ed., *Generals of Israel,* trans. by I. Hannich (Tel Aviv: Hadar Publishing House, 1968).

38. Raphael Patai, ed., *Encyclopedia of Zionism and Israel* (New York: Herzl Press, 1971), 2:864.

39. Seventy-five percent of Israel's population in 1971 was below 40 years of age, *Statistical Abstract of Israel, 1972,* p. 43.

40. Seligman observes "a nervous urgency" animates the policies of the Israeli leadership, see Lester G. Seligman, *Leadership in a New Nation* (New York: Atherton Press, 1964), p. 5.

41. Especially disconcerting was the discrepancy between casualty figures in the October 1973 War.

Chapter 4. Elites in a Charismatic Setting: Egypt

1. For Egyptian politics and history see Rashed al-Barawi, *The Military Coup in Egypt* (Cairo: Renaissance Bookshop, 1952); Anwar El-Sadat, *Revolt on the Nile* (London: Allen Wingate Publishers, 1957); Tom Little, *Modern Egypt* (New York: Frederick A. Praeger, 1967); Jean and Simonne Lacouture, *Egypt in Transition* (New York: Criterion Books, 1958); Amin Sa'id, *Al-Thawrah* [The Revolution] (Cairo, 1957); Ahmad Atiyyat Allah, *Qamus al-Thawrah al-Misriyyah* [Dictionary of the Egyptian Revolution] (Cairo, 1955). For a detailed analysis of bibliographical sources on Jamal Abd al-Nasir, see Khalil I. H. Semaan, "A New Source for the Biography of Jamal Abd al-Nasir," *Muslim World* 58, no. 3 (July 1968): 242–252. Also see, Eliezer Beeri, "On the History of the Free Officers in Egypt," *Hamizrah he-Hadash* 13, no. 3 (1963): xiv–xv; Gamal Abdel Nasser, *The Philosophy of the Revolution* (Buffalo, N.Y.: Economica Books, 1959); Panayotis J. Vatikiotis, *The Egyptian Army in Politics* (Bloomington, Indiana: Indiana University Press, 1961); Robert St. John, *The Boss* (New York: McGraw-Hill Book Co., 1960); Jean Lacouture, *Nasser* (New York: Alfred E. Knopf, 1973); Anthony Nutting, *Nasser* (New York: E. P. Dutton, 1972); and Mohamed Heikal, *The Cairo Documents* (Garden City, New York: Doubleday & Co., 1973).

2. For the competing value systems, see, Charles C. Adams, *Islam and Modernism in Egypt* (London: Oxford University Press, 1933); Malcolm H. Kerr, *Islamic Reform* (Berkeley: University of California Press, 1966); Leonard Binder, *The Ideological Revolution in the Middle East* (New York: John Wiley & Sons, 1964); Albert Habib Hourani, *Arabic Thought in the Liberal Age, 1798–1939* (London: Oxford University Press, 1962); and Nadav Safran, *Egypt in Search of Political Community* (Cambridge, Mass.: Harvard University Press, 1961).

3. Vatikiotis, *The Egyptian Army,* pp. 49–50.

4. Lacouture maintains that Nasir probably became politically conscious at age thirteen. See Lacouture, *Nasser,* p. 26.

5. Vatikiotis, *The Egyptian Army,* pp. 48–49.

6. Nutting, *Nasser,* pp. 12–13.

7. Vatikiotis, *The Egyptian Army,* pp. 48–49.

8. Sadat, *Revolt.*

9. On the concept of leadership as a process of communication, see Karl Wolfgang Deutsch, *The Nerves of Government* (New York: Free Press, 1966), pp. 157–160.

10. Especially after their success in electing their slate in the Officers' Club Affair.

11. Lacouture, *Nasser,* p. 70.

12. Julius Gould and William L. Kolb, *A Dictionary of the Social Sciences* (New York: Free Press of Glencoe, 1964), pp. 653–654.

13. Robert Stephens, *Nasser: A Political Biography* (London: Allen Lane, 1971), pp. 122.

14. Nutting, *Nasser,* pp. 301–303.

15. *Ibid.,* p. 302.

16. Stephens, *Nasser,* p. 385.

17. For parallel accounts of the struggle between Amir and his colleagues, see Stephens, *Nasser,* pp. 359–361 and Nutting, *Nasser,* pp. 308–310.

18. On Muhyi al-Din's "Egypt first" policy, see Miles Copeland, *The Game of Nations* (New York: Simon and Schuster, 1970), pp. 268–269.

19. Data and analysis of the cabinets between 1952 and 1968 are taken from the author's *Egypt Under Nasir* (Albany, N.Y.: State University of New York Press, 1971 and London: University of London Press, 1972).

20. Ahmad Atiyyat Allah, ed., *Al-Qamus al-Siyasi* [Political Dictionary] (Cairo: Dar al-Nahdah, 1968); U.S. Department of State, Embassy in Cairo, *Directory of UAR Personages* (December 1964, December 1965, December 1966); *Who's Who in the Arab World; Keesing's Contemporary Archives; Arab Report and Record; International Who's Who; Cahier d'Orient Contemporain; Europa Yearbook; Whitaker's Almanac; The New York Times;* and *Facts on File.* Also, *Al-Ahram; Al-Akhbar; Akhbar al-Yawm; Akhir Sa'ah; Al-Musawwar; Al-Gumhuriyyah; Al-Nahar; The Scribe; The Daily Star; Ruz al-Yusif;* and *The Arab Observer.*

21. Many of the other officers, including Nasir, had attended civilian colleges and universities; they are excluded from the off-tech category because they left school before completion of academic degrees. On the extent of the military's presence in Egypt's bureaucracies, see the data in United Arab Republic, Bureau of Census and Statistics, *Nashrah Ihsa' Muwazzafi al-Hukumah wa al-Hay'at* [Report on Statistics of Employees of the Government and Agencies] (Cairo, 1962), pp. 52–53. For interpretation of this data, see Dekmejian, *Egypt Under Nasir,* pp. 219–222; also included is data on the ASU elite and its ties to the military, see pp. 271–282.

22. The Syrian leadership is *not* included in the computation.

23. Research in progress in collaboration with Paul Smith on "Cross-national Circulation of Elites: United States, Lebanon, Egypt," Center for Comparative Political Research, State University of New York at Binghamton.

24. Muhammad Hasanayn Haykal, "An al-Tajribah an al-Dimuqratiyyah fi Zamaninah [On Experience in Democracy in Our Times], *Al-Ahram,* 15 November 1968.

25. The activism of the French left and its relatively more cohesive ideology may have contributed to the spread of French leftist intellectual influences in Egypt.

26. Actually this number represents a minimum since data is lacking on several leaders. Table 64 shows a total of 73 foreign degrees granted; but several held more than one foreign degree.

27. Jacob Coleman Hurewitz, *Middle East Politics: The Military Dimension* (New York: Frederick A. Praeger, 1969), p. 127.

28. The final breakdown was checked by a panel of three judges, two Egyptians and one American.

29. Often there was confusion as to where the child was actually born. Note the long debate on whether Nasir was born in Bani Murr, an Upper Egyptian village, or in Alexandria. It was finally determined that he was born in Alexandria after his family's arrival from Bani Murr.

30. Eliezer Beeri, "Social Class and Family Background of the Egyptian Army Officer Class," *Asian and African Studies* 2 (1966): 1–38.

31. Leonard Binder, "Egypt: The Integrative Revolution," in Lucian W. Pye and Sidney Verba, eds., *Political Culture and Political Development* (Princeton: Princeton University Press, 1965), pp. 396–449.

32. Malcolm H. Kerr, "Coming to Terms With Nasser," *International Affairs* 43, no. 1 (January 1967): 67. On the first two years under Sadat see, Richard Hrair Dekmejian, "The Arab World After Nasser," *Middle East Forum* 47, nos. 3 & 4 (Autumn and Winter 1971): 37–46.

Chapter 5. Three Elites in Comparison

1. Farhat Jacob Ziadeh, *Lawyers, the Rule of Law and Liberalism* (Stanford, Calif.: Hoover Institution on War, Revolution and Peace, 1968).

2. Seligman distinguishes between pragmatic and ideological elites in Western politics and the stress placed on negotiation, bargaining, and administrative skills. See Lester G. Seligman, "Elite Recruitment and Political Development," *Journal of Politics* 26, no. 3 (August 1964): 620. American research has shown that certain occupations frequently place their practitioners into bargaining roles. The lawyer is the classic example, although it should be understood that not all lawyers play brokerage roles. See Herbert Jacob, "Initial Recruitment of Elected Officials in the US—A Model," *Journal of Politics* 24, no. 4 (November 1962): 709–710. Moore confirms that during Nasir's regime engineers displaced

lawyers in top political and economic positions; he goes on to stress the engineer's active participation in political demonstrations and their self-view as potential elites. See Clement Henry Moore, "Authoritarian Politics in Unincorporated Society: The Case of Nasser's Egypt" (Paper delivered at American Political Science Association Meeting, Washington, D.C. 5–9 September 1972), p. 15.

3. It should be noted that neither Egypt's ASU nor the Lebanese parties possess political power comparable to Israel's Mapai party.

4. It has been pointed out that in different societies the military is seen as playing different roles—in mass society it can be seen as a conservative force, in an oligarchy it may be a radical; and in a middle-class society it may be a participant and arbiter. See Robert M. Price, "A Theoretical Approach to Military Rule in New States," *World Politics* 23, no. 3 (April 1971): 399–430.

5. R. J. Rummel, "Understanding Factor Analysis," *Journal of Conflict Resolution* 11 (1967): 444–480.

6. For early applications of path analysis in political science, see Hayward Alker, Jr., *Mathematics and Politics* (New York: Macmillan & Co., 1965); Arthur S. Goldberg, "Discerning a Causal Pattern Among Data on Voting Behavior," *American Political Science Review* 60, no. 4 (December 1966): 913–922; Arthur K. Smith, Jr., "Socio-Economic Development and Political Democracy: A Causal Analysis," *Midwest Journal of Political Science* 13, no. 1 (February 1969): 95–125; Donald J. McCrone and Charles F. Cnudde, "Toward a Communications Theory of Democratic Political Development: A Causal Model," *American Political Science Review* 61, no. 1 (March 1967): 72–77.

7. For example, a colleague, Margaret J. Wyszomirski, Cornell University, has tried to use two formulas to calculate a Circulation Index between cabinets: $CI = N$ of Individuals Dropped + N of Individuals Added/ Total N of Individuals in Both Cabinets; or $CI = N$ of positions which have Changed Hands/ Total N of Positions Available in Both Cabinets.

8. For an application of Markov chains in the study of career patterns, see Richard Hrair Dekmejian, "Elite Recruitment, Markov Chains, and Path Analysis: Israel, Egypt, and Lebanon" (Paper delivered at American Political Science Association Meeting, Chicago, Ill., 29 August–2 September 1974).

9. "Declaration of Independence," in *Encyclopedia of Zionism and Israel,* ed. by Raphael Patai (New York: Herzl Press, 1971), p. 244.

10. Amin Iskandar, "Al-Bahth an al-Shakhsiyyah al-Misriyyah" [The Search for the Egyptian Personality], *Al-Jumhuriyyah,* 24 October 1968. One writer had gone as far as to argue that historically the notion of Arab unity and nationalism had been vague among the Egyptian leadership and people and that Arab nationalism did not have strong roots in Egypt. See Abd al-Mun'im Muhammad Badr, *Al-Thawrah al-Arabiyyah al-Ishtirakiyyah* [The Arab Socialist Revolution] (Cairo: n.p., 1967), pp. 317–318. Also, Muhammad Hasanayn Haykal, "An al-Tajribah an al-Dimuqratiyyah fi Zamaninah," [On Experience in Democracy in Our Times], *Al-Ahram,* 15 November 1968.

11. *Ibid.*

12. Daniel Lerner, "A Note on Ambivalent Nationalism and Political Identity," *Public Opinion Quarterly* 20, no. 1 (Spring 1956): 289–292; also Patri-

cia L. Kendall, ''The Ambivalent Nationalism Among Professionals,'' *Public Opinion Quarterly* 20, no. 1 (Spring 1956): 277–288.

13. Richard Hrair Dekmejian, *Egypt Under Nasir* (Albany, N.Y.: State University of New York Press, 1971 and London: University of London Press, 1972), pp. 247–251.

Bibliography

Books

Abdel-Malek, Anouar. *Égypte Société Militaire*. Paris: Editions du Seuil, 1962.

Abdel Nasser, Gamal. *The Philosophy of the Revolution*. Buffalo: Smith, Keynes and Marshall, 1959.

Abu-Lughod, Ibrahim, ed. *The Transformation of Palestine*. Evanston: Northwestern University Press, 1971.

Adams, Charles C. *Islam and Modernism in Egypt: A Study of the Modern Reform Movement Inaugurated by Muhammad 'Abduh*. London: Oxford University Press, 1933.

Agwani, A. S., ed. *The Lebanese Crisis, 1958*. New York: Asia Publishing House, 1965.

Ake, Claude. *A Theory of Political Integration*. Homewood, Ill.: Dorsey Press, 1967.

Allah, Ahmad Atiyyat, ed. *Al-Qamus al-Siyasi* [Political Dictionary]. Cairo: Dar al-Nahdah, 1968.

———. *Qamus al-Thawrah al-Misriyya* [Dictionary of the Egyptian Revolution]. Cairo, 1955.

Alker, Jr., Hayward. *Mathematics and Politics*. New York: Macmillan Co., 1965.

Antonius, George. *The Arab Awakening*. London: Hamish Hamilton, 1955.

Arian, Alan. *Ideological Change in Israel*. Cleveland: Press of Case Western Reserve University, 1968.

Avneri, Uri. *Israel Without Zionists*. New York: Macmillan Co., 1968.

Bachrach, Peter. *The Theory of Democratic Elitism*. Boston: Little, Brown & Co., 1967.

Badi, Joseph. *The Government of the State of Israel*. New York: Twayne Publishers, Inc., 1963.

Baer, Gabriel. *Studies in the Social History of Modern Egypt*. Chicago: University of Chicago Press, 1969.

Bakr, Abd al-Mun'im Muhammad. *Al-Thawrah al-Arabiyyah al-Ishtirakiyyah* [The Arab Socialist Revolution]. Cairo: 1967.

el-Barawy, Rashed. *The Military Coup in Egypt*. Cairo: Renaissance Bookshop, 1952.

Barber, James David. *The Presidential Character*. Englewood Cliffs, N.J.: Prentice-Hall, 1972.

Bayhum, Muhammad Jamil. *Lubnan Bayna Mushriqin wa Maghribin, 1920–69* [Lebanon Between Easterners and Westerners]. Beirut: 1969.

Bell, Daniel. *The End of Ideology.* New York: Free Press, 1952.

Ben Gurion, David. *Israel: The Years of Challenge.* New York: Holt, Rinehart and Winston, 1963.

Ben Shaul, Moshe, ed. *Generals of Israel.* Tel Aviv: Hadar Publishing House, 1968.

Ben Tzvi, Mikha'il. *Reshei Ha-Rishu'yot Ha-Mikomiyot bi-Yisrael* [Heads of Local Councils in Israel]. Tel Aviv: 1971.

Berger, Morroe. *The Arab World Today.* New York: Doubleday, 1962.

————. *Bureaucracy and Society in Modern Egypt: A Study of the Higher Civil Service.* Princeton: Princeton University Press, 1957.

————. *Military Elite and Social Change: Egypt since Napoleon.* Princeton: Princeton University Center for International Studies, 1960.

Binder, Leonard. *The Ideological Revolution in the Middle East.* New York: John Wiley & Son Inc., 1964.

Binder, Leonard, ed. *Politics in Lebanon.* New York: John Wiley & Son Inc., 1966.

Birnbaum, Ervin. *The Politics of Compromise: State and Religion in Israel.* Rutherford, N.J.: Fairleigh Dickinson University Press, 1970.

Bottomore, T. B. *Elites and Society.* London: C. A. Watts, 1964.

Brzezinski, Zbigniew, and Samuel P. Huntington. *Political Power: USA/USSR.* New York: Viking Press, 1964.

Chamoun, Camille. *Crise au Moyen-Orient.* Paris: Gallimard, 1963.

Chiha, Michel. *Politique Interieure.* Beirut: Editions du Trident, 1964.

Churchill, Charles Henry Spencer. *The Druzes and The Maronites Under The Turkish Rule From 1840 to 1860.* London: B. Quaritch, 1862.

Copeland, Miles. *The Game of Nations: The Amorality of Power Politics.* New York: Simon and Schuster, 1969.

Corson, John J. and R. Shale Paul. *Men Near The Top.* Washington: Brookings Institution, 1965.

Dahl, Robert Alan. *Who Governs? Democracy and Power in an American City.* New Haven: Yale University Press, 1961.

Dawson, Richard E. and Kenneth Prewitt. *Political Socialization.* Boston: Little, Brown & Co., 1969.

Dekmejian, R. Hrair. *Egypt Under Nasir: A Study in Political Dynamics.* Albany: State University of New York Press, 1971; and London: University of London Press, 1972.

Deutsch, Karl Wolfgang. *The Nerves of Government.* New York: Free Press, 1966.

Deutsch, Karl Wolfgang and Lewis Joachim Edinger. *Germany Rejoins The Powers.* Stanford, California: Stanford University Press, 1959.

Deutsch, Karl Wolfgang, Roy C. Macridis and Richard L. Merritt. *France, Germany and the Western Alliance: A Study of Elite Attitudes on European Integration and World Politics.* New York: Charles Scribner's Sons, 1967.

Domhoff, George William. *Who Rules America?* Englewood Cliffs, N.J.: Prentice-Hall, 1967.

Eban, Abba. *My Country.* New York: Random House, 1972.

Edinger, Lewis Joachim, ed. *Political Leadership in Industrialized Societies: Studies in Comparative Analysis.* New York: John Wiley and Son Inc., 1967.

Eisenstadt, Shmuel Noah. *Israeli Society.* New York: Basic Books Inc., 1967.

Elon, Amos. *The Israelis: Founders and Sons.* New York: Holt, Rinehart and Winston, 1971.

Etzioni, Amitai. *Political Unification: A Comparative Study of Leaders and Followers.* New York: Holt, Rinehart and Winston, 1965.

Farrell, Robert Barry, ed. *Political Leadership in Eastern Europe and the Soviet Union.* Chicago: Aldine Publishing Co., 1970.

Fenno, Richard F. *The President's Cabinet.* Cambridge, Mass.: Harvard University Press, 1959.

Fisher, Sydney Nettleton, ed. *The Military in the Middle East.* Columbus, Ohio: Ohio State University Press, 1963.

Freudenheim, Yehoshua. *Government in Israel.* Dobbs Ferry, N.Y.: Oceana Publications, 1967.

Frey, Frederick W. *The Turkish Political Elite.* Cambridge: M.I.T. Press, 1965.

Geertz, Clifford, ed. *Old Societies and New States.* New York: Free Press of Glencoe, 1963.

Gibb, Hamilton Alexander Rosskeen and Harold Bowen. *Islamic Society And The West.* London: Oxford University Press, 1950.

Goldmann, Nahum. *Sixty Years of Jewish Life.* New York: 1969.

Gould, Julius and William L. Kolb. *A Dictionary of the Social Sciences.* New York: Free Press of Glencoe, 1964.

Gouldner, Alvin Ward, ed. *Studies in Leadership.* New York: Russell and Russell Inc., 1965.

Greenstein, Fred I. *Personality and Politics.* Chicago: Markham, 1969.

Gurr, Ted Robert. *Politimetrics.* Englewood Cliffs, N.J.: Prentice Hall, 1972.

Guttsman, W. L. *The British Political Elite.* London: MacGibbon and Kee, 1963.

Haddad, George Meri. *Fifty Years of Modern Syria and Lebanon.* Beirut: Dar-al-Hayat, 1950.

Halpern, Ben. *The Idea of the Jewish State.* Cambridge, Mass.: Harvard University Press, 1961.

Halpern, Ben and Shalom Wurm, eds. *The Responsible Attitude: Life and Opinions of Giora Josephtal.* New York: Schocken Books, 1967.

Halpern, Manfred. *The Politics of Social Change in the Middle East and North Africa.* Princeton: Princeton University Press, 1963.

Hargrove, Erwin C. *Presidential Leadership: Personality and Political Style.* New York, Macmillan Co., 1966.

Harik, Iliya F. *Politics and Change in a Traditional Society: Lebanon, 1711–1845.* Princeton: Princeton University Press, 1968.

Heikal, Mohamed. *The Cairo Documents.* Garden City, N.Y.: Doubleday and Co., 1973.

Hertzberg, Arthur, ed. *The Zionist Idea*. Westport, Conn.: Greenwood Press, 1959.

Hitti, Philip Khuri. *Lebanon in History*. London: Macmillan Co., 1957.

————. *A Short History of Lebanon*. London: Macmillan Co., 1965.

————. *The Origin of The Druze People and Religion, With Extracts From Their Sacred Writings*. New York: AMS Press, 1966.

Hourani, Albert Habib. *Arabic Thought in the Liberal Age, 1798–1939*. London: Oxford University Press, 1962.

————. *Minorities in the Arab World*. New York: Oxford University Press, 1947.

————. *Syria and Lebanon*. New York: Oxford University Press, 1946.

Hudson, Michael Craig. *The Precarious Republic*. New York: Random House, 1968.

Huntington, Samuel P. *Political Order In Changing Societies*. New Haven: Yale University Press, 1968.

Hurewitz, Jacob Coleman. *Diplomacy in the Near and Middle East: A Documentary Record (1914–1956)*. Vol. 2. Princeton: D. Van Nostrand Co., 1956.

————. *Middle East Politics: The Military Dimension*. New York: Frederick A. Praeger, 1969.

————. *The Struggle for Palestine*. New York: W. W. Norton & Co., 1950.

Ilchman, Warren Frederick and Norman Thomas Uphoff. *The Political Economy of Change*. Berkeley: University of California Press, 1969.

Ismael, Tareq Y. *Governments And Politics of the Contemporary Middle East*. Homewood, Ill.: Dorsey Press, 1970.

Issawi, Charles. *The Entrepreneur Class*. Ithaca: Cornell University Press, 1955.

Janowitz, Morris. *The Military in the Political Development of New Nations*. Chicago: University of Chicago Press, 1964.

al-Jisr, Basim. *Ri'asah wa Siyasah wa al-Lubnan al-Jadid* [The Presidency, Politics and the New Lebanon]. Beirut: Al-Hayat, 1964.

Jurayj, Gibran. *Haqa'iq an al-Istiqlal Ayyam Rashayya* [Facts about Independence and Rashayya Days]. Beirut: Dar al-Fann, n.d.

Kaplan, Bert, ed. *Studying Personality Cross-Culturally*. Evanston, Ill.: Row Peterson, 1961.

Kerr, Malcolm H., ed. and trans. *Lebanon in the Last Years of Feudalism, 1840–1868* by Antun Dahir al-Aqiqi. Beirut: American University of Beirut, 1959.

————. *Islamic Reform: The Political and Legal Theories of Muhammad 'Abduh and Rashid Rida*. Berkeley: University of California Press, 1966.

Kerstiens, Thom. *The New Elite in Asia and Africa: A Comparative Study of Indonesia and Ghana*. New York: Frederick A. Praeger, 1966.

Khadduri, Majid. *Arab Contemporaries*. Baltimore: Johns Hopkins University Press, 1973.

————. *Political Trends in the Arab World*. Baltimore: Johns Hopkins University Press, 1970.

al-Khalidi, Shaykh Ahmad Ibn Muhammad. *Lubnan fi Ahd al-Amir Fakhr al-Din al-Ma'ani al-Thani* [Lebanon During the Time of Amir Fakhr al-Din al-Ma'ani, The Second]. Beirut: Catholic Press, 1936.

al-Khuli, Lutfi. *Dirasat fi al-Waqi' al-Misri al-Mu'asir* [Studies in Contemporary Egyptian Reality]. Beirut, 1964.

Kornberg, Allan, and Lloyd D. Musolf, eds. *Legislatures In Developmental Perspective.* Durham, N.C.: Duke University Press, 1970.

Lacouture, Jean. *The Demigods.* New York: Alfred A. Knopf, 1970.

————. *Nasser.* New York: Alfred A. Knopf, 1973.

Lacouture, Jean and Simonne. *Egypt in Transition.* New York: Criterion Books, 1958.

Laqueur, Walter Ze'ev, ed. *The Middle East In Transition.* New York: Frederick A. Praeger, 1958.

Lasswell, Harold Dwight, Daniel Lerner and C. Easton Rothwell. *The Comparative Study of Elites.* Stanford, Calif.: Stanford University Press, 1952.

Lasswell, Harold Dwight and Daniel Lerner, eds. *World Revolutionary Elites.* Cambridge: M.I.T. Press, 1965.

Lau-Lavie, Naphtali. *Moshe Dayan.* London: Vallentine, Mitchell, 1968.

Lerner, Daniel and Morton Gorden. *Euratlantica: Changing Perspectives of the European Elites.* Cambridge: M.I.T. Press, 1969.

Lindbloom, Charles E. *The Intelligence of Democracy.* New York: Free Press, 1965.

Lipset, Seymour Martin and Aldo Solari, eds. *Elites in Latin America.* New York: Oxford University Press, 1967.

Little, Tom. *Modern Egypt.* New York: Frederick A. Praeger, 1967.

Longrigg, Stephen Hemsley. *Syria and Lebanon Under French Mandate.* New York: Oxford University Press, 1958.

Love, Kennett. *Suez: The Twice-Fought War.* New York: McGraw-Hill, 1969.

Lyautey, Pierre. *Liban Modérne.* Paris: Julliard, 1964.

Mannhein, Karl. *Man and Society in an Age of Reconstruction.* New York: Harcourt, Brace and World, 1967.

Mardin, Sherif. *The Genesis of Young Ottoman Political Thought.* Princeton: Princeton University Press, 1962.

Matthews, Donald R. *The Social Background of Political Decision-makers.* Garden City, New York: Doubleday & Co., 1954.

Marvick, Dwaine, ed. *Political Decision-Makers.* New York: Free Press, 1961.

Medding, Peter Y. *Mapai in Israel.* London: Cambridge University Press, 1972.

Meo, Leila M. T. *Lebanon, Improbable Nation.* Bloomington, Indiana: Indiana University Press, 1965.

Merritt, Richard L. *Systematic Approaches to Comparative Politics.* Chicago: Rand McNally & Co., 1970.

Mills, Charles Wright. *The Power Elite.* New York: Oxford University Press, 1956.

Moore, Clement Henry. *Tunisia Since Independence.* Berkeley: University of California Press, 1965.

Mosca, Gaetano. *The Ruling Class,* trans. by Hannah D. Kahn, New York: McGraw-Hill Book Co., 1939.

Nashif, Taysir. *A Quantitative Comparative Study of the Jewish and Palestine Arab Elites (1920–48).* Ph.D. Dissertation, SUNY-Binghamton, 1974.

Nutting, Anthony. *Nasser*. New York: E. P. Dutton & Co., 1972.

Parry, Geraint. *Political Elites*. New York: Frederick A. Praeger, 1969.

Patai, Raphael, ed. *Encyclopedia of Zionism and Israel*. 2 vols. New York: Herzl Press, 1971.

Peres, Shimon. *David's Sling*. London: Weidenfeld & Nicolson, 1970.

Perlmutter, Amos. *Military and Politics in Israel*. New York: Frederick A. Praeger, 1969.

Polk, William Roe. *The Opening of South Lebanon, 1788–1840*. Cambridge, Mass.: Harvard University Press, 1963.

Presthus, Robert Vance. *Men at the Top: A Study in Community Power*. New York: Oxford University Press, 1964.

Prittie, Terence. *Eshkol: The Man and the Nation*. New York: Pitman Publ. Corp., 1969.

Pye, Lucian W. and Sidney Verba, eds. *Political Culture and Political Development*. Princeton: Princeton University Press, 1965.

Pye, Lucian W. *Politics, Personality and Nation Building: Burma's Search for Identity*. New Haven: Yale University Press, 1962.

Quandt, William B. *The Comparative Study of Political Elites*. Beverly Hills, Calif.: Sage Publications, 1970.

———. *Revolution and Political Leadership: Algeria 1954–1968*. Cambridge, Mass.: M.I.T. Press, 1969.

Qubain, Fahim Issa. *Crisis in Lebanon*. Washington, D.C.: Middle East Institute, 1961.

Ranney, Austin. *Pathways to Parliament*. Madison: University of Wisconsin Press, 1965.

Roos, Leslie and Noralou Roos. *Managers of Modernization*. Cambridge, Mass.: Harvard University Press, 1971.

Rustow, Dankwart A., ed. *Philosophers and Kings: Studies in Leadership*. New York: Braziller, 1970.

———. *A World of Nations: Problems of Political Modernization*. Washington, D.C.: Brookings Institution, 1967.

El-Sadat, Anwar. *Revolt on the Nile*. London: Allan Wingate, 1957.

Safran, Nadav. *Egypt in Search of Political Community*. Cambridge, Mass.: Harvard University Press, 1961.

St. John, Robert. *The Boss*. New York: McGraw Hill Book Co., 1960.

Salibi, Kamal Suleiman. *The Modern History of Lebanon*. New York: Frederick A. Praeger, 1965.

Schlesinger, Joseph A. *Ambition and Politics: Political Careers in the United States*. Chicago: Rand McNally, 1966.

Segre, V. D. *Israel: A Society in Transition*. New York: Oxford University Press, 1971.

Seligman, Lester G. *Leadership in a New Nation: Political Development in Israel*. New York: Atherton Press, 1964.

Sereno, Renzo. *The Rulers*. Leiden: E. J. Brill, 1962.

Sharabi, Hisham. *Arab Intellectuals and the West: The Formative Years, 1875–1914*. Baltimore: Johns Hopkins Press, 1970.

Shihab, Amir Haydar Ahmad. *Lubnan fi Ahd al-Umara' al-Shihabiyyin* [Lebanon in the Period of the Shihabi Amira]. Beirut: Lebanese University, 1969.

Slutzki, Yehudah. *Toldot Ha-Haganah* [History of the Haganah]. Tel Aviv: Am Oved, 1972.

Smith, Harvey H., et. al. *Area Handbook for Israel*. Washington, D.C.: U.S. Government Printing Office, September 1970.

Stanley, David T., Dean E. Mann, and Jameson W. Doig. *Men Who Govern*. Washington, D.C.: Brookings Institution, 1967.

Stephens, Robert. *Nasser: A Political Biography*. London: Allen Lane, 1971.

Suleiman, Michael W. *Political Parties in Lebanon*. Ithaca, New York: Cornell University Press, 1967.

al-Tahiri, Hamdi Badawi. *Siyasah al-Hukm fi Lubnan* [The Politics of Governance in Lebanon]. Cairo: Dar al-Qawmiyyah, 1966.

Tamir, Nachman, ed. *Anshe Ha-Aliyah Ha-Sheniyah* [The People of the Second Aliyah]. Tel Aviv: Histadrut, 1970, 1971, 1972.

Usabiyus, Salim Butrus. *Dalil Marahil Lubnan Abr al-Tarikh* [Directory of the Historical Stages of Lebanon]. Beirut: n.p., 1955.

Van Nieuwenhuijze, C. A. O. *Social Stratification and the Middle East*. Leiden: E. J. Brill, 1965.

Vatikiotis, Panayotis J. *Conflict in the Middle East*. London: George Allen & Unwin, 1971.

——. *The Egyptian Army in Politics*. Bloomington, Indiana: Indiana University Press, 1961.

——. *The Modern History of Egypt*. London: Weidenfeld & Nicolson, 1969.

Wilkinson, Rupert, ed. *Governing Elites: Studies in Training and Selection*. New York: Oxford University Press, 1969.

Willner, Dorothy. *Nation-building and Community in Israel*. Princeton: Princeton University Press, 1969.

Winer, Gershon. *The Founding Fathers of Israel*. New York: Block Publishing Co., 1971.

Wolfenstein, E. Victor. *Personality and Politics*. Belmont, Calif.: Dickenson Publ. Co., 1969.

——. *The Revolutionary Personality: Lenin, Trotsky, Gandhi*. Princeton: Princeton University Press, 1967.

Wriggins, William Howard. *The Ruler's Imperative: Strategies for Political Survival in Asia and Africa*. New York: Columbia University Press, 1969.

Yoni, Nathan. *Kar'a Batsameret* [Cleavages in the Leadership]. Tel Aviv: Artzi, 1969.

Zeine, Zeine N. *The Emergence of Arab Nationalism*. 3d ed. Delmar, N.Y.: Caravan Books, 1973.

Ziadeh, Farhat J. *Lawyers, the Rule of Law and Liberalism in Modern Egypt*. Stanford, Calif.: Hoover Institution on War, Revolution, and Peace, 1968.

Zidon, Asher. *Knesset: The Parliament of Israel*. New York: Herzl Press, 1968.

Ziegenhagen, Eduard A. and George Bowlby. *Techniques for Political Analysis: A Laboratory Manual*. Boston: Holbrook Press, Inc. 1971.

Zonis, Marvin. *The Political Elite of Iran*. Princeton: Princeton University Press, 1971.

Articles

Akzin, Benjamin. "The Knesset," *International Social Science Journal* 13, no. 4 (1961): 567–82.

Aron, Raymond. "Social Structure and the Ruling Class," *British Journal of Sociology* 1, no. 1 (March 1950): 1–16.

Avineri, Shlomo. "Israel: Two Nations?" in *Israel: Social Structure and Change* ed. by Michael Curtis and Mordechai Chertoff, New Brunswick: Transaction Books, 1973.

Badeau, John S. "The Role in Search of a Hero: A Brief Study of the Egyptian Revolution," *Middle East Journal* 9, no. 4 (Fall 1955): 373–84.

Beck, Carl and James M. Malloy. "Political Elites: A Mode of Analysis," Geneva, 1964.

Beck, Carl. "Aggregative Career Characteristics of Eastern European Political Leaders," Paper delivered at Pittsburgh: International Studies Program, 1968.

Beeri, Eliezer. "On the History of the Free Officers In Egypt," *Hamizrah he-Hadash* 13, no. 3 (1963): xiv–xv.

———. "Social Class and Family Background of the Egyptian Army Officer Class," *Asian and African Studies* 2 (1966): 1–38.

Bill, James. "The Social and Economic Foundations of Power in Contemporary Iran," *Middle East Journal* 17, no. 4 (Fall 1973): 400–13.

Binder, Leonard. "Egypt: The Integrative Revolution," in *Political Culture and Political Development* ed. by Lucian W. Pye and Sidney Verba, Princeton: Princeton University Press, 1966.

———. "Political Recruitment and Participation in Egypt," in *Political Parties and Political Development* ed. by Joseph LaPalombara and Myron Weiner, Princeton: Princeton University Press, 1966.

Blanksten, George I. "Ideology and Nation-building in the Contemporary World," *International Studies Quarterly* 11 (March 1967): 3–11.

Clignet, Remi P. and Philip Foster. "Potential Elites in Ghana and the Ivory Coast: A Preliminary Comparison," *American Journal of Sociology* 70, no. 3 (1965): 349–62.

Crecelius, Daniel. "Al-Azhar in the Revolution," *Middle East Journal* 20, no. 1 (Winter 1966): 3–49.

Crow, Ralph E. "Religious Sectarianism in the Lebanese Political System," *Journal of Politics* 24, no. 3 (August 1962): 489–520.

Czudnowski, Moshe M. "Legislative Recruitment Under Proportional Representation in Israel: A Model and a Case Study," *Midwest Journal of Political Science* 14, no. 3 (May 1970): 216–48.

Dawn, C. Ernest. "The Rise of Arabism in Syria," *Middle East Journal* 17, no. 1 (Winter 1963): 145–68.

Dekmejian, R. Hrair. "The Arab World After Nasser," *Middle East Forum* 47, nos. 3 & 4 (Autumn and Winter 1971): 37–46.

———. "Elite Recruitment, Markov Chains, and Path Analysis: Israel, Egypt, and Lebanon," Paper delivered at the American Political Science Association Meeting, Chicago, Ill., 29 August–2 September 1974.

Dekmejian, R. Hrair and Margaret J. Wyszomirski. "Charismatic Leadership in Islam: The Mahdi of the Sudan," *Comparative Studies in Society and History* 14, no. 2 (March 1972): 193–214.

Dennis, Jack. "Political Socialization to Democratic Orientations in Four Western Systems," *Comparative Political Studies* 1, no. 1 (April 1968): 71–101.

Dodd, C. H. "The Social and Educational Background of Turkish Officials," *Middle Eastern Studies* 1, no. 3 (April 1965): 268–76.

Dogan, Mattei. "Le personnel politique et la personnalite charismatique," *Revue Francaise de Sociologie* 6 (July–September 1965): 305–24.

———. "Les filiéres de la carriére politique," *Revue Francaise de Sociologie* 8 (October–December 1967): 468–92.

———. "Political Ascent in a Class Society: French Deputies 1870–1958," in *Political Decision-makers* ed. by Dwaine Marvick, New York: Free Press, 1959.

Dupree, Louis. "Democracy and the Military Base of Power," *Middle East Journal* 22, no. 1 (Winter 1968): 29–44.

Early, Evelyn Aleene. "The Emergence of an Urban Za'im: A Social Network Analysis," Paper delivered at Middle East Studies Association Meeting, Milwaukee, Wisconsin, 8–10 November 1973.

Eberhard, Wolfram. "Afghanistan's Young Elite," *Asian Survey* 1, no. 12 (February 1962): 3–22.

Edinger, Lewis J. "Political Science and Political Biography: Reflections on the Study of Leadership," *Journal of Politics* 26, no. 2 (May 1964): 420–30.

——— and Donald D. Searing. "Social Background in Elite Analysis," *American Political Science Review* 61, no. 2 (June 1967): 429–45.

Eisenstadt, Shmuel Noah. "Patterns of Leadership and Social Homogeneity in Israel," *International Social Science Bulletin* 8, no. 1 (1956): 36–54.

———. "The Place of Elites and Primary Groups in the Absorption of New Immigration in Israel," *American Journal of Sociology* 57, no. 3 (November 1951): 222–31.

Etzioni, Amitai. "Functional Differentiation of Elites in the Kibbutz," *American Journal of Sociology* 64, no. 5 (March 1959): 476–87.

Gehlen, M. P. and M. McBride. "The Soviet Central Committee: An Elite Analysis," *American Political Science Review* 62, no. 4 (December 1968): 1232–41.

Goldberg, Arthur S. "Discerning a Causal Pattern Among Data on Voting Behavior," *American Political Science Review* 60, no. 4 (December 1966): 913–22.

Grajower, Rebecca. "Zionism and Militarism," *New Left Forum* (September 1967): 32–44.

Gubser, Peter. "The Zu'ama' of Zahlah: The Current Situation in a Lebanese Town," *Middle East Journal* 27, no. 2 (Spring 1973): 173–89.

Halpern, Ben. "The Role of the Military in Israel," in *The Role of the Military in Underdeveloped Countries* ed. by J. J. Johnson, Princeton: Princeton University Press, 1962.

Halpern, Manfred. "Egypt and the New Middle Class: Reaffirmation and New Exploration," *Comparative Studies in Society and History* 11, no. 1 (January 1968): 97–101.

Haykal, Muhammad Hasanayn. "An al-Tajribah an al-Dimuqratiyyah fi Zamaninah" [On Experience in Democracy in Our Times], *Al-Ahram,* 15 November 1968.

Herrmann, Klaus J. "Political Response to the Balfour Declaration in Imperial Germany: German Judaism," *Middle East Journal* 19, no. 3 (Summer 1965): 303–20.

Hess. Jr., Clyde G. and Herbert L. Bodman, Jr. "Confessionalism and Feudality In Lebanese Politics," *Middle East Journal* 8, no. 1 (Winter 1954): 10–26.

Hottinger, Arnold. "Zu'ama' in Historical Perspective," in *Politics in Lebanon* ed. by Leonard Binder, New York: John Wiley & Sons, 1966.

Hurewitz, Jacob Coleman. "Lebanese Democracy in its International Setting," Middle East Journal 17, no. 5 (Autumn, 1963): 487–506.

Iskandar, Amin. "Al-Bahth an al-Shakhsiyyah al-Misriyyah" [The Search for the Egyptian Personality], *Al-Jumhuriyyah* 24 October 1968.

Jacob, Herbert. "Initial Recruitment of Elected Officials in the US—A Model," *Journal of Politics* 24, no. 4 (November 1962): 703–16.

Janowitz, Morris. "The Systematic Analysis of Political Biography," *World Politics* 6, no. 3 (April 1954): 405–12.

Keddie, Nikkie. "The Iranian Power Structure and Social Change 1800–1969: An Overview," *International Journal of Middle Eastern Studies* 2, no. 1 (January 1971): 3–20.

Kendall, Patricia L. "The Ambivalent Nationalism Among Professionals," *Public Opinion Quarterly* 20, no. 1 (Spring 1956): 277–98.

Kerr, Malcolm H. "Coming to Terms With Nasser," *International Affairs* 43, no. 1 (January 1967): 65–84.

———. "Lebanese Views on the 1958 Crisis," *Middle East Journal* 15, no. 1 (Winter 1961): 211–17.

———. "The 1960 Lebanese Parliamentary Elections," *Middle Eastern Affairs* 11, no. 9 (October 1960): 266–75.

———. "Political Decision Making in a Confessional Democracy," in *Politics in Lebanon* ed. by Leonard Binder, New York: John Wiley & Sons, 1966.

Khadduri, Majid. "The Role of the Military in Middle East Politics," *American Political Science Review* 48, no. 2 (June 1953): 511–24.

Khalaf, A. and E. Schwayri. "Family Firms and Industrial Development: The Lebanese Case," *Economic Development and Cultural Change* 15 (October 1966): 59–69.

Khuri, Fuad I. "The Changing Class Structure in Lebanon," *Middle East Journal* 23, no. 1 (Winter 1969): 29–44.

Lacy, Jr., Alex B. "The White House Staff Bureaucracy," *Transaction* 6, no. 3 (January 1969): 50–55.

Landau, Jacob. "Peaceful Change in the Lebanon," *World Today* 9 (April 1953): 162–73.

Lerner, Daniel. "A Note on Ambivalent Nationalism and Political Identity," *Public Opinion Quarterly* 20, no. 1 (Spring 1956): 289–92.

Linz, Juan J. "An Authoritarian Regime: Spain," in *Cleavages, Ideologies, and Party Systems* ed. by Erik Allardt and Yrjo Littunen, Helsinki: Westermarck Society, 1964.

Marr, Phebe Ann. "Iraq's Leadership Dilemma: A Study in Leadership Trends, 1948–1968," *Middle East Journal* 24, no. 3 (Summer 1970): 283–301.

McCrone, Donald J. and Charles F. Cnudde. "Toward a Communications Theory of Democratic Political Development: A Causal Model," *American Political Science Review* 61, no. 1 (March 1967): 72–79.

Miller, William Green. "Political Organization in Iran: From Dowreh to Political Party, Part I and II," *Middle East Journal* 23, no. 2 (Spring 1969): 159–67 and no. 3 (Summer 1969): 343–50.

Moore, Clement Henry. "Authoritarian Politics in Unincorporated Society: The Case of Nasser's Egypt," Paper delivered at the American Political Science Association Meeting, Washington, D.C., 5–9 September 1972.

Moskos, C. C. and W. Bell. "Attitudes Towards Democracy Among Leaders in Four Emerging Nations," *British Journal of Sociology* 15, no. 4 (December 1964): 317–37.

Oren, Stephen. "Continuity and Change in Israel's Religious Parties," *Middle East Journal* 27, no. 1 (Winter 1973): 36–54.

Peretz, Don. "Israel's 1969 Election Issues—The Visible and the Invisible," *Middle East Journal* 24, no. 1 (Winter 1970): 31–46.

Perlmutter, Amos. "The Israel Army in Politics: The Persistence of the Civilian Over the Military," *World Politics* 20, no. 4 (July 1968): 606–43.

Price, Robert M. "A Theoretical Approach to Military Rule in New States," *World Politics* 23, no. 3 (April 1971): 399–430.

Putnam, Robert. "Studying Elite Political Culture," *American Political Science Review* 65, no. 3 (September 1971): 651–81.

Rabin, Albert I. "Personality Study in Israeli Kibbutzim," in *Studying Personality Cross-Culturally* ed. by Bert Kaplan, Evanston, Ill.: Row, and Peterson, 1961.

Remba, Oded. "Income Inequality in Israel: Ethnic Aspects," in *Israel: Social Structure and Change* ed. by Michael Curtis and Mordechai Chertoff, New Brunswick: Transaction Books, 1973.

Rondot, Pierre. "Les structures socio-politique de la nation Libanaise," *Orient* 4, no. 1 (1958): 80–104.

Rummel, R. J. "Understanding Factor Analysis," *Journal of Conflict Resolution* 11, (1967): 444–80.

Rustow, Dankwart. "Who's Who, When and How," *World Politics* 18, no. 4 (1966): 690–717.

Salem, Elie. "Local Elections in Lebanon: A Case Study," *Midwest Journal of Political Science* 9, no. 4 (November 1965): 376–87.

Salibi, Kamal. "Lebanon Since the Crisis of 1958," *World Today* 17, no. 1 (1961): 32–42.

————. "Lebanon Under Fuad Chehab: 1958–1964," *Middle Eastern Studies* 2, no. 3 (April 1966): 211–26.

Salim, Eli. "Cabinet Politics in Lebanon," *Middle East Journal* 21, no. 4 (Autumn 1967): 488–502.

Searing, Donald D. "The Comparative Study of Elite Socialization," *Comparative Political Studies* 14, no 4 (January 1969): 471–500.

————. "Models and Images of Man and Society in Leadership Theory," *Journal of Politics* 31, no. 1 (February 1969): 3–31.

Seligman, Lester G. "Elite Recruitment and Political Development," *Journal of Politics* 26, no. 3 (August 1964): 612–24.

————. "Political Elites Reconsidered," *Comparative Politics* 6, no. 2 (January 1974): 299–314.

————. "The Study of Political Leadership," *American Political Science Review* 44, no. 4 (December 1950): 904–15.

Semaan, Khalil I. H. "A New Source for the Biography of Jamal Abd al-Nasir," *Muslim World* 58, no. 3 (July 1968): 242–52.

Sharabi, Hisham. "The Transformation of Ideology in the Arab World," *Middle East Journal* 19, no. 3 (Summer 1965): 471–86.

Smith, Jr., Arthur K. "Socio-Economic Development and Political Democracy: A Causal Model," *Midwest Journal of Political Science* 13, no. 1 (February 1969): 95–125.

Szyliowicz, Joseph S. "Students and Politics in Turkey," *Middle Eastern Studies* 6, no. 2 (May 1970): 150–62.

Vatikiotis, Panayotis J. "Dilemmas of Political Leadership in the Arab Middle East: The Case of the U.A.R.," *American Political Science Review* 55, no. 1 (March 1961): 103–11.

Wallerstein, Immanuel V. "Elites in French-Speaking West Africa: The Social Bases of Ideas," *Journal of Modern African Studies* 3 (May 1965): 1–33.

Waterbury, John. "Marginal Politics and Elite Manipulation in Morocco," *European Journal of Sociology* 8, no. 1 (1967): 94–111.

Weiker, Walter. "The Ottoman Bureaucracy: Modernization and Reform," *Administrative Science Quarterly* 13, no. 3 (December 1968): 451–70.

Winder, R. Bayley. "Syrian Deputies and Cabinet Ministers, 1919–1959, Part I and II," *Middle East Journal* 16, no. 4 (Autumn 1962): 407–29. and 17, no. 1 (Winter–Spring 1963): 35–54.

Zartman, I. William. "The Study of Elite Circulation," *Comparative Politics* 7, no. 3 (April 1974): 465–488.

General Reference and Government Documents

Arab Report and Record, 1966–1974
Cahier d'Orient Contemporaine
"Chronology" of the *Middle East Journal*
Europa Yearbook
Facts on File

International Who's Who

Al-Intikhabat Khamsin Sanat wa Sanat [Fifty-One Years of Elections], Beirut: Al-Nahar, 1972.

Israeli Government Yearbook, 1952–1970

Keesing's Contemporary Archives

Majmu'ah al-Bayanat al-Wizariyyah al-Lubnaniyyah [Collections of Lebanese Ministerial Pronouncements], Beirut: n.p., 1965.

Middle East and North Africa

Ru'asa' ma Qabl al-Istiqlal [Presidents Before Independence], Beirut: Political Library, 1970.

State of Israel, *Taknon Ha-Knesset* [Regulations of the Knesset] Jerusalem, November 1965.

Statesman's Yearbook

Statistical Yearbook of Israel, 1972

UAR Bureau of Census and Statistics, *Nashrah Ihsa'Muwazzafi al-Hukumah wa al-Hay'at* [Report on Statistics of Employees of the Government and Agencies], Cairo, 1962.

US Department of State, Embassy in Cairo, *Directory of UAR Personages,* December 1964, December 1965, December 1966.

Whitaker's Almanac

Who's Who in the Arab World

Who's Who in Israel, 1952, 1964–65, 1966–67, 1972

Who's Who in Lebanon, 1963–64, 1965–66, 1967–68, 1970–72

Who's Who in World Jewry, 1965

Zionist Yearbook, 1969–70, 1970–71, 1972

Newspapers

Akhbar al-Yawm (Cairo)

Akhir Sa'ah (Cairo)

Ahram Al- (Cairo)

Akhbar, Al- (Cairo)

Hayat, Al- (Beirut)

Jumhuriyyah, Al- (Cairo)

Musawwar, Al- (Cairo)

Nahar, Al- (Beirut)

Ummal, Al- (Cairo)

Arab Observer, The (Cairo)

Daily Star, The (Beirut)

Ha'aretz (Tel Aviv)

Jerusalem Post

Ma'ariv (Tel Aviv)

New York Times, The

Ruz al-Yusif (Cairo)

Scribe, The (Cairo)

Index